# The International Legal Responsibility of the European Union in the Context of the World Trade Organization in Areas of Non-Conferred Competences

Plarent Ruka

# The International Legal Responsibility of the European Union in the Context of the World Trade Organization in Areas of Non-Conferred Competences

Springer

Plarent Ruka
CC Law
Tirana, Albania

Dissertation zur Erlangung des Doktorgrades der Rechtswissenschaft an der Fakultät für Rechtswissenschaft der Universität Hamburg Albrecht Mendelssohn Bartholdy Graduate School of Law
vorgelegt von Plarent Ruka, MLB, LLM
Erstgutachter: Prof. Dr. Armin Hatje
Zweitgutachter: Prof. Dr. Stefan Oeter
Tag der mündlichen Prüfung: 23 August 2016

ISBN 978-3-319-57176-8 ISBN 978-3-319-57177-5 (eBook)
DOI 10.1007/978-3-319-57177-5

Library of Congress Control Number: 2017941639



Printed on acid-free paper

This Springer imprint is published by Springer Nature
The registered company is Springer International Publishing AG
The registered company address is: Gewerbestrasse 11, 6330 Cham, Switzerland

# Preface

The topic of this book was identified during the pre-Lisbon era, while I was working on a research project about the legal challenges that regional trade agreements pose for the World Trade Organization (WTO) agreement. Essentially, from the WTO perspective, the European Union (EU) is deemed to be a preferred art of regionalism as long as the EU common market constitutes an advanced state of economic integration. However, the joint membership of the EU and its member states in the WTO agreement triggers significant legal challenges for this latter in terms of the distribution of the international responsibility for violations of WTO disciplines by the EU or its member states in areas of non-conferred competences. In a more practical level, a question arises about the EU sole participation in the dispute settlement proceedings of the WTO for disputes emerging outside the areas of conferred EU powers. This participation of the EU could provoke significant questions of legality related to the assumption of responsibility for wrongful actions committed by the EU member states while acting within their scope of residual competences. This issue constitutes the main research question of the book. The central assumption is that the way in which the international responsibility of the EU and its member states is distributed sits uneasily with conventional modes provided in international agreements in general. As such, this causes a certain degree of uncertainty for other trading partners, which, by not grasping the constitutional nature of the EU polity, rely on a conventional way of management of the international responsibility. The same problem could be conceived also in light of other international mixed agreements, particularly those operating in the area of international economic law.

The Treaty of Lisbon tackled this issue by consolidating further the common commercial policy of the EU and its member states. As this book was written during the first years of the post-Lisbon era, I explored whether the treaties' amendments truly exhausted the issue of the legitimate assumption by the EU of its member states' responsibility. The more I delved into the legal literature as well as in discussions with EU legal practitioners on this matter, the more I was convinced that the Treaty of Lisbon did not actually settle the question of distribution of international responsibility between the EU and its member states in the context of their joint membership in international mixed agreements for matters of non-conferred competences. Hence, this issue persists even after the redefinition of the common commercial policy in a more advanced format.

Against this background, the book reviews the constitutional fundamentals of the issue of international responsibility of the EU and its member states from the joint participation in the WTO not merely from a theoretical perspective. Rather, the issue of joint responsibility is scrutinized in the context of dispute settlement mechanism of the WTO. With this methodological consideration in mind, the book discovers the failure of the EU's common commercial policy to terminate the state of mixity from practical domain. The main assumption underlying the book is that the joint responsibility regime of the EU and its member states is fallacious. This regime fails to endorse a fair devolution of responsibility to the proper wrongdoer. The book was written with the aim of deconstructing the fallacious model of shared responsibility regime emerging from the joint membership of the EU and its member states in mixed agreements. To that effect, the book proposes a normative model of participation of the EU and its member states in the dispute settlement mechanism of the WTO, which ensures a proper devolution of responsibility to the relevant wrongdoer. This model is conceived on the basis of a constructive approach of integration of the participating legal orders. The book is structured in a comprehensive manner allowing the reader to identify the most relevant predictions from these legal orders which in turn serve to construe the normative model. Accordingly, the book offers firstly a comprehensive overview of the law of international responsibility, the WTO law and the law of mixed agreements, as well as the EU constitutional framework of principles. Only then is the book able to endorse the normative model for addressing the issue of international responsibility of the EU and its member states. Such a normative solution is conceived on the basis of the premises of the WTO agreement. At the same time, to the extent that parallel lines could be drawn with other international mixed agreements without a declaration of powers, this normative solution could be extrapolated to other international agreements, wherever the issue of the fallacious way of devolution of international responsibility arises. Considering the wide scope of matters dealt herein, the book can assist legal practitioners and academics who deal with issues of responsibility in mixed agreements and for which the EU and its member states are apart. The theoretical arguments in the book are discussed by taking into consideration a real case scenario, being the evidence of the practical relevance of the matter.

The book was written during my research at the Albrecht Mendelssohn Bartholdy Graduate School of Law, Faculty of Law, University of Hamburg, Germany. I would like to thank all those who have supported me in this project. My wholehearted gratitude is dedicated to my learned supervisors, Professor Armin Hatje and Professor Stefan Oeter from the Faculty of Law of the University of Hamburg. With their renowned areas of competence, namely, EU law, public international law, and WTO law, Professor Hatje and Professor Oeter have guided me with an immense incitement. Our discussions were always pleasant, inspiring, and productive. In addition to the library of the Faculty of Law at the University of Hamburg, the Max Planck Institute for Comparative and International Private Law in Hamburg, and the German National Library of Economics, I benefited from the kindness of the librarians of Bucerius Law School in Hamburg, who provided me with relevant doctrinal materials and a comfortable place in their library.

Finally, I would like to dedicate this book to my beloved wife, Jola, as a sign of gratitude for accompanying me throughout this project with unconditional patience and care, as well as to my parents and my brother for their support and confidence.

Tirana, Albania Plarent Ruka

# Table of Cases

## Court of Justice of the European Union

### *European Court of Justice*

C-8/55 *Fédération Charbonnière de Belgique v High Authority of the European Coal and Steel Community*, [1956] ECR I-291

C-9/56 *Meroni & Co., Industrie Metallurgiche, SpA v High Authority of the European Coal and Steel Community*, [1958] ECR I-011

C-26/62 *N.V. Algemene Transporten Expeditie Onderneming van Gend en Loos v Nederlandse Administratie der Belastingen*, [1963] ECR I-001

C-6/64 *Flaminio Costa v E.N.E.L.*, [1964] ECR I-585

C-9/69 *Claude Sayag and S.A. Zurich v Jean-Pierre Leduc, Denise Thonnon and S.A. La Concorde*, [1969] ECR I-329

C-11/70 *Internationale Handelsgesellschaft mbH v Einfuhr- und Vorratsstelle für Getreide und Futtermittel, Frankfurt-am-Main*, [1970] ECR I-1125

5/71 *Aktiens-Zuckerfabrik Schöppenstedt v Council of the European Union* [1971] ECR I-975

C-22/70 *Commission of the European Communities v Council of the European Communities* (ERTA), [1971] ECR I-263

Joined Cases C-9 and 11/71 *Compagnie d'approvisionnement, de transport et de crédit SA and Grands Moulins de Paris SA v Commission of the European Communities*, [1972] ECR I-391

Joined Cases C-21-24/72 *International Fruit Company NV et al. v Produktschap voor Groenten en Fruit*, [1972] ECR I-1219

C-57/72 *Westzucker GmbH v Einfuhr- und Vorratsstelle für Zucker*, [1973] ECR I-321

C-4/73 *J. Nold, Kohlen- und Baustoffgroßhandlung v Ruhrkohle Aktiengesellschaft*, [1974] ECR I-491

C-169/73 *Compagnie Continentale France v Council of the European Communities*, [1975] ECR I-117

C-181/73 *R. & V. Haegeman v Belgian State*, [1974] ECR I-449

Joined Cases C-56-60/74 *Kurt Kampffmeyer Mühlenvereinigung KG et al. v Commission and Council of the European Communities*, [1976] ECR I-711

Joined Cases C-3/76, 4/76, 6/76 *Cornelis Kramer et al.*, [1976] ECR I-1279

Joined Cases C-83/76 and 94/76, 4/77, 15/77 and 40/77, *Bayerische HNL Vermehrungsbetriebe GmbH & Co. KG et al. v Council and Commission of the European Communities* [1978] ECR I-1209

C-106/77 *Amministrazione delle Finanze dello Stato v Simmenthal SpA.*, [1978] ECR I-629

C-141/78 *French Republic v United Kingdom of Great Britain and Northern Ireland*, ECR [1979] I-2923

C-238/78, *Ireks-Arkady GmbH v European Economic Community*, [1979] ECR I-203, Opinion of AG Capotorti

C-256/80 *Birra Wührer SpA et al. v Council and Commission of the European Communities*, [1984] ECR I-3693

C-26/81 *SA Oleifici Mediterranei v European Economic Community*, [1982] ECR I-3057

C-104/81 *Hauptzollamt Mainz v Kupferberg*, [1982] ECR I-3641

Joined Cases C-267-269/81 *Amministrazione delle finanze dello Stato v SPI and SAMI*, [1983] ECR I-801

C-327/82 *Ekro BV Vee- en Vleeshandel v Produktschap voor Vee en Vlees*, [1984] ECR I-107

C-59/83 *SA Biovilac NV v European Economic Community*, [1984] ECR I-4057

C-192/84 *Commission of the European Communities v Hellenic Republic*, ECR [1985] I-3967

C-186/85 *Commission of the European Communities v Kingdom of Belgium*, ECR. [1987] I-2029

Joined Cases C-281/85, 283/85, 284/85, 285/85, 287/85 *Federal Republic of Germany et al. v Commission of the European Communities*, [1987] ECR I-3203

C-12/86 *Demirel v Stadt Schwäbisch Gmünd*, [1987] ECR I-3719

C-81/86 - *De Boer Buizen v Council and Commission*, [1987] ECR I-3677

C-204/86 *Hellenic Republic v Council of the European Communities*, [1988] ECR I-5323

C-70/87 *Fédération de l'industrie de l'huilerie de la CEE (Fediol) v Commission of the European Communities*, [1989] ECR I-1781

C-94/87 *Commission of the European Communities v Federal Republic of Germany*, ECR [1989] I-175

C-235/87 *Annunziata Matteucci v Communauté française of Belgium and Commissariat général aux relations internationales of the Communauté française of Belgium*, [1988] ECR I-5589

C-265/87 *Hermann Schräder HS Kraftfutter GmbH & Co. KG v Hauptzollamt Gronau*, [1989] ECR I-2237

C-308/87 *Alfredo Grifoni v European Atomic Energy Community*, [1994] ECR I-341

C-2/88 *J. J. Zwartveld et al.* (Order of the Court), ECR [1990] I-4405

C-68/88 *Commission of the European Communities v Hellenic Republic*, [1989] ECR I-2965

C-70/88 *European Parliament v Council of the European Communities* [1990] ECR I-2041

C-69/89 *Nakajima All Precision Co. Ltd v Council of the European Communities*, [1991] ECR I-2069

Joined Cases C-104/89 and 37/90 *J.M. Mulder et al. v Council of the European Union and Commission of the European Communities*, [1992] ECR I-3061

Joined Cases C-104/89 and 37/90 *J.M. Mulder et al. v Council of the European Union and Commission of the European Communities*, [2000] ECR I-203

Joined Cases C-6/90 and C-9/90 *Francovich and Bonifaci et al. v Italian Republic*, [1991] ECR I-5357

C-316/91 *European Parliament v Council of the European Union*, [1994] ECR I-625

Joined Cases C-46/93 and C-48/93 *Brasserie du Pêcheur SA v Bundesrepublik Deutschland and The Queen v Secretary of State for Transport, ex parte: Factortame Ltd et al.*, [1996] ECR I-1029

C-65/93 *European Parliament v Council of the European Union*, [1995] ECR I-643

C-280/93 *Federal Republic of Germany v Council of the European Union* (Bananas), [1994] ECR I-4973

C-312/93 *Peterbroeck, Van Campenhout & Cie SCS v Belgian State*, [1995] ECR I-4599

Joined Cases C-430/93 and C-431/93 *Van Schijndel* and *Van Veen v SPF*, [1995] ECR I-4705, Opinion of AG Jacobs of 15 June 1995

C-478/93 *Kingdom of the Netherlands v Commission of the European Communities*, [1995] ECR I-3081

C-61/94 *Commission of the European Communities v Federal Republic of Germany*, [1996] ECR I-3989

C-149/96 *Portuguese Republic v Council of the European Union*, [1999] ECR I-8395

C-162/96 *A. Racke GmbH & Co. v Hauptzollamt Mainz*, [1998] ECR I-3655

C-237/98 *Dorsch Consult Ingenieurgesellschaft mbH v Council of the European Union and Commission of the European Communities*, [2000] ECR I-4549

C-287/98 *Grand Duchy of Luxemburg v Berthe Linster, Aloyse Linster and Yvonne Linster*, [2000] ECR I-6917

C-352/98 P, *Bergaderm and Goupil v Commission*, [2000] ECR I-5291

C-357/98 *The Queen v Secretary of State for the Home Department, ex parte Nana Yaa Konadu Yiadom*, [2000] ECR I-9265

C-377/98 *Kingdom of the Netherlands v European Parliament and Council of the European Union*, [2001] ECR I-7079, Opinion of the Advocate General Jacobs of 14 June 2001

C-13/00 *Commission of the European Communities v Ireland*, [2002] ECR I-2943

C-22/00 *Omega Air et al.*, [2002] ECR I-2569

C-224/01 *Gerhard Köbler v Republik Österreich*, [2003] ECR I-10239

C-93/02P *Biret International SA v Council of the European Union*, [2003] ECR I-10497, Opinion of Advocate General Alber of 15 May 2003

C-304/02 *Commission of the European Communities v French Republic*, [2005] ECR I-6263

C-377/02 *Léon Van Parys NV v Belgisch Interventie- en Restitutiebureau (BIRB)*, [2005] ECR I-1465, Opinion of Advocate General Tizzano of 18 November 2004

C-377/02 *Léon Van Parys NV v Belgisch Interventie- en Restitutiebureau (BIRB)*, [2005] ECR I-1465

C-170/03 *Staatssecretaris van Financiën v J. H. M. Feron*, [2005] ECR I-2299

C-239/03 *Commission of the European Communities v French Republic*, [2004] ECR I-598

C-459/03 *Commission of the European Communities v Ireland* (MOX Plant), [2006] ECR I-4635, Opinion of the Advocate General Poiares Maduro

C-459/03 *Commission of the European Communities v Ireland* (MOX Plant), [2006] ECR I-4635

C-316/05 *Nokia Corp. v Joacim Wärdell*, [2006] ECR I-12083

C-402/05P *Kadi and Al Barakaat International Foundation v Council and Commission*, [2008] ECR I-6351, Opinion of the AG Poiares Maduro

Joined Cases C-120/06 and C-121/06 *Fabbrica italiana accumulatori motocarri Montecchio SpA (FIAMM) and Fabbrica italiana accumulatori motocarri Montecchio Technologies LLC (C-120/06 P), Giorgio Fedon & Figli SpA and Fedon America, Inc. (C-121/06 P) v Council of the European Union and Commission of the European Communities*, [2008] ECR I-6513

Joined Cases C-120/06 and C-121/06 *Fabbrica italiana accumulatori motocarri Montecchio SpA (FIAMM) and Fabbrica italiana accumulatori motocarri Montecchio Technologies LLC (C-120/06 P), Giorgio Fedon & Figli SpA and Fedon America, Inc. (C-121/06 P) v Council of the European Union and Commission of the European Communities*, [2008] ECR I-6513, Opinion of the AG Poiares Maduro

C-133/06 *European Parliament v Council of the European Union*, [2008] ECR I-3189

C-195/06 *Kommunikationsbehörde Austria (KommAustria) v Österreichischer Rundfunk (ORF)*, [2007] ECR I-8817

C-308/06 *The Queen, on the application of International Association of Independent Tanker Owners (Intertanko) et al. v Secretary of State for Transport*, [2008] ECR I-405

C-455/06 *Heemskerk BV and Firma Schaap v Productschap Vee en Vlees*, [2008] ECR I-8763

C-246/07 *European Commission v Kingdom of Sweden*, [2010] ECR I-3317

C-370/07 *Commission of the European Communities v Council of the European Union*, [2009] ECR I-8917

## *Court of First Instance*

T-113/96, *Edouard Dubois et Fils SA v Council of the European Union and Commission of the European Communities*, [1998] ECR I-0125

T-383/00 *Beamglow Ltd v European Parliament, Council of the European Union and Commission of the European Communities*, [2005] ECR I-5459

T-240/04 *French Republic v Commission of the European Communities*, [2007] ECR I-4035

## *Opinions and Rulings*

Opinion 1/76 of the ECJ, [1977] ECR I-741, *Opinion given pursuant to Article 228 (1) of the EEC Treaty – 'Draft Agreement establishing a European laying-up fund for inland waterway vessels'*

Ruling 1/78 of the Court of Justice, [1978] ECR I-2151, *Ruling delivered pursuant to the third paragraph of Article 103 of the EAEC Treaty – 'Draft Convention of the International Atomic Energy Agency on the Physical Protection of Nuclear Materials, Facilities and Transports'*

Opinion 1/91 of the Court of Justice, [1991], ECR I-6079, *Opinion delivered pursuant to the second subparagraph of Article 228 (1) of the Treaty – 'Draft agreement between the Community, on the one hand, and the countries of the European Free Trade Association, on the other, relating to the creation of the European Economic Area'*

Opinion 2/91 of the Court of Justice, [1993] ECR I-1061, *Opinion delivered pursuant to the second subparagraph of Article 228 (1) of the EEC Treaty – 'Convention Nº 170 of the International Labour Organization concerning safety in the use of chemicals at work'*

Opinion 1/94 of the Court of Justice, [1994] ECR I-5267, *Competence of the Community to conclude international agreements concerning services and the protection of intellectual property - Article 228 (6) of the EC Treaty (re WTO Agreement)*

Opinion 2/00 of the Court of Justice, *Competence of the Community to conclude Cartagena Protocol*, [2001] ECR I-9713

Opinion 1/00 of the Court of Justice, *Opinion pursuant to Article 300(6) EC - Proposed agreement between the European Community and non-Member States on the establishment of a European Common Aviation Area*, [2002] ECR I-3493

## International Court of Justice

*The Factory at Chorzów*, Jurisdiction, 1927, PCIJ, Series A, No. 9

*The Factory at Chorzów*, Merits, 1928, PCIJ, Series A, No. 17

*Monetary Gold Removed from Rome in 1943* (*Italy v. France, United Kingdom of Great Britain and Northern Ireland and United States of America*), ICJ Reports 1954

*The Corfu Channel Case* (merits) (*UK v Albania*), 1949 I.C.J. Reports, Dissenting Opinion by Judge Azevedo, 78

*Reparation for injuries Suffered in the Service of the United Nations*, Advisory Opinion, I.C.J. Reports 1949, 174

*Interpretation of the Agreement of 25 March 1951 between the WHO and Egypt*, Advisory Opinion, I. C.J. Reports 1980, 73

*Elettronica Sicula S.p.A.* (ELSI) (*United States of America v. Italy*), I.C.J. Reports 1989, 12

*Certain Phosphate Lands in Nauru* (*Nauru v. Australia*), Preliminary Objections, Judgment, I.C.J. Reports 1992, 240

## GATT and WTO

*European Economic Community – Payments and Subsidies Paid to Processors and Producers of Oilseeds and Related Animal-feed Proteins*, GATT doc. C/M/222, 11 July 1988, Minutes of the Meeting of the Council of 16 June 1988

*United States – Standards for Reformulated and Conventional Gasoline*, WT/DS2AB/R, Report of the Appellate Body, 29 April 1996

Minutes of the Meeting of the DSB of 20 March 1997, WTO doc. WT/DSB/M/30 *(re Customs classification of certain computer equipment from United Kingdom and Ireland (items 6, 7 of the Agenda))*

*Australia – Measures Affecting Importation of Salmon*. Recourse to Art. 21.5 by Canada (WT/**DS18**), Report of the Panel of 20 March 2000

*European Communities – Regime for the Importation, Sale and Distribution of Bananas* – Recourse to Arbitration by the European Communities under Article 22.6 DSU, WT/**DS27**/ARB/ECU, 24 March 2000, DSR 2000:V, 2237

*Turkey – Restrictions on Imports of Textile and Clothing Products* (WT/**DS34**), Panel of the Appellate Body of 31 May 1999

*Portugal – Patent Protection under the Industrial Property Act* (WT/**DS37**), settled on 8 October 1996

*European Communities - Customs Classification of Certain Computer Equipment*, Report of the Panel (WT/**DS62, 67, 68**/R), Report of the Panel of 05 February 1998

*Belgium – Measures Affecting Commercial Telephone Services* (WT/**DS80**)

*Ireland – Measures Affecting the Grant of Copyright and Neighbouring Rights* (WT/**DS82**) and *European Communities - Measures Affecting the Grant of Copyright and Neighbouring Rights* (WT/**DS115**), Notification of Mutually Agreed Solution of 13 November 2002 (IP/D/8/Add.1 and IP/D/12/Add.1

*Canada – Measures Affecting the Importation of Milk and the Exportation of Dairy Products* (WT/**DS103** and WT/**DS113**), Report of the Appellate Body of 20 December 2002)

*European Communities – Measures Affecting Asbestos and Asbestos-Containing Products* (WT/**DS135**/1), Request for Consultations by Canada

*European Communities – Measures Affecting Asbestos and Asbestos-Containing Product* (WT/**DS135**), Report of the Panel of 18 September 2000

*European Communities – Measures Affecting Asbestos and Asbestos-Containing Products* (WT/**DS135**/R/Add.1), Addendum to the Report of the Panel, Annex 1

*European Communities – Measures Affecting Asbestos and Asbestos-Containing Product* (WT/**DS135**), Report of the Appellate Body of 12 March 2001

*Korea – Measures Affecting Government Procurement* (WT/**DS163**), Report of the Panel of 19 June 2000

*European Communities – Patent Protection for Pharmaceutical and Agricultural Chemical Products* (WT/**DS153**)

*European Communities – Measures Relating to the Development of a Flight Management System* (WT/**DS172**)

*France – Measures Relating to the Development of a Flight Management System* (WT/**DS173**)

*European Communities – Protection of Trademarks and Geographical Indications for Agricultural Products and Foodstuffs* (WT/**DS174**/R), Report of the Panel of 15 March 2005

*European Communities – Customs Classification of Frozen Boneless Chicken Cuts*, (WT/**DS269**/13 and WT/**DS286**/15), Award of the Arbitrator James Bacchus, ARB 2005-4/21, 20 February 2006

*United States – Measures Affecting Cross-Border Supply of Gambling and Betting Services* (WT/**DS285**), Report of the Panel of 10 November 2004

*European Communities – Measures Affecting Trade in Commercial Vessels* (WT/**DS301**), Report of the Panel of 22 April 2005

## Permanent Court of International Justice

*The 'SS' Wimbledon'*, 1923, PCIJ Series A, No. 1, 4

## International Arbitral Awards

*Affaire des biens britanniques au Maroc espagnol, Great Britain v. Spain*, (1925) 2 R.I.A.A. 615

*Island of Palmas, The Netherlands v. USA*, 4 April 1928, 2 RIAA, 831

*Estate of Jean-Baptiste Caire (France) v. United Mexican States*, (1929) 5 RIAA, 516

*The 'Rainbow Warrior', (France v. New Zealand)*, (1990), 20 RIAA, 215

## German Jurisprudence

*BVerfGE 37, 271 2 BvL 52/71 (Solange I)*, English version available at http://www.utexas.edu/law/academics/centers/transnational/work_new/german/case.php?id=588 (last visited on 24.06.2013)

*Brunner v The European Union Treaty* (Maastricht Judgment) Cases 2 BvR 2134/92 & 2159/92

*Lisbon Treaty Judgment BVerfG*, 2 BvE 2/08 of 30.6.2009, available at http://www.bverfg.de/entscheidungen/es20090630_2bve000208.html (last visited on 25.06.2013)

*Honeywell, BVerfG*, 2 BvR 2661/06 of 06.07.2010, English translation available at http://www.bundesverfassungsgericht.de/en/decisions/rs20100706_2bvr266106en.html (last visited on 24.06.2013)

# Table of Legislative Instruments

## European Union

Treaties Establishing the European Coal and Steel Community in 1951 (ECSC Treaty), the European Economic Community in 1957 (EEC Treaty), and the European Atomic Energy Community in 1957 (EUROATOM Treaty)

Council Directive 76/769/EEC of 27.07.1976 on the approximation of the laws, regulations and administrative provisions of the Member States relating to restrictions on the marketing and use of certain dangerous substances and preparations, OJ L 262, 27.9.1976

Council Resolution of 29.06.1978 on action programme of the European Communities on safety and health at work. Official Journal of the European Communities (OJ) No. C 165, 11.07.1978

Council Directive 80/1107/EC of 27.11.1980, OJ No. L 327, 03.12.1980

Council Directive 83/477/EC of 19.09.1983 on the protection of workers from the risks related to exposure to asbestos at work (second individual Directive within the meaning of Article 8 of Directive 80/1107/EC), OJ No. L 263, 24.09.1983

Council Decision 94/800/EC (of 22 December 1994) concerning the conclusion on behalf of the European Community, as regards matters within its competence, of the agreements reached in the Uruguay Round multilateral negotiations (1986–1994) [1994] OJ L336/1

Commission Directive 1999/77/EC of 26 .07.1999, OJ L 207, 06.08.1999

Presidency Note of the Conference of the Representatives of the Governments of the Member States on the Intergovernmental Conference (IGC 2000) – Extension of the Qualified Majority Voting, Document CONFER 4789/00 of 26 October 2000

Summary of the Progress Report in the Intergovernmental Conference on Institutional Reform, Document CONFER 4790/00 of 3 November 2000

Council Regulation (EC) No 1515/2001 of 23 July 2001, on the measures that may be taken by the Community following a report adopted by the WTO Dispute

Settlement Body concerning anti-dumping and anti-subsidy matters, Official Journal L 201, 26/07/2001

Treaty of Lisbon Amending the Treaty on European Union and the Treaty Establishing the European Community, 13 December 2007, OJ 2007/C 306/01

Regulation (EU) 912/2014 of the European Parliament and of the Council of 23 July 2014 establishing a framework for managing financial responsibility linked to investor-to-state dispute settlement tribunals established by international agreements to which the European Union is party, OJ L 257, 28.8.2014

Regulation (EU) 2015/476 of the European Parliament and of the Council of 11 March 2015 on the measures that the Union may take following a report adopted by the WTO Dispute Settlement Body concerning anti-dumping and anti-subsidy matters, OJ L 83, 27.3.2015

## International Instruments

The Statute of the International Court of Justice, 26 June 1945, 15 UNCIO 355

Vienna Convention on the Law of the Treaties (VCLT) 22 May 1969, 1155 UNTS 331

United Nations Convention on the Law of the Sea (UNCLOS), 10 December 1982, 1833 UNTS 3

International Law Commission Yearbook of the International Law Commission, 1973, Volume II, Documents of the twenty-fifth session including the report of the Commission to the General Assembly

Vienna Convention on the Law of Treaties between States and International Organizations or between International Organizations, 21 March 1986, A/CONF.129/15

International Law Commission Report on the work of its fifty-second session (2000) – Topical summary of the discussion held in the Sixth Committee of the General Assembly during its fifty-fifth session prepared by the Secretariat, [UN Doc. A/CN.4/513], 15 February 2001

International Law Commission Articles on Responsibility of States for the Internationally wrongful acts (2001), adopted by the International Law Commission at its fifty-third session, in 2001, and submitted to the General Assembly, which adopted with the resolution 56/83 of 12 December 2001, and corrected by document A/56/49 (Vol. I)/Corr.4. Available at http://legal.un.org/ilc/texts/9_6.htm

International Law Commission Draft Articles on Responsibility of States for Internationally Wrongful Acts, with Commentaries, 2001, adopted by the International Law Commission at its fifty-third Session (Doc. A/56/10). The report, which also contains commentaries on the draft articles, appeared in the Yearbook of the International Law Commission, 2001, Volume II, Part Two, Documents of the fifty-third session including the report of the Commission to the General Assembly [UN Doc. A/CN.4/SER.A/2001/Add.1 (Part 2)], New York and Geneva, 2007, p. 30, para. 77

Articles on the Prevention of Transboundary Harm from Hazardous Activities, 11 May 2001

International Law Commission Second Report on Responsibility of International Organizations, UN Document A/CN.4/545 re Comments and observations received from international organizations, 25 June 2004

International Law Commission Third Report on Responsibility of International Organizations, by Mr. Giorgio Gaja, Special Rapporteur, [UN Doc. A/CN.4/553], 13 May 2005

International Law Commission Fourth Report on Responsibility of International Organizations, by Mr. Giorgio Gaja, Special Rapporteur, [UN Doc. 2006, A/CN.4/564/, Add.1-2], 28 February, 12 and 20 April 2006

Principles on the Allocation of Loss in the Case of Transboundary Harm Arising Out of Hazardous Activities, 2 June 2006

International Law Commission Draft Articles on the Responsibility of International Organizations, 2011, adopted by the International Law Commission at its sixty-third session, in 2011, and submitted to the General Assembly as a part of the Commission's report covering the work of that session (A/66/10, para. 87). Available at http://legal.un.org/ilc/texts/9_11.htm

International Law Commission Draft Articles on the Responsibility of International Organizations, with Commentaries, 2011, adopted by the International Law Commission at its sixty-third session (Doc. A/66/10). The report, which also contains commentaries to the draft articles (para. 88), will appear in Yearbook of the International Law Commission, 2011, vol. II, Part Two

International Law Commission, Responsibility of International Organizations, Comments and Observations Received from International Organizations, UN Doc. A/CN.4/637 of 14 February 2011

## World Trade Organization/General Agreement on Tariffs and Trade 1947 (GATT)

Agreement Establishing the World Trade Organization, 15 April 1994, 1867 UNTS I-31874 (WTO Agreement)

General Agreement on Tariffs and Trade, 30 October 1947 (GATT 1947) (Annex II-5 of the WTO Agreement)

Agreement on Technical Barriers to Trade (TBT Agreement) (1994) (Annex II-11 of the WTO Agreement)

General Agreement on Trade in Services (1994) (Annex II-16a of the WTO Agreement)

Trade Related Aspects of Intellectual Property Rights (1994) (Annex II-17a of the WTO Agreement)

Understanding on Rules and Procedures Governing the Settlement of Disputes (1994) (Annex II-18 of the WTO Agreement)

Minutes of the Meeting of the Dispute Settlement Body of 7 April 2000, DSB Doc. WT/DSB/M/78, 12 May 2000

## National Legislation

Décret no. 96-1133 *relatif à l'interdiction de l'amiante, pris en application du code de travail et du code de la consummation*, published in the Official Journal of the French Republic on 26.12.1996, 19126 and entered into force on 01.01.1997

Décret n°2001-1316 du 27 décembre 2001 modifiant le décret n° 96-1133 du 24 décembre 1996 *relatif à l'interdiction de l'amiante, pris en application du code du travail et du code de la consommation*, published in the Official Journal of the French Republic on 29.12.2001, 21281 and entered into force on 27.12.2001

Décret n°2002-1528 du 24 décembre 2002 modifiant le décret n° 96-1133 du 24 décembre 1996 *relatif à l'interdiction de l'amiante et le décret n° 96-98 du 7 février 1996 relatif à la protection des travailleurs contre les risques liés à l'inhalation de poussières d'amiante*, published in the Official Journal of the French Republic on 28.12.2002, 21860 and entered into force on 24.12.2002

Gesetz über die Wahrnehmung der Integrationsverantwortung des Bundestages und des Bundesrates in Angelegenheiten der Europäischen Union (Integrationsverantwortungsgesetz—IntVG) of 2 September 2009 (BGBl. I S. 3022), amended through the Article 1 of the Law of 1 December 2009 (BGBl. I S. 3822)

# Contents

# List of Abbreviations

| | |
|---|---|
| ARSIWA | International Law Commission Articles on Responsibility of States for Internationally Wrongful Acts |
| DARIO | International Law Commission Draft Articles on the Responsibility of International Organizations |
| dCoC | Draft of the new protocol on detailed rules for participation by the European Union (European communities and member states) in WTO proceedings |
| DSB | Dispute Settlement Body |
| DSM | Dispute settlement mechanism |
| DSP | Dispute settlement proceedings |
| DSU | Dispute Settlement Understanding |
| ECJ | European Court of Justice |
| ECSC Treaty | The treaty establishing the European Coal and Steel Community (1951) |
| EEC Treaty | The treaty establishing the European Economic Community (1957) |
| EU | European Union |
| EUROATOM Treaty | The treaty establishing the European Atomic Energy Community (1957) |
| ILC | International Law Commission |
| ILO | International Labour Organization |
| PCG | PVA (polyvinyl alcohol), cellulose, and glass fibers |
| TEU | Treaty on European Union |
| TFEU | Treaty on the Functioning of the European Union |
| UNCLOS | United Nations Convention on the Law of the Sea (1982) |
| VCLT | Vienna Convention on the Law of Treaties (1969) |

| | |
|---|---|
| VCLTIO | Vienna Convention on the Law of Treaties between States and International Organizations or between International Organizations (1986) |
| WTO | World Trade Organization |

# Chapter 1
# Introduction

## I. An Introduction to the Membership of the European Union and Its Member States in the WTO

The World Trade Organization (WTO)[1] serves as a common institutional framework for the conduct of trade relations among its Contracting Parties[2] in matters determined in the WTO Agreement and its annexes.[3] The WTO is mainly composed of states, and all the Member States of the European Union (EU)[4] are part of the WTO. In addition, the EU, in its quality as a customs union, is also an original Member of the WTO by having accepted the WTO Agreement and the Multilateral Trade Agreements with the respective Schedules of Concessions and Commitments annexed thereto (Article XI:1 WTO Agreement). Being equally subject to rights and obligations, the EU and its Member States exercise jointly their attributes from the WTO membership. This constitutes one of the major difficulties inherent in the WTO legal system, inasmuch as not all aspects of this joint membership are regulated.[5]

---

[1]The World Trade Organization (WTO) is an international organization founded on the basis of the Agreement Establishing the World Trade Organization (WTO Agreement), which was signed in Marrakesh, Morocco on 15 April 1994. The WTO Agreement is a result of the Uruguay Round of Negotiations (1986–1994), held under the premises of the General Agreement on Tariffs and Trade (GATT) 1947, which has been subsequently integrated in the WTO Agreement. Unless otherwise indicated, the term 'WTO Agreement' in this work shall include all the Multilateral Trade Agreements referred to in Article II:2 of the WTO Agreement.

[2]The concept 'Contracting Party of the WTO Agreement' shall be referred in this work as 'WTO Member State', or as 'WTO Member'.

[3]Article II:1 of the WTO Agreement.

[4]The term 'European Union', referred to as the 'EU' or the 'Union' are used interchangeably in this work with the term 'European Communities', referred to as the 'EC'.

[5]Antoniadis (2004), p. 336.



P. Ruka, *The International Legal Responsibility of the European Union in the Context of the World Trade Organization in Areas of Non-Conferred Competences*,
DOI 10.1007/978-3-319-57177-5_1

Although the WTO and EU legal orders are both part of public international law, and as such, they share common features, in essence they remain very dissimilar and generally pursue different objectives and interests. While the WTO is built upon the traditional model of international organizations, the EU deviates from this idea, inasmuch as it is considered a new legal order of public international law.[6] In the lenses of public international law, the main differences between the EU and the WTO consist in their respective relationships with their Member States. One of these differences concerns the double representation of the EU Member States in the WTO both as direct Members of the WTO and through the EU. This provokes legal uncertainties in terms of decision-making processes and dispute settlement processes. The former are of a political-decisional nature and accommodate the economic and trade interests of the Union polity.[7] The latter have a judicial-normative character and take place when WTO Members request consultations on trade-related measures in the Dispute Settlement Mechanism (DSM).[8]

The legal uncertainty is mainly due to the atypical political and constitutional nature of the EU polity, which creates confusion in terms of the representation of Member States in the Dispute Settlement Proceedings (DSP). Due to its unclear distribution of powers, the Union polity is unable to determine in a definite way the relevant entity that is competent to defend a disputed measure. This is the main reason for the Union to assume answerability for WTO inconsistent measures that

[6]As the Dispute Settlement Body (DSB) has confirmed, the WTO legal order cannot be seen in clinical isolation from public international law, inasmuch as the interpretation of the WTO Agreement by DSB takes into account also customary rules of public international law (Article 3 (2) DSU). See in relation with this statement *United States—Standards for Reformulated and Conventional Gasoline*, WT/DS2AB/R, Report of the Appellate Body, 29 April 1996, 17. See also Stoll (2012), para. 18. For considerations on the EU legal order see Case C-26/62 *N.V. Algemene Transporten Expeditie Onderneming van Gend en Loos v Nederlandse Administratie der Belastingen*, [1963] ECR I-001, 12, para. 4.

[7]The WTO Agreement is characterized of a contract-type rapport between the Members of the club. This informs for a cooperative rather than for a subordination order of relationship between the WTO institutions and its Member States. The fact that the Dispute Settlement Mechanism (DSM) is based on the arbitration model of the settlement of disputes serves as evidence for this kind of relationship. The diverse legal instruments embodied in the WTO Agreement provide for the participating actors the necessary space to exercise political influence for accomplishing their interests. These instruments also play an instrumental role in defending economic interests of WTO actors not only through the decision-making process, but also through the DSM. In this way, the WTO offers a political forum for addressing trade interests, and a dispute settlement forum for providing judicially normative solutions to conflicts among Members.

[8]These proceedings, which often are followed by the establishment of a Panel, may be appealed before the Appellate Body on points of law. The reports have to be approved by the DSB in order to become enforceable, unless it consensually disapproves their conclusions. The WTO Agreement has successfully institutionalized the settlement of disputes. The DSM is considered one of the most successful achievements in public international law; the latter depends upon the willingness of the states, given that any supranational enforcement mechanisms are missing.

are attributed to Member States. The EU has found the way to represent in the DSP the interests of all Member States with one voice.[9] It remains however questionable whether this way is valid for producing legitimate consequences. This question is explored in the following Sections by means of a case study, where it is argued that the WTO membership represents for the EU an uneasy relationship that could become a source of internal tensions, which yet remain virtual.[10] However, these concerns raise questions of both theoretical and practical relevance for the constitutional relations in the Union polity.

The complicated relationship of the legal orders of the WTO, EU and its Member States can be further analyzed from the perspectives of the participating legal orders. From the WTO law perspective, although the EU, as a customs union, constitutes a discriminatory regime for other WTO Members, it still represents a successful and preferred model of regionalism. This is due to the value it has added to international trade in terms of increasing economic welfare, which subsequently offers an additional guarantee for peace, prosperity and political stability. This is the rationale behind Article XXIV GATT, which allows for a closer integration between the economies of the countries, without however increasing trade barriers to other WTO members.

From the EU law perspective, the WTO Agreement can be classified as a mixed agreement, due to the fact that both the EU and its Member States are signatory parties. As such, this Agreement is incorporated simultaneously into the legal orders of the EU and its Member States. The WTO membership of the EU triggers significant constitutional issues in doctrinal and jurisprudential terms. The EU Treaties have awarded a binding value to international treaties. This reflects the monistic line of hierarchy, supported from the argument that international agreements constitute an integral part of the EU legal order and do not, in principle, require any acts of transposition to become effective, depending of course on the nature and the content of the agreement.[11] Additionally, the jurisprudence of the Court of Justice of the European Union ('the ECJ' or, 'the Court') has conceived a higher rank for international agreements concluded by the Union vis-à-vis the secondary legislation; hence endorsing a monistic approach on the relationship.[12] Nevertheless, the ECJ, inspired by a dualistic view on the matter, has rather reserved only a position equivalent to secondary law for the WTO Agreement in the EU legal order by denying the supremacy or any direct effect of this Agreement, and by preserving the autonomy of EU law.[13] Furthermore, any expansionary effect

---

[9]Antoniadis (2004), p. 322.

[10]See also Antoniadis (2004), p. 343.

[11]Eeckhout (2011), pp. 326–327 and Cremona (2012), p. 288.

[12]See for example Joined Cases C-21-24/72 *International Fruit Company NV et al. v Produktschap voor Groenten en Fruit*, [1972] ECR I-1219, paras. 7, 8 and Case C-61/94 *Commission of the European Communities v Federal Republic of Germany*, [1996] ECR I-3989, para. 52. See also Tomuschat (2002), p. 186.

[13]Uerpmann-Wittzack (2010), p. 147. See also Eeckhout (2011), pp. 326–327 and Kuijper and Bronckers (2005), p. 1315.

of the EU powers in the exercise of common commercial policy in relation to the WTO membership has been rejected.[14] These premises preserve the mixed nature of the WTO Agreement, where both the Member States and the EU participate with separate contributions but joint responsibilities.[15]

The mixed nature of the WTO Agreement is an answer to several conflicting factors and trends. On the one hand, the Union polity needs to become more pronounced in the realm of international economic relations. On the other hand, it remains limited from the powers conferred from Member States. By retaining a certain category of residual powers, the latter withhold attributes of sovereign subjects of international law.[16] This tension inherited in the thesis of mixity poses some problems, mainly notable in the pre-conclusion phase (negotiation, conclusion), in the course of institutional management (participation in the decision-making of the Union and Member States, the delineation of competences), as well as in the conflict management (participation in the DSP, attribution of responsibility and the distribution of burden thereof).[17] In particular, the joint responsibility regime associating the majority of mixed agreements may challenge the constitutional prosperity of the polity.[18]

## II. Preliminary Issues of the Joint Responsibility Regime Under the WTO Agreement

The WTO Agreement, with its mixed nature, triggers the question of responsibility for complying with the obligations arising thereof. In relation to this, the general assumption that prevails is that, in the absence of a competence clause or a functionally equivalent declaration on competences, the EU and its Member States are jointly bound by the Agreement vis-à-vis third parties.[19] In addition, the structure of the division of powers between the EU and its Member States is a significant cause for uncertainties in relation to the distribution (apportion) of the areas of responsibilities under the WTO Agreement. Consequently, the EU and its Member States are jointly liable for trade damages caused to other WTO Members for violations of the WTO disciplines, although they are only individually competent for enacting legislation in particular areas covered by the WTO disciplines.

[14]Opinion 1/94 of the Court of Justice, [1994] ECR I-5267, *Competence of the Community to conclude international agreements concerning services and the protection of intellectual property - Article 228 (6) of the EC Treaty* (*re WTO Agreement*), paras. 34, 53, 71, 98 and 105.

[15]See also Hyett (2000), p. 249.

[16]Hillion and Koutrakos (2010), p. xx.

[17]Timmermans (2010), p. 2.

[18]See also Thym (2010), p. 319.

[19]Tomuschat (1983), p. 130.

The joint membership of the EU and its Member States triggers important questions of representation in terms of decision-making processes and dispute resolution. The former issue is essentially addressed by Article IX WTO Agreement, which provides that, in case that the EU, in its quality of a WTO Member, exercises its right to vote, its weight will equal the total number of EU Member States which are WTO Members. The Commission represents the Union and its Member States in decision-making bodies of the EU without prejudices to the internal division of powers in the Union polity.[20] The regulation of EU representation for its Member States in the decision-making process cannot be transposed or applied by analogy to other questions of representation, such as the participation in the DSP, which results unaddressed by any similar instruments. This unregulated aspect of the EU—WTO relationship, leaves space for theoretical interpretations, which also have significant implications in practice. This nexus shall be explored at the outset of this work by analyzing an introductory case, the *EC – Asbestos*.[21]

The central discussion to be addressed in this work is related to the thesis of prior regulation of the EU participation in the DSP, which essentially balances various arguments on the need for legal certainty, as opposed to the unregulated representation. The model of representation is relevant in the context of WTO membership for enhancing the legal certainty in terms of responsibility. However, this model mainly concerns the internal constitutional relations in the EU, and aims to shed light on the way in which the participation of the Union and its Member States in the DSP would ensure an adequate distribution of responsibilities according to the normative expectations of the parties. Indeed, behind the problems of the Union participation in the DSP, one finds the conflicts in the context of vertical division of powers within the Union, which may lead to distortion of responsibility. Such concerns should be addressed internally without implications for the WTO Membership.[22] This demands the elaboration of a 'normative model' of participation of the EU in the DSP based on a *prior regulation*, or on *flexible decisions on representation*. This model may consist of a set of criteria and instruments that stipulate or limit the conditions for the Union participation in the DSP, and it addresses the consequences of this participation for all the EU Member States. The model should not be understood as a closed and rigid setting, but rather as a framework for the accommodation of the normative criteria, as premises for the regulation of the Union participation in the DSP, and the relevant consequences.

---

[20] Antoniadis (2004), p. 328.

[21] *European Communities – Measures Affecting Asbestos and Asbestos-Containing Product* (*EC – Asbestos*), (WT/DS135), Report of the Panel of 18 September 2000 and Report of the Appellate Body of 12 March 2001.

[22] Antoniadis (2004), p. 328.

## III. Introductory Case

A successful theory of law consists of true propositions that adequately explain the nature of law.[23] Various analytical perspectives can be construed for pursuing such propositions, or for proving their adequacy. One of the ways to succeed with a theoretical analysis would be to explore at the outset the practical relevance of a model of the Union participation in the DSP and to suggest certain propositions as guiding normative criteria for construing the model. The elaboration of the relevant issues proposed in this context would be able to provide a plausible legal solution for the issue of the fallacious model of joint responsibility regime. With this prediction in mind, it would be useful to consider the practical relevance of the issue of fallacies of the joint responsibility regime in the context of Union's membership in the WTO Agreement. The following case sheds light on two fundamental premises for this work. Firstly, it highlights the extent to which the scheme of distribution of powers in the EU polity diverts the attribution of responsibilities from the wrongdoer to the Union. Hence, the joint responsibility regime proves to be fallacious inasmuch as it hinders the valid distribution of welfare among the participants, and as such, it constitutes a legal concern for the theory and practice. At a second stage, from a critical assessment of the facts, it is possible to obtain certain true and adequate normative propositions that can in turn be employed to construe a model of the Union participation in the DSP for matters of non-conferred competences.

### *1. Case Brief: EC – Asbestos*

*EC – Asbestos* is a case that illustrates at best the constitutional dimension of the problems related with the EU participation in the DSP, either as a complainant, or as a respondent.[24] This case shows, from a theoretical perspective, how the question of distribution of powers between the EU and its Member States may, under certain circumstances that shall be highlighted in the course of this Chapter, trigger an unfair distribution of international responsibility among the conflicting parties. The dispute adjudicated at the Dispute Settlement Body (DSB) was about a trade measure employed by France, namely the Decree No. 96-1133, dated 24 December 1996 (the Decree) for the prohibition of asbestos and products containing asbestos.[25] This measure was aimed at the protection of the health of workers and

[23]Leiter (2011), p. 3, referring to Dickson and Gardner (2001), p. 17.

[24]Antoniadis (2004), p. 335.

[25]Décret no. 96-1133 *relatif à l'interdiction de l'amiante, pris en application du code de travail et du code de la consummation*, published in the Official Journal of the French Republic on 26.12.1996, 19,126 and entered into force on 01.01.1997. An English translation is provided at *EC – Asbestos*, (WT/DS135/R/Add.1), Addendum to the Report of the Panel, Annexs 1, 3–6.

consumers. Article 1 of the Decree prohibited the manufacture, importation, exportation, possession for sale, placing on the domestic market, the domestic marketing, the offer, the sale, the transfer under any title whatsoever of all varieties of asbestos fibres or products containing asbestos fibres.[26] This ban on asbestos fibres was established for the purpose of protecting workers and consumers. Article 2 of the Decree provided for the exceptions to the ban for certain existing materials, products or devices containing chrysotile fibres (one of the six varieties of asbestos), when no substitute for that fibre would be available, which, on the one hand could pose a lesser occupational health risk to workers handling those materials, and on the other, would provide all technical guarantees of safety corresponding to the ultimate purpose of the use.[27]

Following the negative effects that this measure caused for the exports volume of asbestos (and particularly for chrysotile fibres), Canada requested consultations with the European Communities (EC), aiming to reach a mutual solution regarding the claim that this measure infringed WTO obligations of France.[28] Failing to resolve the dispute amicably, the DSB established on 25 November 1998 a panel to examine the matter referred by Canada. Other WTO members, such as Brazil, the United States of America and Zimbabwe participated as third parties in these proceedings. The final Report[29] of the Panel, which was circulated to WTO Members on 18 September 2000, was appealed from Canada and the EC on certain 'issues of law' and 'legal interpretations'. The Appellate Body issued its Report[30] on 12 March 2001, which was subsequently adopted by the DSB on 5 April 2001.

Canada challenged the ban on chrysotile fibres claiming the incompatibility of the measure with the Agreement on Technical Barriers to Trade (TBT Agreement)[31] and the General Agreement on Tariffs and Trade (GATT).[32] Canada argued that the measures imposed by France violated the national treatment disciplines and the most-favored-nation clause[33]; created unnecessary obstacles to international trade[34]; were not based on effective and appropriate international standards[35]; and did not specify the product requirement in terms of performance,[36] but rather in

[26] *EC – Asbestos*, (WT/DS135/R/Add.1), Addendum to the Report of the Panel, Annexs 1, 4.

[27] *Ibid.*

[28] *EC – Asbestos*, (WT/DS135/1), Request for Consultations by Canada.

[29] *EC – Asbestos*, (WT/DS135), Report of the Panel 18 September 2000.

[30] *EC – Asbestos*, (WT/DS135), Report of the Appellate Body of 16 February 2001.

[31] Agreement on Technical Barriers to Trade (TBT Agreement.

[32] General Agreement on Tariffs and Trade 1994 (GATT 1994) is part of the WTO Agreement and consists of provisions in the General Agreement on Tariffs and Trade, dated 30 October 1947 (GATT 1947). Hereinafter these text will refer to as 'GATT'.

[33] Article 2.1 TBT Agreement.

[34] Article 2.2 TBT Agreement. Articles III.4, IX.1 and XXIII.1(a) or (b) GATT.

[35] Article 2.4 TBT Agreement.

[36] Article 2.8 TBT Agreement.

terms of descriptive characteristics.[37] In addition, Canada argued that the Decree prohibited or restricted the imports of chrysotile fibres and chrysotile-cement products favoring the national industry contrary to national treatment and the 'tariff-only' disciplines of the GATT, namely Articles III:4 and XI:1.[38] Therefore, Canada requested the DSB to recommend to France to bring the Decree in compliance with its WTO obligations.[39] The EC answered to these claims by arguing that *the measures enacted by France* should not be examined in relation with Article XI:1 GATT ('tariff-only' maxim); that *France did not establish less favorable treatment* for similar imported products than for domestic products within the meaning of Article III:4 GATT, and that in any case, *the measures should be considered necessary to protect human health*, within the meaning of Article XX (b) GATT.[40] In addition, EC argued that the measure should not be covered by the TBT Agreement and that in any case it complies with its requirements. It also contradicted the application of Article XXIII:1(b) GATT as inapplicable to these measures. Consequently, EC asked the Panel to reject all arguments presented by Canada.[41]

With regard to the compatibility with the TBT Agreement, Canada claimed that this agreement is applicable and that, under its premises, the French Decree is an unnecessary barrier to trade.[42] The EC, in turn, contradicted the application of the TBT Agreement to the French Decree, given that the Decree constitutes a general prohibition, and in any case, the EC argued that it complies with its provisions.[43] The Panel decided to examine separately the two parts of the Decree, without prejudicing the legal implications of this separation.[44] By employing this approach, the Panel could consider the applicability of the definition of 'technical regulation' of the TBT Agreement upon the prohibition part of the Decree, and at the same time could determine the applicability of the TBT Agreement as a governing act for the dispute. The Panel concluded that the part of the Decree banning the marketing of asbestos and asbestos containing products, does not constitute a 'technical regulation' because its aim serves the general ban of the product, rather than imposing trading arrangements for the product.[45] With regard to the part of the Decree dealing with the exceptions to the general ban, the Panel considered it to be subject to the TBT Agreement.[46] However, the Panel refrained from reaching any

[37] *EC – Asbestos*, Report of the Panel, 5.

[38] *Ibid.*

[39] *Ibid.*

[40] *Ibid.*

[41] *Ibid*, 6.

[42] *Ibid*, 99 (para. 3.245).

[43] *Ibid*, 100–101 (paras. 3.250, 3.252).

[44] *Ibid*, 404 (para. 8.33).

[45] *Ibid*, 411 (para. 8.63).

[46] *Ibid*, 412 (para. 8.70).

conclusion with this respect, in the absence of any claims from Canada.[47] The Appellate Body reversed these findings of the Panel and concluded that the French Decree constitutes a technical regulation in the meaning of the TBT Agreement, but it refrained from examining the Canadian claims for violations thereof.[48]

Further to the legal compliance of the French Decree with the TBT Agreement, the parties argued the compatibility of this act with the GATT. The first issue disputed in this context was whether the French Decree was to be considered a 'border measure' or an 'internal measure' with impacts on the border. In this way, the parties argued on the compatibility of the French Decree with Articles III:4 and XI:1 GATT. The former provides for the principle of non-discrimination between domestic and imported products, whereas the latter provides for the general elimination of quantitative restrictions, namely any border measures other than duties, taxes or other charges. According to Canada, the Decree should be considered both as a border measure and as an internal measure, therefore pointing out the application of both Articles III:4 and XI:1 GATT. This is argued by considering two aspects of the Decree, namely to prohibit the import of all varieties of asbestos (a border measure), and to prohibit the domestic marketing and transfer of all varieties of asbestos and products containing them.[49] The EC contradicted the argument of considering the French Decree as a two-component measure. Instead, it argued that it should be considered as a unique one, which has to be seen as an 'internal regulation' providing for identical treatment of 'like' domestic and imported products within the meaning of Article III:4 GATT. By arguing upon the question of likeness of chrysotile with PCG fibres, the Panel reached the conclusion that they are 'like', and, by allowing for the legal discrimination between products, the French Decree violates Article III:4 GATT.[50] On this issue, the Appellate Body maintained that the competitive relationship between products is crucial for determining 'likeness' under Article III:4 GATT, but nevertheless the health risks associated with chrysotile fibres should be considered under the premises of the physical properties of the product.[51] Utilizing the same criteria employed by the Panel, the Appellate Body, however, reached a different conclusion, namely that the chrysotile fibres are not like products with PCG fibres.[52] After reversing the Panel's findings on the likeness of cement-based products containing chrysotile fibres with cement-based products containing PCG, the Appellate Body concluded that the French Decree is consistent with Article III:4 GATT.[53]

With regard to the violation of Article 3.8 TBT Agreement and Article XXIII:1 (b) GATT, after examining the conditions set out in these Articles, the Panel found that Canada did not establish the existence of nullification or impairment of a

[47] *Ibid*, 465 (para. 9.1(a)).

[48] *EC – Asbestos*, Report of the Appellate Body, 29–31 (paras. 76, 83).

[49] *EC – Asbestos*, Report of the Panel, 147–148 (para. 3.394).

[50] *Ibid*, 431 (paras. 8.155–8.158).

[51] *EC – Asbestos*, Report of the Appellate Body, 37, 45 (paras. 99, 116).

[52] *Ibid*, 48 (para. 126).

[53] *Ibid*, 50 (para. 132).

benefit within the meaning of Article XXIII:(1) GATT as a result of enforcement of the French Decree.[54] The Appellate Body maintained the Panel's reasoning.

A significant issue addressed during the DSP was whether the French measure was justified under the auspices of a health policy, and if yes, whether this measure was appropriate to achieve this end. The *EC maintained that the French Decree is a measure that serves a legitimate objective*, such as the public health, and it is not more trade-restrictive than necessary to fulfill such an objective.[55] The EC argued further that, while no country should be prevented from taking measures necessary for the protection of human health,[56] it is not the necessity of the objective pursued by the measure that should be examined, but whether it was necessary or not to subject the imported products to the measure contested in order to achieve the chosen level of protection.[57] Accordingly, the EC maintained that France was free to choose the level of protection it deemed appropriate in order to halt the spread of the risk linked with the use of asbestos fibres and products containing this material.[58] The Panel heard impartial experts to collect evidences on the health risks of chrysotile asbestos. After having established that the chrysotile fibres, although embodied in other materials, pose an imminent threat to human health, the Panel concluded that the French measure was justified as aiming to protect the public health, thus falling under the criteria of Article XX:b GATT. The Appellate Body upheld this decision.

The overall conclusion of the Panel was that the French Decree violated the GATT disciplines, but this violation was justified under the premises of achieving a legitimate objective. Contrary to this analysis, the Appellate Body reasoned that Canada did not succeed to establish that the French Decree was inconsistent with the EC's obligations under the covered agreements of the WTO.[59] This is a case were both the Panel and the Appellate Body reached the same conclusion, namely that France was not responsible for violation of WTO Agreement, although by employing opposing frameworks of analysis and interpretation.

## 2. A Critical Assessment of EC – Asbestos

### a. A Latent Message of EC – Asbestos and Some Methodological Issues

The *EC – Asbestos* does not constitute a hard case for the issue of responsibility, inasmuch as no violation of the GATT disciplines from the French measure was

[54] *EC – Asbestos*, Report of the Panel, 464 (para. 8.304).

[55] See for example *EC – Asbestos*, Report of the Panel, 108 (para. 3.274).

[56] *Ibid*, 121 (para. 3.313).

[57] *EC – Asbestos*, Report of the Panel, 134 (para. 3.353).

[58] *Ibid*, 134 (para. 3.353).

[59] *EC – Asbestos*, Report of the Appellate Body, 71 (para. 193).

established. Hence, the DSB did not issue any recommendation against the EU and France, but rejected the claims of Canada.[60] Some authors believe that no different result was being expected from such a case, given that the health risk of asbestos is known worldwide, and on the other hand, the WTO law allows for certain discretion to its members in taking preventive measures.[61] Others however explore the relevance of the case in terms of the constitutional limits that can be revealed from the joint responsibility regime for matters of non-conferred competences.[62] From the brief overview of the case, it is obvious that the question of responsibility cannot be examined based on the outcomes of the proceedings, given that no responsibility for the violation of WTO disciplines was established. Nevertheless, this case merits attention not much for its outcome, but rather for the theoretical and practical questions that it would raise, if the French measure would have been found in violation of WTO Agreement. As such it could offer significant predictions in terms of distribution of responsibility had the French measure been found in violation of WTO disciplines and unjustified.

The international responsibility of the EU and its Member States in the WTO framework under the premises of *EC – Asbestos* can be analyzed by observing the dynamics of the participation of the EU in the DSP and the outcomes of this participation. This analysis is done by construing a framework of legal questions which assist in elaborating some aspects of the international responsibility arising out of the EU participation in the DSP. The framework is construed upon the chronological order of actions within the DSP, starting with the request for consultations of a concerned Member of the WTO and concluding with the execution (enforcement) of a DSB ruling or recommendation. After explaining the theoretical significance of the questions, the analysis follows with their practical relevance by means of interpretation of the facts of the *EC – Asbestos*. For those questions, which lack a factual basis, the relevant assumptions are made. In this way, the complete analysis serves as a propositional basis for construing a thesis on the international responsibility of the EU and its Member States in terms of participation in the DSP, where the subject matter of the dispute falls out of the conferred competences of the Union.

The selected analytical framework addresses the following questions: To what extent does the DSB consider the question of the EU legitimation in the proceedings, either by its own initiative or by the request of the parties? Is the measure at question enacted by the EU, or by the concerned Member State? Is the Member State transposing an EU directive, implementing an EU legislative act, or is the justification for the measure based purely on national grounds? Does the object of the claims fall under GATT, TRIPS or other Agreements, and more specifically, does it fall exclusively under competences of the EU, and under which type of

[60] *Ibid*, 71, para. 193.

[61] See for example Horn and Weiler (2003), p. 15, republished at Horn and Weiler (2004), pp. 130–131.

[62] See in particular Antoniadis (2004), pp. 335–336.

competences? How does the EU justify the measure taken by its Member State, if the measure was not a result of an EU legislative act? Does the DSB find the measure in compliance with the WTO obligations, and if not, does it find this measure justified? What would be the consequences of a DSB report/recommendation for the measure found in violation of the WTO obligations and unjustified? Would the EU comply with this kind of report, and at what stage? Could the EU be held liable for measures or rather the Member State alone? Should the liability be deemed as joint, would it be possible to divide it between the EU and its Member State? Could the EU part of responsibility be devolved toward other unrelated Member States of the EU? If the EU would comply with the DSB ruling, would its concerned Member State do the same? Would the EU take any internal remedies in case that the concerned Member State would deny the joint responsibility? What would be the reaction of other EU Member States that have no relation with the disputed measure?

Although the questions derived from the *EC – Asbestos* scenario are limited within the doctrinal persuasions, its premises endorse the thesis that the joint responsibility regime sits uneasily with the mixed nature of the WTO Agreement.[63]

### b. The Missing Passive Legitimation Proceedings of the EU at the EC – Asbestos

The passive legitimation of EU as a litigant in the DSP is of a procedural character and essentially concerns the *ratione personae* for the standing of the EU as a respondent in a case. The EU may participate in the DSP as an active or as a passive litigant whenever the subject matter of the dispute is related with a trade measure enacted by the EU, or any of its Member States, as the practice of DSB has shown.[64] This is the result of the joint responsibility regime of the EU and its Member States in the context of WTO Agreement. This practice implies that the EU is a respondent even in those cases where the measure is not enacted as a result of the EU legislation.[65] Although this question involves substantial issues, at this stage it is important to look at the extent to which the DSB considers the question of the EU legitimation in the proceedings, either by its own initiative or by the request of the parties.

The DSB has never elaborated on the procedural standing of the Union or its Member States in the DSP, hence without questioning the capacity of the party to be

---

[63]See also for general observations in relation with mixed agreements Neframi (2012), p. 339. See further Chap. 3.

[64]See also Bourgeois and Lynskey (2008), p. 204. Additionally, the EU and its Member States may join the consultations as third parties in DSP in cases where they have substantial trade interests in the proceedings (Article 4(11) Dispute Settlement Understanding (DSU)).

[65]This issue shall be analyzed further in the following Chapters.

answerable in a dispute settlement proceeding.[66] The consent of the EU in particular cases has substituted the role of the Member State for the institution of the proceedings.[67] Accordingly, although France denied the consensus on the establishment of a panel, the Union's commitment in this regard made the French denial futile, and as a result, the panel was established.[68] The current Dispute Settlement Understanding (DSU), listed as the Annex 2 of the WTO Agreement, has reinforced the character of mandatory jurisdiction for all Members of the WTO by making the consent for establishment of panels irrelevant. From this, it can be inferred that *the Union has been creeping over the role of the Member States in the DSP by substituting them*. This is obviously in line with the sole representation of the Union in the decision-making processes in the WTO. However, the consequences are obviously not the same. The failure of the DSB in questioning the capacity of the EU to be held answerable also for wrongful measures attributed to the Member States raises the question of the effective capacity of the Union to comply with its rulings, for areas of non-conferred competences.

The status of respondent triggers the issue of international responsibility, because the proceedings can result with both the EU and its Member State (s) being liable for violation of WTO obligations. In principle, the sole participation of the Union in the DSP should not prejudice the incidence that the responsibility is attributed to the Member State, although not present in the proceedings.[69] However, there is no formal or substantial ground to preclude the Union, as an answerable party, from being held responsible for a WTO inconsistent measure. In *EC – Asbestos*, the EU was involved in the DSP to serve the claims of Canada in order to conduct consultations for measures taken by France to ban asbestos and products containing them.[70] Canada did not provide any grounds for the answerability of the EU regarding the measures taken by France. In no procedural step was the legitimation of the EU as a passive litigant questioned. Nevertheless, the EU represented France in these proceedings and defended its interests as they were in a principal-agent relationship. From the procedural point of view, the practice of non-justification of EU's *ratione personae* in the DSP neglects the fact that the EU is not competent for all WTO matters, and that the consequences of such a representation could result in unjustified retaliatory measures for the EU. For this reason, from the *formal* point of view, there should be a *justified answerability* of the EU in the DSP based on the justification of the passive legitimation as a procedural position. This requirement could be suggested as a normative criterion necessary for the model of the Union participation in the DSP, after establishing the

[66]See also Heliskoski (2001), p. 175.

[67]Heliskoski (2001), pp. 174–175.

[68]*European Economic Communities—Payments and Subsidies Paid to Processors and Producers of Oilseeds and Related Animal-feed Proteins*, GATT doc. C/M/222, 11 July 1988, Minutes of the Meeting of the Council of 16 June 1988, 7–17.

[69]Heliskoski (2001), pp. 197, 198.

[70]*EC – Asbestos*, Request for Consultation by Canada.

material relevance of this formal aspect. Either the EU or its Member States may, as a matter of procedure, contest the admissibility of an action by reason of misdirection, which would lead to a better formation of the litigation format.[71]

### c. The Relevance of the Division of Powers for the DSP

The question of answerability would not be raised if a prior regulation would exist, or if from the EU constitutional framework, it would become clear that the EU is fully competent for questions falling within the scope of the WTO. Should this proposition be untrue, it would be then important to look for other normative grounds behind the practice of assuming the answerability from the EU for measures of its Member States. The starting point for this analysis is the subject matter of the dispute. The Court differentiated between the GATT disciplines, for which the EU is exclusively competent, and the GATS/TRIPS disciplines, for which the competence should be exercised from the Member States jointly with the EU.[72] It seems that the Treaty of Lisbon[73] faded this argument out by construing the GATS and TRIPS within the exclusive nature of the Common Commercial Policy.[74] However, the constitutional nature of powers in the Union polity does not favor a full substitution of Member States from the Union.[75]

In case that the object of the claim is related with a border measure, such as the ban of the importation and exportation of asbestos, the claimant may assume the presence of the EU in the proceedings, given that its customs territory covers also the territory of France. In *EC – Asbestos* the request for consultations, as well as the subsequent complaints of Canada, were based on the provisions of the GATT and the TBT Agreement, a fact that suggests that the object of the claim may fall within the domain of EU exclusive competences. This logic suffices to legitimate the EU as a passive litigant and suggests that the EU should be the sole passive litigant in the proceedings. However, this logic presumes that the set of GATT disciplines is fully convergent with the set of exclusive competences of the EU. From a careful analysis of the system of the distribution of powers in the Union polity, it can be

[71]Groux and Manin (1985), p. 144.

[72]Opinion 1/94 of the Court of Justice *re WTO Agreement*, [1994] ECR I-5267, paras. 34, 53, 71, 98 and 105.

[73]Treaty of Lisbon Amending the Treaty on European Union and the Treaty Establishing the European Community, 13 December 2007, 2007/C 306/01.

[74]Article 207(4) of the Treaty on the Functioning of the European Union (TFEU) imposes significant safeguard instruments on the exclusive nature of the Common Commercial Policy. It further requires the unanimity procedure for the negotiation and conclusion of international agreements in the areas of trade in services and intellectual property when these agreements risk the Union's cultural and linguistic diversity, or may hinder the responsibility of the Member States to deliver health and educational services.

[75]The implications of this discourse for the joint membership in the WTO shall be considered further in Chap. 3.

inferred that this assumption is not true, inasmuch as the exclusive competences of the EU are inextricably linked with the competences shared with the Member States, or even the residual powers of the Member States.[76] Hence, the landscape of blurred distribution of powers in the Union polity makes it indispensable for the EU and its Member States to participate jointly in the DSP, in order to prevent a situation where an incompetent litigant would be held answerable for the contested measure. As evidenced also in the DSB practice, the EU seems to assume the role of the representative of its Member States, even in cases where it is not very clear that the EU is fully competent for the subject matter of the measure in dispute. Hence, it can be maintained that the question of competences has a decisive role for the attribution of international responsibility,[77] and as such, it plays a significant role for the format of representation in the DSP.

### d. The Causal Link Between the Disputed Measure and EU Legislation

The status of the joint passive litigants for the EU and the concerned Member State is related with the question of answerability for the disputed measure. From a procedural point of view, the issue of answerability depends on the authorship of the measure. One of the factual arguments provided by the EU during the *EC – Asbestos* proceedings was the legislative activity of the EU and its Member States regarding the restrictive measures on the import of asbestos. EU started to legislate on asbestos at the community level as early as 1980. This was made with the aim of achieving a higher level of health protection and preserving the unity of the single market, particularly in terms of the unification of working standards. Following a Council Resolution of 1978, which urged for feasible community measures in the area of standardization and harmonization of measures for the protection of workers against dangerous substances, including asbestos,[78] the Council issued in 1980 a Directive[79] on the protection of workers from the risks related to exposure against chemical, physical and biological agents at work.

This directive addressed the differences between measures that Member States had employed for protecting workers from chemical, physical and biological agents.[80] In order to harmonize such measures, the Directive provided for the relevant legal instrumentalities that enabled Member States to put in place certain measures for avoiding the exposure of workers to dangerous agents or keeping it at the lowest reasonable level. The Directive listed the measures to be taken into

[76]This issue shall be analyzed further in Chap. 3.

[77]See also Neframi (2012), p. 339.

[78]Council Resolution of 29.06.1978 on action programme of the European Communities on safety and health at work, para. 23 of the Preamble and paras. 3, 5, and 7. Official Journal of the European Communities (OJ) No. C 165, 11.07.1978,1.

[79]Council Directive 80/1107/EC of 27.11.1980, OJ No. L 327, 03.12.1980, 8.

[80]*Ibid*, Preamble, paras. 5–6.

account by the Member States, whereas a later Council Directive (83/477/EC)[81] laid down the limit values and specific requirements for the use of asbestos in working sites. Its particular aim was to protect *workers* against risks to their health, including the prevention of such risks, arising or likely to arise from the exposure to asbestos at work.[82] The risk assessment methodology included the nature and the degree of workers' exposure to dust arising from asbestos or materials containing asbestos. In addition to measures on protection of workers from asbestos, the EU imposed certain restrictions on the placing into market of dangerous substances and preparations. Asbestos have been added to the list of the Directive 76/769/EEC[83] after the Council Directive 83/478/ECC.[84] Hence, the structure of restrictions of asbestos and asbestos containing products in the EU has continuously changed as a result of the evolving scientific knowledge. However, it should be noted that these measures were brought in the proceedings as a matter of example; hence the EU was not answerable for them, as they remained out of the subject matter of the proceedings.

In 1996, when the French Decree was approved, the placing on the market and the use of certain categories of asbestos fibres and products containing these fibres was already prohibited at the EU level. In particular, the placing on the market and the use of chrysotile fibres was prohibited for 14 specific categories of products, which in their end-user form could pose a health risk to the general public. Nevertheless, other chrysotile-containing products, such as *asbestos-cement*, which was the bulk of the dispute between Canada and France, *were not covered* by the scope of the Directive.[85] Only several years after the French Decree, the EU decided to ban the chrysotile asbestos in a total scale, including the *asbestos-cement*, with certain exceptions and transitional arrangements.[86] The full transposition of these measures into domestic legislations was due until 1 January 2005. The measure informed by France regarding the transposition of this Directive was precisely the French Decree 1996-1133 and its amendments, namely the Decree

[81]Council Directive 83/477/EC of 19.09.1983 on the protection of workers from the risks related to exposure to asbestos at work (second individual Directive within the meaning of Article 8 of Directive 80/1107/EC), OJ No. L 263, 24.09.1983, 25.

[82]*Ibid*, Article 1.

[83]Council Directive 76/769/EEC of 27.07.1976 on the approximation of the laws, regulations and administrative provisions of the Member States relating to restrictions on the marketing and use of certain dangerous substances and preparations, OJ L 262, 27.9.1976, 201.

[84]Council Directive 83/478/EEC of 19.09.1983, OJ L 263, 24.09.1983, 33.

[85]Council Directive 76/769/EEC. Cf. Antoniadis (2004), p. 336, who considers the French measure of banning asbestos as being in conformity with the relevant Directive, although the French measure goes beyond the scope of the Directive.

[86]Commission Directive 1999/77/EC of 26 .07.1999, OJ L 207, 06.08.1999, 18.

2001-1316[87] and the Decree 2002-1528.[88] The analysis of the said directives also shows that the ban of asbestos at the EU level aims to harmonize the rules of the internal market for the protection of the health of workers and consumers. These measures were enacted pursuant to the EU powers on internal market, but have side effects in terms of health policy, which is a competence that mainly rests with the Member States and, in principle, is excluded from harmonization.[89]

The establishment of a direct causal link between the contested measure and EU legislation is based on the capacity of the EU to take responsibility for the contested measure. Accordingly, from a *substantive* point of view, there should be established a causal link between the subject matter in the dispute and the activity of the EU in relation to that subject matter. The causal link is responsible for establishing the status of EU as litigant in the proceedings, and as such, it constitutes a significant normative criterion able to define the conditions according to which the EU should participate in the DSP. Additionally, this requirement would influence also the criterion of passive legitimation of the EU as respondent.

### e. Justification of the Contested Measure from the EU

The EU assumes answerability in the DSP as a corollary of the joint responsibility regime, despite its involvement in the disputed measure. This can be regarded as a pragmatic behavior from the EU side, which reflects patterns of the internal constitutional order of the EU polity. Having considered the relevance of the causal link between the EU legislation and the contested measure, it is now turned to the question of justification of the French Decree from the EU in the DSP. The content of this justification may determine the relevance of answerability of the EU as litigant. Given that the measure was not the direct result of the EU legislative infrastructure, the EU could not, and actually did not, respond in its own capacity. Rather the EU served as representative of the French interests when it took over the defense of a measure authored by the French decision-makers strictly grounded on national oriented interests.

Indeed, the EU institutions have exercised a different competence in enacting their directives, and namely the internal market competence, while the French decision-maker has clearly used the public health policy, a competence that in the current state of law still belongs to Member States. The EC maintained that the

---

[87]Décret n°2001-1316 du 27 décembre 2001 modifiant le décret n° 96-1133 du 24 décembre 1996 *relatif à l'interdiction de l'amiante, pris en application du code du travail et du code de la consommation*, published in the Official Journal of the French Republic on 29.12.2001, 21,281 and entered into force on 27.12.2001.

[88]Décret n°2002-1528 du 24 décembre 2002 modifiant le décret n° 96-1133 du 24 décembre 1996 *relatif à l'interdiction de l'amiante et le décret n° 96-98 du 7 février 1996 relatif à la protection des travailleurs contre les risques liés à l'inhalation de poussières d'amiante*, published in the Official Journal of the French Republic on 28.12.2002, 21,860 and entered into force on 24.12.2002.

[89]Article 2(5), para. 2 TFEU.

Decree was a mature reflection upon reliable scientific reports and was reasonably justified as the only proper means for addressing the spread of risks from asbestos among the French population. Accordingly, the EC argued that the prohibition of all types of asbestos was the only possible measure to address the concern, while the level of protection should not be judged as it remained under the discretion of the French authorities.[90] With that, the EU manifested that its position in the DSB had nothing to do with its directives, but rather with its keenness to accept responsibility for whatsoever conduct of its Member States in the context of its WTO membership.[91] By accepting that the French Decree was a health measure, the EU implied that it did not result from an internal market competence. The EU could not claim that the French Decree was a transposition of an internal market directive, because the chrysotile-cement was not falling within the scope of the directive at the time when the French Decree was issued. Amidst this dilemma, the EU has thrived its position as a passive litigant by assuming full answerability for the French Decree, although it would not have been able to justify the legitimacy of this conduct from an EU perspective, and the arguments it provided in the DSP support at best this conclusion.

Although the EC Directives were mentioned in the context of factual arguments presented in the DSP, the parties barely used them to argue for the legal basis of the French Decree. On the contrary, at all stages of the proceedings, the Decree was defended as a national measure, which was enacted as an answer to domestic challenges. This is another argument for concluding that the French Decree was not a corollary of the EU policy, but rather a result of domestic processes that occurred in France. Although the French Decree mentions the EU Directives[92] in its preamble, the total ban of asbestos evidently goes far beyond the limited prohibition that the EU standard had in place in 1996. Therefore, if so required by the procedural arrangements, the EU would barely have succeeded in justifying its direct concern, which triggered its participation in the *EC – Asbestos* proceedings. Nevertheless, this issue was not raised at any procedural stage, hence evading any direct challenge with this regard.

Although the EU is the only interested party in the proceedings to deny answerability for measures falling outside the conferred powers, the EU chooses a different role; it adopts defense strategies as a unified trade actor in order to persuade somehow the counterparties. In case that the justification of the causal link between the disputed measure and the EU legislation would be required in the proceedings, the Commission would hardly be able to justify its procedural position, at least from the EU law perspective. And yet, any elaboration on the intrinsic reasons of the EU for not disclosing the gap between the EU directives and the French measure might

[90]*EC – Asbestos*, Report of the Panel, 176–177 (paras. 3.480–3.483).

[91]See also for this conclusion Eeckhout (2006), p. 463.

[92]Council Directive 76/769/EEC and Council Directive 83/189/EEC of 28 March 1983 laying down a procedure for the provision of information in the field of technical standards and regulations.

go beyond the limits of legal argumentation. However, inasmuch as it could speculated that the defense strategies explain this gap, it could be suggested that they may constitute a relevant criterion to be included in the normative model of the Union participation in the DSP.

### f. Findings on the Contested Measure and Its Consequences

The French Decree was defended as a necessary measure for the protection of the health of workers and consumers. As it has resulted from the findings of the DSB, the French measure affects trade in goods, and supposedly it could violate the discipline of Article III:4 GATT, which addresses the obligation to provide equal treatment to domestic and imported products. However, the DSB found that this measure was a formal implementation of public health policies, a fact that according to Article XX:b GATT could serve as a justification tool for violation of GATT obligations. For these reasons, the *EC – Asbestos* did not establish the international responsibility for France and the EU. Hence, the discussion in the following Sections shall be taken at a theoretical level, in order to develop the relevant assumptions on the conduct of the parties, in case that the French measure would have been found in violation of WTO disciplines and unjustified.

### g. Theoretical Implications of the Membership of the EU and Its Member States in the WTO: The 'Formal-Substantive' Gap

Having established that the measure falls in the domain of public health, it is now turned to the compliance of the regulatory power with GATT disciplines. This question can be addressed by employing an analytical structure as a frame of reference, which combines two essential and distinguishable components of the WTO membership, namely the 'substantial' element and the 'formal' one. Accordingly, under the WTO perspective, there exists a general normative assumption that the WTO obligations are borne by states, which are deemed to have full capacity for exercising governmental authority in all substantive areas included in the WTO Agreement. Each of the Members is responsible for honoring the WTO obligations (concessions) by enacting prudent laws and regulations in compliance with WTO obligations. The ability of states to honor their rights and obligations through the exercise of regulatory authority can be conceived as the *formal element* of the WTO membership. This ensures that the substantive content of the WTO Agreement is duly achieved. The *substantive element* consists of rights and obligations providing for the content of trade regimes and disciplines to the benefit of the WTO Members, mainly included in the table of concessions submitted from each Member. The substantive function of the WTO membership corresponds to the ability of the Members to enjoy the substantial trade benefits.

From the WTO law perspective, no differentiation is made between different facets of the WTO membership, meaning that the states are deemed to have full capacities to make use of the substantive elements offered by the WTO Agreement for whatever discipline. Accordingly, the formal and substantial elements of the WTO membership are fully compatible with each other as long as each WTO Member makes use of the substantive content while the corresponding trade partners honor their formal obligations deriving from the WTO membership. In this way, the substantive element is paired indispensably with the corresponding formal element of the WTO membership. The formal/substantive distinction can be seen as a binary function of the WTO membership. This function accommodates on a normative basis the conduct of trade relations between Members and their ability to honor their international obligations. The WTO law remains silent on the areas for which the EU and its Member States are responsible. Absent a separate regime of responsibilities, the EU and its Member States are presumed jointly responsible for all of their WTO obligations.

From the EU law point of view, the WTO membership sits uneasily with the scheme of the distribution of powers. In the EU legal order, the Member States and the EU institutions exercise the governing power in a different way from the traditional states. The way that the powers are sourced and divided in the vertical relationship between the EU institutions and Member States, constitutes one of the central differentiations between the EU and the traditional states.[93] In view of the frame of reference employed for this analysis, it can be maintained that in the case of the EU, the substantive element is not fully compatible with the formal element of the WTO membership. On the one hand, each Member State of the EU makes use of all the substantive content offered by the WTO membership, while it does not possess all the capacities to honor the obligations deriving from the formal component. On the other hand, the EU makes use of a limited number of benefits (i.e. mainly those deriving from GATT disciplines), and exercises formal obligations that are only limited to these disciplines. In the WTO context the compatibility of substantive and formal components of membership of the EU and its Member States is only possible if and to the extent that they act jointly in an unconditional manner. Given that this can only be possible as long as the trade interests of EU Member States converge, the disparity between the formal and substantive elements would result in a gap, which subsequently triggers the question of responsibility for complying with the WTO Agreement. The formal-substantive gap underlies the construction of the duty of loyalty, as an imperative of the EU Treaties for ensuring the joint participation of the Union and the Member States in the WTO Agreement, and the cross-retaliatory system of the DSU is selected as the prime example with this respect.[94] The underlying thesis of this construction consists of

---

[93] Articles 3, 4, 5 TFEU have classified the powers in three main general categories, namely the group of exclusive competences, the group of shared competences and the group of competences to support, coordinate or supplement the actions of Member States (ancillary powers). This abstract classification does not however exhaust the traditional debates on the vertical division of powers and related issues such as the 'competence creep'. This issue shall be addressed further in Chaps. 3 and 4.

[94] Opinion 1/94 of the Court of Justice *re WTO Agreement*, [1994] ECR I-5267, paras. 108–109.

the fact that the Union and the Member States may have joint obligations under the WTO Agreement. These obligations are inextricably interlinked with each other, and for which, either the Union or the Member States are competent to act.

The WTO Agreement does not fully address this gap, but it is limited to the decision-making process only. The division of powers within the EU polity, which constitutes for the WTO perspective an exception to the general logic, may identify the EU and its Member States as a unified actor, which jointly bear the obligation to honor the WTO obligations. As a result, they are considered to bear the burden of the international responsibility for breaching the WTO law jointly. The *EC – Asbestos* is a case that evidences this relationship. Accordingly, the EU has taken the defense of a national measure, which is not based on the EU conferred powers, but rather on residual competences of France. This constitutes a prime example of the incompatibility between the substantive and formal functions of the WTO membership, inasmuch as the French Decree hinders trade in goods (substantive function), whereas the EU has its (formal) obligation to ensure that trade in goods is not hindered.

In addition, it is also important to emphasize that the question of the consequences of responsibility from the WTO membership for the EU and its Member State, being of a formal or substantive nature, are not addressed under the auspices of the WTO law. Rather, the implication of WTO membership for the legal position of the EU and its Member State remains ultimately a question for EU law, and as such, it has to be addressed in terms of the EU legal order.[95]

### h. From Answerability to Liability

The fact that the *EC – Asbestos* did not establish the violation of WTO disciplines, does not deny the theoretical concerns of a potential responsibility of the EU arising from the violation of WTO disciplines from its Member States. Moreover, the fact that the Panel found the French measure in violation of WTO disciplines is evidence that the question of responsibility, in addition to theoretical concerns, has a practical relevance. Had the measure been found in breach of the WTO obligations and unjustified, the situation could have been significantly different and as such, able to provoke consequences for the formal-substantive gap. The EU could have been found responsible for a measure which evidently was more restrictive than the EU legislation, and furthermore was founded on a legal context which falls outside of the EU set of competences.[96]

This would be the result of the EU answerability, which is understood as the ability of the respondent to serve the petitions of the claimant on a subject matter. As a procedural instrument of international practice, the answerability amounts to the acceptance of jurisdiction of the forum. In view of this, the assumption of

[95]See also Heliskoski (2001), p. 227.

[96]See also Eeckhout (2006), p. 461.

answerability leads to the assumption of responsibility arising out of the proceedings on the matter. This proposition is based on the thesis of the unity of elements of answerability and liability, as constituent elements of responsibility, within the same subject. Accordingly, the subject that is liable, is deemed to be answerable for its role in the causation of damages to the victim. Hence, the answerability of the EU in the DSP triggers joint responsibility, which supposedly would be held jointly with France. In case that the French Decree would be found in violation of WTO obligations, the EU would be liable for damages suffered by Canada from the French measure, and this is a corollary of the joint membership in the WTO Agreement. It is therefore necessary to consider the limits that the assumption of answerability should have, and in view of this, it could be necessary to define this element as a normative criterion that could help the construction of the model of EU participation in the DSP.

#### i. The Attribution of Liability and the Distribution of Burden for Violating WTO Disciplines

The next step after the responsibility, is to define the extent to which the EU and France would share their joint liability. Presumably, in a regime of separated responsibilities, only France should be answerable for its measure. However, based on the current state of the law, given that the contested measure falls under the GATT disciplines, the EU is deemed virtually answerable for the French measure. The joint responsibility regime stipulates *a priori* that the burden of liability should be allocated jointly to the EU and Member States. This is distinguished from the several responsibility regime, which would stipulate that the burden arising out of a contested measure violating WTO disciplines, should be allocated to the responsible authority that holds the substantive competence for enacting the measure. Considering that France, under the formal function of the membership, cannot answer for a GATT-related measure, the abstract result of this would be to hold no party responsible. This in turn is an unacceptable thesis from the international law perspective. In order to prevent a 'no liability' regime, the regime of joint responsibility is adopted. The latter holds the EU answerable, although it lacks the material competences to legislate on the measure.

The EU participation in the DSP triggers complex legal questions of a constitutional nature, particularly in terms of the distribution of the burden of responsibility among various stakeholders.[97] The premises of *EC – Asbestos* illustrate the consequences of the theoretical gap between the substantive and formal functions of the WTO membership, in so far as the EU is held answerable by virtue of the joint responsibility regime for a health measure, for which no competences are conferred in the Treaties. This same conclusion is reached even through a different approach

[97] See also Thies (2013), p. 2.

followed by various authors. According to Eeckhout,[98] the first step to define the liability is to *apportion* the international obligation between the joint parties, and only subsequently to *attribute* the conduct to that party. This approach, by determining international responsibility of joint actors pursuant to their obligations, may seem logical in cognitive terms, but in practice it could result in an improper apportion of responsibility due to the formal-substantive gap. Although GATT is conceived from the ECJ as an exclusive area of the EU, the EU still lacks the adequate powers for controlling all the areas related to GATT disciplines. Consequently, the set of the EU responsibilities and obligations assumed under GATT does not correspond to the effective control of the EU over all the areas covered by this Agreement, which in turn makes the model of joint responsibility fallacious. Therefore, in *EC – Asbestos* the fallacy of the proposed model is explained by the fact that the conduct is attributable to France, while the responsibility for this conduct would be attributed to the EU, because the GATT-related formal obligations fall *a priori* within the EU competences.[99] At the same time, the premises of *EC – Asbestos* illustrate the missing capacity of the EU to satisfy the formal obligations, because the necessary powers on public health policies rest with the Member States.

The model of attribution of liability can be further construed under certain premises that consider the conduct of the EU and its Member States as complementary to each other. Accordingly, although the EU has its own international legal personality, it should not be perceived as an alien entity to its Member States. The Member States, as primary stakeholders of the EU polity, play a significant role in the decision-making system and supply its institutions with resources in exchange of benefits of a public nature. Accordingly, the EU and its Member States should be considered as a single but heterogeneous polity, whose internal rules should be able to track the apportion of the conduct to the constituent units. Only after apportioning the conduct, it would be possible to attribute the responsibilities related to this conduct. The responsibility arising out of the EU participation in the DSP, which is due to its formal WTO obligations (*ipso iure*) and not to its conduct in relation to the wrongful measure, should be attributed to the conduct that led to the proceedings. This mechanism could serve as an appendix to the joint responsibility thesis, which would be able to address the formal-substantive gap and its related fallacies.

The central variables, which are common for both the formal-substantive gap of the WTO membership and the joint responsibility regime, rest upon two systemic grounds, which are defined in the EU constitutional framework. Firstly, the vertical distribution of powers in the Union polity is blurred, hence not clear enough to define a separated responsibility regime. Secondly, the competences of the EU and its Member States are inextricably linked, and as such, the performance of the formal functions of the WTO membership is not clearly attributed to the Union or

[98]Eeckhout (2006), p. 461.

[99]Eeckhout (2006), p. 461.

its Member States. This constitutes a premise for the formal-substantive gap of the WTO membership of the Union. In light of these arguments, it can be maintained that the joint responsibility regime is the logical consequence of the need to ensure full compliance of the Union polity with the WTO obligations, which is able to compensate for this gap. The example of the mechanism of cross-retaliation evidences this claim. Accordingly, the ultimate result of the DSP, which holds the EU and its Member States responsible for the violation of WTO disciplines, may entitle a WTO Member to institute countervailing measures not merely within the same area of a disputed measure, and against the relevant EU Member State, but also in other covered WTO Agreements, which may fall under the responsibility of the EU.[100] Under a separated responsibility regime, and taking into account the systemic concerns of the distribution of powers, the cross-retaliatory measures would not be possible to be employed in full scale, inasmuch as the ultimate attribution of responsibility should follow the rules of attribution of conduct for the wrongful act. Hence, the retaliation should be made only against the Member to which the wrongful conduct is attributed, and the cross-retaliation would be limited only to those areas for which this Member is competent. This would make the system of retaliation ineffective, considering that a limited cross-retaliation might not suffice to induce the responsible party to cease the wrongful conduct. Therefore, the regime of joint responsibility is indispensable for ensuring the full scale of effectiveness of the system of retaliation, as a guarantee for compliance with the WTO Agreement.

Building on the premises of *EC – Asbestos*, in case that the EU would have been found responsible for violating the WTO obligations, certainly it would have been faced with the obligation to withdraw the instituted measure, and if this would not be possible, it would become subject to retaliatory measures by Canada amounting to the damages that Canada has suffered from the French measure. Obviously, the EU part of liability would be devolved to its Member States in addition to France. This liability could be held on a solidarity basis only to the extent that the law so provides, or if the affected parties so accept. Otherwise, the solidarity method of distributing a burden that is essentially caused by one of the parties could stimulate defective behaviors in the club, or could cause tension in the Union. All these facets of international responsibility and its attribution pursuant to the rules of attribution of conduct could be relevant for a normative model of the EU participation in the DSP. This model should ensure a proper attribution of liability for violation of WTO disciplines and the allocation of burden based on the authorship of the contested measure, as opposed to the distribution of burden upon solidarity basis, or to the attribution of conduct pursuant to the *a priori* allocation of responsibilities, which is quite an abstract exercise. As it shall be shown further in Chap. 2, the elaboration of these criteria could have normative relevance for the model of participation of EU in the DSP.

---

[100]See also MacLeod et al. (1996), p. 159.

### j. Complying with the DSB Rulings or Recommendations

Another aspect that derives from the attribution of liability to the EU is related to the way in which the EU would oblige a Member State to enact or withdraw a law or a measure that falls outside the conferred powers of the EU. Building on the premises of *EC – Asbestos* this would mean that, in case that the EU would have been found responsible for the trade measures against Canada, the EU would have to require France to withdraw the measure by terminating the effects of the Decree for the prohibition of asbestos and products containing asbestos. However, in case that France would refuse, in its own right, to comply with the DSB ruling, the entire polity could be faced with countervailing measures from Canada. In this case, the EU could initiate infringement proceedings against France.[101] The main question related with this option would be, on what basis could the Union institute such proceedings? Here again the question of competences would come into play, and under a 'state-of-law' community, the issue would be only resolved by the ECJ if France would refuse to comply.[102] Presumably, some constitutional principles of the EU polity, such as the principles of loyalty, effectiveness, primacy, subsidiarity, institutional balance, might assist in compensating for the fallacies of the joint responsibility regime in terms of devolution of liabilities to the unrelated Member States of the Union for matters falling out of the conferred areas of EU powers. However, the question is whether these principles would suffice to resolve the formal-substantive gap and the consequences of the Union participation in DSP for questions of non-conferred competences.

A similar problem has not escaped the attention of the ECJ while providing its opinion on the question of competence of the EU or its Member States on particular issues of the WTO Agreement. The Court has considered that both the EU and the concerned Member States need to cooperate when taking cross-retaliatory measures, given that the EU exclusively covers the scope of GATT, whereas they share competences covering the scope of GATS/TRIPS. Hence, the ECJ conceived the duty to cooperate as an imperative 'way out' that can address the inability (in law) of the EU and its Member States to implement alone the WTO Agreement.[103] This position underlines the fallacy of the joint responsibility regime with regard to the abstract attribution of responsibilities in the vertical relationship between the EU and its Member States and the relevance the distribution of powers can have for this issue. It furthermore suggests significant hints in favor of conceiving a self-regulatory mechanism that can compensate somehow the negative externalities of the joint responsibility regime for the WTO Agreement.

However, the fact that the ECJ conceived this mechanism only for cross-retaliatory measures that would ensure the realization of interests of the Union

---

[101] Antoniadis (2004), p. 335.

[102] See also Eeckhout (2006), pp. 463–464.

[103] Opinion 1/94 of the Court of Justice *re WTO Agreement*, [1994] ECR I-5267, para 109. See also Hyett (2000), p. 249 *et seq.*

and its Member States in their position as active litigants defines this mechanism as incomplete and as a premature model of the distribution of responsibilities. This mechanism can nevertheless become useful if it will be associated also with the ability to address the consequences of participation in the DSP for questions of non-conferred competences. In this way, the fallacies of the joint responsibility regime and the formal-substantive gap that arise out of the WTO membership can be thoroughly addressed through a system of predetermined rules, which combine the general propositions regulating the Union participation in the DSP with the flexible decision-making on managing particular situations.

Obviously, the mechanism conceived by the ECJ for dealing with cross-retaliatory measures is based on the principle of loyalty. In this regard, due consideration should be made to the fact that the principle of loyalty alone may not prove sufficient to ensure the duty to perform international obligations arising out of the DSB decisions.[104] Since the principle of loyalty is not a justiciable legal principle, its normative value in this context may be questionable.[105] Therefore, whether the duty of loyalty can have ultimate normative effects in addressing these concerns remains subject to doctrinal speculations, inasmuch as the practice has proven scarce in this direction.[106]

This jurisprudential conception *in abstracto* on the question of responsibility for compliance with the WTO Agreement reflects however the practical relevance of the theoretical questions raised above. The question of attribution of responsibility in the context of the interlinked obligations of the Union and the Member States in relation with the mixed agreements constitutes a poorly elaborated domain, not only from the normative perspective, but also from the judicial one,[107] and as such, it has become subject to doctrinal discourse.[108] At the same time, this discourse manifests the insufficiency of the dogmatic constructions, such as the duty of cooperation, to provide definite solutions to the question of international responsibility of the EU in terms of the participation in DSP for non-conferred competences. Therefore, another normative criterion that would assist in the definition of a model for the EU representation in the DSP would be related to the element of compliance with the DSB rulings and recommendations, based on the duty to perform international obligations. This duty could allegedly be construed in light of the principle of loyalty, whose normative value, as well as its limitations, should be duly evaluated.[109]

---

[104]See also Antoniadis (2004), p. 328.

[105]Heliskoski (2001), p. 231.

[106]Antoniadis (2004), p. 328.

[107]See also Heliskoski (2001), p. 247.

[108]See particularly on the matter Timmermans (2000), Heliskoski (2001), Antoniadis (2004).

[109]See further Chap. 4 Section Iv.4.

## IV. Concluding Remarks and the Structure of the Work

Generally, certain cases become landmarks when causing a notable shift in jurisprudence, legal doctrine, governance, or legal practice. Others may still attain this status due to the attention or controversies that their reasoning causes in the concerned communities. The *EC – Asbestos* can be considered such a case due to its capability in bringing new perspectives of thinking to the regulators and adjudicators in the application of the central disciplines of the GATT to the regulatory activity of governments.[110] However, this case should not be valued more for the outcomes, but rather for what it did not unveil. Its reasoning values are well known among the academic community, while it is essential to emphasize that the *EC – Asbestos* would have brought into focus significant constitutional questions, had the result not been in favor of France. The issue of international responsibility of the EU and its Member States, which was construed upon its premises, can nevertheless prove relevant not only for the context of the WTO Agreement but also for other mixed agreements of the same kind.

The questions raised in this Chapter aimed to provide a framework of analysis that introduces the problem of attribution of the responsibility from the WTO membership of the Union for areas of non-conferred competences. This analysis considered the way in which the responsibility from the WTO membership would be devolved among the participants in the EU polity, in case that the EU would be held accountable and liable for violation of WTO obligations from a particular EU Member State. The issues of the fallacies of the joint responsibility regime and the formal-substantive gap of the WTO membership of the EU and its Member States, seen in light of the vertical distribution of powers in the EU, are raised not only from a theoretical dimension, but have practical implications, as the analysis of *EC – Asbestos* purported to highlight. The fact that the jurisprudence has only partially addressed this gap by conceiving a self-regulatory mechanism for cross-retaliatory measures, without however elaborating further the question of distribution of joint responsibility, reaffirms the practical relevance anchored in this theoretical problem. Hence, these issues constitute the essential assumptions of this work, which shall permeate the entire structure of the analysis.

In view of these theoretical and practical concerns, this work aims to address the question of the joint responsibility of the EU and its Member States in the context of their WTO membership, under the thesis of the blurred structure of competences in the EU. The ultimate aim is to conceive a normative model for the EU participation in the DSP for matters of non-conferred competences, which is able to address the fallacies of the joint responsibility regime. This model should include propositions that ensure the legal certainty; ensure a proper answerability compatible with the distribution of powers; honor the WTO obligations of the Union polity; provide for a proper allocation of burden and welfare based on the rules of attribution; and take account of the current WTO practice.

[110] Horn and Weiler (2003), pp. 14–15, republished at Horn and Weiler (2004), pp. 129–130.

Chapter 2 elaborates on the joint responsibility regime and its fallacies from the perspective of public international law. The question of joint responsibility in the context of international mixed agreements, with a focus on the WTO Agreement, is then analyzed in Chap. 3. In Chap. 4, the question of international legal responsibility is considered in light of the internal constitutional structure of the Union polity. In this Chapter, the prospect of constitutional principles to address the fallacies of the joint responsibility regime is analyzed on the premises of the rule of law principle and its sub-principles. The constitutional framework of principles is employed as an instrument for criticizing the state of the law and practice of the joint responsibility regime, and as a framework for construing relevant normative predictions for the model of the Union participation in the DSP for matters of non-conferred competences. Chapter 5 elaborates the model of participation of Union in the DSP as a normative context for addressing the fallacies of the joint responsibility regime in the context of WTO membership. This builds on the premises elaborated in the preceding Chapters, and conceives the normative model as an aggregate of: (a) considerations of the legal responsibility as perceived from the international law perspective; (b) the relevant predictions from the context of mixed agreements; and (c) the relevant predictions from the constitutional principles of the EU polity. This approach is justified by the need to address the challenges of the joint responsibility of the EU and its Member States in the WTO Agreement from a new perspective of the legal scholarship, which cultivates the analysis beyond the traditional lines that pursue the solution for the problems within isolated areas of law, such as international law of responsibility, or the law on mixed agreements alone.[111] Chapter 6 concludes.

## References

Antoniadis, Antonis. 2004. The Participation of the European Community in the World Trade Organization: An External Look at European Union Constitution-Building. In *European Union Law for the Twenty-First Century: Rethinking the New Legal Order*. Vol. 1: Constitutional and Public Law: External Relations, ed. Takis Tridimas and Paolisa Nebbia, 321–344. Oxford: Hart.

Bogdandy, Armin von. 2010. Founding Principles. In *Principles of European Constitutional Law*, ed. Armin von Bogdandy and Jürgen Bast, 2nd ed., 11–54. Oxford, Portland, OR; München, Germany: Hart; CH Beck.

Bourgeois, Jacques H.J., and Orla Lynskey. 2008. The Extent to Which the EC Legislature Takes Account of WTO Obligations: Jousting Lessons from European Parliament. In *Law and Practice of EU External Relations: Salient Features of a Changing Landscape*, ed. Alan Dashwood and Marc Maresceau, 202–223. Cambridge: Cambridge University Press.

[111]This approach follows the thesis that the doctrine of principles in the EU legal discourse "contribute[s] to a more reflective legal scholarship exploring the dimensions, foundations and functions of principles in European legal discourse [...] strengthen[s] the role of courts vis-à-vis politics [... and] promotes the project of a European scholarship". Bogdandy (2010), p. 12.

Cremona, Marise. 2012. Member States Agreements as Union Law. In *International Law as Law of the European Union*, ed. Enzo Cannizzaro, Paolo Palchetti, and Ramses A. Wessel, 288–324. Studies in EU external relations, vol. 5. Boston: Martinus Nijhoff.

Dickson, Julie, and John Gardner. 2001. *Evaluation and Legal Theory*. Legal theory today. The Hague: Hart.

Eeckhout, Piet. 2006. The EU and Its Member States in the WTO - Issues of Responsibility. In *Regional Trade Agreements and the WTO Legal System*, ed. Lorand Bartels and Federico Ortino, 449–464. International economic law series. Oxford: Oxford University Press.

———. 2011. *EU External Relations Law*. 2nd ed. Oxford EU law library. Oxford, New York: Oxford University Press.

Groux, Jean, and Philippe Manin. 1985. *The European Communities in the International Order*. The European perspectives series. Brussels, Washington, DC: Commission of the European Communities; European Community Information Service [distributor].

Heliskoski, Joni. 2001. *Mixed Agreements as a Technique for Organizing the International Relations of the European Community and Its Member States*. The Hague, New York: Kluwer Law International.

Hillion, Christophe, and Panos Koutrakos, eds. 2010. *Mixed Agreements Revisited. The EU and Its Member States in the World*. Modern studies in European law, vol. 21. Oxford [England], Portland, OR: Hart.

Horn, Henrik, and Joseph H.H. Weiler. 2003. EC-Asbestos: European Communities - Measures Affecting Asbestos and Asbestos-Containing Products. In *The WTO Case Law of 2001*, ed. Henrik Horn and Petros C. Mavroidis. American Law Institute reporters' studies. Cambridge, New York: Cambridge University Press.

———. 2004. EC-Asbestos: European Communities - Measures Affecting Asbestos and Asbestos-Containing Products. *World Trade Review* 3 (1): 129–151.

Hyett, Stephen. 2000. The Duty of Cooperation: A Flexible Concept. In *The General Law of E.C. External Relations*, ed. Alan Dashwood and Christophe Hillion, 248–253. London: Sweet & Maxwell.

Kuijper, Pieter Jan, and Marco Bronckers. 2005. WTO Law in the European Court of Justice. *Common Market Law Review* 42: 1313–1355.

Leiter, Brian. 2011. The Demarcation Problem in Jurisprudence: A New Case for Scepticism. *Oxford Journal of Legal Studies* 31 (4): 663–677.

MacLeod, I., I.D. Hendry, and Stephen Hyett. 1996. *The External Relations of the European Communities. A Manual of Law and Practice*. Oxford, New York: Clarendon Press; Oxford University Press.

Neframi, Eleftheria. 2012. Mixed Agreements as a Source of European Union Law. In *International Law as Law of the European Union*, ed. Enzo Cannizzaro, Paolo Palchetti, and Ramses A. Wessel, 325–349. Studies in EU external relations, vol. 5. Boston: Martinus Nijhoff.

Stoll, Peter-Tobias. 2012. World Trade Organization (WTO). In *The Max Planck Encyclopedia of Public International Law*, ed. Rüdiger Wolfrum, VII. New York, NY: Oxford University Press.

Thies, Anne. 2013. *International Trade Disputes and EU Liability*. Cambridge studies in European law and policy. New York.

Thym, Daniel. 2010. Foreign Affairs. In *Principles of European Constitutional Law*, ed. Armin von Bogdandy and Jürgen Bast, 2nd ed., 309–343. Oxford, Portland, OR; München, Germany: Hart; CH Beck.

Timmermans, Christiaan. 2000. Organising Joint Participation of E.C. and Member States. In *The General Law of E.C. External Relations*, ed. Alan Dashwood and Christophe Hillion, 239–247. London: Sweet & Maxwell.

———. 2010. Opening Remarks - Evolution of Mixity Since the Leiden 1982 Conference. In *Mixed Agreements Revisited: The EU and Its Member States in the World*, ed. Christophe Hillion and Panos Koutrakos, 1–8. Modern studies in European law, vol. 21. Oxford [England], Portland, OR: Hart.

Tomuschat, Christian. 1983. Liability for Mixed Agreements. In *Mixed Agreements*, ed. David O'Keeffe and Henry G. Schermers, 125–132. Deventer, Boston: Kluwer Law and Taxation Publishers.

———. 2002. The International Responsibility of the European Union. In *The European Union as an Actor in International Relations*, ed. Enzo Cannizzaro, 177–191. The Hague, New York: Kluwer Law International.

Uerpmann-Wittzack, Robert. 2010. The Constitutional Role of International Law. In *Principles of European Constitutional Law*, ed. Armin von Bogdandy and Jürgen Bast, 2nd ed., 131–167. Oxford, Portland, OR; München, Germany: Hart; CH Beck.

# Chapter 2
# Perspectives from the International Law of Responsibility on the Joint Responsibility Regime of the EU and Its Member States

## I. Introduction

The responsibility of the EU and its Member States from their WTO membership is analyzed upon the lines of the international law of responsibility. The international law of responsibility constitutes a substantial pillar for the normative value of the international legal order. With a view to ensure an adequate level of normativity, the analysis of the joint responsibility regime in light of the general predictions of international law shall aim to shed light on some central propositions for the management of the problems resulting from such a regime. This Chapter considers the nature, definition, and the main elements of international law of responsibility. These shall in turn serve as relevant tools for the analysis, interpretation, and construction of the model of participation of the EU and its Member States in the WTO Agreement and the processes related with it. In view of that, this Chapter first offers a general overview of the theoretical aspects of international responsibility. It then highlights the main predictions of the *legi generali* and *legi speciali* on international responsibility and the joint responsibility regime, which are instrumental for the elaboration of the model of EU participation in DSP.

## II. Theoretical Aspects of the International Law of Responsibility

### *1. General Insights on International Responsibility*

The increasing interdependence between states and other entities of international law demands consolidated rules of international responsibility, and a better



P. Ruka, *The International Legal Responsibility of the European Union in the Context of the World Trade Organization in Areas of Non-Conferred Competences*,
DOI 10.1007/978-3-319-57177-5_2

cooperation between states, in order to prevent the dominance of the interests of the group (community) over the individual interests of its constituent entities.[1] The equal protection of interests of all participants from the wrongful conduct of particular entities is an indispensable guarantee for the international legal order.[2] The general aim of international responsibility, is to "(a) prevent or minimize (by deterrence) breach of obligations prescribed by law; [and] (b) to provide remedies for those subjects whose legal rights have been infringed due to such violations".[3]

The legal responsibility is considered "the corollary of international law, the best proof of its existence and the most credible measure of its effectiveness".[4] As a particular category of international law, the international responsibility protects its main subjects, such as states and international organizations, from any invasion of legal interests from other participants.[5] An invasion of legal interests consists of "acts and omissions [that] may be categorized as illegal by reference to the rules establishing rights and duties".[6] The main normative framework determining the conditions for the qualification of a wrongful act and its consequences is mainly regulated in specific international treaties in which these subjects participate (*lex specialis*).[7] However, the general international law is also relevant for defining the elements of legal responsibility, namely the attribution of responsibility, the breach of obligations, the excuse of the breach, and consequences of the breach, such as the reparation and response to the breach (invocation).[8] Each of these elements provides the cognitive function of determining the responsibility in cases of internationally wrongful acts, and can be further combined with the respective propositions in *lex specialis*, namely the treaty determining the content of obligations that are breached from a state or international organization. In addition, the regimes of responsibility under *legi speciali* cannot be construed in total isolation from the general propositions of international law of responsibility.[9] The propositions of *legi generali* can still be applicable given that any violation of state

[1]Eagleton (1928), pp. 228–229 (further considering the increasing human and international intercourse as a cause for the interdependence; hence, the risk of dominance of the interests of the group over the individual is greater. The system of responsibility constitutes a means for precluding dominance and abuse against less fortunate members, and the main challenge remains as to the "most efficient machinery for interpreting, administering, and enforcing that responsibility").

[2]Quigley (1987), p. 131.

[3]Hirsch (1995), p. 8. See also Dupuy (1989), pp. 105–106.

[4]Pellet (2010), 3.

[5]Brownlie (1998), p. 435.

[6]Brownlie (1998), p. 436.

[7]Crawford (2010), p. 20.

[8]Crawford (2010), p. 20 and Crawford (2008), p. 540.

[9]This issue shall be elaborated further in the following Chapter. See further Simma and Pulkowski (2010).

obligations gives rise to state responsibility,[10] hence suggesting a pluralist construction of the rules of responsibility.

The international responsibility is considered an attribute of state sovereignty,[11] inasmuch as states are by nature obliged to protect their authority over their territories and the rights of their populations, and as such, they are responsible for performing their duties.[12] In this quality, the international legal responsibility can be considered a corollary of sovereignty as long as it stands as a guarantee for the realization of rights and obligations among states, which are prerogatives of sovereignty.[13] Subsequently, the responsibility is construed upon these prerogatives of states, which in the international level are further protected by the principles of *pacta sunt servanda* and *bona fide*. These principles, being rooted in the capacity of states and international organizations to enter into treaties and to honor them in good faith,[14] serve as instruments for safeguarding the normative value of international responsibility. This normative value rests on the ability of international rules to trigger foreseeable consequences in case of their violation.[15] This construction confirms the predictions of the Latin maxim '*ubi responsibilitas, ubi ius*', inasmuch as the legal responsibility constitutes a premise for ensuring the legal certainty for all participants.

## *2. The Legal Definition and the Content of International Legal Responsibility*

Before addressing the definition of the international responsibility from a legal perspective, it is relevant to consider certain linguistic connotations of the concept,[16] without nevertheless adopting any comparative analysis of its meaning in

[10]Crawford (2010), p. 21. See also *The 'Rainbow Warrior', (France v. New Zealand),* (1990), 20 RIAA, 215, 251, para. 75. See also Brownlie (1998), p. 438.

[11]*The 'SS' Wimbledon'*, 1923, PCIJ Series A, No. 1, 4, 25. International responsibility serves as "the inevitable regulatory mechanism through which [a] conflict is mediated and the rights of each State may be opposed to those of all others". See further, Pellet (2010), p. 4.

[12]*Island of Palmas, The Netherlands v. USA*, 4 April 1928, 2 RIAA, 831, 839. See further Koskenniemi (2010), p. 47.

[13]Pellet (2010), pp. 4–5, referring also to International Law Commission Draft Articles on Responsibility of States for Internationally Wrongful Acts, with Commentaries, 2001 ('ILC Commentaries to Draft ARSIWA'), Commentary to Article 2 ARSIWA, para. 2, 177.

[14]Crawford (2010), p. 18. See also Vienna Convention on the Law of Treaties between States and International Organizations or between International Organizations (VCLTSIO), 21 March 1986, A/CONF.129/15, art. 26. (Not in force until 09.05.2014). NB: The VCLTSIO is not ratified from the EU and its Member States; therefore, in the context of this work it shall be used as an instructive document.

[15]Pellet (2010), p. 4.

[16]See also Pellet (2010), p. 11, and International Law Commission Yearbook of the International Law Commission, 1973, Volume II, Documents of the twenty-fifth session including the report of the Commission to the General Assembly, 169.

different languages. The elaboration of the concept of 'responsibility' is relevant for discovering any connotations it has for different categories of international responsibility.[17] The concept of 'responsibility' in the sense of 'accountability' suggests the following synonyms: "accountableness, [...] answerability, bounden duty, boundness, burden, chargeability, commitment, compulsion, culpability, duty, encumbrance, engagement, imperative duty, liability, obligation, obligatoriness, pledge, promise, *rationem rei*, subjection to, that which is owing".[18] The term 'responsibility' refers essentially to 'liability'.[19] The main connotations that the concept of responsibility implies are developed in the context of private and criminal national law. In these legal disciplines, the concept of responsibility may imply that "under legal rules [someone] is liable to be made either to suffer or to pay compensation in certain eventualities [...] for his own actions or the harm he has done, [... or] for the actions of other persons [amounting to] 'legal accountability'".[20] Additionally, the concept of responsibility includes also "the capacity, so far as this is a matter of a man's mind or will, which normal people have to control their actions and conform to law".[21]

These facets of the concept of responsibility influence the meaning of the legal responsibility in international law. The concept of international responsibility is based on the premises of state sovereignty, such as the ability of states to assert rights and to discharge obligations. By keeping a significant distance from different understandings of the concept of responsibility in national law, the international law has developed its own concept of legal responsibility. The evolutionary course of this concept has started with the definition of responsibility as an "obligation to make reparation",[22] which implies the necessity to objectively determine the 'damage' that the injured state has incurred. The jurisprudence has maintained this approach, by stating that "it is a principle of international law, and even a general conception of law, that any breach of an engagement involves an obligation to make reparation", while the "reparation is the indispensable complement of a failure to apply a convention".[23] Obviously, the definition of responsibility as an obligation to make reparation is rather limited to those breaches of international law for which an actual damage is sustained. The concept of responsibility was expanded in the course of evolution to include damages to moral interests in addition to those to economic interests, and furthermore, it was regarded as a

[17]The reason for this limitation, more than conditioned from the research question, is related with the difficulties that this concept entails in various languages, such as in English, French, Albanian, etc.

[18]See the entry 'Responsibility' in Burton (1998), p. 469.

[19]Garner and Black (1999), p. 1314, entry "Responsibility".

[20]Hart (1968), pp. 196–197.

[21]Hart (1968), p. 197.

[22]Pellet (2010), p. 5, referring also to Grotius et al. (2005), Ch. CVII, para. 1 (Vol. II, 884), and Jouannet (1998), p. 407.

[23]*The Factory at Chorzów*, Merits, 1928, PCIJ, Series A, No. 17, 29, and *The Factory at Chorzów*, Jurisdiction, 1927, PCIJ, Series A, No. 9, 21.

corollary of an internationally wrongful act, which is considered a more general concept that includes damages from injuries.[24]

By expanding the concept of international responsibility beyond damages to economic interests, its normative scope is increased not only quantitatively, by protecting more areas of primary relations, but also qualitatively, by adopting an 'objective' rather than a 'subjective' approach for the conception of international responsibility. This approach allows for the construction of responsibility on a relationship basis and neglects any substantial contribution that the element of fault may have for attributing the legal responsibility on states, despite the role that the elements of intention (*dolus*) and negligence (*culpa*) might have in the scale of damages.[25] According to the doctrine of 'objective responsibility', states are responsible for acts committed by their officials or their organs, despite the absence of fault on their part and regardless of whether these organs where acting within the limits of their powers or not.[26] The 'objectivization' of international responsibility predicts that,

> [the] international law must be respected independently of the consequences of a violation and any breach entails the responsibility of its author, while the content of such responsibility, its concrete effects, varies according to whether or not the internationally wrongful act has caused damage, and according to the nature of the norm breached.[27]

The function of distinguishing between the primary relationship of the parties, which includes their rights and obligations, from the secondary relationship that emerges as a result of an internationally wrongful act infringing this primary relationship, is instrumental for addressing the consequences of this violation. The concept of internationally wrongful act is fundamental for the content of legal responsibility. This concept is described as an act that is forbidden or disallowed by an international rule, and as such, it is not permissible in any circumstances.[28] The prohibited conduct constitutes the legal reason against performing an internationally wrongful act; hence, such act should not be done, and if done, its performance should cease in order to bring the state of illegality to an end.[29] This framework constitutes a theoretical standard for developing normative judgments whenever states or international organizations commit internationally wrongful acts. Subsequently they may face restrictions on their sovereignty, in order to restore the injured legal order.

Both the traditional and the current definitions of the concept of responsibility have a common feature in terms of the way in which they are conceived. Accordingly, the traditional understanding of the internationally wrongful act regards it as

---

[24]ILC Commentaries to Draft ARSIWA, Commentary to Article 3 ARSIWA, paras. 12 183.

[25]Brownlie (1998), pp. 439 and 444.

[26]Brownlie (1998), p. 440, referring to *Estate of Jean-Baptiste Caire (France) v. United Mexican States*, (1929) 5 RIAA, 516, 529.

[27]Pellet (2010), p. 9.

[28]Crawford and Watkins (2010), p. 286.

[29]Crawford and Watkins (2010), p. 286.

a violation of an international obligation, "accompanied by the appearance of a *new legal relationship* between the State to which the act is imputable, which is obliged to make reparation, and the State with respect to which the unfulfilled obligation existed, which can demand reparation".[30] Similarly, the International Law Commission (ILC) Articles on Responsibility of States for Internationally Wrongful Acts (2001),[31] (ARSIWA), which have codified the progressive development of the international law of state responsibility, regard the term "international responsibility" [as covering] the *new legal relations* which arise under international law by reason of the internationally wrongful act of a State".[32] In both these definitions, the responsibility is considered as part of a 'new legal relationship', which results from the fact of the infringement of an international obligation by an internationally wrongful act. This relationship is distinguished from the contest of rights and obligations between parties, which gave rise to this relationship, and as such, can be addressed in light of a separate set of rules and norms which regulate the regime of responsibility.

The content of treaties, which are binding on states, constitutes the object of the legal relationship protected by the legal institution of international responsibility. The internationally wrongful act, defined as the act violating this content and the obligations prescribed in the treaties, constitutes the juridical fact that gives rise to the new relationship of international responsibility, which is presumed to be regulated from the general norms of international law on responsibility (*legi generali*). This presumption can be reversed only in the presence of more specific propositions (*lex specialis*), which would take precedence over the *legi generali*.[33] These propositions can be part of the violated treaty and regulate the relationship of responsibility in an exclusive manner.

## 3. The Nature of International Responsibility

The international legal responsibility constitutes a new legal relationship that arises as a corollary of the internationally wrongful act. The consequences of an internationally wrongful act may differ pursuant to the nature of the primary obligations

---

[30]Pellet (2010), p. 5, referring to Anzilotti (1999), p. 467. (Emphasis added). The concept of 'imputability' has the same meaning with the concept of 'attributability', and may in this work be used interchangeably. On a further terminological discussion see Condorelli and Kress (2010), p. 233.

[31]Adopted by the International Law Commission at its fifty-third session, in 2001, and submitted to the General Assembly, which adopted with the resolution 56/83 of 12 December 2001, and corrected by document A/56/49(Vol. I)/Corr.4.

[32]Commentary to Article 1 ARSIWA, paras. 1, 32 (emphasis added). See also General Commentary to ARSIWA, paras. 1, 31.

[33]The distinction between *legi generali* and *lex specialis* shall be considered in the following Section.

provided in the treaty. Accordingly, one can distinguish between different kinds of obligations of the parties.[34] An obligation of conduct (or means) refers to an obligation to endeavor, to strive, or to put the best efforts, for achieving a particular result, but without an ultimate commitment.[35] This is to be distinguished from an obligation of result (or end), which refers to a burden on the addressee to attain a precise result, hence to guarantee the outcome.[36] The distinction between these categories is relevant for the regime of responsibility, inasmuch as it determines the nature of reparations of the consequences of the wrongful act.[37]

In principle, only the internationally wrongful acts are able to trigger international responsibility. This means that lawful acts may be subject to another type of liability, which includes compensation, but triggers no responsibility, since the element of illegality is missing.[38] This regime can be particularly useful to ensure that the operators under the jurisdiction of the defecting states are held liable for damages caused by them, in order to provide prompt, adequate, and effective compensation to the victims of the hazardous activities.[39] Furthermore, one can distinguish also obligations that do not cause damages, but still trigger international responsibility. While in the case of mere responsibility (with reference to no damages) the main consequence is the obligation to comply, in the case of liability, the main consequence of incurring responsibility is the obligation to make reparation. Both these situations may give rise to reprisal relationships, such as countermeasures, which are regarded as methods aiming to enforce compliance with primary or secondary obligations.

One of the properties of international responsibility is the element of answerability contained therein. The concept of responsibility may entail 'answerability'

---

[34]This art of classification of obligations is inspired from the civil law tradition. See for a thorough analysis for the impact of this classification for the law of international responsibility Dupuy (1999). Although the implications of this classification for the regime of responsibility may not be quite obvious, the theoretical implications may be considered useful for emphasizing the normative nature of various formulations of responsibility regimes, as shall be later elaborated in Chap. 5.

[35]Dupuy (1999), pp. 375, 378. See also Crawford (1999), p. 21, para. 57.

[36]Dupuy (1999), pp. 375, 378.

[37]There may be however cases where formulations of obligations of conduct seem to depend on the achievement of the result as a proof that the obligation of conduct is observed (due diligence of a state in committing an act). See further Dupuy (1999), pp. 378–380.

[38]This differentiation is endorsed from the practice of the ILC, which has distinguished ARSIWA (2001), addressing the consequences of breach of international obligations through internationally wrongful acts, from the Articles on the Prevention of Transboundary Harm from Hazardous Activities (2001) and the Principles on the Allocation of Loss in the Case of Transboundary Harm Arising Out of Hazardous Activities (2006), which address liability from lawful acts. The regime of liability in the vein of the latter documents is regarded as complementary to the regime of responsibility of states. See further Boyle (2010), pp. 94, 99.

[39]Principles 3, 4, 6 of the ILC Principles on the Allocation of Loss in the Case of Transboundary Harm Arising Out of Hazardous Activities (2006). This category is excluded from the scope of this work, considering that the non-compliance with WTO obligations includes an illegal element.

for a wrongful act, which consists of an obligation to call into account a subject for its conduct and to make it respond to any moral or legal charges.[40] Although answerability may be conceived as a capacity for establishing accountability, it might not necessarily lead to liability, given that the subject taken into account might offer a valid justification for his conduct.[41] The concept of responsibility as liability includes those situations where the breach has been established and imputed to responsible subjects, which shall be held liable for violating their international obligations. This entails a response of community against the wrong-doer by means of punishment, censure, or enforced compensation.[42] The state of liability consists of principles that determine the legal consequences of the breach of international obligations, and shape the judicial response against the violation of international norms.[43] Such liabilities can be found in regimes of civil or criminal liability against states, international organizations, or nationals.[44]

This distinction between accountability and liability as two facets of responsibility has significant procedural implications. Answerability finds its place in the rules determining the *locus standi* and the admissibility of claims, and concerns preliminary phases of the legal process.[45] The claimant state calls into account the respondent state aiming to make it morally or legally accountable for conduct that allegedly violates an international norm. The parties have to justify their legitimation in the proceedings, by justifying the connection of the claimant with the consequences of the internationally wrongful act, and the connection of the respondent with the authorship of this act.

The process of answerability is complemented with the element of liability, inasmuch as from the proceedings it becomes clear that the respondent should be held accountable for the internationally wrongful act. The regime of accountability entails two main predictions. In the first place, this regime forbids the internationally wrongful act by means of an international rule. This implies that an internationally wrongful act "is not a permissible act for which a price is charged or an act which a state is entitled to perform so long as it provides adequate reparation for any resulting harms; it is an act which should not be done; if done and the performance is ongoing [. . .], it should cease".[46] In the second place, the regime of accountability predicts that the consequences of an internationally wrongful act should be

---

[40]Crawford and Watkins (2010), p. 283.

[41]Crawford and Watkins (2010), p. 283.

[42]Crawford and Watkins (2010), p. 284.

[43]Crawford and Watkins (2010), p. 284.

[44]Crawford and Watkins (2010), p. 284. The concept of nationals includes the natural and legal persons.

[45]Crawford and Watkins (2010), p. 284.

[46]Crawford and Watkins (2010), p. 286.

undone to the highest possible extent.[47] Both these predictions could possibly remain in cases of difficulty to reestablish the *status quo ante*.[48] The abstract nature of these predictions is present also in the WTO system of international responsibility. The first prediction would imply that, once a measure instituted by a WTO Member is regarded WTO inconsistent, it should be withdrawn immediately, as there can be no price to be charged for keeping it in place. However, this legal presumption can be reversed on a temporary basis by allowing the victim to suspend concessions for the wrongdoer, without recovering nevertheless the suffered damages; hence, it lets the losses lie where they fall. This system challenges the model of international responsibility, as it provides no incentives for defecting Members to terminate the state of illegality.

The answerability and liability, as elements of responsibility, are significant for the EU participation in the DSP. The EU is called into DSP whenever a Member State is claimed to have committed an internationally wrongful act in terms of its WTO obligations. Without taking into consideration the relevance of the joint responsibility regime in this regard, the predictions on the *locus standi* suggest that the EU should be able to justify its procedural position as a respondent. This justification is usually evaded for a number of normative and non-normative reasons related with the way the EU polity works. A normative reason is the joint responsibility regime, which predicts *a priori* that the EU and its Member States shall be jointly responsible for their obligations arising out of the mixed agreements, such as the WTO Agreement.[49] A non-normative reason is the political tendency of the EU institutions to represent the EU in the international trade as a consolidated block in order to gain greater global power. This coincides with the interests of Member States, which prefer to be represented by the EU in order to show in the proceedings more power against the claimant. Nevertheless, the failure of the EU to justify its procedural position does not prejudice its ability to answer, hence to be called accountable for the disputed subject matter. Indeed, as it happened with *EC – Asbestos*, the EU was held answerable during the proceedings for measures instituted by France. Following the predictions on answerability, it could be argued that the EU should not be called into account for a measure that is instituted by its Member States as long as this measure is not instituted in the context of EU legislation. This would constitute a paradox for the regime of answerability. Hence, the status of accountability and liability are attributed to the EU *ex relatione* rather than subjectively. The WTO legal system has been so far indifferent to this contradiction; it has employed the regime of joint responsibility of the EU and its Member States.

---

[47] Crawford and Watkins (2010), p. 286.

[48] Crawford and Watkins (2010), p. 286.

[49] See *infra* Chap. 3.

## III. International Responsibility According to *legi generali*

From the above overview, it becomes clear that international responsibility refers to the secondary relationship emerging after a subject of international law has breached its obligations instituted in the primary relationship. The following elaborates on the elements of the responsibility of states and international organizations according to *legi generali*, as a premise for analyzing the joint responsibility regime of the Union and its Member States from the WTO membership.

The fragmentation of public international law, mainly resulting from a missing hierarchical structure of norms and a unified constitutional source, carries its effect also in terms of the international responsibility of states and international organizations. As there is, so far, no general binding treaty regulating the matter of international responsibility, this work shall take into account the customary law on the state responsibility, as codified from the ILC. The products of this codification are particularly the ARSIWA and the ILC Draft Articles on the Responsibility of International Organizations (2011) (DARIO).[50] These instruments have not yet received the status of the treaty law, as long as they are not adopted from states. Nevertheless, they express the authority of customary international law,[51] and as such, they may be qualified as recognized sources of international law pursuant to Article 38 of the Statute of the International Court of Justice (1945).[52] From a functional perspective, these rules "can usefully be seen as embodying higher-order decisions about the reason-giving and loss-shifting functions of international legal prohibitions".[53] From a systematic point of view, the ARSIWA provides a systematization of the system of responsibility of states. The DARIO follows the same structure of ARSIWA, and as such, these instruments contain similar (if not identical) legal institutions and principles.[54]

### *1. The Internationally Wrongful Act and the Attribution of Conduct to States and International Organizations*

The international responsibility of states and international organizations is triggered from their wrongful conduct, which is defined in Articles 2–3 ARSIWA and 4–5

[50] Adopted by the International Law Commission at its sixty-third session, in 2011, and submitted to the General Assembly as a part of the Commission's report covering the work of that session (A/66/10, para. 87).

[51] Crawford (2008), p. 540.

[52] The Statute of the International Court of Justice, 26 June 1945, 15 UNCIO 355, constitutes an integral part of the Charter of United Nations pursuant to Article 92 of the Charter.

[53] Crawford and Watkins (2010), p. 287.

[54] For this reason, the main elements of international responsibility of states and international organizations provided in these instruments shall be considered jointly in the following Sections.

DARIO respectively. This conduct consists of actions and omissions in violation of international obligations that can be attributed to states or international organizations, and as such, give rise to international responsibility (Articles 1, 2 ARSIWA and 3, 4 DARIO). The rules of attribution address the way in which the internationally wrongful conduct is attributed to states and international organizations. The element of attribution plays a primary role in establishing a connection between the internationally wrongful act and the state or the international organization (Articles 2(a) ARSIWA and 4(a) DARIO). The second condition of the internationally wrongful act refers to the breach of an international obligation, which should be attributed to the state or international organization (Articles 2(b) ARSIWA and 4 (b) DARIO). Additionally, it may also be suggested that a third element for triggering international responsibility is the inability to justify the internationally wrongful conduct pursuant to any of the grounds precluding wrongfulness, which are provided in Articles 20–25 ARSIWA and 20–25 DARIO.[55] Although constituting distinct normative operations, these elements are cumulatively employed to determine the state of wrongfulness of conduct.[56]

ARSIWA have classified the different configurations of attribution in four main categories, while DARIO only partially follows this scheme. The first category (Articles 4–7 ARSIWA and 6–8 DARIO) addresses the conduct of *de jure* organs of a state or international organization, the conduct of persons or organs exercising elements of governmental authority, the conduct of organs of a state or organs and agents of an international organization placed at the disposal of another state or international organization, and the excess of authority (*ultra vires* action) or contravention of instructions. Article 4 ARSIWA considers as an act of the state the conduct of any state organ, whether exercising legislative, executive, judicial, or any other functions, whatever the position in the organizational structure of the state and its character as an organ of the central or local government. Similarly, Article 6 DARIO provides that a wrongful conduct of the organs or agents of an international organization is attributed to the organization itself, whatever their position in this organization. Article 5 ARSIWA provides that the wrongful conduct is attributed to a state, even if the person or entity is not an organ of the state, but exercises elements of governmental authority in that particular conduct.[57] In this way, the companies commissioned by states to perform public services, as well as other entities controlled by states, may be regarded as state organs if they commit internationally wrongful acts.[58] Furthermore, states have to maintain their international obligations irrespective of the role of the private parties in conducting internationally wrongful acts.[59] According to Articles 6 ARSIWA and 7 DARIO,

[55] Condorelli and Kress (2010), p. 224.

[56] See also Stern (2010a), pp. 201–202.

[57] See also Dupuy (2010), p. 176.

[58] See also Crawford (2008), p. 544.

[59] *Canada – Measures Affecting the Importation of Milk and the Exportation of Dairy Products* (WT/DS103 and WT/DS113), Report of the Appellate Body of 20 December 2002).

the conduct of an organ of a state, or an organ, or an agent of an international organization, which is placed at the disposal of another state or international organization, shall be regarded as conduct of the state or organization at the disposal of which the organ or agent is placed. The exercise of governmental functions remains the central element that matters in attributing the responsibility to states, and prevails over any justifications for excess of authority from governmental authorities in violating obligations of states and international organizations (Article 7 ARSIWA and Article 8 DARIO). Hence, the excess of powers (*ultra vires* action), which pursuant to the municipal law of states, or the internal rules of international organizations, could amount to a legal reason for the invalidity of the act, does not constitute an excuse for justifying states or international organizations for the breach of their international obligations.[60]

The following provisions address the conduct of persons or entities, which behave as *de facto* organs of states. Accordingly, the second category concerns the conduct of persons directed or controlled by a state. Pursuant to Article 8 ARSIWA, the conduct shall be attributed to a state if a person or a group of persons is under the control or the instructions of that state. In this configuration, the basic element for establishing the attribution of conduct to a state is the exercise of the 'effective control', while a wide interpretation could include also the exercise of the 'overall control'.[61] Furthermore, Article 9 ARSIWA provides that the state is also responsible for the conduct of persons exercising governmental authority in absence or in default of the official authorities. Here the emphasis is put on the 'effective organization' of state activity, which takes precedence over the formal organization of the state.[62] The third category includes the conduct of an insurrectional or other movement, which, pursuant to Article 10 ARSIWA, is attributed to the state, whose government is formed by this movement, being that an existing or a new state. In this way, the wrongful conduct of the movement is connected with the organs of the state succeeding the movement. The fourth category refers to the conduct that is acknowledged and adopted by a state as its own, and, pursuant to Article 11 ARSIWA, is attributed to that state if the preceding configurations fail to apply.

The question of attribution of conduct becomes quite complex in the context of international obligations of states and international organizations. The international organizations appear as actors in international law similarly to states, although they lack territory, population, and the relevant sovereignty; hence, they can be described as abstract creations of states. International organizations are recognized as legal entities, and as such, they are distinguished by states. Any allegations for

[60](Article 27 VCLT and Articles 3, 32 ARSIWA and Articles 5, 32 DARIO). See further Condorelli and Kress (2010), p. 230.

[61]Condorelli and Kress (2010), p. 230.

[62]Condorelli and Kress (2010), p. 231.

their consideration as 'superstates' are denied.[63] Rather, international organizations are considered subjects of international law, which are bound by any obligations incumbent upon them by virtue of general rules of international law, their constitutions, or under international agreements to which they are parties.[64] From this, it can be inferred that international legal responsibility is not an exclusive attribute of states. International organizations, as derivatives of states, may also bear international responsibility. State responsibility serves as a cognitive model for the responsibility of international organizations.[65] Indeed, international organizations cannot claim their abstract nature to ensure them to escape international responsibility.[66]

The connection between the state responsibility and the responsibility of international organizations results from their constitutional compound. In view of this, international organizations incur responsibility as a corollary of their legal personality, which has ensured them the capacity to assert rights and to discharge obligations.[67] Hence, the international organizations have the ability to invoke the responsibility of other entities, and at the same time, to guarantee their obligations with full responsibility.[68]

One of the central criteria for the internationally wrongful acts entailing the responsibility of international organizations is the establishment of the link between the organization and the organ, agent, or person that has committed the wrongful act. One way to establish this connection is to analyze their formal relationship; the other way would be to consider the exercise of control from the organization upon the agent or organs.[69] The internationally wrongful act should fall under the control or the scope of the organs or agents of the international organization in order for the conduct to be attributed to it.[70] The evaluation of the criterion of control receives particular interest, in that it should "comprise a series of competences and attributions, the various elements of which need not necessarily be present in each and every case but which, taken as a whole, must be sufficiently strong and coherent to justify effective allegiance [...] of the agent or entity of the organization".[71] Additionally, in order to be attributable to the organization, it is also necessary that the wrongful conduct is committed in the framework of the official function of

---

[63] *Reparation for injuries Suffered in the Service of the United Nations*, Advisory Opinion, I.C.J. Reports 1949, 174, 179.

[64] *Interpretation of the Agreement of 25 March 1951 between the WHO and Egypt*, Advisory Opinion, I. C.J. Reports 1980, 73, 89–90, para. 37.

[65] Crawford (2010), p. 17.

[66] See also Tomuschat (2002), p. 179.

[67] See in particular, *Reparation for injuries Suffered in the Service of the United Nations*, Advisory Opinion, 179. See also Pellet (2010), pp. 4–6.

[68] See also Pellet (2010), p. 7.

[69] Klein (2010), p. 298.

[70] Klein (2010), p. 304.

[71] Klein (2010), p. 300 (with further reference).

the agent or the body of international organization.[72] The responsibility can be also attributed to the organization in cases of *ultra vires* action of its agents. Accordingly, the illegality of conduct pursuant to the internal rules of the organization due to the violation of material competences or procedural rules, or due to the action beyond the limits of the prescribed instructions set to the agent, does not preclude the responsibility of organization.[73] Hence, the official function remains a criterion *sine qua non* for attributing the international responsibility to the organization.[74]

The international responsibility of international organizations is nevertheless subject to a number of limitations. On the one hand, international organizations remain instruments of states, and on the other, states take the central decisions on the course of the organization in the capacity of their stakeholders.[75] Furthermore, the conferred powers constitute another crucial limitation for the scope of the organizations. This limitation is central for the question of international responsibility, and is designated as the principle of specialty, which characterizes the competences of international organizations.[76] In the presence of the limited resources, these elements predict a 'limited responsibility' regime for the international organizations. In view of these limitations, the responsibility of international organizations is obviously a derivative of the limited legal personality, which allows these organizations to undertake international obligations that trigger responsibility only for the entrusted functions.

In light of these general observations, it is noteworthy to consider the relevance of the general predictions of responsibility for international organizations for the EU. The EU is considered to be very close to statehood, and this suggests that the Union must be subject to the regime of international responsibility similar to states and international organizations.[77] However, due to many differentiating factors, the EU is considered neither a state, nor an international organization. In light of these factors, it can be maintained that the general rules of responsibility of international organizations may partly apply to the EU, particularly in terms of the relationship with the Member States. The affinity of the EU with the statehood may further suggest that the Union may be also subject to general rules of international responsibility applicable to states.[78]

The hybrid nature of the EU as an international organization and as a 'Union of States' is reflected also in the concomitant application of rules of international responsibility of states and international organizations. The nature of constitutional relationship in the Union polity is not without implications for the WTO obligations of the EU and its Member States. The responsibility from this membership is

---

[72]Klein (2010), p. 304.

[73]Klein (2010), p. 304.

[74]Klein (2010), p. 306.

[75]Condorelli and Kress (2010), p. 222.

[76]Pellet (2010), p. 7.

[77]Tomuschat (2002), p. 183.

[78]Tomuschat (2002), p. 183.

attributed to the EU and is further devolved to Member States, in that they are the ultimate holders of the burden of responsibility. Obviously, the question of the vertical distribution of powers (Chap. 3) has a say in this context. The limitation imposed from the vertical distribution of powers discloses a further state of tension in terms of the way in which the Member States and the EU control the actions of each other in the context of their WTO membership. Accordingly, the Union cannot control the WTO action of the Member States for matters falling within their residual powers, while the Member States could control the Union only for the part of the conferred powers. From this, following the predictions of the criterion of control and the principle of specialty for the attribution of responsibility, it can be inferred that the responsibility from the WTO membership should be attributed to the Union for the part of the conferred powers. The complexity of this thesis is further stressed in light of *ultra vires* actions of the EU or its Member States in the context of the WTO obligations. Accordingly, considering that *ultra vires* is not among the reasons for avoiding responsibility, the responsibility from the WTO membership is attributed to the Union and its Member States jointly, despite the fact whether they are acting within the legitimate areas of powers or not.

From a general consideration of these predictions, it becomes clear that the principle of attribution of conduct entails the unity between the conduct and the wrongdoer, as a premise for incurring international responsibility. As a normative operation, the attribution of conduct aims to establish that a wrongful conduct is attributed to a state for the purpose of responsibility, without prejudicing its legality.[79] The attribution of conduct ensures that the internationally wrongful conduct of nationals is imputed to the state as a subject of international law, on behalf of which they are acting.[80] The elements of control or disposition (agency) are crucial in this operation. From these predictions, it could be inferred that the principle of attribution does not entail situations in which the states could be qualified as wrongdoers for conduct, which has been committed out of their control or authorization. In the premises of the *EC – Asbestos* scenario, this would imply that the Union cannot, in principle, assume the authorship for a measure which has been instituted out of its control or agency, hence without its authorization, inasmuch as the French Decree is not transposing EU legislation.

The question of attribution of powers can be further analyzed in view of the law of the treaties. The doctrine of substitution provides for the succession or the continuity of rights and obligations from international treaties in cases where a state member into a treaty joins a federal state or an international organization. With the premises of *EC – Asbestos* scenario in mind, the question to be addressed is whether the doctrine of substitution would apply to the WTO membership of the EU and its Member States. Furthermore, could this doctrine be able to explain the sole participation of the EU in the DSP and the attribution of responsibility for all the WTO inconsistent measures? In light of Article 30 Vienna Convention on the

[79]ILC Commentaries to Draft ARSIWA, Commentary to Article 4.

[80]Stern (2010a), p. 202.

Law of Treaties (1969) (VCLT), the Member States may not absolve their responsibility toward third parties by transferring their powers to the EU institutions, inasmuch as the GATT 1947 precedes the EU Treaties, unless the EU would assume the relevant obligations, and the responsibility of the Member States would not be compromised.[81] This proposition suggests that the assumption of obligations from the EU absolves the Member States from their responsibilities toward third parties.

The transfer of powers from Member States to the EU level may entail an '*ipso jure*' succession of certain treaty rights and obligations in relation with the third parties in this treaty.[82] In the context of WTO obligations, this could imply that the EU is entitled to participate in the DSP only for matters falling within the areas of the transferred powers. Only in this way, the obligations arising out of this participation would be legitimate for the Union polity. In practice, since the EU has not assumed all the relevant obligations of Member States from the GATT, it cannot succeed the Member States in all aspects of the WTO membership. Hence, for matters falling within the scope of residual competences of the Member States, the EU is not entitled to assume such obligations as long as no transfer of powers has taken place, and as a result, the duty to comply with the WTO obligations has remained with the Member States. In this way, the sole participation of the Union in the DSP is not explained from the doctrine of substitution alone. Following the rules of attribution, the wrongful conduct of the Member States, from a normative perspective, should not be attributed to the Union, in cases that this conduct is part of the residual powers of the Member States.

## 2. The Breach of International Obligations

The second element of the international responsibility refers to the breach of international obligations from states or international organizations (Articles 2 (b) ARSIWA and 4(b) DARIO). The element of breach is defined as a situation in which an act of a state or international organization is not in conformity with what is required of them by an international obligation (Articles 12 ARSIWA and 10 DARIO). The breach is objectively assessed by comparing the conduct that the state or international organization is expected to have pursuant to the normative predictions of the obligation, with the actual conduct the subject has committed.[83] In this way, the international breach is determined by the relationship of two

[81] See also Hirsch (1995), pp. 53–54.

[82] Pescatore (1979), pp. 637–638. For a further analysis of the succession or continuity of treaty rights and obligations in traditional theories see O'Connell (1963), p. 54 *et seq*.

[83] Stern (2010a), p. 209.

elements: the conduct as a material fact, and the rule of law determining the 'ought-to' conduct of the state or international organization (as a matter of law).[84] In this relationship the action, as a positive act, or the omission, as a negative act, are respectively juxtaposed to the international obligation, which consists of a duty to commit a certain act or to refrain from a forbidden conduct.[85] This comparison evidences the wrongful character of a conduct as an operation of the rules of attribution. While in cases of wrongful actions, the operation of attribution is established from the relationship between the cause (the action) and the effect (the event), in the case of omissions, where the action is missing, the attribution of wrongful act is evidenced by the fact that the required action would have prevented the event that breached the international obligation.[86]

The subjective elements of wrongful conduct, as understood in the municipal legal orders, are excluded from the concept of breach in international law. However, occasionally the element of intention may assist in determining particular expressions of breach, such as in the cases of genocide, trade barriers, etc.,[87] where the subjective elements of intention and negligence are necessary for determining the quantum of reparation (Articles 39 ARSIWA and 30 DARIO).

The international obligations are part of the primary relationship of the subjects of international law. Obviously, in order for an international obligation to become a reference point for determining internationally wrongful conduct, it should first constitute a binding obligation for the state or the international organization at the time when the conduct occurs (Articles 13 ARSIWA and 11 DARIO). Yet, the determination of breach on behalf of the internationally wrongful act "depends on the precise terms of the obligation, its interpretation and application, taking into account its object and purpose and the facts of the case."[88] The temporal dimension of the commission of the internationally wrongful act is therefore crucial for determining the fact whether the conduct of the state or international organization can be regarded as violating the obligation or not.

Articles 13 ARSIWA and 11 DARIO provide that an act of a state or international organization does not constitute a breach of international obligations unless the state or the organization is bound by that obligation at the time when the act is committed. This proposition is a manifestation of the principle of intertemporal law, *tempus regit actum*.[89] The primary function of the principle is to ensure that the subject of international law can be held responsible for breach of binding

[84]Stern (2010a), p. 209 referring also to Anzilotti (1906).

[85]See further Latty (2010), pp. 356–357, 360.

[86]Latty (2010), p. 361, referring also to Ago, Roberto, *Le délit interntional*, 1939-II, Recueil des Cours, 415, 503.

[87]See also Stern (2010a), p. 209.

[88]ILC Commentaries to Draft ARSIWA, Commentary to Article 12 ARSIWA, paras. 1, 54.

[89]This principle, which implies that an act performed according to the law in force at the time of performance, refers mainly to the laws of procedure in civil or criminal jurisdictions of continental legal systems, such as Italy and Spain. See for an example of application of this principle Bariffi (2012), para. 9.

obligations. Furthermore, this principle might entail a certain degree of retroactivity when indicating that these subjects remain responsible even if the obligation is not in force any more due to the operation of the doctrine of substitution.[90] Notwithstanding the limits of this discussion, the principle *tempus regit actum* predicts that a state or international organization cannot be held responsible for a breach of an obligation that was not binding at the time of the wrongful conduct. This prediction is quite relevant for addressing the fallacy of the EU responsibility, which is entailed for acts that were falling within the competences of Member States, but which were unionized in the course of the integration. Accordingly, to consider the EU answerable for enacting a ban on asbestos on the grounds of public health, a measure that initially was enacted by France and was followed by the EU several years after the *EC – Asbestos* ruling was delivered, contradicts the predictions of the principle of intertemporal law. Hence, the EU participation in the DSP with reference to French measures is not justified upon the predictions of the principle *tempus regit actum*, inasmuch as the EU could be held responsible for a measure enacted outside the scope of EU legislation. As a result, the burden of this responsibility would be devolved to the other EU Member States.

## *3. The Rules of Justification of the Internationally Wrongful Act*

The observance of international agreements constitutes a general obligation of international law, as an expression of the principle *pacta sunt servanda*, according to which the treaties in force are binding upon the parties and must be performed by them in good faith.[91] Furthermore, the parties are precluded from invoking the provisions of their internal law, or the rules of international organizations, as a justification for their failure to perform the treaties.[92] Indeed, international law is essentially undetermined from municipal law, and *vice versa*. This thesis finds its expression in Article 3 ARSIWA, which provides that: "[t]he characterization of an act of a State as internationally wrongful is governed by international law. Such characterization is not affected by the characterization of the same act as lawful by internal law." This rule, which is recognized in the doctrine as 'the reciprocal indetermination of legal orders',[93] may suggest that the contrary proposition is also true. Accordingly, an act that violates municipal law may fully comply with international law. The logic for this argument is essentially based on the disjunction (detachment) of international law from the municipal legal orders.[94] The ICJ has

---

[90] Tavernier (2010), p. 399.

[91] Article 26 VCLT and Article 26 VCLTSIO.

[92] Article 27 VCLT and Article 27 VCLTSIO.

[93] Dupuy (2010), p. 174 *et seq*.

[94] Stern (2010a), p. 211.

also maintained that the fact that an act of public authority may have been unlawful in municipal law does not necessarily mean that that act was unlawful in international law, as a breach of a treaty or otherwise.[95]

The observance of international obligations could however be hindered by virtue of facts which are considered lawful, or which do not depend on the will of the party that violates the obligations. The circumstances precluding wrongfulness constitute the third element that is necessary for triggering international responsibility. These rules establish the grounds for justifying the commitment of internationally wrongful acts, which otherwise would be qualified as illegal. Articles 20–25 ARSIWA and 20–25 DARIO provide that the wrongfulness is precluded by virtue of consent, self-defense, legally instituted countermeasures, *force majeure*, distress, or necessity. Rather than grounds that absolve states and international organizations from their international obligations, these rules can be considered as legal reasons that justify the wrongfulness in case that the predetermined criteria established in these provisions are satisfied.

## *4. The Content and Implementation of the Regime of International Responsibility*

The content of the international responsibility regime refers to the legal consequences for the responsible entity due to the violation of primary obligations. This regime is part of the secondary relationship emerging out of this violation. The legal consequences of an internationally wrongful act are preceded from certain tools that aim at saving the primary relationship. Accordingly, Articles 29, 30 ARSIWA and 29, 30 DARIO, as tools of *legi generali*, serve to the principle *pacta sunt servanda*, inasmuch as they aim to ensure that the continuous performance of primary obligations is not prejudiced from the emergence of the secondary relationship. Hence, the defaulting entity should cease the wrongful conduct, if it is continuing, or offer the guarantees of non-repetition, if the conduct has been terminated. The cessation and the guarantees for non-repetition constitute the primary legal consequences of any internationally wrongful act, and aim to restore the injured legal order, notwithstanding the presence of damages. These instruments, as additional tools of the duty of performance, are a strong mechanism for ensuring the rule of law in the international legal order. They aim to terminate any wrongful conduct, and exclude any possibility for the compensation to be used for justifying the breach of international obligations. This would constitute a threat for "the binding

[95] *Elettronica Sicula S.p.A. (ELSI) (United States of America v. Italy)*, I.C.J. Reports 1989, 12, 74, para. 124.

force of primary rules themselves and endanger the validity, certainty and effectiveness of international legal relations".[96]

The duty of cessation and the guarantees for non-repetition are instruments that can be invoked also from states or international organizations other than the injured ones. This is possible if the primary obligation is owed to a group of states (including the claimant) or an international organization that is established for the protection of a collective interest of the group, or is owed to the international community as a whole (Articles 48 ARSIWA and 49 DARIO).[97] While the duty of cessation can be requested only to the benefit of the injured subject, the guarantee of non-repetition can be awarded to the benefit of third parties that are not directly affected from the internationally wrongful act.[98] The risk of repetition, the gravity of the wrongful act and the nature of the breached obligation fall under the main criteria for determining the need to employ an obligation of guarantee for non-repetition.[99]

While the duty of cessation and non-repetition guarantees are designed as remedies for any kind of injuries of the international legal order, with or without damages, the obligation of reparation is reserved for internationally wrongful acts that have caused damage. Such damage may consist of moral or material injuries, and its presence entails the obligation of the wrongdoer to make full reparation for the injury caused by the internationally wrongful act (Articles 31 ARSIWA and 31 DARIO). Furthermore, Articles 42 ARSIWA and 43 DARIO entitle an injured state or international organization to invoke the responsibility of another entity, in case that the breached obligation is owed to that subject individually, or is owed to a group of states, international organizations, or to the international community as a whole. The latter is subject to the condition that the internationally wrongful act *specially affects this subject*, or is of such a character as to *radically change the position* of all the other states or international organizations to which *the obligation is owed* with respect to *the further performance of the obligation*.[100]

The qualification of a state or international organization as 'injured' refers to a legal status which is obviously distinguished from subjects 'other than the injured state or international organization' provided in Articles 48 ARSIWA and 49 DARIO, which do not have direct or indirect individual legal interests in

[96]Commentary to draft Article 6 of the Report of the ILC, 45th Session, *ILC Yearbook 1993*, Vol. II(2), [UN Document A/CN.4/SER.A/1993/Add.l (Part 1)], 56, para 6. See further Corten (2010), p. 548.

[97]See further Corten (2010), p. 548.

[98]Barbier (2010), p. 557.

[99]Report of the International Law Commission on the work of its fifty-second session (2000)—Topical summary of the discussion held in the Sixth Committee of the General Assembly during its fifty-fifth session prepared by the Secretariat, [UN Doc. A/CN.4/513], 15 February 2001, 15, para. 57.

[100]Articles 42 ARSIWA and 43 DARIO. Emphasis added.

terms of the breach, but is nevertheless influenced from the legal injuries incurred from the holders of the collective interests.[101] Both of these categories are entitled to invoke responsibility of the wrongdoer, but the legal consequences of their status are fundamentally different. Accordingly, whereas both categories can demand the cessation of the internationally wrongful act, as well as the assurances and guarantees of non-repetition, the category of non-injured subjects cannot claim other direct benefits. Such a category can demand the performance of the obligations only to the benefit of the injured subjects, and is limited to any further reparations. Furthermore, this category cannot impose countermeasures for the implementation of the international responsibility, which are reserved as instruments in the discretion of the injured subjects only (Articles 49 ARSIWA and 51 DARIO).[102]

As it has been maintained in jurisprudence,

> [the] reparation must, as far as possible, wipe out all the consequences of the illegal act and reestablish the situation which would, in all probability, have existed if that act had not been committed. Restitution in kind, or, if this is not possible, payment of a sum corresponding to the value which a restitution in kind would bear; the award, if need be, of damages for loss sustained which would not be covered by restitution in kind or payment in place of it – such are the principles which should serve to determine the amount of compensation due for an act contrary to international law.[103]

Following these predictions, Articles 34–37 ARSIWA and 34–37 DARIO provide that the damages, being moral and/or material, shall be fully repaired by means of restitution, compensation, and satisfaction.

Full reparation includes, but is not limited to, the restitution or its equivalent, given that they constitute only the principal remedy which might not suffice to redress the damages incurred due to the internationally wrongful act. Restitution aims to re-establish the situation that existed before the wrongful act was committed, subject to the conditions that this operation is possible, and is proportional to the loss (Articles 35 ARSIWA and 35 DARIO). Restitution may have a material or a legal nature; the latter denoting a measure that aims the alteration or revocation of judicial, legislative, executive or constitutional acts violating international obligations.[104] If this restitution is not possible, the obligation for reparation shall consist of the obligation to compensate the damage, including loss of profits (Articles 56 ARSIWA and 36 DARIO). The amount of compensation is therefore calculated by measuring the difference of the actual financial position, and the position that would have been achieved absent to the wrongful act.[105] Compensation is limited to

---

[101] See further on this distinction Stern (2010b), pp. 567–568 and ILC Commentaries to Draft ARSIWA, Commentary to Article 48, para. 2.

[102] See further Stern (2010b), p. 568.

[103] *The Factory at Chorzów*, Merits, 1928, 29, and *The Factory at Chorzów*, Jurisdiction, 1927, 47.

[104] Gray (2010), pp. 590–591.

[105] See further Barker (2010), p. 601.

the injury actually suffered and requires the causal link between the internationally wrongful act and the incurred damages, as a precondition for this modality.[106] In case that the restitution and compensation are not possible, the obligation for satisfaction can be applied as a residual reparation tool for the injury. This obligation may consist of an acknowledgement of the breach, an expression of regret, a formal apology, or another appropriate modality (Articles 37 ARSIWA and 37 DARIO). In any case, this obligation should be proportional to the injury and not humiliating to the wrongdoer.

The reparation of injuries follows a certain course of priorities in the selection and application of means. The main rule in this course provides that the reparation must be adequate and that the restitution in kind is preferable against the reparation by equivalence.[107] The adequacy criterion, mentioned in *The Factory at Chorzów*, is followed by 'full reparation' as provided in Articles 31 ARSIWA and 31 DARIO, inasmuch as it aims to restore the situation that existed before the wrongful act was committed; hence wiping out all the consequences of an internationally wrongful act.[108] Additionally, the reparation has to be proportional, in that the burden for the wrongdoer that is charged with the restitution, must not be disproportional to the benefit of the victim; a situation which would otherwise prefer compensation against satisfaction.[109]

The rule of adequacy, with its dimensions of 'full restoration' and 'proportionality', can be regarded as a function of the injury caused by the wrongdoer, in that the seriousness of the wrongful conduct and the will to terminate the defection of primary obligations should be considered the main determinants for the reparation mode.[110] The satisfaction would be regarded an adequate form of reparation for moral and no-damage injuries, which can be associated with the cessation and the guarantees for non-repetition, while the material damages can request, in addition to these forms, also the restitution and/or compensation.[111] This combination of means of reparation is based on the predictions of Articles 34 ARSIWA and 34 DARIO. Any order of priority between these means is established pursuant to the systematic interpretation of the provisions, which allow for the application of means if the more preferred one has not proven sufficient (Articles 36, 37 ARSIWA and 36, 37 DARIO). Yet, this order is subject to factual assessment from courts or tribunals, given that the determination of means is a function of the injury. The nature of damages may further restrict the criteria of adequacy and proportionality.

The implementation of international responsibility refers to the operative part of the secondary relationship that succeeds the finding of an internationally wrongful

---

[106]Stern (2010b), p. 567.

[107]Kerbrat (2010), p. 579.

[108]*The Factory at Chorzów*, Merits, 1928, 29, and *The Factory at Chorzów*, Jurisdiction, 1927, 21 and 47.

[109]Articles 35(b) ARSIWA and 35(b) DARIO. See further Kerbrat (2010), p. 579.

[110]Kerbrat (2010), pp. 579–580.

[111]See further Kerbrat (2010), pp. 580–581.

act and the subsequent attribution of that act to a wrongdoer. The regime of responsibility has to be enforced in order to achieve its normative aims. The traditional instruments of enforcement include the use of force, diplomatic and economic sanctions, etc. However, international agreements may provide for other systems of enforcement of international responsibility, in order to oblige the wrongdoer to comply with its obligations and/or to repair the injuries. The enforcement means may include the suspension of rights from the international agreement, the institution of countermeasures, and/or the imposition of penalties. While the violation of the obligation constitutes an internationally wrongful act, the institution of countermeasures from the injured party is qualified as a legal act inasmuch as it aims to ensure the cessation of the wrongful act. In this respect, it should be emphasized that the primary function of countermeasures remains the obligation of the wrongdoer to comply with the primary obligations pursuant to the treaty.[112]

The system of countermeasures established in Chapter II ARSIWA (Articles 49–54) is designed to ensure that the parties in a treaty comply with their primary and secondary obligations. As a means of reprisals in a regime that lacks a hierarchical or centralized system of enforcement, the countermeasures allow the injured party to temporary derogate from its treaty obligations.[113] Obviously, these measures cannot be considered a punishment for the breach of international law, but rather as reciprocal measures at the disposal of an injured state. Typically, the system of countermeasures is embodied in the DSU as a tool for enforcing the DSB rulings and recommendations. However, it should be mentioned that this system might not be an effective tool in the hands of states with a comparatively lower trade power in the relationship. In such cases, the countermeasures do not accomplish their aim, given that the imposition of barriers might not suffice to ensure the injured state to accrue its lost benefits from the wrongful act, or might even damage its economic position in the global trade.

Most of the predictions of the regime of responsibility pursuant to the *legi generali* do not find application in the context of WTO Agreement. This is not only due to the fact that the WTO legal order constitutes *lex specialis*, but also due to the normative choice of this system. Accordingly, the regime of responsibility in the WTO legal order is adopted to its nature as a forum of negotiations. As such, the responsibility is centered on the cessation of the WTO inconsistent measures. The concept of damages is not recognized, and as a result the restitution, satisfaction, and compensation of damages do not find application. Furthermore, the system of retaliation is designed as a tool for enforcing the DSB rulings and recommendations. Hence, the retaliatory or cross-retaliatory measures are temporary and do not aim to compensate for the loss. Indeed, from the economic point of view, none of the parties would be interested in the long-term to impose trade measures, because the overall trade loss would be greater than the short-term benefits of such measures. Even the option of compensation of damages which can be adopted in the

[112]The countermeasures are analysed further in the following Sections.

[113]Verhoeven (2010), pp. 110–111.

course of retaliatory measures, does not aim to legitimize the wrongful measures, and is based on the mutual agreement of the parties; hence, it differs from the compensation provided in the *legi generali*, which is mandatory and is imposed from the tribunal or the court.

## IV. General Rules of Joint Responsibility of States and International Organizations

The above observations suggest that the regime of international responsibility is triggered by committing internationally wrongful acts in breaching binding international obligations. From this, it can be presumed that the incurrence of responsibility would be, generally, individual, in that the subjects of international law incur responsibility as a result of their own wrongful acts. This presumption can be reversed to the benefit of the joint responsibility regime, which the states and international organizations may incur due to joint wrongful conduct. The following elaborates further the normative conditions in which the joint responsibility regime is incurred. This, in turn, shall serve as a significant premise for conceiving a model for the WTO membership of the EU and its Member States.

### *1. The Content of the Joint Responsibility Regime*

Two or more subjects of international law may be held responsible for the same wrongful conduct, inasmuch as they have participated through distinct acts and omissions that can be attributed to them. The regime of joint and several liability in international law is duly distinguished from analogies in municipal.[114] The basic conception of joint responsibility stems from the joint action of a plurality of states in committing an internationally wrongful conduct, which subsequently leads to a state of responsibility that is borne jointly and severally (*solidaire*) from each of the participants in the conduct. The joint responsibility of distinct entities is based on their collaboration or complicity in the commitment of internationally wrongful conduct.[115]

Where several states are responsible for the same internationally wrongful conduct, the responsibility of each state may be invoked in relation to that act (Article 47 ARSIWA). The compensation is limited to the amount of the suffered damages, and the damages can be claimed against each of the participants. Article 48 DARIO provides similar predictions for the joint responsibility of more than one entities composed of international organizations and states, which are held jointly

[114]Crawford (2008), p. 554.

[115]Orakhelashvili (2010), p. 647.

responsible for the same internationally wrongful act. Additionally, this provision distinguishes between the entity bearing the primary responsibility, from the one bearing the subsidiary responsibility, and which may be invoked only in case that the holder of the primary responsibility has failed to provide reparation.[116] In light of this differentiation, it is obvious that the position of each of the entities involved in the wrongful conduct might not be the same. This differentiation has implications for the allocation of remedial duties between jointly responsible entities in the course of implementation of the responsibility regime. This shall be further explored by considering the various modes for incurring joint responsibility.

## 2. *The Modes of Incurring Joint Responsibility*

The standard mode for incurring joint responsibility includes those situations in which two or more subjects of international law breach their obligations that are prescribed in the treaty or other sources of international law. The fact whether these entities have made a prior declaration of responsibility determines whether the subjects should incur joint or several responsibility. The standard nature of this mode consists of the fact that the breach of joint obligations is triggered from the joint internationally wrongful conduct of participating entities, and both entities maintain a certain role in this conduct. The joint responsibility consists of concerted or independent conduct of the states and international organizations in breach of international obligations in a single or a series of events.[117] As a general principle, the rules of attribution constitute the main normative criterion for establishing joint responsibility. The attribution of joint responsibility to a plurality of states would be, in principle, subject to similar conditions of attribution as in individual cases of responsibility, where every participating state in the joint internationally wrongful act would be responsible if it has contributed to that act.[118]

The direct relationship of an entity with the wrongful conduct is not always a condition for triggering joint responsibility. States or international organizations may incur responsibility by virtue of a certain relationship with another subject that commits an internationally wrongful act.[119] This art of incurring responsibility is particularly present in cases of aid, direction, or coercion of a state or an international organization for committing internationally wrongful acts (respectively Articles 16, 17, 18 ARSIWA and 14, 15, 16 DARIO). Obviously, these acts exceed the

---

[116]Article 48(2) DARIO. See further International Law Commission Draft Articles on the Responsibility of International Organizations, with Commentaries, 2011, adopted by the International Law Commission at its sixty-third session (Doc. A/66/10) ('ILC Commentaries to DARIO'), Commentary to Article 48 DARIO, para. 3.

[117]See further Noyes and Smith (1988), pp. 228–229.

[118]Dominicé (2010), p. 282.

[119]See also Dominicé (2010), pp. 281–282.

mere incitement to wrongful acts.[120] Indeed, unless otherwise provided by a particular legal instrument, a mere incitement or encouragement to commit an internationally wrongful act would not constitute a ground for responsibility *per se*, and should be distinguished from the complicity.[121] From these provisions, it becomes clear that the law of responsibility is particularly concerned about the idea of a state or international organization instrumentalizing another state.[122] Therefore, these cases of participation of a state or international organization in the commitment of an internationally wrongful act constitute autonomous grounds for incurring responsibility, in that they remain independent from the main internationally wrongful act. This mode of incurring responsibility bypasses the rules of attribution and as such, the incurrence of responsibility by virtue of complicity is designed as a primary source of responsibility.[123]

In the course of its evolution, there have been attempts to distinguish the concept of joint responsibility from complicity. Accordingly, while complicity is reserved for conduct of states facilitating other states in committing wrongful acts, the joint responsibility is invoked for cases where both states act as principals in committing internationally wrongful acts.[124] Notwithstanding these connotations, the ARSIWA and DARIO have endorsed the inclusion of aid and assistance, as typical forms of complicity, under the umbrella of the joint responsibility regime.[125]

The incurrence of international responsibility by virtue of complicity is subject to two conditions. First, the participating state intends to collaborate in the act despite its awareness about the circumstances of wrongfulness. Second, the act would still be wrongful even if committed by the participating state itself.[126] While the second condition can be assessed objectively, the element of intention constitutes a juridical fact, which might be particularly difficult to be evidenced in certain cases, and would conflict with the objectivization of the international responsibility by bringing into the scene particular subjective elements.[127] Therefore, the element of knowledge about the circumstances on wrongfulness should be interpreted restrictively in order to preserve a standard of objective responsibility for establishing the responsibility of the accomplice for the contribution to the internationally wrongful act.

---

[120]Dominicé (2010), p. 285.

[121]Quigley (1987), pp. 80–81. See also ILC Commentaries to Draft ARSIWA, Commentaries to Article 14, para. 13 and Article 15, para. 9. As an example of incitement as a ground for international responsibility, see Article III of the Convention on the Prevention and Punishment of the Crime of Genocide (1948) and Article 4 of the International Convention on the Elimination of All Forms of Racial Discrimination (1965).

[122]Kuijper (2010), p. 218.

[123]Kuijper (2010), pp. 218–219.

[124]Quigley (1987), pp. 78, 80.

[125]Articles 16 ARSIWA and 14 DARIO.

[126]See further Dominicé (2010), pp. 285–287.

[127]Orakhelashvili (2010), pp. 650–651.

States may incur joint responsibility also outside the context of an international treaty. In these cases, it is essential that they exercise a joint wrongful conduct, which is carried out by a single action where each state contributes with a particular role.[128] A single action, which may entail joint international responsibility, could be the establishment of a joint organ empowered with governmental authority in the meaning of Article 5 ARSIWA.[129] The burden of joint responsibility can be attributed to the participating states, in case that such an organ acting on their behalf commits an internationally wrongful act.[130]

Joint international responsibility may also be incurred in a 'principal-agent' relationship, where the breach from an agent-state of international obligation in the course of performance of a mandated action from the principal, may trigger the joint responsibility of both states.[131] In these cases, should the agent commit an internationally wrongful act, the principal may also incur international responsibility.[132] However, the principal-agent relationship should be only valid for those cases when the agent is appointed as such by the principal.[133] In this way, not every joint responsibility scenario can be construed upon this relationship model.

A similar relationship is revealed also in cases of protectorates, where the joint responsibility may be attributed on the basis of a 'mandate' relationship.[134] However, a distinction should be made in these cases, given that the protector incurs international responsibility by virtue of the legal relationship between the states. As such, the concept of vicarious (indirect) rather than joint responsibility could better respond to the attribution of responsibility among states, although the difference between these two alternatives might not be always obvious.[135] Yet, the element of international legal capacity is particularly relevant for distinguishing joint responsibility from cases of protectorates, where a state takes over the obligations of an international character belonging to the protected state. In such cases, the protecting state bears international responsibility of the protected state *ipso lege*,[136] i.e. by virtue of the legal relationship between them. This is distinguished from the joint responsibility regime in the classic sense, where the responsibility is invoked on the basis of the relationship of the contributory entity in the wrongful act, hence on autonomous grounds of responsibility.

The regime of vicarious responsibility constitutes a legal framework for shifting the responsibility of one state to another, and this is significantly different from the

---

[128]Dominicé (2010), pp. 282–283.

[129]Dominicé (2010), p. 283.

[130]See further Dominicé (2010), p. 283.

[131]Dominicé (2010), p. 283.

[132]See further *Certain Phosphate Lands in Nauru (Nauru v. Australia)*, Preliminary Objections, Judgment, I.C.J. Reports 1992, 240, 258–259, para. 48.

[133]See further Orakhelashvili (2010), pp. 655–656.

[134]Dominicé (2010), p. 283.

[135]Quigley (1987), p. 80.

[136]Quigley (1987), p. 80.

joint responsibility regime, which predicts shared responsibility of multiple entities. The rationale for shifting the burden of responsibility is that the responsibility cannot be diminished on a unilateral basis from the putative states.[137] Furthermore, the protected state cannot act without an intermediary at the international level, and the protecting state must bear the responsibility of the protected state at least on the basis of vicarious liability.[138] The vicarious responsibility regime is similar with the responsibility that the Union may incur due to its participation in the DSP as a representative of the concerned Member State. In this way, based on the premises of *EC – Asbestos*, it can be suggested that the EU could become vicariously responsible for the French measure which *ex hipothesi* would be inconsistent with the WTO disciplines. The responsibility of the Union conceived in this way, is similar to the model of vicarious responsibility only in terms of the effects, because in essence, the Union is not a protecting state for the Member States; they still maintain their own international legal personality. Nevertheless, this art of responsibility could be of a theoretical relevance for modeling the participation of the Union in the DSP (to be discussed further in Chap. 5).

## *3. The Sources of Joint Responsibility of International Organizations and Their Member States*

From the brief overview of the modes of incurring international responsibility, it became clear that the rules of attribution might not always ensure that the wrongdoer becomes responsible for the wrongful act. Rather, a state and the organization where it belongs may randomly become jointly responsible for internationally wrongful acts that they never committed or intended to commit. Hence, the joint responsibility regime does not include only those situations where both the responsible entities play a role in the wrongful act, but also those where one of the parties incurs responsibility *ex relatione*. This reveals the fallacies of a joint responsibility regime. For the Union polity, this would suggest that the Union might become responsible for wrongful conduct attributed to Member States, and *vice versa*. The following shall explore such fallacies by considering the relationships that trigger the joint responsibility.

The main fallacy of the joint responsibility regime is related with the thesis of 'double attribution', which entails the cumulative responsibility of both the state and the international organization where they are part of.[139] The problems related with the cumulative responsibility can be analyzed in two different settings. In the first setting, one could consider the predictions of the cumulative responsibility for

---

137 *Affaire des biens britanniques au Maroc espagnol, Great Britain v. Spain*, (1925) 2 R.I.A.A. 615, 648–649. See further Crawford (2008), p. 553.

138 Crawford (2008), p. 553.

139 Condorelli and Kress (2010), p. 222.

a member state of an international organization, while the latter has entered an international treaty with third subjects of international law, such as states or other international organizations. The standard regime of a cumulative responsibility would suggest that the state and the organization are held jointly responsible in case that they violate jointly their obligations. Such a regime is perfectly compatible with the rules of attribution. However, another possibility is that the organization engages its own responsibility due to conduct that is attributable to the member state alone.[140] In this case, the regime of cumulative responsibility disregards the predictions of the rules of attribution, and in view of this, it could prove fallacious. This fallacy could be overcome to the extent that the failure of the state to comply with the international obligations of the organization to which it belongs is construed as a breach of the internal rules of the organization, which should prevent member states from breaching international obligations.[141] This approach is compatible with the objective nature of the international responsibility. Accordingly, the regime of cumulative responsibility *ex relatione* provides that not only the wrongdoer is responsible, but also the organization itself, which has the burden to discharge obligations, despite the role of *dolus* and *culpa* in the wrongful conduct.

In a second setting, the predictions of the cumulative responsibility can be considered in terms of the joint membership in an international treaty of a state and an international organization where it is part of. One could distinguish between two different variations in this setting, namely the joint membership with or without a declaration of responsibility of the state and the organization. In a membership with a declaration of separated responsibilities, the legal responsibility for breach of international obligations should be allocated to the subject to whom the internationally wrongful conduct is attributed. This is possible in those mixed agreements, where the member state and the organization have a clear separation of powers, and enter into the mixed agreement with their individual contributions that are easily identifiable. In a more complex situation, where the member state and the organization have interrelated or interdependent powers, they enter into international treaties with a configuration of mixed and complementary contributions. This is based on the thesis that the inability to separate clearly the powers in an identifiable way triggers the regime of joint responsibility. This is the case of the WTO Agreement, which is designed as a mixed agreement. The inability to make a declaration of powers in the majority of the mixed agreements entered into by the Union and its Member States is based on the fact that the powers conferred to the Union may be inextricably linked or may have repercussions over the residual powers of the Member States.[142] Such a regime contains all the premises for challenging the rules of attribution, given that in a regime of mixed competences it is rather difficult to apportion the conduct, and to attribute it to one of the participants in a certain way. Therefore, the joint responsibility regime accommodates in a pragmatic way the fallacies of the rules of attribution.

---

[140] Condorelli and Kress (2010), p. 222.

[141] Condorelli and Kress (2010), p. 222.

[142] See also Heliskoski (2001), p. 229.

The cumulative responsibility in these settings remains superficial, in that it does not explain the causes and the consequences of the failure of the rules of attribution to impute the responsibility in a proper way. Rather, the joint responsibility regime is conceived as an artificial infrastructure for ensuring that the obligations of the parties are discharged, notwithstanding the allocation of responsibilities related with them. With the proviso that this infrastructure entails the fallacious allocation of burden in the Union polity, it might be useful to elaborate on the sources of the joint responsibility for acts attributed respectively either to the international organizations, or to its member states.

#### a. Joint Responsibility for Acts Attributed to International Organizations

The internationally wrongful acts committed by an international organization trigger international responsibility that is imputed pursuant to the rules of attribution. However, the member states of this organization may become jointly responsible either by virtue of their participation in the wrongful conduct, or *ex relatione*. Indeed, while the joint responsibility of states often depends on their joint wrongful conduct, the rule of joint responsibility of states and international organizations typically occurs when the organizations institute wrongful acts and their member states implement them without denying the state of unlawfulness.[143] The fact that the rules of attribution fail to preclude a joint responsibility regime is mainly explained from the constitutional nature of the relationship between the international organization and its member states. Accordingly, it might be quite difficult to identify cases in which member states are detached from the internationally wrongful conduct of the organization in one way or another. This is true for both forms of joint responsibility, the one that is incurred *ex relatione*, as well as the one that is established by virtue of complicity between the state and the organization.

One of the challenges of the joint responsibility regime is to distinguish between the facts whether the member states are acting in the conditions of complicity, or whether they become jointly responsible by virtue of the law or the fact. A state committing an internationally wrongful act pursuant to the binding decisions of an international organization, which *ex hipothesi* violate international obligations, is held responsible for its part in the wrongful action.[144] The main reason behind this proposition could be based on the assumption that the act of the organization giving rise to international responsibility is either in violation of the internal legal framework (hence null and void), and as such cannot be qualified as lawful in light of implied powers, or violates peremptory norms of international law.[145] For these reasons, the member states are under their own international obligations not to

[143]Hirsch (1995), p. 86.

[144]Orakhelashvili (2010), p. 655.

[145]Orakhelashvili (2010), p. 655.

implement such an act. This uncertainty could be complicated further in cases where the distribution of powers in the organization is not clear enough to indicate whether the organization exercises its own exclusive powers, or the powers that are retained from the member states.

The member states of international organizations may become responsible also by virtue of facts, which trigger joint responsibility, although they lack the necessary normative infrastructure in this respect. The answerability of the EU in front of the DSB for disputes that are not related with the conduct of the EU institutions, could serve as a factual circumstance triggering the international responsibility for the Member States. This theoretical conception can be applied in the settings of the *EC – Asbestos* scenario, where the EU has participated in the DSP for a measure, which was instituted by France allegedly in violation of WTO obligations, and had no connection with the EU legislation at the time of enactment (in view of the principle of intertemporal law). Had the EU been found responsible for a measure attributed to France, it would have to bear the burden for that act. This responsibility would be jointly borne by all the EU Member States. In this regard, the wrongfulness consists of the premise that the EU lacks the full and unconditional authorization to participate in DSP on behalf of the Member States. Such wrongfulness has an internal nature, and as such, it should be addressed from a constitutional point of view (see infra Chaps. 4 and 5).

The EU institutions have continuously defended their attributes as the sole bearer of the international responsibility for acts of the institutions that *ex hipothesi* are regarded as internationally wrongful acts. Accordingly, the EU has acknowledged its responsibility for measures related to its areas of responsibility (e.g. tariff concessions) even if such measures are instituted by organs of the Member States, with the argument that such areas are part of the exclusive competences of the EU. Hence, the EU is the only entity in a position to repair the possible breach, i.e. in the capacity to ensure the possible restitution of the injured legal order under the DSU.[146] This claim is essentially based on the argument defended by the EU that,

> [pursuant] to its *sui generis* domestic constitutional arrangements that Community laws are generally not executed through authorities at Community level but rather through recourse to the authorities of its [Member] States which, in such a situation, "act *de facto* as organs of the Community, for which the Community would be responsible under WTO law and international law in general".[147]

Obviously this argument is sustained from the rules of attribution, insofar as the EU holds the sole responsibility for questions falling within its exclusive domain of

[146]International Law Commission, Responsibility of International Organizations, Comments and Observations Received from International Organizations, UN Doc. A/CN.4/637 of 14 February 2011, Section II.B.7, 24.

[147]*European Communities – Protection of Trademarks and Geographical Indications for Agricultural Products and Foodstuffs* (WT/DS174/R), Report of the Panel of 15 March 2005, paras. 7.98 and 7.725.

powers. This argument constitutes the normative basis for the EU participation in DSP where a measure instituted by its Member States is at stake.

However, the question is, to what extent could the Union assume responsibility for disputed measures that are instituted from Member States within the scope of their residual powers? Indeed, the argument maintained from the Union that the Member States act as functional organs of the Union refers *a priori* to all measures instituted from Member States, and as such, it disregards the vertical distribution of powers in the Union polity. This constitutional element is not without implications for the WTO membership of the EU and its Member States.[148] As a result, the approach followed from the Union with regard to the participation in the DSP suggests that the attribution of responsibility should not follow the general rules of attribution, but rather involves special arrangements for avoiding such rules.[149] This would be in line with the predictions of the principle of *lex specialis* (Articles 55 ARSIWA and 64 DARIO), which allows special regimes to prevail over the *legi generali*. The WTO Agreement and its Annex agreements, and particularly the DSU, do not regulate explicitly the question of participation of the EU in the DSP. Rather, this participation follows an unwritten rule that the EU represents its Member States in the DSP on the ground that the WTO Agreement is regarded as a mixed agreement, which lacks a declaration of competences and as such, entails a regime of joint responsibility for both the EU and its Member States.[150]

In general, a declaration of powers is deemed to instruct the third states to a certain extent to whom they can invoke international responsibility for breaches of international obligations, as in the case of the United Nations Convention on the Law of the Sea of 10 December 1982 (UNCLOS).[151] The joint participation of the EU and its Member States in the UNCLOS is essentially based on a separate regime of responsibility, which is carefully negotiated among parties in the negotiation process.[152] The declaration of competences, submitted with the signature of the convention from the EU, is the basis for the model of mixity offered by UNCLOS. In addition, Annex IX to the Convention regulates the participation of international organizations, by providing among others the extent of participation and the rights and obligations. However, the missing declaration of powers may leave the choice

[148]This argument is analyzed further in Chap. 3.

[149]International Law Commission Third Report on Responsibility of International Organizations, by Mr. Giorgio Gaja, Special Rapporteur, [UN Doc. A/CN.4/553], 13 May 2005, 10, para. 12.

[150]The internal distribution of powers, being the decisive element of the conduct of the EU and its Member States in mixed agreements, may influence the conduct of membership in one of two alternatives, either by providing a declaration of powers, or by entering the agreement with joint responsibilities. These alternatives give rise to the discourse on the advantages and disadvantages of a flexible system *versus* a formalized system of responsibility, which shall be considered further in Chap. 5.

[151]Pursuant to Article 2 of the Annex IX to the UNCLOS, the EU has made a declaration of competences transferred from the Member States and their extent of application in terms of the provisions of UNCLOS. See also Neframi (2002), p. 195.

[152]See for the historic perspectives on the EU in UNCLOS Simmonds (1989), pp. 108–109.

of the responsible entity to the injured state.[153] With the proviso that the obligations under UNCLOS are assumed partly from the EU and partly from the Member States, the responsibility model instituted therein is based on a formal procedure, which precedes the joint or several liability of the Union and its Member States (Article 6(2) Annex IX UNCLOS). According to this model, the Union and the Member States have an 'optional standing' as to the participation in the settlement of disputes with third countries, which allows them to decide the party to which the claim can be addressed.[154]

The essential features of joint responsibility regime predict that a missing declaration of powers should not work to the detriment of third states and that their legitimate confidence should be protected.[155] In the context of WTO Agreement, this could imply that the WTO Members may invoke either the responsibility of the Union or of the Member States, or of both of them, with reference to any stipulations set forth in the WTO Agreement, since the Union and its Member States have assumed responsibility over the whole breadth of the substantive scope of this Agreement.[156] This practical arrangement lacks a normative regulation in the legal orders either of the WTO or of the EU. However, this deficiency has not precluded the Union or its Member States to incur international responsibility for breaches of the WTO Agreement. As much as the rapport between the declaration of powers and the regime of responsibility is concerned, it can be suggested that the attribution of international responsibility aligns to the declaration of powers as an objective parameter; hence assisting third states in mixed agreements to enhance their legitimate expectations in terms of responsibility.[157]

### b. Joint Responsibility for Acts Attributed to Member States

International responsibility may also arise due to internationally wrongful acts, which are attributed to member states directly as a result of breach of their international obligations, and this may entail also the responsibility of the organization *ex relatione*.[158] The joint responsibility in this context can emerge in four different modes, which are elaborated in turn.

---

[153] Tomuschat (2002), p. 185.
[154] Heliskoski (2001), p. 166.
[155] Tomuschat (2002), p. 185.
[156] Tomuschat (2002), p. 185.
[157] Neframi (2012), p. 340.
[158] Klein (2010), p. 306.

### i. Direct Participation of the Member State in the Internationally Wrongful Act

In this mode of relationship, a member state would be deemed responsible for the breach of an international obligation if it would carry out activities jointly with the international organization where it is part of, by violating international obligations binding on both of them. This situation may be regarded as a 'parallel responsibility' given that the state co-authors the internationally wrongful conduct with the international organization.[159] This mode has a great theoretical relevance in that it construes the primary (direct) line of international responsibility of member state parallel to the secondary (indirect) line of responsibility of member state for the breach of its international obligation against third parties in relation with the internal rules of the organization. Hence, the member states are also responsible for making the organization violate its obligations. This distinction is nevertheless not very obvious, insofar as the breach is jointly attributed to both the state and the organization, and this simplifies the process of attribution of conduct. This mode of relationship could be relevant for construing the joint responsibility of the EU and France in the scenario of *EC – Asbestos*. Accordingly, in case that, by virtue of its sole participation in the DSP and the abstract assumption of answerability, the EU would be held solely responsible for the inconsistency of the French Decree, France would be also designated as a jointly responsible state. This is because France has violated the internal rules of organization by making the Union violate its international obligations.

### ii. Complicity of Member States in the Internationally Wrongful Act of the Organization

This mode of relationship predicts that a state is internationally responsible if it provides aid or assists its international organization to commit an internationally wrongful act (Article 58 DARIO). This responsibility is subject to the conditions that the complicity is provided willfully and with the intention to breach international obligations of the organization (willfulness criterion), and that the breach would be qualified as such even if the conduct would be committed by that state (qualification criterion). The institutional (decision-making) framework of the organization, which *ex hipothesi* adopts acts in violation of international obligations of the organization, could be one expression of this mode.[160] This construction presumes that the role of the state was indispensable for the internationally wrongful act, and that the state has been aware for the consequences of the vote, which is characterized of a high standard of care that states generally pay for the decisions in the international organizations.[161] Indeed, the duty of care is entrusted on any

[159] See further Klein (2010), p. 307.
[160] Klein (2010), p. 308.
[161] Klein (2010), p. 308.

entity, whose complicit actions may lead to the performance of an internationally wrongful act. This may require the conduct of relevant inquiries from the complicit state in order to increase the level of knowledge about the wrongful utilization of aid or assistance from the wrongdoer.[162]

The complicity doctrine, although theoretical, should be construed in a more narrow sense, by considering the member state not as a constituent element of the organization, but rather as a separate entity that aids or assists the organization to commit an internationally wrongful act.[163] In this way, the process of attribution occurs in two distinct levels: the primary level, which concerns the main breach of an international obligation from the international organization; and the secondary level, which addresses the influential role of the member state in this process, and which obviously is more than a mere incitement. These two levels are distinguished from a methodological point of view, and entail theoretical relevance in terms of allocating the responsibility pursuant to the role of each participant. For the *EC – Asbestos* scenario, this would imply that in case that the French Decree would be found WTO inconsistent and unjustified, France would be the primary holder of responsibility, while the EU would be held responsible on the basis of complicity, in case that its complicit role would be established.

### iii. Coercion of an International Organization by Its Member States

This mode of relationship, which is provided in Article 60 DARIO, suggests that the member state, which exercises such a control over the organization as to coerce it to commit an internationally wrongful act, is deemed responsible, subject to the criteria of willfulness and qualification. In practice, it might prove difficult to evidence the mechanism of control or direction of the international organization by a member state. This is because the simple membership, the direct participation in decision-making, or the management of the organization, can hardly lead to the influence through coercion of an organization, which is considered an autonomous entity of international law with its own legal personality.[164] Nevertheless, although the grounds of responsibility in cases of coercion are very narrow and quite theoretical, should the influence be proven, it certainly entails derived responsibility for the state, which is attributed to it due to the internationally wrongful act of the organization.[165] In the Union polity, this mode of incurring joint responsibility might be difficult due to a consolidated level of checks and balances in the decision-making process, which allows for a sound equilibrium of interests among Member

[162] Quigley (1987), pp. 119–120.

[163] International Law Commission Fourth Report on Responsibility of International Organizations, by Mr. Giorgio Gaja, Special Rapporteur, [UN Doc. 2006, A/CN.4/564/, Add.1–2], 28 February, 12 and 20 April 2006, para. 62.

[164] Klein (2010), p. 309.

[165] Klein (2010), p. 310.

States. Indeed, the decision-making process is subject to horizontal and vertical control mechanisms, which would hardly allow a single Member State to coerce or control the entire Union to commit an internationally wrongful act. The actions of the Union are subject to a qualified majority of Member States, and this precludes the possibility of coercion or control of the Union as an instrumentalizing strategy for breaching international obligations.

iv. Joint Responsibility by Reason of Failure of Due Diligence by Member States

The duty of member states to exercise due diligence over the activities of the organization constitutes an obligation for the states, which is separated from the duty of organization to respect its own international obligations. This suggests that the failure by a member state of acting in a diligent manner in relation to an act of the organization, which *ex hipothesi* breaches its international obligations, would constitute a separate breach attributed to the member state.[166] The construction of this mode as a negligent or passive approach toward the wrongful acts of the organization, distinguishes this mode from other modes of complicity, which are mainly based on the active participation of the state in the wrongful activities of the organization.[167] The obligation of due diligence predicts for the state's duty to observe the activities of the organization, and particularly those taking part in its territory, and to exercise the necessary territorial control in order to prevent such activities from happening. This duty inherits the general presumption that states are obliged by international law not to use their territory against the interests of other states.[168]

This construction of responsibility has found place in Article 61 DARIO, where it is provided that:

> a state, member of an international organization, incurs international responsibility if, by taking advantage of the fact that the organization has competence in relation to the subject matter of one of state's international obligations, it circumvents that obligation by causing the organization to commit an act that, if committed by the state, would have constituted a breach of the obligation.

This applies "whether or not the act in question is internationally wrongful for the international organization". The predictions of Article 61 DARIO provide for an autonomous source of international responsibility for a state, by reason of actively breaching its own international obligations, with the argument that it is not competent to take diligent measures in that area. This means that the international responsibility of states is not engaged by means of internationally wrongful acts of the organization *per se*, but rather by reason of states failing to diligently observe

[166] Klein (2010), p. 310.
[167] Klein (2010), p. 311.
[168] Klein (2010), p. 310.

their own treaty obligations.[169] For the EU – Member States relationship, this could imply that the Member States would incur international responsibility if they would induce the Union to take actions, which also for the Member States would constitute a violation of international obligations. In the context of WTO membership, this may suggest that the Union acting in areas of residual powers of the Member States would make Member States responsible for any breaches of their individual WTO obligations, because, with their missing diligence, they induce the Union to breach the WTO obligations of the Member States.

### 4. General Limitations on the Attribution of Joint Responsibility

The regime of joint responsibility may be subject to general procedural limitations for the same reasons applicable to the individual responsibility. A particularly relevant limitation is the international law principle of the lack of compulsory jurisdiction for states and international organizations. As reaffirmed in the *Monetary Gold Case*, the international jurisdiction (of the ICJ) can be exercised only with the consent of the state.[170] The *Monetary Gold* principle predicts for the court a self-restrictive approach for adjudicating on the rights and responsibilities of an entity, which has not provided the consent for the proceedings. This is reaffirmed in *Nauru Case*, where the International Court of Justice employed the *Monetary Gold* principle as a jurisdictional standard to determine the connectivity between the subject matter at the dispute and the third parties not present in the dispute.[171] Similarly, the jurisdictional limitations may influence the establishment of joint responsibility for acts committed jointly from different entities in those cases where any of the participants rejects or denies the jurisdiction of the court or the tribunal. This concern is particularly relevant for cases where the causal link between the internationally wrongful act and the alleged wrongdoer are not clearly evidenced. In the context of WTO membership, this concern is overcome by means of the mandatory jurisdiction of the DSB over any material disputes in relation with the WTO disciplines.

[169]Klein (2010), p. 314.

[170]*Monetary Gold Removed from Rome in 1943 (Italy v. France, United Kingdom of Great Britain and Northern Ireland and United States of America)*, ICJ Reports 1954, 19, 31–32.

[171]*Certain Phosphate Lands in Nauru (Nauru v. Australia)*, Preliminary Objections, Judgment, 240, 259–262, particularly para. 55.

## *5. Division of Reparations in Joint Responsibility Regimes*

The process of attribution of responsibility in the course of the secondary relationship is followed by the allocation of the remedial duties between the joint responsible entities.[172] The regime of joint responsibility is construed in the context of secondary relationship as a set of rights and obligations that aim to ensure the restitution of the injured legal order by means of reparation of damages in addition to the cessation of wrongful act or the relevant guarantees of non-repetition. Articles 47 ARSIWA and 48 DARIO provide that in cases of a plurality of responsible entities for the same internationally wrongful act, the responsibility of each entity can be invoked in relation to that act. This rule reveals the principle of the discretionary freedom of the victim to invoke responsibility from each of the injurers. In the *Corfu Channel* case, Judge Azevedo has disclosed this side of joint responsibility by indicating that: "The victim retains the right to submit a claim against one only of the responsible parties, *in solidum*, in accordance with the choice which is always left to the discretion of the victim, in the purely economic field".[173] Hence, the joint responsibility represents a regime based on solidarity in order to ensure due reparation of damages.

The fact that the ARSIWA and DARIO provide no specific regulation on the division of reparations, may suggest that the parties, namely the victim and the injurers, have to resolve the reparation of damages on a bilateral basis.[174] However, the amount of reparation and the apportioning of reparations among jointly responsible entities could fall under the discretion of the *forum* that addresses the dispute. The contribution of responsible entities to the wrongful act, in principle, should play a role in the apportioning of responsibility.[175] The construction of complicity as a separate wrongful act allows for a certain autonomy in the distribution of responsibility pursuant to the merits of the conduct.[176] This is probably the only area of international responsibility where the subjective elements of responsibility play a role in addition to its objective elements, such as the causal link and the level of participation in the wrongful act.

These predictions on the distribution of responsibility are relevant not only for the cases of joint responsibility due to complicity in the commission of the internationally wrongful act, but also for the joint responsibility in the context of mixed agreements where no declaration on competences or apportion of reparations is made.[177] This suggests that these Articles can produce normative effects in terms of joint responsibility for violations of obligations of a mixed agreement by the

[172]See also Orakhelashvili (2010), pp. 647–665.

[173]*The Corfu Channel Case* (merits) (*UK v Albania*), 1949 I.C.J. Reports, Dissenting Opinion by Judge Azevedo, 78, 92.

[174]See also Orakhelashvili (2010), p. 657.

[175]Orakhelashvili (2010), pp. 658–659.

[176]See also Quigley (1987), p. 129,

[177]ILC Commentaries to DARIO, Commentary to Article 48, para. 1.

member states of an organization, although the wrongful conduct is attributed *ex hipothesi* to the organization where these states are members. The central assumption in this relationship is that the organization does not conduct alone the internationally wrongful act, and that its member states are *ex relatione* involved in this action. From this, it could be inferred that, in addition to the integral relationship between the international organization and the member states, there should exist also a certain degree of complicity in the conduct of the internationally wrongful act. This complicity may exist either in the decision-making process of the organization, or in the material contribution that one or more member states provide for the commitment of the internationally wrongful act. This construction constitutes a significant legal argument for both the attribution and the allocation of joint responsibility.

The question of distribution of responsibility further depends on the fact whether the author state maintains a certain degree of freedom in the commission of the internationally wrongful act, or whether it is entirely subordinated to the participating state. In the former case, the joint responsibility is more probable, whereas in the latter, the participating state should be deemed individually responsible for the breach.[178] The fact that the damages may not be caused by all the responsible entities, but only by a part of them, may suggest that the responsibility should also be allocated pursuant to the principle of attribution. Obviously, the responsible part of jointly responsible entities might be capable to provide the necessary remedies as the primary responsible subjects. However, in terms of the joint responsibility regime, the law of responsibility entitles the victim to request reparation from each of the responsible parties. This is particularly necessary where the primary entity does not provide the relevant reparations in an efficient way. Article 48 (2) DARIO entitles the victim to invoke subsidiary responsibility from the remaining entities. In cases of subsidiary responsibility, one of the jointly responsible parties bears all the burden of reparation. This may be the case also in other modes of joint responsibility where no subsidiary rule applies, but only one party takes the burden of reparation for all the others on solidarity basis. In these cases, the entity providing reparation has the right of recourse against the other entities (Articles 47(2)(b) ARSIWA and 48(3)(b) DARIO).

In light of the above observations, it could be inferred that in case that the Union is held jointly responsible for violation of WTO disciplines for matters falling within the residual areas of Member States powers, the Union may have the right of recourse against the wrongdoer. The right of recourse, in the context of responsibility from the WTO membership, may consist of taking the relevant measures that ensure the cessation of the violation of WTO disciplines. Therefore, although a domain that is essentially regulated from *lex specialis*, the rules of joint responsibility pursuant to *legi generali* could provide a sound normative framework that complements the WTO or the EU legal orders in this respect.

[178] Dominicé (2010), pp. 288–289.

## *6. Indirect Devolution of Responsibility Among the Membership of the International Organization by Virtue of Vicarious Responsibility*

Apart from the incurrence of international responsibility by virtue of the joint conduct of internationally wrongful acts, there could also exist other forms for a member state to incur responsibility for the wrongful acts of the organization. One way for incurring responsibility would be by means of subsidiarity responsibility, which constitutes a possibility in the hands of the injured parties to recover the damages from the entities that are not primarily responsible for the wrongful conduct. Hence, the second in the row is considered responsible for the reparations. Article 48(3)(b) DARIO provides the right of recourse of the secondary responsible entity against the primary jointly responsible entities. Article 62 DARIO provides that a member state of the organization is responsible for an internationally wrongful act of the organization, if it has accepted responsibility for the internationally wrongful act, or has led the injured party to rely on its responsibility. This constitutes a prime example of subsidiary responsibility, and reaffirms the legal presumption that the member states of an organization are *prima facie* not responsible for the acts of the organization, unless they satisfy the relevant criteria.

This construction of responsibility does not however explore much the distribution of joint responsibility within the organization. Member states may effectively incur responsibility through the membership in international organizations. Accordingly, the international organizations, being considered derivations of their member states, in terms of the international legal personality are considered artificial (legal) entities, which represent the interests of their main stakeholders. The member states establish the organizations, determine their mission and objectives, endow them with powers and the relevant international capacity to act, and provide the necessary resources (territory, human and financial resources) for accomplishing their mission.[179] In this quality, the international organization can be seen as a second grade entity, which does not exist as an autonomous body, but represents its member states on the basis of a limited mandate that is embodied in the catalogue of conferred powers. In light of this, the international organization can be compared with a business entity, which is created by the shareholders to pursue their interests. Hence, the member states remain the ultimate holders of the rights over the organizations, and they control its course of action in relation with third parties by means of participation in the decision-making processes within the structure of the organization. The delegation of powers to these organizations is followed by the responsibility of the states for the consequences of this delegation.[180] In this way, it can be inferred that an international organization represents a compound of joint interests of its member states, and as such, the organization cannot be detached

[179]See also Orakhelashvili (2010), p. 653.

[180]Orakhelashvili (2010), p. 663.

from them. The separate legal personality of the organization does not necessarily immunize the member states from the responsibility of the organization in international relations, particularly for actions in which they contribute in a direct or indirect way.[181] Hence, the member states are bound by the activity of the organization in an inextricable manner, and bear in this regard the responsibility deriving from this activity.

In addition to the joint and several responsibility of the organizations and their member states for common actions, the regime of subsidiary responsibility may also allow for an implied regime of joint responsibility, insofar as the organization, as a primary responsible entity, fails to meet its liabilities with its own resources. In such a situation, although the organization is deemed the primary responsible entity for an internationally wrongful act, the member states may only incur responsibility to the extent that the organization cannot repair the injured legal order. In such circumstances, the member states shall step in for meeting the residual liabilities of the organization pursuant to the level of their contributions.[182] This mode of incurring joint responsibility, as an implicit result of the doctrine of derivative personality of organizations, supports the view that the organization is a creation of the member states and any responsibility incurred from this creation should not vanish behind the veil of its separate legal personality.[183] Accordingly, the regime of joint and several responsibility could be a proper way for ensuring effective remedies and legal certainty in the international legal order.[184]

The proposition that the international organization is responsible alone for its own wrongful conduct can be regarded as a ‘fiction’, if the relationship with its member states would be taken into account. Accordingly, any benefit from the international action serves the interests of the stakeholders, namely the member states. Similarly, any obligations that the organization creates in the international relations should be also regarded as a virtual obligation for the member states. Subsequently, the responsibility of the organization can be regarded as virtually apportioned to the members of the organization. In view of this, one can think of a ‘virtual devolution’ of the burden of the international organization to the member states. The question of the division of reparations between the constituent entities of the international organization, either because of the delegated character of powers, or due to the territorial element, is inherent in the legal nature of the organization; the latter triggers the responsibility of the member states *ex relatione*, absent of the direct attribution.[185]

In light of these observations, it can be inferred that the joint responsibility regime constitutes an imperative for establishing clear rules of devolution of the international responsibility between the participants of the Union polity. Obviously,

[181]See also Orakhelashvili (2010), p. 662.

[182]Orakhelashvili (2010), p. 662.

[183]Orakhelashvili (2010), pp. 662–663.

[184]Orakhelashvili (2010), p. 662.

[185]Orakhelashvili (2010), p. 648.

there exists a state of tension between the fact that the responsibility of member states is in principle subject to their acceptance (Article 62 DARIO), and the fact that the virtual devolution of burden is the natural result of the international organization representing its member states. In light of these contradictory claims, the international law of responsibility remains, in principle, quite indifferent toward any relationship of devolution. Such a relationship is governed by the constitutional charter of the international organization. Hence, it is the duty of this framework to accommodate also the predictions of the rules of attribution, as a premise for the internal peace in the polity.

The question of devolution of joint responsibility of the Union from its WTO membership, which underlines the entire research question of this work, is construed as an internal constitutional matter of the EU polity. However, inasmuch as the Union represents features of an international organization, the predictions of *legi generali* could help in complementing the normative framework in addressing the fallacies of the joint responsibility regime. A pluralist approach on the matter could produce a model of participation of the Union in the DSP, which would be more sustained from the normative point of view. Hence, in case that, by virtue of its participation in the DSP for defending the French Decree, the Union would be found responsible for violating WTO obligations, the burden of responsibility would be devolved to all Member States, which are designated as virtually responsible in this case. France would be the ultimate responsible party in this relationship. Following the predictions of Article 62 DARIO, the unconcerned Member States could escape this devolution in case that they deny the responsibility toward the injured party (Canada). On the other hand, France cannot escape responsibility, considering that it is precisely the French measure that led Canada to rely on the responsibility of France for violating the WTO obligations. Hence, the Union's responsibility could well be allocated to France. This responsibility is particularly relevant for the cessation of the wrongful act, and remains quite theoretical in relation with the countermeasures, given that the latter are applied against the entire Union. In case that these measures cannot be devolved explicitly to French products, particularly in cases of cross-retaliatory measures, then the other Member States may also face trade barriers. As a result, this fallacy could only be addressed in the internal institutional context of the polity.

## V. International Legal Responsibility in the Context of *lex specialis* Regimes

The international responsibility of the Union and its Member States in the context of their WTO membership manifests the interference of various legal orders. From the international law perspective, the WTO Agreement and the EU legal order constitute particular examples of *lex specialis*, which determine the conditions, the content, and the implementation of the international responsibility. The normative framework of the *legi generali* on responsibility allows for, and gives priority to, the application of the *lex specialis* regimes of responsibility. Articles 55 ARSIWA and 64 DARIO provide that the special rules determining the conditions for the existence of an internationally wrongful act, or the content of implementation of the international responsibility, prevail over the *legi generali*. For the EU – Member States relationship, as well as for the relationship of the WTO with its Members, this means that the internal rules of organizations regulate exclusively the issues of responsibility for violation of international obligations. However, the provisions of *legi generali* remain at least instructive for the construction of a model of responsibility for the participation of the Union in the DSP. The following shall elaborate on the regimes of responsibility of the WTO and the EU legal orders, in order to point out some necessary predictions for addressing the fallacies of the joint responsibility regime.

## *1. The WTO Agreement as* lex specialis *for the International Legal Responsibility*

The WTO Agreement constitutes a significant part of the international legal order, inasmuch as it institutionalizes the trade relations among its Members, and its global outreach is beyond any doubt. In terms of the responsibility of the EU and its Member States, this Agreement represents the main source of the entire picture of the interaction of the legal orders. The content of the WTO Agreement, embodied in multilateral and plurilateral agreements, regulates the primary relationship between Member States that have accepted them.[186] The obligations contained therein have been initially conceived as state obligations, and have later been expanded for customs territories, such as the European Union (Article XII WTO Agreement). The obligations of the WTO Agreement, unlike in many other international treaties, are preserved from a specific regime of dispute settlement, which governs the conditions and the implementation of the international responsibility emerging out of the violation of these obligations from the Members.

With the institutionalization of the judicial system of adjudication of trade disputes, the tendency of self-containment resulting from the process of continuous fragmentation of international law is diminishing.[187] The WTO law has not escaped this process either. The DSU constitutes an exclusive system (hence a *lex specialis*) for addressing the international responsibility in the context of WTO Agreement. Nevertheless, the DSM remains only *prima facie* autonomous inasmuch as it cannot be seen in clinical isolation from the *legi generali*.[188] Indeed, the DSB in several cases has adopted the *legi generali* rules of attribution of international

[186] Article II WTO Agreement.

[187] Eeckhout (2011), p. 345.

[188] *US – Gasoline*, Report of the Appellate Body, 17. See also Stoll (2012), para. 18.

responsibility.[189] The main WTO legal framework is conceived not merely as a traditional subsystem of international law, based on treaties governing the trade relations of sovereign states. Article 3.2 DSU recalls the customary rules of international law as an aiding tool of interpretation of the WTO Agreements, hence serving as an implied reference rule for the application of the VCLT.[190] Hence, the *legi generali* on the international responsibility cannot be completely displaced in favor of *lex specialis*, but rather these two bodies of rules apply in a complementary way.[191] This construction allows for the general rules of international responsibility to apply insofar as the matter is not regulated from the WTO regime of responsibility. This constructive way of interpretation is based on the combination of Articles 55 with 56 ARSIWA and Articles 64 with 65 DARIO. Accordingly, the *lex specialis* does not explicitly exclude the application of *legi generali*, but only substitutes the regime of responsibility with its own specific rules.

The DSM constitutes an advanced system of responsibility in the context of international law. Its automatic and compulsory jurisdiction, the right of appeal before the Appellate Body, the time limits for the resolution of disputes, and a specific system of retaliation, make the DSM distinctively more efficient than other comparable systems in the law of international organizations.[192] A further distinction is drawn in terms of the remedies for injuries of WTO obligations. The system of retaliation aims the cessation of the wrongful measures, rather than the reparation of damages incurred from the victims.

The DSM may be activated not merely for breach of WTO obligations amounting to nullification or impairment of trade benefits for WTO Members, but also for the application of trade measures that do not conflict with WTO obligations.[193] Article XXIII(1) GATT provides for the right of reparation not only for violation of WTO obligations through internationally wrongful acts (violation complaints), but also for impairment or nullification of benefits or the impediment of the objectives of WTO Agreement due to lawful acts of Member States (non-violation complaints).[194] The right to invoke reparations for injuries caused

---

[189] See for example *Australia – Measures Affecting Importation of Salmon*. Recourse to Art. 21.5 by Canada (WT/DS18), Report of the Panel of 20 March 2000, paras. 7.12–7.13; *Turkey – Restrictions on Imports of Textile and Clothing Products* (WT/DS34), Panel of the Appellate Body of 31 May 1999, paras. 9.41–9.43; *Korea – Measures Affecting Government Procurement* (WT/DS163), Report of the Panel of 19 June 2000, para. 6.5; and *United States – Measures Affecting Cross-Border Supply of Gambling and Betting Services* (WT/DS285), Report of the Panel of 10 November 2004, para. 6.128.

[190] See also Gomula (2010), p. 792.

[191] Gomula (2010), pp. 792–793.

[192] See also Antoniadis (2004), p. 330.

[193] Article XXIII(1)(b, c) GATT.

[194] See further Gomula (2010), pp. 793–394. The 'non-violation complaints' are further detailed in Article 26 DSU, while the majority of the WTO system of responsibility is mainly concerned for 'violation complaints', hence regulating the secondary relationship.

from lawful acts is part of the primary relations among parties. The failure to observe these obligations may be regarded as a violation of the primary obligations, which subsequently triggers legal responsibility due to internationally wrongful acts.[195] This constitutes an exception from the structure of responsibility according to *legi generali*, which addresses the international responsibility as a result of the commitment of an internationally wrongful act only.

With the proviso that the violation of WTO obligations constitutes an internationally wrongful act (Article XXIII GATT), it can be suggested that the DSB should follow the rules of attribution in order to establish the breach of obligations. The procedural rules do not include these rules, and for this reason, the *legi generali* on the international responsibility of states and international organization, respectively ARSIWA and DARIO, could complement the *lex specialis* with reference to these elements of responsibility from the WTO membership. Obviously, this construction would reject any argument that considers DSM as a self-contained regime.[196] Nevertheless, the DSM constitutes a *lex specialis*, inasmuch as it limits and displaces the remedies provided in *legi generali* by defining only specific consequences that are allowed to flow.[197]

Article 3(7) DSU provides the main elements of the DSM. This system aims to achieve a positive solution to a dispute, which is mutually acceptable to the parties and consistent with the covered agreements. Absent a mutually agreed solution, the DSB conducts a process aiming the withdrawal of a WTO inconsistent measure. Pursuant to Articles 3(7) and 22(1) DSU, the cessation of the wrongful measures excludes the compensation of victims in the classic sense. Hence, the reparation of injuries is not part of the restitution of the injured legal order. Indeed, the possibility of compensation provided in the DSU is subject to the condition that the cessation is impracticable. The compensation is designated as a temporary measure conditioned upon the termination effects of the cessation. Additionally, Article 22 DSU provides that the compensation remains a voluntary measure. As such, compensation in the WTO context differs from compensation as a reparation instrument for the injury pursuant to the *legi generali*. The rationale behind this mode is to avoid the stimulation of state decisions aimed at pursuing pragmatic behavior by trading with their concessions. Hence, the WTO system of reparation aims to achieve the restitution of the legal injuries by terminating the internationally wrongful act, rather than reallocating the loss from the impairment or nullification of benefits by means of *restitutio in integrum*, its equivalent (compensation), or satisfaction.

The lack of an obligation for reparation is due to the special conception of the legal injury in the WTO legal order.[198] As it results from Article 3(7) DSU, the main thread of the system of remedies is to ensure the performance of the WTO obligations, and the enforcement of the DSB rulings for the declaration of wrongful

---

[195] ILC Commentaries to Draft ARSIWA, General Commentary para. 4(c).

[196] See further Gomula (2010), pp. 794–795 and Villalpando (2002), p. 395.

[197] ILC Commentaries to Draft ARSIWA, Commentary to Article 55, para. 3.

[198] Gomula (2010), p. 798.

(inconsistent) measures mainly relies on voluntary compliance. In light of this, the restitution by equivalence is seen as a temporary measure, while the possibility of suspending the application of concessions under the authorized retaliatory measures, is regarded as a measure of last resort. Whereas compensation is conceived as a voluntary measure, the suspension of concessions is not subject to the voluntary acceptance from the wrongdoer. The retaliatory measures are enacted for ensuring the enforcement of DSB rulings or recommendations. The process of retaliation may be shifted from the domain where the violation of WTO disciplines has occurred, into another area, where it can be deemed more efficient for achieving compliance with DSB decisions.[199] This cross-retaliation is based on the principle of exhaustion of prior stages of retaliation. Accordingly, the complainant should first seek the suspension of concessions with respect to the same sector in which the WTO inconsistent measure was instituted, and if this is not found practicable or effective, resort can be made to another sector of the same agreement (Article 22 (3) (a, b) DSU). If the same party finds that the same sector is still impracticable and ineffective to achieve the aims of retaliation, and if the circumstances are serious enough, it may seek to suspend the concessions or other obligations under another covered agreement (Article 22 (3) (c) DSU). This option is applied for the first time in the *EC – Banana* Case. In this case, the DSB authorized the cross-retaliation in an area other than the one where the inconsistent measures were instituted, after realizing that the primary area of retaliation would not suffice for the claimant to exercise the relevant pressure over the EU to withdraw the inconsistent measures.[200] For the EU, the system of cross-retaliation might prove quite disadvantageous. Accordingly, the EU may incur suspension of concessions from a WTO Member, although the WTO inconsistent measure is instituted from a Member State in the exercise of its residual powers. This fallacious situation is not prevented by the WTO law, and remains to be addressed from an internal perspective of the EU legal order.

The institution of unilateral countermeasures is outlawed from the WTO legal order.[201] Article 23 DSU recalls in particular that the only lawful way for Members of the WTO to seek redress for their violated rights is through the DSM. Hence, any measure outside these procedures, which unilaterally attempts to restore the balance of rights and obligations by seeking withdrawal of WTO inconsistent measures, by seeking compensation, or by suspending WTO concessions, although in compliance with the WTO Agreement, can be considered to be in violation of Article 23 (1) DSU.[202] The suspension of concessions or other obligations under the covered

[199]See also MacLeod et al. (1996), p. 159.

[200]See further *European Communities – Regime for the Importation, Sale and Distribution of Bananas* (*EC – Bananas*), Recourse to Arbitration by the European Communities under Article 22.6 DSU, WT/DS27/ARB/ECU, 24 March 2000, DSR 2000:V, 2237, paras. 174–175.

[201]See also Gomula (2010), p. 798.

[202]See in particular *European Communities – Measures Affecting Trade in Commercial Vessels* (WT/DS301), Report of the Panel of 22 April 2005, in particular paras. 7.195, 7.207 and 7.220.

agreement is subject to the prior approval of the DSB, which should take into consideration certain principles and procedures that aim to minimize the adverse effects of retaliatory measures. These principles should be able to balance the need of retaliatory measures to exercise the relevant pressure on the wrongdoer for compliance with WTO obligations with the need to protect the reciprocity levels in the institution of trade measures. The rationale behind this balance is to discourage discriminatory measures as long as they increase the overall trade loss, without compromising however the restitution of the injured legal order.

The institution of countermeasures raises further the question of their impact on the relationship between the EU and its Member States. As a general principle, the system of countermeasures should not affect the rights of third parties.[203] The institution of countermeasures, pursuant to *legi generali*, follows the principle of attribution, in that it provides for the right to institute countermeasures only against the state which is responsible for the internationally wrongful act (Article 49 (1) ARSIWA and 51(1) DARIO). When reflecting on the relevance of these predictions for the membership of the EU and its Member States in the WTO, an important question can be raised. Should the Member States of the EU, which are not related with a DSP, be considered as third states in relation with the countermeasures? With this respect, it is maintained in the doctrine that a possible construction of either the Union or its Member States as a third party in a DSP, raises concerns in relation with the joint responsibility regime.[204] A disputed measure falling within the scope of the conferred powers of the Union has, in principle, no connection with the residual powers of the Member States. Hence, following the predictions of the *legi generali* on the application of countermeasures, the DSP, and particularly the countermeasures in such cases, should not affect the rights of the Member States, which can be regarded as third parties. Should this construction gain normative moment, the regime of joint responsibility would become questionable in its entirety. As a result, the DSP may become hostage of the vertical distribution of powers in the Union polity. However, the WTO legal system precludes the possibility that the enforcement of DSB rulings and recommendations become futile and subject to conditions. The cross-retaliation constitutes the ultimate form of the countermeasures (Article 22 (3) DSU), and as such, it is unconditionally accepted from all Members of the WTO (Article XI:1 WTO Agreement).[205] In this way, the construction of the EU or its Member States as third parties in the DSP hinders the effectiveness of the WTO Agreement.

This analysis reveals the relevance of the internal constitutional issues of the Union polity for the DSP. The DSB lacks the jurisdiction to judge on internal matters of the Union polity. Moreover, no procedural provision of the DSU entitles the DSB to verify the standing of the Union or its Member States in the DSP

[203] ILC Commentaries to DARIO, General Commentary of Chapter II (Countermeasures), 129, para. 6.

[204] Heliskoski (2001), pp. 222–223.

[205] See also Heliskoski (2001), pp. 223–224.

according to the conferred powers. This procedural moment constitutes a concern for the Union polity, given that the procedural legitimation of the Union as a representative of the Member State should be able to reflect the mandate of representation, in the absence of a concrete linkage between the disputed measure and the Union law.[206] This issue gains further relevance for the attribution of responsibility of the Union in the course of the DSP.

From a general observation of the DSM, it can be inferred that this system is based on the negotiation between the concerned parties to pursue a mutually agreed solution of the disputes, inasmuch as the entire system depends on the voluntary withdrawal of inconsistent measures from the wrongdoer, although at the costs of its own economy. The option of compensation is subject to mutual agreement and the institution of countermeasures is only a reciprocal tool for inducing the wrongdoer to comply with the DSB rulings or recommendations. The reciprocal nature of the dispute resolution system makes it relatively flexible and, as such, unpredictable. Indeed, the flexible elements of the DSM can weaken the normative character of the WTO obligations, and subject their enforcement to the pragmatic behavior of the participants.

Nevertheless, there is no doubt that the DSB rulings and recommendations are binding upon the parties, and the mechanism for their compliance through compensation or suspension of concessions remains temporary.[207] In the realm of public international law, the DSM is regarded as a quite sophisticated and advanced system of enforcement, precisely due to its compulsory jurisdiction and the clarity of the regime of compliance.[208] The DSB rulings are binding on the WTO Members and give rise to an obligation to bring WTO-inconsistent measures in conformity with their obligations under the covered agreements, and must be implemented promptly in order to ensure effective resolution of disputes to the benefit of all Members (Article 21.1 DSU).[209] The GATT 1994 system of enforcement inherits nevertheless some downsides from its predecessor, GATT 1947. Accordingly, the enforcement mechanism of the DSB rulings and recommendations is limited to trade sanctions in the form of retaliatory measures. In economic terms, this solution is not efficient, given that the trade damages caused from internationally wrongful acts are not mitigated; rather they are multiplied and spread to additional victims of trade wars. Hence, the overall loss is greater than any short time benefits. The lack of compensation of victims may constitute a reason for not motivating the wrongdoers to comply with adverse DSB rulings and recommendations. Nevertheless, if

[206]On the basis of these premises, it might be possible to develop an internal procedure to deal with the jurisdictional standing of the Union or its concerned Member State in a particular DSP. This question underlies the discourse of the normative model of representation of the EU and its Member States and is further elaborated in Chap. 5.

[207]Eeckhout (2011), p. 378.

[208]Eeckhout (2011), p. 378.

[209]*European Communities – Customs Classification of Frozen Boneless Chicken Cuts*, (WT/DS269/13 and WT/DS286/15), Award of the Arbitrator James Bacchus, ARB 2005-4/21, para. 55.

construed from a general public international law perspective, the DSM remains fairly successful.

## *2. The EU Legal Order as* lex specialis *for the International Responsibility*

The EU legal order constitutes the other important element that plays a role in the general picture of the interaction of legal orders, inasmuch as the question of responsibility from the WTO membership of the EU and its Member States is concerned. Although the WTO Agreement remains the primary normative framework for construing the joint responsibility regime of the Union and its Member States, the EU constitutional infrastructure has a complementary relevance for managing particular aspects of this regime. The legal and institutional relationship of the Union institutions and its Member States influences the joint responsibility regime in two different aspects. On the one hand, the constitutional infrastructure that manages the issues of responsibility within the Union polity provides the premises and the conditions for the participation of the Union in the DSP. On the other hand, this infrastructure could serve as a relevant framework for managing the fallacies of the joint responsibility regime, and particularly the devolution of responsibility among the participants.

The regime of responsibility in the EU legal order is independent from other international regimes of responsibility and as such, it may be regarded as a clear *lex specialis* with strong features of a self-contained regime. The norms of the *legi generali* on international responsibility, in principle, do not apply in addressing the consequences of internationally wrongful acts of the Member States or the Union institutions. The normative ground for this assumption is the self-sufficiency of the EU legal order in regulating the secondary relationship of legal responsibility. An obvious equivalence of the EU regime of responsibility with the *legi generali* is missing.[210] However, this system cannot be fully detached from the *legi generali* on responsibility, at least from a theoretical point of view. The main argument for this is based on the overwhelmingly reiterated formula that the EU is conceived as a new legal order of international law.[211] In light of this, it can be presumed that the principles and institutions of international responsibility in *legi generali* can, to some extent, be employed in the EU legal order for addressing the fallacies of the international legal responsibility in this system.

The system of international legal responsibility, as codified in the *legi generali*, is however distinguished from the legal responsibility in the EU legal order. The latter entails a general obligation of the Member States to take any appropriate

[210] See also Thouvenin (2010), p. 861.

[211] Case C-26/62 *Van Gend en Loos v Administratie der Belastingen*, [1963] ECR I-001, 12, para. 4.

measures to ensure the fulfillment of obligations arising out of the Treaties or resulting from the Union acts (Article 4(3) para. 2 Treaty on European Union (TEU). This obligation is conceived as an expression of the principle of loyalty, and is essentially based on the abstract obligation of the Member States to comply with the Union's primary and secondary legislation.[212] The duty of loyalty provides for the (positive) obligation of the Member States to facilitate the achievement of the Union's tasks and the (negative) duty to refrain from any measures jeopardizing the attainment of the Union's objectives (Article 4(3) para. 3 TEU). These obligations endorse the proposition that the Union is heavily dependent on the compliance of Member States with the EU law, reaffirming in this way the thesis that the Union does not exist as a detached entity from its constituent Member States.

Similar to the *legi generali*, the regime of legal responsibility in the EU legal order can be conceived as a secondary relationship, which is engaged with the violation of the primary norms. The object of legal responsibility in the EU legal order refers to the protection of primary norms, which impose obligations on Member States and exceptionally on their nationals (mainly in the competition domain).

The EU legal order has a multidimensional infrastructure for the management of the issues of responsibility. The EU is not a unitary entity, but a Union of sovereign states, which have unionized a number of areas of governance by conferring powers on the Union, and which have withheld residual powers on the remaining areas. The infrastructure that addresses the questions of responsibility is composed of two main layers, which are combined with each other. The main institutional layer addressing the responsibility of Member States and EU institutions consists of the Union's judicial branch and provides the necessary remedies for the application of Union law. The ECJ has jurisdiction on infringement proceedings initiated from the Commission or Member States against other Member States that allegedly fail to fulfill their Treaty obligations (Articles 256, 258–260 of the Treaty on the Functioning of the European Union (TFEU)). The other layer is composed of the courts or tribunals of the Member States, which have jurisdiction on disputes where the Union institutions are party, if the Treaties do not reserve it to the ECJ (Article 274). The exclusive jurisdiction of the ECJ is reserved for any disputes between Member States related to the interpretation of the Treaties (Article 273 TFEU). This jurisdiction includes the preliminary rulings on questions raised before the courts and tribunals of the Member States on the interpretation of the Treaties and the validity and interpretation of acts of EU institutions (Article 267 TFEU). The ECJ has jurisdiction in actions for compensation of damages against the Union institutions pursuant to Articles 256, 268 and 340 TFEU. Similarly, Member States may incur non-contractual liability for breach of Union law, and are obliged in this regard to redress the injured rights.[213] This remedy can be activated in cases where the nationals claim liability of Member States for breach of EU law.

[212]The duty of loyalty shall be analyzed in more detail in Chap. 4.

[213]Joined Cases C-6/90 and C-9/90 *Francovich and Bonifaci et al. v Italian Republic*, [1991] ECR I-5357, paras. 33 and 35.

From this configuration of jurisdiction in the EU legal order, it can be inferred that the institutional infrastructure where the regime of responsibility operates, is distributed among the ECJ and the national courts of the Member States. While the determination of breach of Union law is determined at the Union level, the determination of liability is conducted at the national level pursuant to domestic norms.[214] This system of responsibility may be regarded as an effective machinery for compliance with the EU law, inasmuch as it vests on the subjects the relevant rights to invoke responsibility, in addition to the infringement procedure conducted by the Commission under the control of the ECJ.[215] The national legal orders ensure that their nationals may invoke the responsibility of states for complying with EU law. The preliminary ruling proceedings serve as a further guarantee for a homogeneous application of EU law among the Member States. Additionally, the Union institutions can also be held responsible vis-à-vis Member States for the violation of the principle of conferral to the detriment of the residual powers of the Member States.[216] This possibility in the hands of Member States can be construed in view of the legality review procedure pursuant to Article 263 TFEU.

In order to ensure compliance with the Union law, the most that the system of responsibility in the EU legal order may achieve, is to impose a lump sum and/or (daily) penalty payments for non-compliance with the judicial decisions declaring the wrongfulness and requiring the cessation of the act (Article 260(2) TFEU). Such monetary obligations may be imposed also for cases of failure of transposition of directives from the Member States (Article 260(3) TFEU). This is another *differentia specifica* of the system of responsibility in the *legi generali* and the WTO law, from the responsibility for breach of Union law. From the legal nature of these sanctions, it can be inferred that, although imposed in the context of responsibility for the breach of EU law, they are not construed in the function of reparation of damages, as they are not designed as direct measures of punishment for the breach. Rather, these sanctions are conceived as methods of enforcement, or as constraining tools for complying with the obligation to restitute the injured legal order through cessation.

Although the infringement proceedings are not construed in the context of the regime of responsibility, as no damages are taken into consideration,[217] they may still be regarded as a form of (partial) restitution of the injured legal order through the cessation of the wrongful act. The options of pecuniary measures provided in Article 260 TFEU aim at inducing the wrongdoer to comply with the judgment establishing the breach.[218] This is similar to the responsibility pursuant to *legi*

---

[214] Thouvenin (2010), p. 866.

[215] Case C-26/62 *Van Gend en Loos v Administratie der Belastingen*, [1963] ECR I-001, 13, para. 5.

[216] Tomuschat (2002),185–186.

[217] Thouvenin (2010), p. 866.

[218] Case C-304/02 *Commission of the European Communities v French Republic*, [2005] ECR I-6263, para. 80.

*generali*, which is not always about the compensation of damages. The incurrence of damages does not appear to be a decisive condition for the incurrence of responsibility. The objectification doctrine prevailing in this relationship is mostly concerned with compliance. The EU legal order has adopted a similar approach, by construing a system of compliance with the EU obligations, which is quite effective in ensuring compliance through cessation of the wrongful conduct (Articles 258–260 TFEU). However, the EU legal order is distinguished from international law, inasmuch as it acknowledges the right of any natural or legal persons to invoke directly the pecuniary responsibility of the wrongdoers, subject to the condition that the wrongful act should be serious and must concern a conferred right.[219] This difference does not concern the responsibility *per se*, but rather the conditions for establishing the secondary relationship between the parties.

The fact that the EU Member States are the main subjects of the regime of responsibility is inspired from the idea that they are the masters of the Treaties. As such, they remain the responsible bodies for the breach of EU Treaties. The normative ground behind this legal presumption is mainly Article 4 TEU, which provides for the obligation of Member States to ensure the fulfillment of the obligations arising from the Treaties. This obligation, as an expression of the principles of *pacta sunt servanda* and loyalty, is reaffirmed by the jurisprudence in several cases, as a basis for the identification of the substantial obligations of Member States.[220] The ECJ has advanced these abstract predictions into well-established conditions for the responsibility of Member States toward their nationals. In this way, they can be held liable not only for the obligations arising from the Treaties, but also for damages incurred from nationals due to failure to comply with their obligations.

The system of responsibility in the EU legal order, in addition to the responsibility of Member States, includes also a particular regime of responsibility for the Union institutions. Article 340 TFEU provides that, in addition to contractual liability, the Union shall be liable in cases of non-contractual liability to make good any damage caused by its institutions or its servants. Although the determination of liability is made in accordance with the general principles common to the laws of the Member States, pursuant to Articles 256 and 268 TFEU, the jurisdiction in the disputes relating to compensation is reserved for the ECJ, which acts as a court of first instance. This is due to the fact that the Union cannot be condemned by the Member States' courts to the extent that the non-contractual liability is concerned.

In order for the EU to be held responsible, the breach of the rule of law should be attributed to its institutions, or the agents that acted in its name.[221] The acts of the Member States, which are stemming from the primary legislation, do not entail the

[219]Thouvenin (2010), p. 868.

[220]Edward and Lane (2012), p. 45. See also Case C-246/07 *European Commission v Kingdom of Sweden*, [2010] ECR I-3317, para. 69.

[221]Thouvenin (2010), p. 867.

responsibility of the Union, as long as they constitute inter-state law and, as such, they are not attributable to the Union.[222] However, the responsibility of the Member States cannot be excluded in this context.[223] Furthermore, there should exist a causal link between the wrongful conduct, which *ex hipothesi* is attributed to the Union, and the alleged damage.[224] In cases of individual claims, they have also the obligation to prove the damages that they have incurred as a result of the Union's unlawful act; the element of real damages suffered from the individuals is a *conditio sine qua non* for the pecuniary responsibility.[225] In jurisprudence, it is clearly established that omissions by the Union institutions, similarly to active actions, give rise to liability on the part of the Union.[226] Therefore, the pecuniary responsibility of the Union institutions is reserved for those acts that infringe the conferred rights of the individuals and cause damages upon them.

As to the element of attribution of the wrongful conduct to the Union institutions, the ECJ has maintained that the Union is liable for actions, which, by virtue of an internal and direct relationship, are the necessary extension of the tasks entrusted to the institutions.[227] The vicarious responsibility of the Union in relation with wrongful acts of its agents and servants is therefore limited only to actions or omissions committed by them during the performance of their duties.[228] The responsibility of the Union's agents, which is incurred outside the scope of their commissioned duties, should be claimed on a personal basis before the national courts where the wrongful act has occurred.[229]

The invocation of responsibility in the Union polity constitutes another area of interest, particularly in terms of the allocation of burden for breach of obligations. The subjects entitled to invoke the legal responsibility of states in the Union polity

[222]Case T-113/96, *Edouard Dubois et Fils SA v Council of the European Union and Commission of the European Communities*, [1998] ECR I-125, paras. 41 and 57.

[223]*Ibid*, para. 57.

[224]Case C-169/73 *Compagnie Continentale France v Council of the European Communities*, [1975] ECR I-117, para. 22.

[225]Case C-26/81 *SA Oleifici Mediterranei v European Economic Community*, [1982] ECR I-3057, para. 16.

[226]This liability can be established only where those institutions have infringed a legal obligation to act under a provision of Union law, which can either be any formal rule of Union law, or any general principle of law, by virtue of which the Union would be obliged to compensate a person who has been subject to a measure expropriating his property or restricting his freedom to enjoy his right to property, since the Union cannot be obliged to make good damage caused by acts which cannot be imputed to it. See further, Case T-113/96, *Edouard Dubois et Fils SA v Council and Commission*, [1998] ECR I-125, paras. 56 and 57.

[227]Case C-9/69 *Claude Sayag and S.A. Zurich v Jean-Pierre Leduc, Denise Thonnon and S.A. La Concorde*, [1969] ECR I-329, para. 7.

[228]Thouvenin (2010), p. 868.

[229]Thouvenin (2010), p. 868. See also Case C-9/69 *Sayag et al. v Leduc et al.*, [1969] ECR I-329, para. 7.

are not only states, but also individuals holding subjective rights conferred by the Treaties.[230] This constitutes a strong differentiation factor from the legal responsibility in international law, where individuals are only exceptionally recognized as subjects of international treaties (mainly in the domains of international law of human rights and international criminal law). The EU legal order recognizes the right of individuals to invoke the responsibility of Member States for non-compliance with the EU norms, as long as their subjective rights are seriously violated from acts or omissions in violation of the EU norms.[231] The main criteria required for sustaining the right of invocation include the fact that the breach of a rule of law conferring rights on individuals, the sufficiently serious nature of the breach, and the existence of a causal link between the breach and the harm suffered from the injured individual rights.[232]

While the elements of breach of a rule of law and the evidence of a causal link can be determined more objectively, the element of seriousness requires more attention. In order to determine whether a breach is sufficiently serious,

> the competent court may take into consideration [...] the clarity and precision of the rule breached, the measure of discretion left by that rule to the national or Community authorities, whether the infringement and the damage caused was intentional or involuntary, whether any error of law was excusable or inexcusable, the fact that the position taken by a Community institution may have contributed toward the omission, and the adoption or retention of national measures or practices contrary to Community law.[233]

With a view to the rule of law, the EU legal order acknowledges the right of natural or legal persons to invoke the review of legality of legislative acts or other acts of the institutions. This is possible for legislative acts if they are addressed to the natural or legal persons, or if they are of direct and individual concern to them, or for regulatory acts which do not entail implementing measures and are of a direct concern to these persons (Article 263(4) TFEU). In the course of determining the responsibility, the EU legal order requires that the wrongful act should be serious, in that it must be manifest and grave. These elements can be assessed in terms of the margin of appreciation that the wrongdoer has when committing the wrongful

---

[230] See also Thouvenin (2010), p. 861.

[231] Thouvenin (2010), pp. 868–870. See also Case 5/71 *Aktiens-Zuckerfabrik Schöppenstedt v Council of the European Union* [1971] ECR I-975, paragraph 11; Joined Cases C-83/76 and 94/76, 4/77, 15/77 and 40/77, *Bayerische HNL Vermehrungsbetriebe GmbH & Co. KG and others v Council and Commission of the European Communities* [1978] ECR I-1209, paragraph 6; Joined Cases C-104/89 and 37/90 *J.M. Mulder et al. v Council of the European Union and Commission of the European Communities*, [1992] ECR I-3061, paragraph 12.

[232] Joined Cases C-46/93 and C-48/93 *Brasserie du Pêcheur SA v Bundesrepublik Deutschland and The Queen v Secretary of State for Transport, ex parte: Factortame Ltd. et al.*, [1996] ECR I-1029, para. 51.

[233] *Ibid*, para. 56.

act.[234] When the margin of appreciation is small, the breach of Union law is qualified as sufficiently serious for triggering responsibility,[235] without suggesting, however, that a wide margin of appreciation would enable the wrongdoer to escape the responsibility for the wrongful act.

The preservation of effectiveness of the EU legal order, demands that the system of international responsibility, in terms of the protection of subjective rights, goes as far as acknowledging the right of individuals to obtain redress for the infringed rights.[236] This however presumes that the individuals have incurred damages, being the only juridical fact that gives rise to responsibility. In order for the damages to be compensable, they should be real, certain, actual, unusual, special and should exceed the ordinary risk of economic activity.[237] Given that the compensation of damages aims the highest extent of *restitutio in integrum*, the determination of damages incurred by individuals, in addition to the loss suffered from the wrongful conduct, may take into consideration, depending on the circumstances, also the loss of earnings, the loss of a chance as well as the moral harm.[238]

The regime of responsibility in the EU legal order is, in principle, not only reserved for wrongful conduct, but also for lawful acts, which may cause damages even without injuring the legal order. The incurrence of non-contractual liability for lawful conduct is questioned from the ECJ. Even if it would be recognized, this art of liability could be subject to several conditions, such as the existence of actual damages, a causal link between the damage and the conduct, and the unusual and special nature of the damage.[239] Even more exceptional would be the legal responsibility for legislative acts when the economic choices are concerned, unless a sufficiently serious breach of a superior rule of law for the protection of individual

[234]Thouvenin (2010), pp. 868–869.

[235]Thouvenin (2010), p. 869.

[236]Joined Cases C-6/90 and C-9/90 *Francovich et al. v Italy*, [1991] ECR I-5357, paras. 33 and 35.

[237]Cases C-256/80 *Birra Wührer SpA et al. v Council and Commission of the European Communities*, [1984] ECR I-3693, para. 15 and C-59/83 *SA Biovilac NV v European Economic Community*, [1984] ECR I-4057, para. 28. See also Thouvenin (2010), p. 872.

[238]Case C-308/87 *Alfredo Grifoni v European Atomic Energy Community*, [1994] ECR I-341, para. 40, Joined Cases C-104/89 and 37/90 *J.M. Mulder et al. v Council of the European Union and Commission of the European Communities*, [2000] ECR I-203, paras. 51, 63. See further Thouvenin (2010), p. 871.

[239]Cases C-237/98 *Dorsch Consult Ingenieurgesellschaft mbH v Council of the European Union and Commission of the European Communities*, [2000] ECR I-4549, para. 19 and T-383/00 *Beamglow Ltd. v European Parliament, Council of the European Union and Commission of the European Communities*, [2005] ECR I-5459, para. 174. See further Joined Cases C-120/06 and C-121/06 *Fabbrica italiana accumulatori motocarri Montecchio SpA (FIAMM) and Fabbrica italiana accumulatori motocarri Montecchio Technologies LLC (C-120/06 P), Giorgio Fedon & Figli SpA and Fedon America, Inc. (C-121/06 P) v Council of the European Union and Commission of the European Communities*, [2008] ECR I-6513, paras. 167, 169.

rights would have occurred.[240] This may obviously amount to a deny of any right to compensation to individuals incurring damages within reasonable limits, even if the measure is declared null and void due to its unlawful nature, unless the institution has manifestly and gravely disregarded the limits on the exercise of its powers.[241] However, the non-contractual liability may be incurred for acts violating the individual right of property or the freedom to pursue trade or profession. This is to the extent that the concerned legislative measure has impaired the very substance of those rights in a disproportionate and intolerable manner, precisely because no compensation is awarded to avoid or remedy such impairment.[242] As already confirmed in jurisprudence, the individual right to property and the freedom to pursue trade and profession are not absolute and must be viewed in relation to their social function. They may be restricted to the benefit of general interest, with the condition that such restrictions do not constitute a disproportionate and intolerable interference, thereby impairing the very substance of the rights guaranteed by the EU legal order.[243]

The element of damages remains a distinguishing factor for the responsibility resulting from wrongful acts or lawful acts. The damages in a wrongful conduct can be certain, and this includes the likeness that the damage will occur in the future as well. In the cases of lawful acts, the responsibility cannot be triggered unless the damage is actually incurred and has harmed the individual interests.[244] The rationale for incurring responsibility for non-actual but certain damages, is based on the need to prevent even greater damage by bringing the matter before the court as soon as the cause of damage is certain.[245]

In the cases of harm due to lawful acts, the responsibility of the author is triggered by virtue of the damages it has caused. For this reason, the circumstances in which the damages are incurred have to be considered more carefully. The regime of responsibility for lawful acts would constitute a restriction for the governing authorities, inasmuch as it makes responsible the states or the Union for their lawful conduct, such as in the case of legislative or executive acts. Such a restriction must be justified, given that the general interests behind these lawful acts

---

[240]Joined Cases C-83/76 and 94/76, 4/77, 15/77 and 40/77, *HNL and others v Council and Commission* [1978] ECR I-1209, para. 5. See also Joined Cases C-120/06 and C-121/06 *FIAMM and Fedon v Council and Commission*, [2008] ECR I-6513, paras. 171–172.

[241]Joined Cases C-83/76 and 94/76, 4/77, 15/77 and 40/77, *HNL and others v Council and Commission* [1978] ECR I-1209, para. 6.

[242]Joined Cases C-120/06 and C-121/06 *FIAMM and Fedon v Council and Commission*, [2008] ECR I-6513, paras. 183–184.

[243]Case C-4/73 *J. Nold, Kohlen- und Baustoffgroßhandlung v Ruhrkohle Aktiengesellschaft*, [1974] ECR I-491, para. 14. See also Case C-265/87 *Hermann Schräder HS Kraftfutter GmbH & Co. KG v Hauptzollamt Gronau*, [1989] ECR I-2237, para. 15 and Case C-280/93 *Federal Republic of Germany v Council of the European Union* (Bananas), [1994] ECR I-4973, para. 78.

[244]Joined Cases C-56-60/74 *Kurt Kampffmeyer Mühlenvereinigung KG and others v Commission and Council of the European Communities*, [1976] ECR I-711, para. 6.

[245]*Ibid.*

can be hindered. Therefore, the jurisprudence has maintained that the subjects of the Union law may be responsible for their lawful acts if their actions cause damages of an 'unusual and special' nature, which is defined as a situation in which the victims incur a less-favorable treatment in comparison with other operators.[246] For the regime of responsibility to be established, the victim should be injured in a different way, and much more seriously than all other traders and producers. This criterion refers to the unusual element of harm. Furthermore, the damages should not be suffered as a result of the normal course of business; hence the damages should exceed the limits of the economic risks inherent in the concerned sector, which would qualify the harm as special.[247] Therefore, the risks associated with the normal course of business serve as an abstract limitation for the legal responsibility in relation with the lawful acts due to unusual and special damages incurred by individuals. Particularly, the general interest, which is mainly observed in legislative acts, could serve as a strong argument against the responsibility regime for lawful acts.[248]

Notwithstanding the option for damage compensation, the effectiveness of the EU system of responsibility relies particularly on the cessation of wrongful acts. Pursuant to Article 259 TFEU, Member States are entitled to invoke compliance with EU obligations against another Member State, which has *ex hipothesi* failed to fulfill the obligations of the Treaties. The way in which this mechanism is conceived, suggests that the system of responsibility has employed only a partial scheme for the restitution of the injured legal order, by limiting the consequences of the wrongful act to the cessation, rather than by providing for all the relevant forms of reparation of damages. The Commission plays a central role within the system of responsibility in the EU legal order, namely that of the 'guardian of the Treaties'. Hence, under the control of the ECJ, the Commission oversees the application of the Union law, and initiates the infringement procedure to this end (Article 258 TFEU). The course of responsibility in this procedure is limited to the invocation of compliance, rather than to any reparation of damages from the wrongful act.

The regime of responsibility in the Union polity has also several shortcomings. The reliance of compliance with EU law on the incidence of cases from concerned individuals, in addition to the inability of the Commission to oversee the application of an increasingly amount of legislation in an ever expanding and diverse territory, makes the system of compliance vulnerable, although not in a considerable scale. This downside is further associated with a systemic deficiency of the system of

---

[246]Joined Cases C-9 and 11/71 *Compagnie d'approvisionnement, de transport et de crédit SA and Grands Moulins de Paris SA v Commission of the European Communities*, [1972] ECR I-391, para. 45, Case C-237/98 *Dorsch v Council*, [2000] ECR I-4549, paras. 18, 19.

[247]Case C-59/83 *SA Biovilac NV v European Economic Community*, [1984] ECR I-4057, paras. 27, 28.

[248]Joined Cases C-120/06 and C-121/06 *FIAMM and Fedon v Council and Commission*, [2008] ECR I-6513, paras. 49–56, 132–133, 176–188. See further Chalmers et al. (2010), p. 655. See further Thouvenin (2010), p. 873.

responsibility, lacking the obligation of reparations as a complete way of restitution of the injured legal order. Nevertheless, the possibility of individuals to claim reparations may, in particular situations, exercise a positive pressure to the defaulting Member State. Accordingly, the wrongdoer may be charged with an obligation of cessation, as well as with an obligation of reparation of damages against individuals in the form of *restitutio in integrum* or restitution by equivalence (compensation of material damages).[249]

In addition, one can point out a structural issue, which arises from the fact that the entire system of responsibility in the EU legal system depends on the enforcement mechanisms in the municipal legal orders of the Member States, and particularly from the national courts and tribunals. The Member States are obliged to repair the loss and damages pursuant to their national laws on state liability, and this constitutes a requirement of EU law.[250] Hence, this element of the system of responsibility, which includes reparation of damages, relies on the Member States' judicial systems, as a constituent part of the system of enforcement of the EU legal order. This structure is able to offer the relevant remedies to individuals for violations of their subjective rights, and is based on the attributes of EU law as directly applicable.[251] Even in those cases where the transposition is needed to give domestic power to the directives, the EU law has the relevant guarantees that the rights conferred to individuals shall not be hindered by the omission of Member States (the implied direct effect of the directives). In principle, there is a potential risk that the Member States may find loopholes to evade their obligations.[252] However, the monitoring function of the ECJ through the preliminary proceedings ensures a certain degree of homogeneity in the uniform application of EU law, and ensures strong and impartial guarantees in the implementation of law.

Overall, it can be maintained that the system of responsibility in the Union polity is quite developed and sophisticated. As such, it can provide a sound contribution for conceiving the model of participation of the Union polity in the DSP. It further can offer an adequate framework for addressing the fallacies of the joint responsibility regime from the WTO membership, particularly in terms of the devolution of responsibility, which shall be elaborated in Chap. 5.

## VI. Conclusion

This Chapter aimed at highlighting some relevant propositions of the international law of responsibility of states and international organizations pursuant to the *legi generali* and *lex specialis*. These serve as normative premises for addressing the

249 See further on this issue Schermers (1989), pp. 886–888.

250 Joined Cases C-6/90 and C-9/90 *Francovich et al. v Italy*, [1991] ECR I-5357, paras. 38 and 45.

251 Thouvenin (2010), p. 862.

252 Schermers (1989), pp. 886–888.

fallacies of the joint responsibility regime of the Union and its Member States in the context of their WTO membership. Amid the increasing fragmentation of international law, the regime of responsibility has a crucial role for preventing the breach of obligations, as well as for providing the relevant remedies for the injured rights. However, these aims are often challenged by a plurality of normative sources that compete with each other. In order for the aims of the responsibility regimes not to be hindered, the competing legal orders could be accommodated in a constructive way. This (constructive) approach results from the unity of normative sources of international legal responsibility.[253] In this way, the provisions of the *legi generali* allow for the *lex specialis* to take precedence in the regulation of the international responsibility of states and international organizations. The latter could be also construed in such a way that allows for particular provisions of the *legi generali* to resolve the paradoxes that may be created from the specific regimes, such as the joint responsibility regime from the WTO membership of the EU and its Member States.

One of the central factors causing this art of fallacy, results from the deficiency of the application of the rules of attribution of international responsibility in the context of WTO membership. By failing to establish a connection between the WTO inconsistent measures of the Member States and the Union as a sole participant in the DSP, the Union may be held responsible for inconsistent measures of the Member States, although they may result from actions that, *ex hypothesi*, fall out of the areas of the conferred powers. The answerability of the Union in DSP involving such measures, is not without implications for the attribution of responsibility and for the devolution of burden to the Union and its Member States. The fallacies of the joint responsibility regime influence at most the individual claims of sovereignty of each of the participants, as an ability to assert rights and to discharge obligations. Accordingly, the Member States are concerned of their ability to assert sovereign rights over residual powers. Their counterparts in the WTO are also concerned of their sovereign rights, which could be affected from the inability of the Union to discharge obligations in relation with powers that could be held virtually from the Union, and effectively from its Member States. Furthermore, the formal-substantive gap of the WTO membership is a potential argument for the Member States to reject any consequences from the participation of the Union in the DSP for matters falling with their residual powers. The Union may also claim its ultimate rights in terms of the representation of the entire polity, inasmuch as these proceedings may influence indirectly its conferred powers. However, given that the doctrine of substitution is not fully applicable for the Union participation in the WTO proceedings, due to the incomplete transfer of powers at the EU level, this claim of the Union could only be explained on the basis of other premises, such as the constitutional ones.

Obviously, the constitutional infrastructure of the EU, and particularly the vertical distribution of powers, seem to be the ultimate factors that trigger the

[253] See also Crawford (2010), p. 21.

fallacies of the joint responsibility regime. The joint responsibility is, however, not only part of the problem, but also part of the solution for construing stable relationships of the EU polity with the outer world. This is the case not only with the WTO Agreement, but also with UNCLOS, the EU partnership and cooperation agreements, as well as the investment treaties. These international agreements are adopted in a mixed form from both the Union and its Member States. The question then is whether all these agreements should inherit the same fallacies in terms of the distribution of responsibility, as the WTO Agreement? Mixed agreements regulate subject matters that may fall partly within the competences of states, and partly within the conferred powers of international organizations.[254] Obviously, when mixed agreements or its associated documents do not determine the parties that should be held responsible for breach of obligations that *ex hipothesi* could belong both to the international organizations and its member states, the responsibility can be distributed in any of the following alternatives. The first alternative, which serves as a general assumption widely accepted in the doctrine and practice, is that the international organization and its member states shall be held jointly responsible in case that the distribution of powers is not clearly defined by a declaration of powers.[255] A second alternative could be the attribution of responsibility following the apportionment of powers pursuant to the respective declaration.[256] A third alternative could be the attribution of responsibility to the organization, which decides subsequently on the apportionment of responsibility within the polity pursuant to internal rules.[257] All these alternatives inform that, in principle, the responsibility for breach of international obligations in a mixed agreement should lie with that party to whom the internationally wrongful act is attributed, which is the entity that holds the competence on the subject matter at dispute.[258]

However, the law of international responsibility does not always succeed in attributing the conduct to the real author of the wrongful act. The level of responsibility may very much depend on the level of participation, the complicity, and the causal link between the wrongful act and the conduct of the participating state.[259] In this way, states are held responsible not merely for wrongful acts committed due to their direct participation, but also by means of their indirect contribution. In these circumstances, the responsibility is attributed by virtue of complicity, which constitutes an internationally wrongful act *per se*. Nevertheless, this prediction is not valid for the EU participation in the DSP, which participation could trigger the responsibility of the Union for Member States' measures *ex relatione*, hence in the

---

[254] Schermers and Blokker (2003), pp. 1121–1127; Hirsch (1995), p. 19 *et seq.*; and Neframi (2002). See further on mixed agreements Chap. 3.

[255] Hirsch (1995), p. 24.

[256] Hirsch (1995), p. 24. See also Dolmans (1985), pp. 81–85.

[257] Hirsch (1995), p. 24. See also Schermers (1983), p. 830.

[258] Hirsch (1995), p. 24.

[259] Orakhelashvili (2010), pp. 658–659.

absence of any form of complicity. This art of responsibility is further analyzed in the following Chapter, which addresses the joint responsibility as a regime of mixed agreements in general, and pays a special focus to the WTO Agreement.

## References


Antoniadis, Antonis. 2004. The Participation of the European Community in the World Trade Organization: An External Look at European Union Constitution-Building. In *European Union Law for the Twenty-First Century: Rethinking the New Legal Order. Vol. 1: Constitutional and Public Law: External Relations*, ed. Takis Tridimas and Paolisa Nebbia, 321–344. Oxford: Hart Publishing.

Anzilotti, Dionisio. 1906. La Responsabilité Internationale des Etats à Raison des Dommages Soufferts par des Étrangers. *RGDIP* 10: 5–29.

———. 1999. *Cours de Droit International*. Les introuvables. Paris: LGDJ; Université Panthéon-Assas.

Barbier, Sandrine. 2010. Assurances and Guarantees of Non-repetition. In *The Law of International Responsibility*, ed. James Crawford, Alain Pellet, Simon Olleson, and Kate Parlett, 552–561. Oxford, New York: Oxford University Press.

Bariffi, Francisco J. 2012. Scilingo Case. In *The Max Planck Encyclopedia of Public International Law*, ed. Rüdiger Wolfrum, VII. New York, NY: Oxford University Press.

Barker, John. 2010. The Different Forms of Reparation: Compensation. In *The Law of International Responsibility*, ed. James Crawford, Alain Pellet, Simon Olleson, and Kate Parlett, 599–611. Oxford, New York: Oxford University Press.

Boyle, Alan. 2010. Liability for Injurious Consequences of Act Not Prohibited by International Law. In *The Law of International Responsibility*, ed. James Crawford, Alain Pellet, Simon Olleson, and Kate Parlett, 95–104. Oxford, New York: Oxford University Press.

Brownlie, Ian. 1998. *Principles of Public International Law*. 5th ed. Oxford, New York: Clarendon Press; Oxford University Press.

Burton, William C. 1998. *Burton's Legal Thesaurus*. 3rd ed. New York: Macmillan Library Reference.

Chalmers, Damian, G.T. Davies, and Giorgio Monti. 2010. *European Union Law. Cases and Materials*. 2nd ed. Cambridge: Cambridge University Press.

Condorelli, Luigi, and Claus Kress. 2010. The Rule of Attribution: General Considerations. In *The Law of International Responsibility*, ed. James Crawford, Alain Pellet, Simon Olleson, and Kate Parlett, 221–236. Oxford, New York: Oxford University Press.

Corten, Olivier. 2010. The Obligation of Cessation. In *The Law of International Responsibility*, ed. James Crawford, Alain Pellet, Simon Olleson, and Kate Parlett, 545–549. Oxford, New York: Oxford University Press.

Crawford, James. 1999. Second Report on State Responsiblity. DOCUMENT A/CN.4/498 and Add.1-4, date 17 March, 1 and 30 April, 19 July 1999.

———. 2008. *Brownlie's Principles of Public International Law*. 8th ed. Oxford: Oxford University Press.

———. 2010. The System of International Responsibility. In *The Law of International Responsibility*, ed. James Crawford, Alain Pellet, Simon Olleson, and Kate Parlett, 17–25. Oxford, New York: Oxford University Press.

Crawford, James, and Jeremy Watkins. 2010. International Responsibility. In *The Philosophy of International Law*, ed. Samantha Besson and John Tasioulas, 283–298. Oxford, New York: Oxford University Press.

Dolmans, Maurits J.F.M. 1985. *Problems of Mixed Agreements. Division of Powers Within the EEC and the Rights of Third States*. The Hague: Asser Instituut.

Dominicé, Christian. 2010. Attribution of Conduct to Multiple States and the Implication of a State in the Act of Another State. In *The Law of International Responsibility*, ed. James Crawford, Alain Pellet, Simon Olleson, and Kate Parlett, 281–289. Oxford, New York: Oxford University Press.

Dupuy, Pierre-Marie. 1989. The International Law of States Responsibility: Revolution or Evolution. *Michigan Journal of International Law* 11: 105.

———. 1999. Reviewing the Difficulties of Codification: On Ago's Classification of Obligations of Means and Obligations of Result in Relation to State Responsibility. *European Journal of International Law* 10 (2): 371–385. doi:10.1093/ejil/10.2.371.

———. 2010. Relations Between the International Law and Responsibility in Municipal Law. In *The Law of International Responsibility*, ed. James Crawford, Alain Pellet, Simon Olleson, and Kate Parlett. Oxford, New York: Oxford University Press.

Eagleton, Clyde. 1928. *The Responsibility of States in International Law*. New York: New York University Press.

Edward, David A.O., and Robert C. Lane. 2012. *Edward and Lane on European Union Law*. Cheltenham: Edward Elgar.

Eeckhout, Piet. 2011. *EU External Relations Law*. 2nd ed. Oxford EU law library. Oxford, New York: Oxford University Press.

Garner, Bryan A., and Henry Campbell Black. 1999. *Black's Law Dictionary*. 7th ed. St. Paul, Minn: West Group.

Gomula, Joanna. 2010. Responsibility and the World Trade Organization. In *The Law of International Responsibility*, ed. James Crawford, Alain Pellet, Simon Olleson, and Kate Parlett, 791–801. Oxford, New York: Oxford University Press.

Gray, Christine D. 2010. The Different Forms of Reparation: Restitution. In *The Law of International Responsibility*, ed. James Crawford, Alain Pellet, Simon Olleson, and Kate Parlett, 589–597. Oxford, New York: Oxford University Press.

Grotius, Hugo, Jean Barbeyrac, and Richard Tuck. 2005. *The Rights of War and Peace. Natural Law and Enlightenment Classics*. Indianapolis: Liberty Fund.

Hart, H.L.A. 1968. *Punishment and Responsibility. Essays in the Philosophy of Law*. Oxford: Clarendon Press.

Heliskoski, Joni. 2001. *Mixed Agreements as a Technique for Organizing the International Relations of the European Community and Its Member States*. The Hague, New York: Kluwer Law International.

Hirsch, Moshe. 1995. *The Responsibility of International Organizations Toward Third Parties. Some Basic Principles*. Dordrecht, Boston: Martinus Nijhoff.

Jouannet, Emmanuelle. 1998. *Emer de Vattel et l'émergence doctrinale du droit international classique*. Publication de la Revue générale du droit international public, vol. 50. Paris: Pedone.

Kerbrat, Yann. 2010. Interaction Between the Forms of Reparation. In *The Law of International Responsibility*, ed. James Crawford, Alain Pellet, Simon Olleson, and Kate Parlett, 573–587. Oxford, New York: Oxford University Press.

Klein, Pierre. 2010. The Attribution of Acts to International Organizations. In *The Law of International Responsibility*, ed. James Crawford, Alain Pellet, Simon Olleson, and Kate Parlett, 297–315. Oxford, New York: Oxford University Press.

Koskenniemi, Martti. 2010. Doctrines of State Responsibility. In *The Law of International Responsibility*, ed. James Crawford, Alain Pellet, Simon Olleson, and Kate Parlett, 45–51. Oxford, New York: Oxford University Press.

Kuijper, Pieter Jan. 2010. International Responsibility for EU Mixed Agreements. In *Mixed Agreements Revisited: The EU and Its Member States in the World*, ed. Christophe Hillion and Panos Koutrakos, 208–227. Modern studies in European law, vol. 21. Oxford [England], Portland, OR: Hart.

Latty, Franck. 2010. Actions and Omissions. In *The Law of International Responsibility*, ed. James Crawford, Alain Pellet, Simon Olleson, and Kate Parlett, 355–363. Oxford, New York: Oxford University Press.

MacLeod, I., I.D. Hendry, and Stephen Hyett. 1996. *The External Relations of the European Communities. A Manual of Law and Practice*. Oxford, New York: Clarendon Press; Oxford University Press.

Neframi, Eleftheria. 2002. International Responsibility of the European Community and of the Member States under Mixed Agreements. In *The European Union as an Actor in International Relations*, ed. Enzo Cannizzaro, 193–205. The Hague, New York: Kluwer Law International.

———. 2012. Mixed Agreements as a Source of European Union Law. In *International Law as Law of the European Union*, ed. Enzo Cannizzaro, Paolo Palchetti, and Ramses A. Wessel, 325–349. Studies in EU external relations, vol. 5. Boston: Martinus Nijhoff.

Noyes, John E., and Brian D. Smith. 1988. State Responsibility and the Principle of Joint and Several Liability. *Yale Journal of International Law* 13: 225.

O'Connell, D.P. 1963. State Succession and the Effect Upon Treaties of Entry into a Composite Relationship. *British Year Book of International Law* 39: 54.

Orakhelashvili, Alexander. 2010. Division of Reparation Between Responsible Entities. In *The Law of International Responsibility*, ed. James Crawford, Alain Pellet, Simon Olleson, and Kate Parlett, 647–665. Oxford, New York: Oxford University Press.

Pellet, Alain. 2010. The Definition of Responsibility in International Law. In *The Law of International Responsibility*, ed. James Crawford, Alain Pellet, Simon Olleson, and Kate Parlett, 3–16. Oxford, New York: Oxford University Press.

Pescatore, Pierre. 1979. External Relations in the Case-Law of the Court of Justice of the European Communities. *Common Market Law Review* 16: 615.

Quigley, John. 1987. Complicity in International Law: A New Direction in the Law of State Responsibility. *British Yearbook of International Law* 57 (1): 77–131. doi:10.1093/bybil/57.1.77.

Schermers, Henry G. 1983. International Organizations as Members of Other International Organizations. In *Völkerrecht als Rechtsordnung, Internationale Gerichtsbarkeit, Menschenrechte: Festschrift für Hermann Mosler*, ed. Hermann Mosler and Rudolf Bernhardt, 823–838. Beiträge zum ausländischen öffentlichen Recht und Völkerrecht, vol. 81. Berlin, New York: Springer.

———. 1989. The Suit for Damages as a Means of Pressure on the Member States of the European Community. In *Staat und Völkerrechtsordnung: Festschrift für Karl Doehring*, ed. Karl Doehring, Kay Hailbronner, Georg Ress, and Torsten Stein, 883–888. Beiträge zum ausländischen öffentlichen Recht und Völkerrecht, vol. 98. Berlin, New York: Springer.

Schermers, Henry G., and Niels Blokker. 2003. *International Institutional Law. Unity Within Diversity*. 4th ed. Boston: Martinus Nijhoff.

Simma, Bruno, and Dirk Pulkowski. 2010. *Leges Speciales* and Self-Contained Regimes. In *The Law of International Responsibility*, ed. James Crawford, Alain Pellet, Simon Olleson, and Kate Parlett, 139–163. Oxford, New York: Oxford University Press.

Simmonds, Kenneth R. 1989. The European Economic Community and the New Law of the Sea. In *Recueil des cours: Collected Courses of the Hague Academy of International Law*, VI, 9–166. Collection, Tome 218. Dordrecht: Martinus Nijhoff.

Stern, Brigitte. 2010a. The Elements of an Internationally Wrongful Act. In *The Law of International Responsibility*, ed. James Crawford, Alain Pellet, Simon Olleson, and Kate Parlett, 193–220. Oxford, New York: Oxford University Press.

———. 2010b. The Obligation to Make Reparation. In *The Law of International Responsibility*, ed. James Crawford, Alain Pellet, Simon Olleson, and Kate Parlett, 563–571. Oxford, New York: Oxford University Press.

Stoll, Peter-Tobias. 2012. World Trade Organization (WTO). In *The Max Planck Encyclopedia of Public International Law*, ed. Rüdiger Wolfrum, VII. New York, NY: Oxford University Press.

Tavernier, Paul. 2010. Relevance of Intertemporal Law. In *The Law of International Responsibility*, ed. James Crawford, Alain Pellet, Simon Olleson, and Kate Parlett, 397–403. Oxford, New York: Oxford University Press.

Thouvenin, Jean-Marc. 2010. Responsibility in the Context of the European Legal Order. In *The Law of International Responsibility*, ed. James Crawford, Alain Pellet, Simon Olleson, and Kate Parlett, 861–875. Oxford, New York: Oxford University Press.

Tomuschat, Christian. 2002. The International Responsibility of the European Union. In *The European Union as an Actor in International Relations*, ed. Enzo Cannizzaro, 177–191. The Hague, New York: Kluwer Law International.

Verhoeven, Joe. 2010. The Law of Responsibility and the Law of Treaties. In *The Law of International Responsibility*, ed. James Crawford, Alain Pellet, Simon Olleson, and Kate Parlett, 103–113. Oxford, New York: Oxford University Press.

Villalpando, S.M. 2002. Attribution of Conduct to the State: How the Rules of State Responsibility May Be Applied Within the WTO Dispute Settlement System. *Journal of International Economic Law* 5 (2): 393–420. doi:10.1093/jiel/5.2.393.

# Chapter 3
# International Responsibility in Mixed Agreements: The Case of the WTO Agreement

## I. Introduction

After having considered the general predictions of public international law on legal responsibility, it is now turned to the issue of responsibility in the context of WTO Agreement, as a preliminary step for analyzing the management of problems of responsibility in the EU polity. The responsibility of the EU and its Member States from the joint participation in international agreements in general, and in the WTO Agreement in particular, is discussed in view of mixed agreements. A mixed agreement, in the context of this work, shall be defined as a multilateral treaty concluded between, on the one hand, the EU as an international organization and any or all of its Member States, and, on the other hand, other states and/or international organizations. The mixed nature is determined due to the fact that the international agreements cover certain matters which fall indubitably within the competences of the EU and its Member States, and which they exercise on an exclusive or shared basis.[1] The main legal argument for this participation is explained by the fact that the international organization alone may lack the full and autonomous capacity to participate in the treaty, or that the international organization and its member states are competent for different areas of governance covered by the international treaty. Hence, they complement each other with their joint participation in this treaty. This is the case of the WTO Agreement, where the Union and its Member States contribute jointly and complementarily with their own and shared powers.

Mixed agreements, as much as their implementation is concerned, represent a formula for accommodating both the concerns of the Union, its Member States, and third states in relation with the vertical distribution of powers in the EU polity. The

[1] See further on a similar definition Cremona (1982), p. 411; MacLeod et al. (1996), p. 143; and Weiler (1999), p. 132.



P. Ruka, *The International Legal Responsibility of the European Union in the Context of the World Trade Organization in Areas of Non-Conferred Competences*,
DOI 10.1007/978-3-319-57177-5_3

internal competition of powers in the EU polity plays a controversial role in terms of maintaining the state of uncertainty over the entire lifecycle of the agreement. At the same time, it explains at best the necessity for a joint responsibility regime as a premise for addressing the problems from the competition of powers in the Union polity.[2] The ultimate reasons for this formula are found in the EU constitutional infrastructure. This infrastructure precludes the EU and its Member States to enter independently into international agreements without any implications for each other.[3] In light of this, the responsibility of the EU and its Member States from their WTO membership constitutes an issue indispensably related with the internal nature of the Union polity. The vertical distribution of powers plays a significant role for the major legal challenges related with this issue.[4] In light of these observations, it can be maintained that the issue of legal responsibility in the context of WTO membership of the EU and its Member States is shaped from the interplay of two main factors: the constitutional nature of the EU polity with its vertical division of powers, and the nature of the WTO legal order with its effects on the legal orders of the EU and its Member States. The combination of these factors leads to the prevalence of a joint responsibility regime, which entails various fallacies in terms of the distribution of burden of responsibility among the EU and its Member States.

This Chapter elaborates on particular facets of the joint responsibility by analyzing in general terms the factors that determine this regime. This serves as a theoretical framework for elaborating the premises and the conditions of the participation of EU and its Member States in the DSP for matters of non-conferred competences, as well as for managing the problems of responsibility of the EU and its Member States in relation with this participation. This approach justifies the need for an inquiry on the structure of powers in the EU polity, which explains the joint participation of the EU and its Member States in the WTO Agreement (Section II). With the proviso that the WTO Agreement has limited effects on the legal orders of EU and its Member States, Section III elaborates on eventual implications for the issue of responsibility. These factors are construed as determinant premises for the joint responsibility regime in the context of WTO membership. Such premises entail particular fallacies in terms of the distribution of burden of responsibility among the EU and its Member States (Section IV). This discourse, together with the framework of the constitutional principles in the EU polity (Chap. 4), aims to explore the relevant framework for a normative model for managing the concerns of responsibility in the course of the WTO membership of the EU and its Member States. This model should be able to provide for adequate premises and conditions for the participation of the EU and its Member States in the DSP for matters of non-conferred competences, and for managing the eventual international responsibility from this participation (Chap. 5).

[2]See also Neframi (2012), p. 339.

[3]See also Bourgeois (1997), p. 85 and Dashwood (1997), p. 93.

[4]See also Cremona (2008), pp. 68–69.

# II. The Relevance of the Vertical Distribution of Powers for the WTO Agreement

The constitutional nature of the EU polity and the vertical relationship between the Union and its Member States is decisive for their joint participation in mixed agreements, and notably in the WTO Agreement. A further elaboration on the vertical relationship in the Union polity, with a view on the distribution of powers, would be useful for distinguishing the determining factors of the joint responsibility regime.

Mixed agreements constitute a significant instrument in the hands of the Union polity for conducting the external relations with the outer world. They manifest the intermediate nature of the Union as a polity 'in between' an international organization and a federation.[5] The main argument behind the Union resorting to mixity is the contest of powers between the Union and its Member States, a metamorphic process characterized of a notable dynamic and, to some extent, unpredictable nature. Amid this contest, one could distinguish the capacity of the Union and its constituent Member States to undertake international obligations, as well as their legislative capacity to comply with the obligations of the respective agreement.[6] These challenges in the Union polity emanate from the predictions of the principle of conferral, and particularly from the unstable nature of distribution of powers between the Union and its Member States. The underlying background of the state of mixity is therefore characterized of a "combination of parallelism, preemption, and material expansion" of powers.[7] Before considering the way in which the competition of powers affects the WTO membership of the Union and its Member States, as a framework for analyzing the concerns raised from the joint responsibility regime, it is firstly useful to provide an overview of the structure of powers in the Union polity.

## *1. Overview of the Structure of Powers in the EU Polity*

The distribution of powers in the Union polity constitutes a central constitutional moment, which serves as an ultimate source of legitimacy. The scheme of powers represents a certain balance of interests of all participants in the polity. The general categories of the Union powers are determined in specific terms in the TFEU and represent a vertical relationship between the Union institutions and Member States. The Treaties have defined the powers in three main categories, namely powers that are exclusive for the Union (Member States' action in these areas is excluded);

[5]Weiler (1999), pp. 131–132.

[6]Weiler (1999), p. pp. 133–134. See further for the mixed procedure of conclusion of mixed agreements Heliskoski (2001), p. 25 *et seq.*

[7]Weiler (1999), p. 175.

powers that are shared between the Union and its Member States (with a preemption character in favor of the Union); and ancillary (or complementary) powers, which shall be exercised by Member States with the coordination, support or supplementary action of the Union (Article 2 TFEU).

Pursuant to Article 3 TFEU, the Union shall have exclusive competence in the areas related to the customs union, competition in the internal market, monetary policies for the zone of monetary union, conservation of marine biological resources under common fisheries policy, and the common commercial policy. With respect to the exclusive powers, it should be emphasized that the TFEU provides a more comprehensive outline on the content of the conferred powers and the way in which they are exercised. Accordingly, focusing on the common commercial policy, Article 207 TFEU provides that the conduct of the common commercial policy includes particularly the conclusion of tariff and trade agreements (such as, GATT 1947), service agreements (GATS), and commercial aspects of intellectual property (TRIPS). This understanding of the common commercial policy was introduced with the Treaty of Lisbon, which expanded further the scope of this exclusive competence with additional areas, such as the commercial aspects of intellectual property, services, and foreign investments. The designation of the common commercial policy as an exclusive competence, and furthermore, the inclusion within its scope of the containing areas of the WTO Agreement, recasts the question of the Member States' competences for entering the WTO Agreement at all. This question, which was already settled in the Opinion 1/94 of the ECJ, influences largely the problem of the distribution of responsibility between the EU and its Member States, as resulting from their WTO membership in the course of conduct of the common commercial policy.[8] Furthermore, the concern is raised in relation with the limits of the areas covered from the exclusive competences, as well as in terms of their ability to be fully exercised at the Union level.

As to the nature of exclusivity, Article 2(1) TFEU provides that only the Union may legislate and adopt legally binding acts in these areas, while the Member States may do so only if so empowered by the Union, or for implementing Union acts, hence in cases of delegation or enforcement of EU law. These areas constitute exclusive domains of the Union institutions, which decide autonomously on them. The exercise of powers in such areas at the Member State level in a unilateral manner is essentially precluded. One could hardly speak of residual powers in these areas, inasmuch as the sovereignty of Member States is transferred to the Union.

In addition to the outlined exclusive competences, this category includes several uncertain applications. The Union shall have exclusive competence for concluding international agreements pursuant to legislative acts of the Union, or as a necessary means to enable the Union to exercise its internal competences, or in so far as their conclusion may affect common rules or alter their scope.[9] The state of exclusivity in

[8]A more detailed analysis of this question shall be taken in the following Section.

[9]This approach is in line with the *ERTA* doctrine (see n 405 *infra*). See also Timmermans (1981), p. 19.

the external dimension of the internal powers of the Union is acknowledged to the Union also for other unionized areas falling within the shared powers, in addition to the exclusive ones. This mechanism implies for the Member States an obligation to observe diligently the unionized areas during their external action, in order not to hinder the exclusivity of the Union in this context. This would mean that the Member States can still enter international agreements in areas of shared powers as long as they are not unionized, thus the EU has not exercised them.[10]

Articles 2(2) and 4 TFEU provide for a category of powers which, in principle, are shared by the Union and its Member States,[11] in that they may, as a matter of capacity, legislate and adopt legally binding acts in the areas falling within this category. Nevertheless, this potential capacity cannot be exercised simultaneously, because a parallel action would prove either overlapping or exclusionary for the authority. In order to address this concern, Article 2(2) TFEU stipulates a rule-preemption regime, according to which, Member States may exercise their potential authority as long as the Union has not exercised these powers. Once a shared area of power is unionized, Member States should cease to enact legislation in this area. This regime combines the principle of primacy with the principle of loyalty by giving deference to the unionized competence.[12] Obviously, this method is able to turn into '*de facto* exclusive' any measure falling within the shared areas of competences, although no formal transformation of powers has taken place. This method allows, however, for the repatriation of unionized competences in the future. This scheme of powers is quite dynamic, given that in different periods, the powers that were initially exercised from the Member States, can be unionized, and as such, can only be exercised at the Union level in the future, unless the Union itself instructs otherwise.

As a result of the preemption doctrine, Member States are precluded from exercising such powers individually. This course of integration resembles to a spillover process that centralizes continuously the powers at the Union level,

---

[10]This approach would essentially be in line with the *Kramer Case*, Joined Cases C-3/76, 4/76, 6/76 *Cornelis Kramer et al.*, [1976] ECR I-1279, para. 39. See also Timmermans (1981), p. 19.

[11]Pursuant to Article 4 TFEU, the powers falling in this category include mainly: internal market; social policy, for the aspects defined in the TFEU; economic, social and territorial cohesion; agriculture and fisheries, excluding the conservation of marine biological resources; environment; consumer protection; transport; trans-European networks; energy; areas of freedom, security and justice; common safety concerns in public health matters, for the aspects defined in the TFEU. Additionally, the Union shall have the competence to carry out activities, and particularly to define and implement programs in the areas of research, technological development and space, and to conduct a common policy in the areas of development cooperation and humanitarian aid, without preventing Member States from their own powers in this regard. This means that although falling within the category of shared competences, these areas preclude the rule-preemption doctrine from being applied. The language of Article 4 implies that the areas listed therein do not constitute an exhaustive list of powers, and in this regard other powers not mentioned in the Treaties can potentially fall within the category of shared powers, subject to limitations from the principle of conferral.

[12]See also Rossi (2012), p. 100.

without amending the Treaties. In this way, the Union polity decides on a pragmatic basis what areas to unionize. However, the Member States have the primary role in this regard inasmuch as they participate in the decision-making institutions of the Union; hence exercise the decision-making attributes in the common domain of the Union polity. Due to this dynamic scheme, it is hardly possible to declare *a priori* with their entry into mixed agreements the powers that shall be exercised at the Union level, and those residual with the Member States. Nevertheless, this difficulty may be overcome by means of updating arrangements in mixed agreements, which oblige the Union and the Member States to inform the changes in the scheme powers, although this cannot correct the unpredictability that is inherent in this ever-changing scheme.

The Treaties are silent as to the category of powers that Member States have not conferred to the Union, but remain inherent as attributes of their sovereignty (residual powers). Article 5 TFEU provides for the Member States' duty of coordination in the areas of economic policies, employment and social policies, which in principle remain an exclusive domain of the Member States and are subject to a low level of integration. In view of Article 2(5) TFEU the competence of the Union to support, coordinate or supplement the actions of the Member States, should not supersede the powers of Member States in these areas. Any acts in relation to these competences should not entail harmonization of Member States' laws and regulations. Article 4(1) TEU has a significant contribution in this regard, given that it ensures that areas falling in the category of supporting competences (Article 6 TFEU)[13] shall not be shared between the Union and Member States, thus excluded from the harmonization and unionization. From this, it can be inferred that the harmonization and the lack of preemptive character serve as general limitations on the Union with respect to these areas of residual powers.[14]

Further to these categories of powers, the Union shall have competences to define and implement a common foreign and security policy, including the progressive framing of a common defense policy (Article 2(4) TFEU). However, this competence is mainly subject to unanimity in the European Council and the Council of the EU (Article 24(1) TEU). Most importantly, the enactment of legislative acts and the general jurisdiction of the ECJ for the majority of acts are excluded. This indicates for a powerful claim of national authority in these areas.

These observations show that the delineation of the competences conferred to the Union is essentially difficult to be established in a definite way and at a given period, inasmuch as the scheme of distribution of powers remains quite dynamic. This results with the powers conferred to the Union being inextricably linked with residual powers of the Member States, hence amounting to a limitation of each of these participants to act in a way that would not affect to a certain extent the

[13]The category of ancillary powers includes an exhaustive list: the protection and improvement of human health; industry; culture; tourism; education, vocational training, youth and sport; civil protection; and administrative cooperation.

[14]Rossi (2012), p. 101.

interests of the other. The fact that Member States retain in relation with certain WTO areas powers which they must be able to exercise on their own, could cause complications of a constitutional nature for the Union.[15] Hence, the joint action of the Union and its Member States is often the safe alternative ensuring the execution of powers in the internal and external dimensions of the polity.

## 2. *The Significance of the Exclusive Competence of Common Commercial Policy for the WTO Membership*

The designation of the common commercial policy as an exclusive competence changes, in principle, the conditions of membership in the WTO Agreement, inasmuch as it affects the vertical distribution of powers between the EU and its Member States. In light of this, it could be expected that the EU would substitute the Member States in their external action, and the Union alone would enter international agreements, which no longer need to be mixed. This is the direct consequence of exclusivity, which provides for the Union an attribute to legislate and adopt legally binding acts solely and to the exclusion of Member States (Article 2 (1) TFEU). In view of the Opinion 1/94, this could mean that the Member States, ceasing to be competent for GATS and TRIPS, are bound by the obligations of these agreements only by virtue of their EU membership, and not as a result of their residual powers.

In light of these observations, it would be useful to elaborate on particular facets of the effects that this constitutional change would have for the WTO membership. Would that mean that the Member States of the EU should withdraw from their WTO membership? While there may be various strategic and political reasons for not doing so, the question then is, whether this withdrawal would prove sufficient from a normative point of view. Member States cannot easily accept their diminishing role in international relations, which is considered their essential attribute as sovereign states.[16] Furthermore, if they would withdraw from the WTO membership, the number of votes of the EU in the WTO decision-making bodies would be reduced to one single vote. Hence, this option is not a desired one. For such reasons, the state of mixity seems to be more advantageous than the requalification of the WTO Agreement as a Union Agreement.[17]

Beyond the reasons underlying this discourse, the state of mixity is mostly justified on certain constitutional grounds inherent in the Union polity. The Union is exclusively competent to conduct the common commercial policy. By including the GATS and TRIPS within the scope of this competence, it is maintained (mostly in the post-Lisbon doctrine) that the reasons permeating the Opinion 1/94 of the

[15] Kuijper (1995b), p. 99.

[16] See also Hilf (1995), p. 245.

[17] See also Antoniadis (2004), p. 337.

ECJ, which conceived the thesis of the joint participation of the Union and Member States in the WTO Agreement, became obsolete.[18] If that would suggest that the Union became competent to participate as a sole participant in the WTO, the question then is, what explains the unanimous action of the Council for the conclusion of international agreements in the field of trade in services and the commercial aspects of intellectual property (Article 207(4) TFEU)? This safeguard mechanism is of a procedural nature, and essentially refers to the requirement of unanimity voting in the Council for matters of common commercial policy, such as trade in services and commercial aspects of intellectual property, where such agreements include provisions for which unanimity is required in the adoption of internal rules (Article 207(4) para. 2 TFEU).

This provision reaffirms the doctrine of parallelism of competences, whereby the Union's external competences are construed as parallels of the internal powers, as long as the external action serves to the internal powers' exercise.[19] Further to the doctrine of parallelism, Article 207(4) TFEU provides that the limitation on the Union's exclusive powers in terms of the common commercial policy may emerge from the condition of the unanimous voting in the Council for areas covered by international agreements in the field of trade of cultural and audiovisual services. This is so, when these agreements risk to prejudice the Union's cultural and linguistic diversity (para. 3(a)), or could affect the trade in social, education and health services by risking seriously to disturb the national organization of such services and prejudice the responsibility of Member States to deliver them (para. 3 (b)). With this 'open-end' formulation, this limitation is likely to restrict largely the Union's action in most of the common commercial policy directions, and could jeopardize the Commission's effectiveness in the negotiation of international agreements in these areas.[20]

In relation with the significance of the requirement of unanimity for the EU membership in the WTO Agreement, it should be emphasized that the requirement for unanimous voting does not deny the constitutional change in terms of vertical distribution of powers *per se*, and as such, it should not be overestimated. However, the unanimity requirement indicates the presence of strong interests, which Member States intend to observe in a strict way. Accordingly, although the Member States conferred the material competence to the Union, they still withhold the instruments for exercising them; hence pushing the achievement of the lowest common denominator in the decision-making process to extremes. Obviously, there can be no action of the Union in conducting the common commercial policy without satisfying the interests of each Member State in these areas.

However, the predictions of Article 207(4) TFEU are particularly relevant for the residual powers of Member States, by reemphasizing their responsibility in delivering services in particular areas, including health policy. This reaffirms the

[18]Geiger et al. (2015), p. 758.

[19]See also Antoniadis (2004), p. 324.

[20]Antoniadis (2004), p. 324.

relevance of the *EC – Asbestos* scenario on the constitutional argument in relation with the residual powers of Member States. Accordingly, although the competence of the Union in the areas of common commercial policy is virtually an exclusive competence of the Union, the measures in the areas of social policy, education and health remain the sole responsibility of Member States. Such powers are not conferred to the Union (Articles 5(3) and 6 TFEU), and for this reason, the limitations in Article 207(4) TFEU have to be construed as an exception to (or even a breach of) the doctrine of parallelism, in that the Union's external action is not justified in terms of the internal conferred powers.[21] Rather, the content of the ancillary powers of the Union corresponds to the residual powers of the Member States, and the unanimity voting in the Council serves as a guarantee that the interests of the Member States are duly observed from the Union when concluding international agreements falling within these powers.

The residual powers of Member States may become prominent in the execution and implementation of particular obligations, which are implemented in the Member State level despite the fact that they are part of the common commercial policy. Furthermore, the Union may authorize the Member States to act in such areas, or these areas could be deemed as absolute prerogatives of Member States' sovereignty, which, by virtue of their nature cannot be delegated at the Union level, such as the protection of public moral or public health. These limitations concern not only the newly added areas of common commercial policy, such as trade in services and commercial aspects of intellectual property, but also the traditional exclusive competence on the trade in goods. It is for these reasons that the determination of the common commercial policy as an exclusive competence, does not suffice to terminate the state of mixity of the WTO Agreement, at least from a substantive point of view.

The safeguard mechanism reaffirms a further constitutional restriction of the common commercial policy in terms of harmonization of residual powers of the Member States, and particularly the areas where the Union has only ancillary powers.[22] The fact that the Union is not allowed to harmonize actions in the area of protection and improvement of human health, industry, culture, tourism, education, vocational training, youth, sport, civil protection, and administrative cooperation (Article 6 TFEU), shows that the Union is precluded from external actions, which could affect the Member States' autonomy in these areas. This is also in line with the predictions of Article 207(6) TFEU, which precludes any effects of the common commercial policy on the internal delimitation of powers, and particularly the harmonization of ancillary powers.[23] Such constitutional limitations are also manifested in the Union's relationship with the WTO.[24] Since the internal competence of the Union is limited only to ancillary functions, such as the support,

[21]See also Antoniadis (2004), p. 325.

[22]Antoniadis (2004), p. 325.

[23]See also Antoniadis (2004), p. 325.

[24]Antoniadis (2004), pp. 321–322.

coordination, or supplementation of the role of Member States in these areas, based on the doctrine of parallelism, the Union cannot supersede the limits of the conferred internal powers in the conduct of its external action.

For the WTO obligations, these predictions are of great relevance. Even if the Union would be required to act in the ancillary areas of powers, in the internal domain it cannot exercise more than the available ancillary functions conferred in the Treaties. For this reason, any obligation of the Union from the external action, although virtually conceived under the exclusive competences of the Union, could be construed as inextricably linked with the attributes of Member States to exercise their residual powers in these areas. Therefore, the Union and the Member States have to act jointly due to their inextricable linkage of their competences.[25] This makes the EU virtually competent for areas falling within the common commercial policy in the external action, but internally the Member States maintain the residual powers that they actually exercise. As a matter of example, one can recall the residual power of France to regulate the trade with asbestos on the grounds of public health policy, although the GATT has been a prerogative of European Economic Community since its very inception in the 1950s. Hence, the scope of substantive matters covered from the WTO Agreement remains broader than the common commercial policy, even after its designation as an exclusive competence of the Union.[26]

The common commercial policy could barely amount to a normative basis for justifying the succession of Member States from the Union in the context of their WTO membership. All the limitations on the exclusive powers of the Union in particular areas of the common commercial policy, although not prejudicing the state of exclusivity *per se*, ensure that all Member States actively participate in the exercise of the common commercial policy from the Union as a guarantee for their residual powers. Therefore, the common commercial policy continues to inherit the systemic deficiencies of the vertical distribution of powers in the EU. This is so even after the expansion of the scope of exclusivity with new areas, such as the trade in services, foreign investments and trade-related aspects of intellectual property.

## *3. Implications of the Distribution of Powers for the Joint Membership in the WTO*

From the overview of powers in the Union polity, it became clear that an absolute delimitation of powers at the vertical level remains difficult due to the inextricable linkage of competences conferred to the Union with the residual powers of the Member States. Furthermore, the common commercial policy could barely prove

[25] Timmermans (2000), p. 245.

[26] See further on a pre-Lisbon discourse on the matter Antoniadis (2004), pp. 322–323.

sufficient to ensure an autonomous action of the Union in the international arena without the joint consent of the Member States. In view of these observations, the joint participation of the Union and its Member States in the WTO Agreement addresses at best the concerns of the vertical distribution of powers in terms of its implementation.

The joint membership in the WTO Agreement is a precondition for the joint responsibility regime. The elaboration of the joint membership regime assists in identifying the main premises and conditions for the participation of the EU and its Member States in the DSP. By elaborating on the implications of the vertical distribution of powers for the definition of the joint participation of the EU polity in the WTO Agreement, this Section analyzes the mechanism and the extent to which the joint membership regime accommodates the concerns raised from the scheme of powers.

The nature of a mixed agreement depends from the nature of competences, which are affected from its scope, and particularly from their ownership. In light of this, it is useful to distinguish between, on the one hand, the "*classic* or *real mixity*", where the exclusive competence of the Union is clearly distinguished from the residual competences of the Member States, and, on the other hand, the "*quasi* or *sometimes even false mixity*", where the Union is competent for its exclusive competences, while the remaining areas covered by the agreement may be shared with the Member States or are residual with them.[27] According to the latter, the EU could be virtually competent for non-exclusive competences conferred upon it, but not yet unionized. The quasi mixity represents a highly interesting case, inasmuch as the shared or residual competences are inextricably linked with their exercise from both the Union and its Member States; hence, their separated exercise is excluded.[28] Given that the quasi mixity underlies the entire relationship of the EU and its Member States in the context of WTO, it might be useful to consider the mechanism in which the distribution of powers leads to such a circumstance.

The internal and external relations in the Union polity may hinder each other, and the allocation of powers constitutes a mutual concern for both of these spheres. Accordingly, the EU, in the course of its external relations, may impede the allocation of powers by assuming responsibilities that are prerogatives of the Member States. In this way, the EU behaves as if it owned those powers in reality. This triggers the issue of legitimacy for assuming internal powers by means of undertaking external obligations. As a result of these obligations, the Union may require the Member States to take actions conforming to these obligations. In order for this to be legitimate, the identification of ownership of powers affected from the agreement is indispensable. Indeed, the legitimate assumption of powers does not depend on the nature of powers *per se*, i.e. whether they are exclusive for the EU, shared with the Member States, or residual on them, but rather on their very

[27]Timmermans (2000), p. 241.

[28]Timmermans (2000), p. 241.

existence.[29] However, the distribution of powers in three categories constitutes the path for the identification of ownership of powers in the polity.

The vertical distribution of powers may influence the external action of the Union in various ways. The ownership of powers is important for determining whether the international obligation in relation to a disputed issue is attributed to the participation of the Member State in the international agreement or to the participation of the Union therein. The main premise for this, is however a regime of separated competences, where the powers of the Union could be easily identified. In the Union polity, this cannot be easily outlined. In a regime of separated competences, the EU and its Member States would be held responsible for their individual obligations as a function of their own competences. As long as the EU and its Member States can only implement their own obligations from the agreement by executing their own powers (respectively, conferred and residual), the implementation of mixed agreements should follow the same principles that guide the distribution of powers, as in the internal framework of the Union.[30] Therefore, the Union's institutions are only entitled to observe the part of obligations arising out of the mixed agreements, which are largely covered by the EU powers.[31] The Member States should observe their own obligations corresponding to their residual powers. Nevertheless, the prediction of separated obligations following the regime of separated powers cannot be easily implemented in the domain of shared powers. In practice, it is difficult to distinguish between the competences of the EU and Member States in the context of mixed agreements, and the shared competences increase the difficulty in this process.[32] These concerns can be addressed from the principle of complementarity, which is inherent in the very nature of mixed agreements and serves as a tool of compensation for the different ownerships of powers covered by the same agreement.

In principle, mixed agreements should not expand the EU competences to the detriment of the Member States' ones. In the course of the EU integration, the areas of EU exclusive powers have continuously expanded and the activity of the EU institutions in the areas of shared competences has significantly increased. While the EU is competent to undertake international obligations for matters falling within the exclusive areas of powers, the situation differs for areas in which the Union shares competences with the Member States, due to their preemptive nature. Accordingly, Article 2(2) TFEU has conceived shared competences in a specific area as a real capacity for the Member States to legislate *as long as* the Union has

---

[29]Eeckhout (2011), p. 236.

[30]Eeckhout (2011), p. 260. See also the ECJ's Ruling 1/78 of the Court of Justice, [1978] ECR I-2151, *Ruling delivered pursuant to the third paragraph of Article 103 of the EAEC Treaty – 'Draft Convention of the International Atomic Energy Agency on the Physical Protection of Nuclear Materials, Facilities and Transports'*, para. 36.

[31]Case C-13/00 *Commission of the European Communities v Ireland*, [2002] ECR I-2943, para. 20 and C-239/03 *Commission of the European Communities v French Republic*, [2004] ECR I-598, paras. 27–31. See also Weiler (1999), p. 181.

[32]See also Eeckhout (2011), p. 256.

not legislated. From this, it can be inferred that once the Union has exercised its capacity to legislate, that area is unionized and the Member States cease to legislate autonomously, unless instructed from the EU legislation otherwise. This allows also for the repatriation of competences, if the Union ceases to legislate. Hence, the exercise of shared competences from the Union is crucial for the conduct of its external relations, particularly when mixed agreements include areas of shared competences.[33]

Amid this unsustainable scheme of powers, one could distinguish an additional element for uncertainty. This is related with the qualification of the unionized areas as premises for the Union to enter into international agreements. Often, the qualification of the Union's competence may be determined by way of quantification of the legislative measures enacted by the Union. The Union may be qualified as 'competent' in an area although it has not exhaustively legislated on it. Hence, in such situations, a disputed matter may not be regulated from the Union but from the Member State. The largely regulated areas of EU law can be a significant argument for the classification of shared competences as unionized powers.[34] This allows the Union to enter into international agreements covering these areas, which subsequently shall be binding on the Member States.[35] This leads the Union to assume obligations for non-conferred areas of competence. Such obligations are virtual for the Union, but real for the Member States.

The *EC – Asbestos* scenario confirms the relevance of this theoretical issue. Accordingly, when France enacted the measure banning the import of asbestos products, the EU had largely legislated in the area by enacting a variety of restrictions on trade with asbestos based on internal market competences (not on public health grounds), although not banning them entirely. The French measure, if assessed in terms of the EU legislation, would very likely qualify as a national measure based on the prerogatives of France to protect public health, given that it went beyond the EU legislation by banning any trade with asbestos products.[36] Obviously, the application of two different standards of analysis for the same measure, produces two different propositions, which could be both true. This paradox is explained from the inability to outline a delimitation zone between the conferred and residual powers in the polity. This constitutes the basis for the

[33]See also Eeckhout (2011), p. 239.

[34]See with regard to environmental competences C-239/03 *Commission v France*, [2004] ECR I-598, paras. 27–31.

[35]This mechanism should however be distinguished from the implied powers doctrine, which acknowledges the right of the Union to enter into international obligations absent a conferred external power in the area, but is *necessary* to enable the Union to exercise its internal competence (Articles 3(2) and 216(1) TFEU). See also Case C-22/70 *Commission of the European Communities v Council of the European Communities*, [1971] ECR I-263, also referred to in the literature as '*ERTA* or *AETR* judgment'. See also Eeckhout (2011), p. 239.

[36]In light of these arguments, the French measure, if found WTO inconsistent, would have triggered the joint responsibility of France and the EU, even though the measure was regarded as a purely national one.

substantive gap between the WTO obligations of the Union and the WTO privileges of the Member States, which do not fully converge with each other. In order for the paradox not to shift its external effects to third parties, the Union polity has denied the regime of separated obligations following the separated powers, and has rather adopted a joint membership in the WTO, which is followed by obligations that should be observed jointly. The concept of observation does not merely include the jurisdiction of the ECJ to interpret provisions of mixed agreements with joint interest for both the EU and the Member States, but also the implementation and application of such provisions.[37] This construction may require also from Member States to take measures, or to act in a particular way in terms of their EU obligations.[38] In this way, Member States are obliged to take measures not only by reason of their own membership in the international agreement, but also by reason of their membership in the Union.

Taking into account the role of the distribution of powers in the Union polity for the joint membership regime, which is decisive for the construction of the international responsibility based on joint or several terms, it is useful to consider the way in which this vertical relationship is incorporated in the formal aspects of the membership in mixed agreements. The international treaties concluded jointly from the EU and its Member States are the prime example of mixed agreements. Indeed, mixed agreements can create two different regimes of responsibility, which functionally depend on the vertical distribution of powers in the Union. The WTO Agreement is concluded as a mixed agreement where both the EU and Member States have made no declaration of powers, and as such, are deemed jointly responsible for the WTO obligations.[39] In the presence of a declaration of powers, the EU would be responsible only for the competences conferred by the Member States.[40] Therefore, the declaration of competences, in principle, excludes the application of a joint responsibility regime to the benefit of a regime of separated responsibilities of the parties. The WTO Agreement and its annexed agreements are silent as to the vertical distribution of powers in the Union polity.[41] As a general consideration, it could be suggested that the vertical distribution of powers between the Union and its Member States does not entail a separated responsibility regime where no declaration of powers or responsibilities is made on the concerned treaty.[42] The joint responsibility regime is presumed to be the default alternative

[37]See for example C-239/03 *Commission v France*, [2004] ECR I-598, paras. 27–31 where the ECJ employed a broad interpretation of the environmental competences of the EU to include areas residual within the powers of Member States. See also Eeckhout (2011), p. 304.

[38]Eeckhout (2011), pp. 260–261.

[39]ILC Commentaries to DARIO, Commentary to Article 48 DARIO, para. 1. See for example Case C-316/91 *European Parliament v Council of the European Union*, [1994] ECR I-625, para. 29.

[40]See also Neframi (2002), p. 195.

[41]See also Heliskoski (2001), p. 176.

[42]Neframi (2002), p. 198.

in the absence of a declaration of powers, which would otherwise trigger a several responsibility regime following the ownership of competences.

However, the declaration of powers is only a formal explanation of the way in which the consequences of mixed agreements should be addressed. The declaration of competences in the course of the signature of mixed agreement would be determined from the distribution of powers and the compatibility of the subject matter of the agreement with the scheme of powers. Certainly, the dynamic scheme of powers in the Union polity challenges this relationship. Furthermore, the declaration of competences, although in principle follows the scheme of the distribution of powers, could prove scarce in terms of a separated responsibility regime in cases where the internationally wrongful act is attributed to a party that has committed it beyond its declared competences over the subject matter. Accordingly, the Union may be held responsible for violating an obligation by virtue of an internationally wrongful conduct attributed to its actions, although the matter may fall within the residual powers of the Member States.[43]

Obviously, a declaration of powers in the context of WTO Agreement could have been quite unrealistic when the Agreement was signed in 1994. At that time, the ECJ delivered an Opinion, in which the propositions of the GATS and TRIPS Agreements were found in the joint competence of the EU and its Member States, unlike GATT, which was the sole competence of the EU.[44] Here, the Court distinguished particular aspects covered by GATS and TRIPS from the common commercial policy of the Union. Article 207 TFEU, reformulated with the Treaty of Lisbon (2007), reversed the structure conceived from the ECJ, by expanding the scope of common commercial policy with the commercial aspects of intellectual property, trade in services and foreign investments. The change in the vertical structure of powers of the Union polity would have led to the necessity of modification of the declaration of powers, should it have existed. However, it remains doubtful whether this formal modification of the declaration of powers would have essentially resolved the substantive gaps inherent in the structure of powers.[45]

Having considered the implications of the vertical distribution of powers for the declaration of powers, and the relevance of the constitutional changes in this scheme for the declaration of powers, it is furthermore useful to consider the implications of these constitutional changes for the membership of the EU and its Member States in the WTO. The EU integration process has resulted in the transfer of powers from the Member States to the Union level, a process that in the language of the Treaties refers to the principle of conferral (Articles 4(1), 5(1) TEU). The transfer of powers in some areas may amount to a transfer of sovereignty to the Union, which, pursuant to the doctrine of substitution, assumes the rights and obligations of Member States in these areas. In terms of the WTO Agreement, the

[43]Neframi (2002), p. 196.

[44]Opinion 1/94 of the Court of Justice *re WTO Agreement*, [1994] ECR I-5267, paras. 34, 46, 47, 98, 103–105.

[45]See also Schermers (1983), p. 829.

transfer of sovereignty has lead the Member States to withdraw their individual schedules of concessions to the benefit of the Union's single schedule of concessions for the areas of conferred powers.[46] This constitutes a clear case of the application of the doctrine of substitution in that the EU continues and succeeds the WTO obligations of the Member States. The latter keep making use of the rights provided in this Agreement either by virtue of their direct participation therein, or by virtue of derivation as EU Members. However, the fact that the WTO areas are increasingly converging with the Union's competences may nevertheless not suffice for the succession from the EU of the Member States membership in the WTO. The claim that the Treaty of Lisbon has expanded the Union's external competences in order to exhaust the need for a mixed membership in the WTO Agreement,[47] should be taken seriously but not in absolute terms. The scheme of powers, the decentralized nature of their exercise, and the incomplete federalization of the Union polity, make it indispensable for the Union and its Member States to participate jointly in mixed agreements. Hence, the Member States remain reluctant to surrender their influence in international organizations to the benefit of the EU, as a safeguard for their sovereignty claims.[48]

In light of the doctrine of substitution, a question would arise as to the effects that its predictions have over the residual powers of the Member States. The transfer of powers in the selected areas has resulted in the reduction of rights and obligations of the Member States in these areas.[49] As a result, the position of the Member States in the WTO has been substituted by the Union only for the areas conferred in the Treaties, whereas for the residual powers, the Member States should, in principle, observe their own obligations. Hence, in terms of obligations, the Member States share with the EU their responsibilities either individually or jointly, following the structure of powers. As much as the category of rights is concerned, the Member States do not only enjoy their own rights, but also the Union rights, which they derive by virtue of their EU membership. This framework explains the formal-substantive gap of the WTO membership of the EU and Member States, which remains a plausible argument for the joint membership regime.

The joint participation of the EU and its Member States in the WTO Agreement should be considered also in terms of their participation in the DSP. Such a participation presents particular concerns, irrespective of the fact whether the EU takes part as a complainant or as a respondent. The EU has participated in the DSP not only for matters falling within the areas of conferred powers, but also for matters that are residual with the Member States. Potential conflicts in relation

[46]*European Communities – Customs Classification of Certain Computer Equipment* (*EC – Computer Equipment*), Report of the Panel (WT/DS62, 67, 68/R), Report of the Panel of 05 February 1998, para. 4.10.

[47]See for such claims Eeckhout (2011), p. 231.

[48]Eeckhout (2011), p. 223, Sack (1995), p. 1233 and Weiler (1999), pp. 168–169.

[49]*EC – Computer Equipment*, (WT/DS62, 67, 68/R), Report of the Panel of 05 February 1998, para. 4.14.

with this problem have been avoided in practice with the participation of the concerned Member States in the proceedings.[50] However, from a theoretical perspective, the retaliatory processes may disclose potential tensions, as long as concerned Member States may institute retaliatory measures in their own right, contrary to the intention of the Council.[51] In other scenarios, the Union may be unable to take countermeasures for areas falling within the residual powers of the Member States, and the contrary holds true for the Member States as well.[52] Similarly, a state of tension could be further created if defaulting Member States, whose measures have been ruled as WTO inconsistent, would refuse, in their own right, to comply with the DSB rulings and recommendations, although *ex hipothesi* they would be positioned against the majority of the other Member States in the Council. It remains further unclear whether a Member State may institute proceedings against a third state in the DSB, should the Union refuse to do so on behalf of the affected Member State.[53]

All these drawbacks of the retaliatory system, which are not addressed from the DSU, may lead to inequitable results.[54] All the Member States may incur trade losses from the increased barriers in the course of cross-retaliatory measures, if the defaulting Member State has not complied with DSB rulings and recommendations within the grace period. Obviously, the participation of the Union in the DSP can be regarded as one of the legal causes for this burden. Indeed, the cross-retaliation in the course of suspension of concessions constitutes the ultimate instrument, after failing to identify within the same area of the inconsistent measure, the proper concessions that ensure the victim to accrue most effectively the trade benefits amounting to impaired rights. This is an instrument of constraint for the wrongdoer to cease the wrongful act. This principle, which is enshrined in Article 22(3) DSU, can however be criticized on grounds of the methodology of application, which raises concerns in terms of misuse of rights. Accordingly, in the first case of authorization of cross-retaliatory measures,[55] the Union was concerned about the weak reasoning as a basis of authorization of cross-retaliatory measures, particularly in the area of intellectual property rights, which is regarded quite specific and delicate.[56] The concerns are particularly raised at a procedural level, namely on due process considerations, rather than on material grounds concerning the vertical distribution of powers in the Union. However, the concerns in relation with the inequitable effects of cross-retaliation, which are based on the fear that the

[50]See further Antoniadis (2004), p. 332.

[51]Antoniadis (2004), p. 332.

[52]See also Heliskoski (2001), p. 215.

[53]Antoniadis (2004), pp. 332–333.

[54]Heliskoski (2001), p. 215.

[55]*EC – Bananas*, Recourse to Arbitration by the European Communities under Article 22.6 DSU, WT/DS27/ARB/ECU, 24 March 2000, DSR 2000:V, 2237, paras. 174–175.

[56]DSB Doc. WT/DSB/M/78 of 12 May 2000, Minutes of the Meeting of the Dispute Settlement Body of 7 April 2000, item 3 of the Agenda, 9, para. 38.

"division in the external relations competence sits uncomfortably with the [DSU]",[57] remain theoretical, inasmuch as no significant conflicts have emerged in the course of the WTO practice. So far, the option of cross-retaliation has not succeeded to raise significant constitutional questions for the EU polity.

From a procedural point of view it should be emphasized that, although the DSB has barely questioned the capacity of the Union to be held answerable and responsible for inconsistent measures attributed to Member States, the distribution of powers can influence, at least theoretically, the standing of the EU as a respondent in the DSP. The Commission (hence the Union), has represented the Member States in the DSP as of 1974 for all trade disputes involving a Member State, notwithstanding the origin of the disputed measure that nullified or impaired trade benefits of the WTO Members.[58] Developed on a *de facto* basis, this practice, which bypasses the answerability of those Member States that have imposed the wrongful measure, is deemed legally doubtful in terms of WTO law.[59] Even in terms of the general rules of attribution, this practice is questionable. Nevertheless, inasmuch as this practice reflects the constitutional choice of the Union polity, this perspective is crucial for the analysis. In this regard, it has prevailed the argument that the Union has considered itself bound by GATT and has, in its own name, exercised the rights, and carried out the obligations of Member States as far as those rights and obligations fall within its compass, which is practically the case with respect to all areas governed by GATT.[60] The assumption of GATT 1947 obligations from the Communities, in the absence of a formal ratification, is conceived from the ECJ as a constitutional construction based on the inductive logic of derived obligations. This customary practice is now embodied in the current practice by means of Article XVI:1 WTO Agreement, which allows the disputes to be brought against the EU, at least in terms of trade in goods.[61]

The ownership of exclusive and other conferred powers makes the Union fully responsible for complying with WTO obligations. This implies that the Union should be the sole respondent in all cases where the Union measures are invoked as WTO inconsistent. In view of this, measures falling within the exclusive competence of the Union should be addressed to the Union.[62] The question is whether from this practice it could be inferred that the Union is not answerable for measures that do not fall within the conferred powers? If the distribution of powers would be the explanatory variable for the question of participation of the

[57]See also Kuijper (1995a), p. 242 and Heliskoski (2001), p. 215.

[58]Petersmann (1986), p. 47.

[59]See also Antoniadis (2004), p. 333.

[60]Joined Cases C-21-24/72 *International Fruit Company NV et al. v Produktschap voor Groenten en Fruit*, [1972] ECR I-1219, 1224. See also paras. 10–12 in the same ruling.

[61]See also Antoniadis (2004), p. 334.

[62]Minutes of the Meeting of the DSB of 20 March 1997, WTO doc. WT/DSB/M/30 *(re Customs classification of certain computer equipment from United Kingdom and Ireland*, items 6 and 7 of the Agenda.

Union as a respondent in the DSP, the answer for this question would remain quite uncompromised from the arbitrary practice of the joint responsibility regime. Indeed, the joint responsibility is understood as a premise for triggering the participation of the Union also for matters falling within the non-conferred powers of the Union. In view of the third parties, and particularly in the context of their quest for legal certainty, this way of understanding is plausible. In addition, from the perspective of the Union's pursuit for preserving the common interests and the autonomy of the legal order, and considering the broad conception of the Union competences under the WTO Agreement, the participation of the Union as a sole representative of Member States is again justified.[63]

However, from the Member States' perspective, considering the normative argument of residual sovereignty over the non-conferred areas, the Union should not represent the Member States for measures falling within their residual powers. Rather, the Union could be co-defendant with the Member States that have instituted the disputed measures. This model would answer at best the challenges of cross-sector mixity. By preserving the residual powers of Member States, this model designates the Union as a sole representing body of the entire polity, while involving the concerned Member States in DSP where their interests are at stake.

This approach has effects similar to those of the model of *vertical mixed agreement*, which allows the EU to represent the entire bloc in external relations, but at the same time, not to gain internal legislative implementing competences, which remain with the Member States.[64] This model remains theoretical, as long as the Member States would incur international obligations in areas of residual powers, although not being part of international agreements, which, from the traditional international law perspective, would be inconceivable. Furthermore, from the EU law perspective, the model would hardly get the relevant level of legitimacy, inasmuch as it construes the vertical relationship between the Union and Member States in a function subordinate to the external dimension. As a result, the model of vertical mixed agreements remains a hypothetical alternative of the joint membership regime with a combined representation in the DSP.

In light of the above, given that in the course of a WTO proceeding it might not be very easy to distinguish beforehand the ownership of the competences related to the disputed measure, and taking into account that the wide scope of EU powers is increasing continuously, the joint membership regime might be plausible in the interest of legal certainty. This construction seems to be missing a compelling legal logic.[65] Yet, it could be regarded as pragmatic, inasmuch as it ensures that the Union has the opportunity to observe its own prerogatives in relation with the WTO law in all cases. Accordingly, the participation of the Union in the DSP could avoid the possibility that any procedural constellations in the DSM address measures for which the Union may be even partially competent. As to the potential implications

[63]See also Heliskoski (2001), pp. 182–183, 188.

[64]Weiler (1999), p. 187.

[65]Heliskoski (2001), pp. 189–190.

of this participation for the Member States, this could be addressed further from an internal point of view by means of constitutional principles of the Union.

Amid the problems and challenges of cross-sector mixity and the fallacies of the joint membership regime in the WTO, and moreover, in light of the constitutional principles of the Union polity, one could distinguish the principle of loyalty as a significant proposition for aligning the interest of the Member States and the Union into a common position. The pursuit of a common position remains, from a procedural point of view, the main normative outcome of this principle.[66] The conclusion to be drawn from these problems is that the distribution of powers plays a significant role for the implementation of the WTO Agreement and for the regime of joint responsibility.

## III. The Effect of the WTO Agreement on the Legal Orders of EU and Its Member States

The international legal responsibility of the EU and its Member States is defined from the complex relationship of the elements and factors that are embodied in the very nature of the Union polity, as well as in the constitutional nature of mixed agreements. As to the WTO Agreement, it can be suggested that its constitutional nature is decisive for the definition of the joint responsibility regime, inasmuch as it assists in shaping the pluralistic relationship of the legal orders of the WTO, EU, and the EU Member States. This relationship can be explored by analyzing the way in which the WTO Agreement is received in the EU legal order.

### *1. The Interpretation of Mixed Agreements from the ECJ and Issues of Jurisdiction*

In general, it could be presumed that the legal effects of mixed agreements should follow the distribution of powers, in that the effect of the agreement in the EU legal order should be limited to those areas for which the Union is competent. By virtue of this presumption, the institutional capacity of the Union and the jurisdiction of ECJ for the interpretation and application of these agreements are limited within the areas of conferred powers.[67] The question to be addressed in this regard is whether the WTO Agreement would have a full or a limited extent of application in the EU legal order. Hence, would the ECJ be competent to decide on matters falling within the residual powers of the Member States in relation with disputes concerning the application and interpretation of mixed agreements? The ECJ has not provided a

[66]MacLeod et al. (1996), pp. 148–149 and Antoniadis (2004), p. 328.

[67]See also Eeckhout (2011), p. 278.

direct answer to these questions, but it has confirmed that it has jurisdiction to interpret a mixed agreement, including the provisions for which the Member States are competent.[68] However, the ECJ cannot ignore the limitation of its jurisdiction on the questions falling within the residual powers of the Member States.[69] This constitutes a significant premise for the non-expansionary effects of mixed agreements on the structure of powers in the Union polity.

Mixed agreements may lead to theoretical paradoxes, inasmuch as issues of jurisdiction and responsibility are concerned. The WTO Agreement provides a prime example of such paradoxes, in that a strict interpretation of the normative framework could, under theoretical conditions, lead to deadlocks. Accordingly, in terms of jurisdictional issues, there can be situations in which the WTO Agreement does not seem to converge with the EU legal order. Pursuant to Article 23.1 DSU, the Contracting Parties are not allowed to resort to any dispute settlement mechanism other than the WTO Agreement. Similarly, Article 344 TFEU provides for the jurisdictional monopoly of the ECJ in the adjudication of disputes between Member States for issues related with the Treaties. In light of these provisions, two Member States of the EU cannot institute proceedings in relation to a dispute covered by both legal orders (e.g. trade measures) in any of these fora without violating the provisions of the other agreement.[70] Certainly, this paradox can be resolved by way of the practical deference to any of the fora against the other. The ECJ, although inclined to protect the autonomy of the EU legal order, may still submit to the practice of the international courts, such as the DSM or the European Court of Human Rights, provided that these fora do not rule on internal matters of the Union, such as the distribution of powers, interpretation of Treaties, or other EU legislation.[71] However, a provision in the mixed agreement addressing this paradox would be a safer normative solution for avoiding jurisdictional clashes. Article 282 UNCLOS, for example, entails a pluralist approach toward the forum shopping, by bringing external procedural arrangements for dispute settlement into its own jurisdictional scheme.[72] However, considering that the jurisdictional conflicts are not new in the course of an increasing fragmentation of international law, general rules governing the conflict of laws might be useful to address these concerns, absent of specific rules in this regard.

As to the paradoxes in relation to competences, the mixed agreements have a tendency to create systemic maladministration of responsibility in terms of the principle of attribution. The joint responsibility regime serves as a normative framework for attributing the responsibility for breach of international obligation not only to the party to whom the internationally wrongful act is attributed, but also to other participants, which are deemed jointly responsible due to their joint

[68]Case C-12/86 *Demirel v Stadt Schwäbisch Gmünd*, [1987] ECR I-3719, para. 9.

[69]See also Eeckhout (2011), pp. 278, 303, 304.

[70]See also Eeckhout (2011), p. 240.

[71]Eeckhout (2011), p. 241.

[72]Salles (2014), pp. 174–175.

membership in the agreement. This fallacy is further associated with missing mechanisms for redistributing responsibility. This is particularly obvious in the context of WTO Agreement, where the responsibility for breach of WTO obligations does not amount to pecuniary damages, although the economic damages from trade loss might be obvious.

The discourse on the international responsibility of the EU and its Member States in the context of WTO membership cannot be detached from the general considerations on the effects of mixed agreements in the EU legal order. In principle, the effects of the WTO Agreement in the legal orders of the EU and its Member States can be organized on the basis of monist or dualist lines, as an expression of the relationship between international and municipal legal orders.[73] While this relationship has not been clearly defined in the EU constitutional framework, the jurisprudence has not adopted a uniform approach either. The issue of responsibility for violation of WTO obligations relates to this discourse, inasmuch as the effect of the WTO Agreement on the legal orders of the EU and its Member States determines the conditions for the management of problems caused from the fallacy of the joint responsibility regime in the context of WTO membership. In the general discourse of effects, it might be also useful to distinguish the effect of the DSB rulings and recommendations.

The institutional frameworks established by mixed agreements create for the EU and its Member States binding international obligations. As such, they produce rules of conduct that may influence the internal relationship in the Union polity.[74] The creation of an institutional framework, including the dispute settlement system, in principle complies with the EU legal order. By virtue of being an integral part of the EU legal order, the decisions of DSB are binding upon the Union institutions and the Member States.[75] However, insofar as the system of courts established pursuant to a mixed agreement may interfere with the Union legal order, and particularly with the vertical distribution of powers in the Union polity, by means of interpretation of the allocation of responsibilities provided by the Treaties, that system would not be compatible with EU law. This would constitute a violation of Articles 19(1) TEU and 344 TFEU, which prohibit Member States to submit the jurisdiction for interpretation of Treaties to any fora other than the ECJ. By establishing a 'jurisdictional monopoly' of the ECJ, these provisions preclude

[73]According to Dowrick, "(i)n the mid twentieth century, legal philosophers who have advanced general theories of law have assumed that all modern laws belong either to the sphere of international law or to municipal, alias national, legal systems, and have speculated on their relations inter se, on monist or dualist lines". See further, Dowrick (1983), p. 170.

[74]Article 216(2) TFEU.

[75]Opinion 1/91 of the Court of Justice, [1991], ECR I-6079, *Opinion delivered pursuant to the second subparagraph of Article 228 (1) of the Treaty – 'Draft agreement between the Community, on the one hand, and the countries of the European Free Trade Association, on the other, relating to the creation of the European Economic Area'*, paras. 37, 39, 40. See further for arguments on the position of the provisions of mixed agreements as an integral part of the EU legal order, Case C-181/73 *R. & V. Haegeman v Belgian State*, [1974] ECR I-449, para. 5.

Member States to resort to external methods of dispute settlement.[76] Any institution and pursuit from Member States of proceedings before international tribunals involves a risk of affecting the jurisdictional order laid down in the Treaties, and consequently, the autonomy of the EU legal order, when the proceedings concern the interpretation of EU norms.[77] In this way, the Union and its Member States should not become subject to international obligations which conflict with the obligations and responsibilities provided in the Treaties.[78] Mixed agreements anchor propositions that may be interpreted against the Union's interests. It is on this basis that the ECJ assumed authority to interpret the effects of an international agreement in the EU legal order, including the national law, notwithstanding the fact that the implementation may be the responsibility of the Member State.[79] The main reason underlying this normative proposition rests with the necessity to preserve the autonomy of the EU legal order through homogeneous and uniform interpretation.[80] From this, it could be inferred that the possibility for Member States to invoke the compliance of WTO obligations against each other in front of the DSB is excluded, as long as it would constitute a violation of the Union law.

The main canon for preserving the institutional autonomy of the EU legal order from interactions with mixed agreements consists in the clear institutional separation of the Union from other contracting parties. This is a guarantee for the Union to remain unaffected from any changes in the scheme of powers or from the interpretation of the Union law.[81] Indeed, the question of competences is decisive for the existence of a mixed agreement and for its implementation. The fact that the Union has not full exclusive competences in the areas governed by the WTO Agreement is conditional for its joint conclusion from the EU and its Member States.[82] The conclusion of a mixed agreement *per se* does not transform the nature of competences from shared into exclusive, while the competences determine the principal entity that is responsible for the implementation of obligations from this agreement.[83] Although the ECJ has asserted exclusive jurisdiction for the interpretation

---

[76]Case C-459/03 *Commission of the European Communities v Ireland* (MOX Plant), [2006] ECR I-4635, para. 152. See also Opinion of the Advocate General Poiares Maduro, para. 9 in the same case. See also Eeckhout (2011), p. 239.

[77]Case C-459/03 *Commission v Ireland* (MOX Plant), [2006] ECR I-4635, para. 154.

[78]Cases C-104/81 *Hauptzollamt Mainz v Kupferberg*, [1982] ECR I-3641, para. 13, C-12/86 *Demirel v Stadt Schwäbisch Gmünd*, [1987] ECR I-3719, para. 11 and C-13/00 *Commission v Ireland*, [2002] ECR I-2943, para. 15. See also Eeckhout (2011), p. 260.

[79]Case C-104/81 *Hauptzollamt Mainz v Kupferberg*, [1982] ECR I-3641, paras. 11–14. See also Eeckhout (2011), p. 334.

[80]Opinion 1/91 of the ECJ *re Agreement on the European Economic Area* [1991], ECR I-6079, paras. 37–47.

[81]Opinion 1/00 of the Court of Justice, *Opinion pursuant to Article 300(6) EC – Proposed agreement between the European Community and non-Member States on the establishment of a European Common Aviation Area*, [2002] ECR I-3493, para. 6.

[82]Opinion 1/94 of the Court of Justice *re WTO Agreement*, [1994] ECR I-5267, paras. 34, 46, 47, 98, 103–105. See also Neframi (2012), p. 330.

[83]Neframi (2012), pp. 331–335.

of mixed agreements as a guarantee for their uniform implementation, the implementation of the provisions of mixed agreements related with non-conferred powers should remain with the Member States.[84]

In this way, it can be ensured that the EU legal order remains unaffected from the jurisdictional outreach of the international dispute settlement mechanisms established with mixed agreements. The risk of negative effects in this regard is based on the provisions of mixed agreements, which are a constitutive part of the EU legal order and, as such, able to produce adverse effects.[85] Nevertheless, the binding effect of international agreements for the Union and its Member States (Article 216(2) TFEU) does not necessarily mean that mixed agreements, as much as the methods of interpretation are concerned, are automatically and fully assimilated in the EU legal order.[86] A full monistic approach is not deemed compatible with the EU legal order, and neither with the legal traditions of the majority of the Member States.[87] The ECJ has mostly adopted a teleological approach for the interpretation of mixed agreements; hence stressing the objectives pursued by the provision, and leading to a broader scope of interpretation.[88]

The issue of effect of the WTO Agreement in the EU legal order has been mainly elaborated in the context of the ECJ's jurisdiction for the interpretation of the Agreement. Mixed agreements may become subject to the legality review procedure pursuant to Article 263 TFEU insofar as their compatibility with the EU legal order is concerned. Illegality may arise not only from an act of institutions concluding the mixed agreement, but also from actions of the Union violating the agreement.[89] In both these courses of action, the protection of legality regime concerns acts of Union institutions, being legislative acts or other acts intended to produce legal effects *vis-á-vis* third parties (Article 263(2) TFEU). The ECJ has jurisdiction to review legality on the grounds of lack of competence, infringement of an essential procedural requirement, infringement of the Treaties or of any rule of law relating to their application, or misuse of powers (Article 263(2) TFEU). The ECJ has assumed extensive jurisdiction in the interpretation of international agreements, which is regarded questionable in terms of law, but arguably, desirable in the interest of the rule of law in the plurality of the legal orders that intersect with the EU legal order.[90] The ECJ has justified its authority to interpret international agreements on the ground of uniform application and legal certainty, although the Member States may be in charge for their implementation.[91]

---

[84]Neframi (2012), p. 337.

[85]Cases C-13/00 *Commission v Ireland*, [2002] ECR I-2943, para. 14 and C-459/03 *Commission v Ireland* (MOX Plant), [2006] ECR I-4635, para. 84.

[86]Eeckhout (2011), p. 304.

[87]Eeckhout (2011), p. 327.

[88]Eeckhout (2011), p. 305.

[89]Eeckhout (2011), p. 287 *et seq.*

[90]Jacobs (2008), p. 14.

[91]MacLeod et al. (1996), p. 140. See also Neframi (2012), pp. 327–328.

The review of legality in relation with an international agreement is subject to two conditions: the provisions of that agreement must firstly bind the Union, and secondly, they must be capable of conferring rights on citizens of the Union, which they may invoke before the courts.[92] The ECJ has assumed jurisdiction to interpret GATT notwithstanding the fact whether the measure in question was part of the Union law or Member State law.[93] Hence, the ECJ considered the Union to be bound by the GATT 1947 by virtue of derived obligations from Member States, although the Communities where not party thereto.[94] The main argument for this is based on the fact that the majority of areas covered by GATT 1947 were conferred from the Member States to the Union as a category of exclusive powers, which led to a 'functional succession' of the obligations of the Member States.[95]

## 2. *The Effect of the WTO Agreement on the Legal Orders of the EU and Its Member States*

The legality review in the context of mixed agreements has raised the question of direct effect of those agreements in the municipal legal order. Notwithstanding the wide interpretative jurisdiction of the ECJ, the direct effect of the WTO Agreement in terms of the legality review of the Union's conduct is denied, even in cases where a DSB ruling or recommendation has affirmed the WTO incompliance of the measure.[96] The ECJ has maintained that the WTO provisions are not among the rules in light of which the ECJ is to review the legality of measures adopted by the Union institutions. According to the ECJ, the review of legality depends on the direct effect of the Agreement, as a precondition for establishing the standing of parties to invoke illegality of secondary legislation.[97] In addition to the jurisprudence, the institutions have also clearly denied the direct effect of the WTO Agreement (particularly GATS and TRIPS) as an opportunity of being invoked in

---

[92] Joined Cases C-21-24/72 *International Fruit Company NV et al. v Produktschap voor Groenten en Fruit*, [1972] ECR I-1219, paras. 7, 8.

[93] Joined Cases C-267-269/81 *Amministrazione delle finanze dello Stato v SPI and SAMI*, [1983] ECR I-801, para. 15. The concerns in relation with the dimension of the jurisdiction of the ECJ shall nevertheless remain outside the scope of this work.

[94] Joined Cases C-21-24/72 *International Fruit Company NV et al. v Produktschap voor Groenten en Fruit*, [1972] ECR I-1219, paras. 10–15.

[95] Cremona (2012), p. 294.

[96] Geiger et al. (2015), p. 174.

[97] Joined Cases C-21-24/72 *International Fruit Company NV et al. v Produktschap voor Groenten en Fruit*, [1972] ECR I-1219, para. 27 and Case C-149/96 *Portuguese Republic v Council of the European Union*, [1999] ECR I-8395, para. 47. See also Joined Cases C-120/06 and C-121/06 *FIAMM and Fedon v Council and Commission*, [2008] ECR I-6513, para. 111. For an overview of the evolution of the direct effect of international agreements in the EU legal order, see Jacobs (2008), pp. 13–33. See also Bogdandy (2005), p. 47 *et seq.*

EU's or Member States' courts.[98] This is in line with the same approach that other trading partners comparable to EU, such as the USA, Japan, and Canada, have maintained in relation with the direct effect of the WTO Agreement in their legal orders.[99]

The missing direct effect implies that the Member States cannot remedy their injured rights from the Union actions violating the WTO Agreement.[100] While for the individuals this denied opportunity is not new (with certain exceptions considered below), given that it converges also with the approach of national courts denying the direct effect of the WTO Agreement, for the Member States this results in a missing opportunity to resort to judicial tools for addressing conflicting obligations from the WTO Agreement.[101] The arguments behind the denial of direct effect are mainly based on the spirit and nature of the WTO Agreement. This is mainly based on the principle of negotiation of reciprocal concessions and mutually advantageous arrangements; hence, distinguished from other mixed agreements creating some asymmetry of obligations or establishing special relations of integration of third countries with the Union.[102] Obviously, the ECJ follows a double standard in assessing the direct effect of the WTO Agreement. On the one hand, for the denial of direct effect, the ECJ considers as a normative argument the nature and the spirit of the WTO Agreement as part of the EU legal order and binding on it. On the other hand, based on the same argument, the ECJ denies the direct effect of the same Agreement for reviewing the legality of secondary acts of the Union.

The ECJ has not distinguished between the direct effect of substantive obligations of the WTO Agreement and the direct effect of DSB rulings enforcing such obligations.[103] Therefore, the review of legality of secondary acts on the basis of DSB rulings is not possible.[104] As to the compliance with the recommendations and rulings of the DSB, the ECJ has not considered them as capable to confer rights that can be invoked in courts from individuals.[105] The doctrine and some Advocate

---

[98]Council Decision 94/800/EC (of 22 December 1994) concerning the conclusion on behalf of the European Community, as regards matters within its competence, of the agreements reached in the Uruguay Round multilateral negotiations (1986–1994) [1994] OJ L336/1, last recital of the Preamble. See also Schedule of Specific Commitments of European Communities and their Member States, GATS/SC/31, 15 April 1994, Introductory note, 1, para. 3.

[99]See further Thies (2013), pp. 180–186.

[100]Tomuschat (2002), p. 188.

[101]See for this critic Case C-377/98 *Kingdom of the Netherlands v European Parliament and Council of the European Union*, [2001] ECR I-7079, Opinion of the Advocate General Jacobs of 14 June 2001, para. 147.

[102]Case C-149/96 *Portugal v Council*, [1999] ECR I-8395, para. 42. See also Case C-104/81 *Hauptzollamt Mainz v Kupferberg*, [1982] ECR I-3641, para. 22.

[103]See also Eeckhout (1997), pp. 51–55 and Eeckhout (2011). p. 367.

[104]Joined Cases C-120/06 and C-121/06 *FIAMM and Fedon v Council and Commission*, [2008] ECR I-6513, paras. 125–127.

[105]*Ibid*, para. 115. See also Case C-377/02 *Léon Van Parys NV v Belgisch Interventie- en Restitutiebureau (BIRB)*, [2005] ECR I-1465, para. 41.

Generals have advocated the idea of distinguishing the WTO Agreement from the rulings and recommendations of the DSB in terms of the direct effect.[106] Nevertheless, the jurisprudence has disagreed, by maintaining that the DSB rulings, as instruments enforcing material provisions of the WTO Agreement, cannot have more power than the WTO provisions themselves, and as such, cannot confer rights on individuals. This is due to the fact that the resolution of disputes in the WTO legal order is essentially based on negotiations between trading partners, a dynamic rather than static process. In addition to the withdrawal of wrongful measures, this process takes into account also temporary options, such as the settlement, payment of compensation, or suspension of concessions.[107]

With respect to the effect of the WTO Agreement in relation with the reparation of injuries suffered from individuals, it can be maintained that the ECJ has been consistent in excluding any liability for inconsistent trade measures enacted from the Union and its Member States. This is particularly so when the EU institutions enact trade measures in the context of WTO. Accordingly, economic operators incurring damages must be aware of the temporary nature of economic benefits. Such benefits may terminate due to changed circumstances resulting from measures suspending concessions as a reaction against the position taken by economic partners, which enjoy a significant margin of discretion in selecting the measures.[108]

The violations of the WTO Agreement are characterized of unpredictability in the reallocation of burden. Accordingly, certain economic operators in the EU, in their ordinary course of business, may not be interested in a particular DSP, as long as it may not be related with the industry where they operate. However, in case that the dispute persists and as a result, the EU or its Member States refuse to take measures pursuant to a ruling or recommendation of the DSB, the trading partner may become entitled to enact cross-retaliatory measures, which may affect these economic operators in an unpredictable way. The course of business of the victims of retaliation could be significantly affected due to decreased trade volumes, or due to measures taken to prevent the loss of foreign market, such as the shift of production in another country, if the nature of the industry so allows. These operations may result in considerable damages. The economic operators, whose products are included in retaliatory lists, would benefit from the immediate compliance of the EU or its Member States with DSB rulings and recommendations.[109]

---

[106] Eeckhout (1997), pp. 51–55 and Eeckhout (2011), p. 367. See further Case C-93/02P *Biret International SA v Council of the European Union*, [2003] ECR I-10497, Opinion of Advocate General Alber of 15 May 2003, paras. 74–81; Case C-377/02 *Van Parys* [2005] ECR I-1465, Opinion of Advocate General Tizzano of 18 November 2004, para. 73.

[107] Cases C-149/96 *Portugal v Council*, [1999] ECR I-8395, paras. 36–39 and C-22/00 *Omega Air et al.*, [2002] ECR I-2569, para. 89.

[108] Joined Cases C-120/06 and C-121/06 *FIAMM and Fedon v Council and Commission*, [2008] ECR I-6513, paras. 185, 186. See also Case C-280/93 *Germany v Council* (Bananas), [1994] ECR I-4973, para. 79.

[109] Thies (2006), p. 1162.

In this way, the burden of loss and damages will be reallocated to the detriment of a particular export related industry. Obviously, the 'direct victims' of a DSB ruling, which have to rely on the direct effect of primary WTO law, are to be distinguished from the 'retaliatory victims', which rely on rights conferred from temporary measures of retaliation.[110] The legal significance of this difference consists in the ability of each of these categories of victims to prove their direct concern in relation with the DSB ruling or the act authorizing cross-retaliatory measures, as preconditions for claiming the review of legality of EU secondary legislation pursuant to Article 263 TFEU. In this discourse, it should be recalled that the victims of retaliation may claim remedies only insofar as the concerned acts have direct effect, hence conferring rights upon them.[111] This condition is quite impossible to be established in the course of retaliation. Therefore, the fallacy of the retaliatory system in diverting the real burden, remains a systemic deficiency of the system of retaliation.

In light of these arguments, it can be inferred that the expiry of the 'grace' period granted by the DSB to withdraw inconsistent measures, constitutes the triggering moment for starting the negotiations for reaching an acceptable solution. Being aware of the importance of the bargaining power of the parties in negotiations, the ECJ has employed a judicial 'self-restrictive' approach in relation with the review of legality of secondary EU legislation. Accordingly, the ECJ has left leeway to legislative and executive institutions of the Union to reach an agreement on reciprocal basis with the trading partners.[112] The ECJ has reaffirmed in this way, that the discretion and scope for negotiations of EU institutions vis-à-vis their trading partners derives from the nature of the WTO Agreement, and especially from the reciprocity and flexibility characterizing it.[113] It remains however questionable whether the deterrent effect through the financial burden caused from the legality review process of the ECJ, is the ultimate ground for denying liability for breach of the WTO Agreement in the EU polity. Obviously, the main justification for this argument seems to be morally rather legally based, inasmuch as the Union, being aware of the breach of the WTO law, may continue its course based on politically, rather than legally oriented decisions.[114]

The nature of the DSM is considered another argument for denying the direct effect of the WTO Agreement, in that it constitutes a platform of perennial negotiations between the injured state and the wrongdoer. From an international law perspective, the fact that the defecting parties may continue, subject to

---

[110]Thies (2006), p. 1162.

[111]See also Thies (2006), p. 1162.

[112]Case C-149/96 *Portugal v Council*, [1999] ECR I-8395, paras. 43–46. See also Case C-377/02 *Van Parys*, [2005] ECR I-1465, paras. 51, 53 and Joined Cases C-120/06 and C-121/06 *FIAMM and Fedon v Council and Commission*, [2008] ECR I-6513, paras. 117, 119.

[113]Joined Cases C-120/06 and C-121/06 *FIAMM and Fedon v Council and Commission*, [2008] ECR I-6513, para. 130.

[114]See further on this discussion Thies (2006), p. 1158.

compensation or countervailing measures, their non-compliance with the DSB rulings and recommendations, despite the expiry of the reasonable time of compliance, cannot legitimize the wrongful conduct.[115] Indeed, the DSB rulings and recommendations are binding upon the parties, notwithstanding their missing capability of being invoked in courts. This confirms that the lack of direct effect is not a ground for neglecting the effects of the WTO Agreement and DSB rulings in the EU legal order. With all their limitations in terms of direct effect, the WTO Agreement in its entirety, and the DSB rulings and recommendations in particular, remain binding upon institutions of the Union and Member States, as part of their international obligations.[116] In light of this, it could be useful to elaborate on the implications of the denial of direct effect of the WTO Agreement on the issue responsibility. This constitutes the central reason for denying the responsibility of the Union and its Member States for violation of WTO disciplines in relation with the damages incurred by individuals.

Amid the unsuccessful actions for damages, the question would arise whether the denial of direct effect precludes also the actions for legality review of the Union and Member States in light of the WTO Agreement. The lack of direct effect of the WTO Agreements in the EU legal order does not preclude the adoption of measures from the EU institutions implementing the obligations assumed within the context of this Agreement. Such acts could, in principle, become subject to legality review from the Court.[117] This affirms a differentiated regime of effects of the WTO Agreement, which allows for the observance of obligations of the EU and its Member States under the Agreement. In principle, the lack of direct effect should not be an obstacle for reviewing the legality of secondary acts based on primary law, insofar as such acts intend to implement WTO obligations. The principle of implementation is recognized in the ECJ jurisprudence as an exception to the limitations caused from the lack of direct effect of the WTO Agreement, as much as the legality review is concerned. Accordingly, when the Union intends to implement a particular obligation in the context of WTO Agreement, or if its secondary acts expressly refer to specific provisions of this Agreement, the Court may review the legality of acts from the perspective of the WTO Agreement.[118] Since the WTO Agreement is part of the EU legal order, the judicial review is justified by the principle of legality, which the ECJ is bound to observe.[119] The

---

[115] Eeckhout (2011), p. 378.

[116] Tancredi (2012), p. 250.

[117] Case C-280/93 *Germany v Council* (Bananas), [1994] ECR I-4973, paras. 106–112, and Case C-149/96 *Portugal v Council*, [1999] ECR I-8395, para. 27.

[118] Referred also as the '*Nakajima/Fediol*' exceptions, pursuant to Cases C-70/87 *Fédération de l'industrie de l'huilerie de la CEE (Fediol) v Commission of the European Communities*, [1989] ECR I-1781, paras. 19–22; Case C-69/89 *Nakajima All Precision Co. Ltd. v Council of the European Communities*, [1991] ECR I-2069, para. 31; and C-149/96 *Portugal v Council*, [1999] ECR I-8395, para. 49. See also Case C-280/93 *Germany v Council* (Bananas), [1994] ECR I-4973, para. 111.

[119] See also Eeckhout (2011), p. 360.

construction of the principle of implementation of the WTO Agreement as a premise for the legality review of the Union actions, could amount to a certain degree to an indirect effect of the WTO Agreement in the EU legal order.[120] This observation is in line with the principled view that the ECJ can review the legality of the conduct of Union institutions on the basis of international agreements as long as this is not precluded by the agreement itself, and when their provisions are unconditional and sufficiently precise.[121] If the Union has not agreed on the effects that an agreement shall enjoy within the EU legal order, then the court that has jurisdiction is entitled to interpret the provisions of an international agreement to that effect.[122] Such an interpretation cannot be determined without taking into account the origin of the provisions in question.[123]

A particular question to be addressed in this context is related with the circumstances in which an act of the Union or its Member States can be qualified as intended to implement a particular WTO obligation or referring to a specific provision of the WTO Agreement. Would a DSB ruling requiring the EU or its Member States to withdraw a measure enacted in violation of the WTO Agreement be sufficient to grant this Agreement adequate direct effect for the legality review? The undertaking of the EU to comply with a DSB ruling has not been regarded from the ECJ as capable for justifying the WTO rules as a standard for the legality review of EU actions. This is due to the wide margin of discretion for the implementation of the ruling and due to the necessity to preserve a sound and reciprocal bargaining power for the Union's institutions.[124] Therefore, the ECJ has denied the right of an economic operator to claim damages by reason of the invalidity of Union's measures, even when a DSB ruling has established that the EU measure is incompatible with the WTO Agreement.[125]

---

[120]Eeckhout (2011), p. 329.

[121]Case C-308/06 *The Queen, on the application of International Association of Independent Tanker Owners (Intertanko) et al. v Secretary of State for Transport*, [2008] ECR I-405, para. 45. See also Joined Cases C-120/06 and C-121/06 *FIAMM and Fedon v Council and Commission*, [2008] ECR I-6513, para. 110.

[122]Cases C-104/81 *Hauptzollamt Mainz v Kupferberg*, [1982] ECR I-3641, para. 17 and C-149/96 *Portugal v Council*, [1999] ECR I-8395, para. 34.

[123]*Ibid.*

[124]Joined Cases C-120/06 and C-121/06 *FIAMM and Fedon v Council and Commission*, [2008] ECR I-6513, paras. 49, 101.

[125]Case C-377/02 *Van Parys*, [2005] ECR I-1465, para. 54 and Joined Cases C-120/06 and C-121/06 *FIAMM and Fedon v Council and Commission*, [2008] ECR I-6513, para. 111.

### 3. The Effect of the WTO Agreement in Light of the Challenges of Legal Pluralism

The principles developed by the ECJ in terms of the implementation and effect of the WTO Agreement are neither fully monist, nor fully dualist.[126] Obviously, a misinterpretation of the reception of international obligations in the EU legal order could lead to different claims of authority from municipal (EU and Member States) and international (WTO) legal orders. This can easily amount to a source of normative ambiguity and conflicts.[127] The denial of direct effect of WTO law in the EU legal order reinforces the thesis of dualism in the reception of international law, whose superiority is decided by the EU courts.[128] The principle of implementation, as a premise for judicial review of EU secondary acts, takes the role of balancing between the monist and dualist lines, and ensures a sort of internalization of WTO obligations in the EU legal order.[129]

In this balancing function, the judicial-normative processes of the ECJ cannot escape the challenges of the legal pluralism. The observation of the WTO obligations represents a normative process where many conflicting interests compete with each other. Among these interests can be listed the right of the Member States to regulate in their public interests, the right of trading partners to enjoy trade benefits, the right of individuals to be immune from trade restrictions, or moreover, to get compensation for injuries from retaliatory measures. The DSB constitutes a forum for addressing such competing normative claims also through negotiation processes. The ECJ, when required to address particular claims in this process, could interfere with a different kind of conflict resolution, which integrates the political elements in the judicial-normative processes. Hence, the multiplication of competing legal orders and their jurisdictional claims, and the expansion of relevant legal sources, can lead to normative conflicts that are to be resolved by courts.[130]

One way to deal with the challenges of pluralism would be to employ an interpretation that gives priority to one norm over the others. Accordingly, the principle of implementation, which balances the effect of the WTO Agreement in the EU legal order against the immunity of EU and its Member States from consequences of violation of WTO disciplines, gives preference to WTO obligations as opposed to immunity. More than a sign of openness toward the WTO Agreement, this approach construes the WTO obligations in the context of the EU legal order, and justifies in this way the exclusive approach against other alternatives.

[126]Eeckhout (2011), p. 374.

[127]Dani (2010), pp. 336–337.

[128]Tancredi (2012), p. 264.

[129]Eeckhout (2011), p. 361.

[130]Maduro (2009), pp. 366–367.

An exclusive approach requires the ECJ to employ a mono-dimensional conceptualization of the conflict in terms of any of the alternatives, such as the respect for the international rule of law, allocation of costs between economic actors, exposure of the EU budget toward possible burden of breaches of WTO obligations, legal implications inherent in each of the available judicial solutions, political room of maneuver, and accountability of political institutions.[131] The general approach that the WTO law does not confer rights on individuals, resulting in the denial of direct effect and of the legality review of secondary acts of Union and its Member States,[132] constitutes a ground for justifying an exclusive approach. This approach overweighs one factor against the others, as opposed of integrating all the factors within one single judicial-normative process.

Alternatively, the court could employ an inclusive approach, which is based on a particular model of interpretation that is open to complex economic, social, and political arguments. Here, the normative argument is construed in competition and/or in cooperation with other institutions, such as the political processes and other jurisdictions. This could be achieved by means of teleological interpretation, guided by a clear articulation of the systemic understanding of the legal order.[133]

## *4. The Consequences of the Denial of Direct Effect of the WTO Agreement*

The inclusive approach for addressing the challenges of legal pluralism could enrich the judicial-normative constructions of the courts, by endowing them with more acceptance, but cannot escape certain criticism. In terms of democratic legitimacy, overweighing the political room of maneuver against other elements could constitute a significant fallacy of the judicial-normative process, as much as the consequences in terms of the allocation of burden of responsibility are concerned. Obviously, the ECJ remains unconcerned about the legitimacy of the actions of the EU institutions after the expiry of the grace period, and about the subsequent burden of trade sanctions from countervailing measures, particularly the cross-retaliatory measures. Indeed, from a normative point of view, the preservation from the ECJ of the political room of maneuver of the EU institutions in the negotiations constitutes a temporary violation of the principle *pacta sunt servanda* and Article 216(2) TFEU. This is because the binding effect of the WTO Agreement and the relevant DSB ruling enforcing the covered agreements is hindered.[134]

Another consequence of the denial of direct effect of the WTO Agreement is the incapability of the Member States to invoke by judicial means the obligation of the

[131] Dani (2010), p. 337.

[132] Eeckhout (2011), p. 349.

[133] Maduro (2009), pp. 367–368.

[134] Eeckhout (2011), p. 381.

Union to comply with its WTO obligations, and particularly in cases involving the judicial review of EU secondary legislation.[135] In the absence of adequate remedies to Member States for challenging the Union's incompliance with international obligations, it could be suggested that an enforcement action, akin to that in the disposition of Commission (Articles 258 *et seq* TFEU), would be more appropriate in terms of legal consequences.[136] Accordingly, an enforcement action would be able to produce *ex nunc* effects, which would be limited to the cessation of the internationally wrongful act from the Union and the compliance with WTO obligations, rather than *ex tunc* effects of the action for annulment.[137] Article 265 TFEU could prove relevant in obliging the Union institutions to act, if this action could be construed also in light of the international obligations of the Union.[138]

In light of the above, it can be inferred that the review of legality of secondary acts, when leading to their annulment and voidance *ab initio*, would create *ex tunc* effects, amounting not only to cessation of the wrongful measures, but also to possible reimbursement when aiming to restore the wrongful consequences of the act (*restitutio in integrum*).[139] This action would include damage compensation, as long as the restoration of the negative effects of the illegal act may so require. This regime would not be possible under the judicial enforcement of DSB rulings or recommendations, given that they are limited to prospective effects only, which in turn could be preserved from the invalidation of the wrongful legislation.[140]

With respect to the effects of judicial review of secondary legislation in light of the WTO Agreement, it is obvious that such review could amount to an obligation of the wrongdoer to remedy the illegal measures.[141] This is not without implications for the legislative and executive processes within the Union's institutional framework. Accordingly, from the very nature of the WTO institutional framework, it can be inferred that it provides a forum of negotiations on trade relations, including the disputes arising in this context (Article III(2) WTO Agreement). Indeed, the process of consultation and negotiation permeates the entire dispute settlement system of the WTO. As such, the bargaining power constitutes a significant prerogative of the parties, which should be preserved during the entire process of settlement. In this respect, the ECJ has interpreted the Union law so as to preserve the necessary prerogative of its institutions to the benefit of a stronger polity in comparison with other trading partners. This underlying ground has direct implications on the legislative and executive activity. As maintained in the jurisprudence, even when the legality of measures is subject to judicial review, any prospective actions for damages against the Union should not hinder the legislative activity in pursuing the

[135]Eeckhout (2011), p. 322.

[136]Eeckhout (2011), p. 322.

[137]Eeckhout (2011), p. 322.

[138]Eeckhout (2011), p. 322.

[139]See also Eeckhout (2011), p. 369.

[140]Eeckhout (2011), p. 369.

[141]Joined Cases C-120/06 and C-121/06 *FIAMM and Fedon v Council and Commission*, [2008] ECR I-6513, para. 119. See further Eeckhout (2011), p. 300.

general interest.[142] As a result of this, no liability can be incurred from the Union for conduct falling within the sphere of its legislative competence, as long as any failure to comply with the WTO obligations cannot be invoked before the Union courts. This is particularly so when the Union enjoys a wide margin of discretion, unless the concerned institution has manifestly and gravely disregarded the limits in exercising its powers.[143]

It is questionable whether the pecuniary character of actions for compensation due to non-contractual liability of the Union could have any real deterrent effect on the institutions to change their political action in relation with DSB rulings.[144] Indeed, actions for compensation could barely lead to the annulment of EU measures.[145] However, the ECJ has been particularly aware of any potential limitations of the bargaining power of the EU institutions that would put them in a disadvantage against their counterparts. In view of that, the ECJ has abstained from any possibility of depriving the legislative or executive organs from maintaining any measures inconsistent with the WTO Agreement, to the benefit of a greater bargaining power toward other trading partners.[146] In light of this, although, in principle, the denial of direct effect does not prejudice the prerogatives of the judiciary to review the legality of actions of Union institutions, it still allows potential measures to violate individual interests to the benefit of the interests of the entire Union.

Whether the same construction could be employed to review the actions of Member States in terms of the WTO obligations, this is a different question, which remains subject to speculations insofar as the practice proves scarce in this direction. In principle, the ECJ has jurisdiction to adjudicate actions against Member States in violation of their Treaty obligations. In terms of the infringement proceedings, the obligation of the Union under the WTO can be designated as a concomitant obligation of the Member State under the same Agreement (Article 216(2) TFEU). Furthermore, even if the concerned WTO obligation falls within the exclusive powers of the Union, this obligation can be further extrapolated as an internal obligation of the Member State not to hinder the ability of the Union to comply with the WTO obligations, as an expression of the duty of loyalty pursuant to Article 4(3) TEU.[147] Indeed, the internal rules of organizations entail a 'good

---

[142] Joined Cases C-120/06 and C-121/06 *FIAMM and Fedon v Council and Commission*, [2008] ECR I-6513, para. 174.

[143] Joined Cases C-83/76 and 94/76, 4/77, 15/77 and 40/77, *HNL and others v Council and Commission* [1978] ECR I-1209, paras. 5, 6. See also Joined Cases C-120/06 and C-121/06 *FIAMM and Fedon v Council and Commission*, [2008] ECR I-6513, paras. 174, 176.

[144] See further on this argument Thies (2006), p. 1158.

[145] Thies (2006), p. 1166.

[146] Case C-149/96 *Portugal v Council*, [1999] ECR I-8395, paras. 40, 46.

[147] See further for an application of this principle in terms of the extrapolation of the international obligations of the Union as internal obligations of the Member States to the Union which has assumed responsibility for the due performance of the agreement Case C-13/00 *Commission v Ireland*, [2002] ECR I-2943, para. 15 and Opinion 1/94 of the Court of Justice *re WTO Agreement*, [1994] ECR I-5267, paras. 108–109. See further Eeckhout (2011), p. 302 and Wessel (2008), p. 180.

faith' obligation for the Member States not to hinder the effective enforcement of international agreements, in which the organization has lawfully entered.[148] This goes in line with the duty of loyalty of Member States to assist the Union in fulfilling its international obligations.

Amid various normative and non-normative reasons against the direct effect of the WTO Agreement in the EU legal order, without prejudicing its binding nature, one could also distinguish some systemic grounds supporting this line of arguments. Accordingly, the recognition of direct effect of the WTO Agreement in the EU legal order would nonetheless be compatible with the constitutional structure of the EU legal order. One of the first implications of recognition of direct effect would be the possibility of effective actions of individuals for damages or legality review in the ECJ pursuant to the WTO Agreement. This would subsequently transform the ECJ into an agency of the WTO judicial branch, without nevertheless offering the proper guarantees for correct interpretation of WTO law.[149] Since this institution is missing in the WTO level, it would be quite redundant for the EU legal order to provide more than the WTO Agreement provides. Furthermore, in a disintegrated system of adjudication, the direct effect would allow for proceedings being raised before the ECJ without first being submitted to the domestic courts. This would not only supersede the relevant jurisdiction of the Member States, but would also conflict with contradictory rulings of the DSB.[150] In such circumstances, not only would the principle of *res judicata* become obsolete, but also an overexertion of the judicial system in the EU legal order would possibly exceed any expectations of the WTO Agreement itself. Furthermore, this approach could interfere with the rationale and the *modus operandi* of the DSM,[151] which remains deferent to mutually accepted solutions, as an indicator of the positive solution of disputes (Article 3(7) DSU).

Obviously, a mutual acceptance of the DSB rulings and recommendations can be better achieved from a 'mediation-like' instrument, rather than by purely judicial organs. In view of this, the philosophy of a dispute settlement system may also allow for greater flexibility in the interpretation of WTO law, and as such, it may achieve a lower common denominator in the clash between compliance with WTO obligations and responsibility for breach of these obligations. Clearly, this goes to the detriment of legal certainty, clarity, precision, and conciseness, which are significant premises of an efficient direct effect regime.[152]

---

[148] Wessel (2008), p. 180.

[149] See further Eeckhout (2011), p. 376.

[150] Eeckhout (2011), p. 376.

[151] See also Eeckhout (2011), p. 377.

[152] Eeckhout (2011), p. 377.

As a conclusion, it can be maintained that the missing direct effect of the WTO Agreement in the EU legal order does not prejudice its binding effect upon the Union and its Member States. The constitutional nature of the WTO Agreement and its reception within the legal orders of the Union and its Member States constitute an additional argument in favor of the joint membership regime. The way in which the WTO normative processes operate requires the indispensable participation of both the Union and the concerned Member States, given that they supplement each other in the observation of WTO obligations to the best possible extent.

## IV. The Joint International Responsibility of the EU and Its Member States in the WTO Agreement

The joint responsibility regime is primarily a consequence of the inevitable joint membership of the EU and its Member States in the WTO Agreement, which is determined from a dynamic and unclear distribution of powers. Furthermore, the joint responsibility results also from the constitutional nature of the WTO Agreement, as a negotiations forum for the maintenance of trade concessions, and as unable for entailing a direct effect in the municipal legal orders. In light of these observations, this Section elaborates on particular facets of the joint responsibility regime, focusing on the fallacies of the distribution of burden of responsibility among participants. The question in this respect would be to consider how mixed agreements, and particularly the WTO Agreement, address the joint responsibility regime and the fallacies related with it.

From the above Sections, it became clear that the implications of the vertical distribution of powers on mixed agreements are a theoretical problem with practical relevance, although so far, practice has shown no significant cases with obvious negative consequences.[153] In principle, the attribution of responsibility to the EU or its Member States should be a simple exercise following the general rules of attribution of conduct pursuant to the distribution of competences. Intuitively, it could be proposed that the allocation of international responsibility between the Union and its Member States in cases of mixed agreements without a declaration of competences should follow the vertical division of powers.[154] This proposition constitutes however a weak argument, which is not supported from the doctrine and jurisprudence. The justice of this argument, mainly based on the claim that a wrongdoer should be held responsible for matters falling within the domain of its powers, cannot overcome the imperatives of structural deficiency in the Union polity. The underlying reason for this deficiency is based on the dynamic nature of competences in the Union, which may continuously alter the scheme of powers in the life cycle of a mixed agreement. In case that the attribution of responsibility

[153] See also Eeckhout (2011), p. 257.

[154] Eeckhout (2011), p. 262.

would be based on the criterion of apportion of competences, the distribution of responsibility may remain hostage of the complexity of the vertical distribution of powers in the EU polity.[155] The missing declaration of powers can be considered an indication that the parties have assumed the joint responsibility regime.[156] However, the presence or not of a declaration of powers *per se* cannot explain the regime of responsibility, given that such a regime is determined from systemic rather than formal reasons.

Indeed, the identification of the exact line dividing the matters falling within the conferred powers of the Union from the matters falling within the residual powers of Member States is quite difficult.[157] This difficulty precludes the adoption of a responsibility regime based on the distribution of powers. In this way, the thesis that the absence of a declaration of powers presumes the joint responsibility of the EU and its Member States aims to compensate for the structural deficiency of the Union polity.

The regime of responsibility could alternatively be identified based on the nature of obligations, whether they are undertaken jointly or independently from the EU and its Member States. The nature of obligations is determined indirectly from the ownership of competences on a particular area, whether they belong to the Union, the Member States, or are shared between them. In light of this, the determination of the quality of competences matters for the entire system of responsibility, and takes a particular relevance in the dispute settlement mechanism. Accordingly, the Member States may not be entitled to institute proceedings against third parties in a mixed agreement, if the competence for a disputed area is conferred to the Union. Similarly, a Member State may become subject to DSP in an international forum and, as such, it cannot refuse the proceedings on the ground that the EU is competent on the matter.[158] Even a declaration of competences would not sustain the refusal of Member States to be held answerable in such proceedings.[159] Hence, the separated powers regime in a mixed agreement does not necessarily lead to a regime of separated responsibilities, but may, in certain cases, lead to joint responsibility.

The inclusion within the joint responsibility regime of the responsibility related with the separated powers constitutes a sort of paradox. On the one hand, the regime of joint responsibility constitutes a regime that targets mainly the areas falling in the shared powers, as well as the powers of the EU and its Member States that are inextricably linked with each other. On the other hand, this regime includes also the responsibility that is attributed to one of the participants individually following the separated powers paradigm. If it would be possible to resolve this paradox,

[155]See for a similar logic on the relationship of the criterion of competence and the jurisdiction of ECJ Eeckhout (2011), p. 279.

[156]See for example Case C-316/91 *Parliament v Council*, ECR I-625, para. 29.

[157]Tomuschat (2002), p. 183.

[158]Eeckhout (2011), p. 240.

[159]Eeckhout (2011), p. 240.

obviously one could conceive a mixed model of responsibility. The joint responsibility would refer to the joint obligations with reference to shared powers, and other indistinguishable powers, while the several responsibility would correspond to areas for which the separation of powers would be possible. Instead, the joint responsibility regime has prevailed, in that the regime of joint responsibility appears to be a greater set that involves, in addition to its targeted powers, also the virtual regime of separated responsibility. As such, the correlation of this regime with the areas of powers that can be distinguished separately remains virtual. However, considering the ability to distinguish, on the basis of the ownership of competences, the powers of Member States from the powers of the Union, it is then possible to supplement the system of joint responsibility with a regime of several responsibility, whereby the owner of separated powers should be deemed responsible for its wrongful acts. The concepts of primary and subsidiary responsibility answer at best to this model.

The joint participation of the EU and its Member States in a mixed agreement, and furthermore, the absence of a declaration of powers in its signature, are strong indicators of the parties' failure to agree on an acceptable scheme of powers affected from the scope of the agreement. The missing declaration of powers in mixed agreements in general, and in the WTO Agreement in particular, entails the joint and several responsibility of the Union and its Member States.[160] The claims of third states for the breach of WTO obligations either from the EU or any of its Member States, particularly when the matter in dispute covers overlapping competences of both these entities, may be invoked jointly against the EU and the relevant Member States, but also severally against each of them.[161] The several responsibility of the Union and its Member States in the framework of the WTO Agreement became concrete when the United States of America invoked violation of TRIPS obligations against Ireland (WT/DS/82) and the European Communities (WT/DS/115) severally.[162] However, a mutually agreed solution on the dispute between the three parties avoided several DSPs to take place, hence without testing this option in practice. Hence, the joint responsibility regime remains so far the principal alternative confirmed in jurisprudence.

The joint responsibility regime cannot escape criticism in terms of the justice it does to the interests of Member States in relation with the distribution of the burden of responsibility. Accordingly, by attributing the responsibility to the parties that have taken joint obligations in the mixed agreements, notwithstanding the role of each of these parties in the wrongful conduct, this regime oversimplifies a structural problem in the Union polity caused by the vertical division of powers. Obviously,

---

[160]Case C-316/91 *Parliament v Council*, ECR I-625, para. 29.

[161]Hirsch (1995), pp. 24–25 and Neframi (2002), pp. 202–203.

[162]See *Ireland—Measures Affecting the Grant of Copyright and Neighbouring Rights*, (*Ireland – Copyright*), (WT/DS82) and *European Communities – Measures Affecting the Grant of Copyright and Neighbouring Rights* (WT/DS115), Notification of Mutually Agreed Solution of 13 November 2002(IP/D/8/Add.1 and IP/D/12/Add.1).

this regime echoes the prevailing thesis of objectification of international responsibility to the detriment of the subjective responsibility. Hence, the regime of joint responsibility ignores any requirements for the apportionment of obligations pursuant to the rules of organization,[163] which could lead to the apportionment of responsibility following the principle of the division of powers. Furthermore, the regime of joint responsibility may extend *de facto* the competences of the Union, given that Member States may have to accept responsibility for an act for which the Union is deemed *a priori* responsible, although they have never consented to, or do not have any legal or actual means to control the wrongful conduct.[164]

The joint and several responsibility regime in the context of international law can also be criticized, in that it inherits the same paradoxes as in the municipal legal order where it is conceived. In municipal law, the joint and several liability protects the injured party by imposing upon each wrongdoer an obligation to pay compensation for the entire injury, including the share of harm under the responsibility of another party.[165] In the context of international law, the parties are states, which by default remain quite concerned about the violation of their sovereignty, which in turn, might be encroached by the attribution of responsibility that should be attributed to another state.[166] However, the concerns on state sovereignty are not the only critics of the fallacious nature of joint and several responsibility in international law. Indeed, the joint responsibility regime constitutes a theoretical possibility for extending the outreach of the Union's scope of action toward areas that are not conferred to the Union, by diminishing in this way the authority of the Member States.

The fallacies of the joint responsibility regime from the EU law perspective, are based on the possibility of holding responsible a party for a wrongful act, which cannot be attributed to its wrongful conduct under the rules of attribution.[167] While this possibility is inconceivable in terms of the normative framework, this way of understanding is already confirmed from the doctrine and jurisprudence. Article 216(2) TEU provides that the Agreements concluded by the Union are binding upon the institutions of the Union and on its Member States. Given that mixed agreements, including the WTO one, are also binding upon the Union, any breach from the side of the Union's bloc would entail the responsibility to comply. The designation in mixed agreements of a proposition addressing the responsibility of the Union for breaches of Member States in the exercise of their residual powers would probably go too far. The doctrine has already acknowledged that the joint responsibility regime is indifferent as to the element of attribution of conduct.[168] As a

[163] Article 2(b) DARIO provides that the 'rules of the organization' include the constituent instruments, decisions, resolutions and other acts of the international organization adopted in accordance with those instruments, and the established practice of the organization.

[164] Heliskoski (2001), p. 151.

[165] Noyes and Smith (1988), p. 259.

[166] Noyes and Smith (1988), p. 259.

[167] See also Neframi (2002), p. 202.

[168] Neframi (2002), p. 202.

result, the Union may be held responsible for the implementation of the entire agreement, despite the fact that the wrongful conduct is attributed to its Member States, while the latter are responsible toward the Union for honoring their international obligations.[169] Furthermore, the Member States, as individual members of the mixed agreement, may be held responsible concurrently with the Union, if the rules of attribution should be duly followed.[170]

In the external dimension, the joint participation may be considered as an implicit mandate of the Union and its Member States to act in the areas of competence of each other.[171] When looking closely at this action, it is useful to emphasize that this implicit mandate cannot be absolute in both directions. Accordingly, the substantive rights of the Union from the WTO membership may be freely exercised from the Member States without any limitations, and this is due to the fact that the Member States of the EU are the main stakeholders of the EU as a customs union. The Union can hardly make use of the substantive rights of Member States. It rather exercises attributes of their formal obligations, particularly in terms of the answerability in DSP. In the international law context, this implied mandate is construed in light of the joint responsibility regime. In the context of EU law, this construction constitutes a fallacy, inasmuch as the formal obligations may be followed by secondary relationships leading to subsequent obligations, such as the cross-retaliatory measures that may be suffered from the Member States due to the Union participation in the DSP. Furthermore, the compliance of the Union with the formal obligations of the Member States in the context of WTO Agreement, insofar as the cross-retaliatory measures are concerned, has implications for the internal equilibrium of powers. The obligations that the Union may incur in the course of DSP may distress the residual powers of Member States, and as such may trigger internal tensions in the polity in case that not all Member States are willing to comply with the DSB rulings.

As to the submission to responsibility, the practice with the DSP has shown that the EU has assumed responsibility for wrongful actions of Member States falling within the exclusive powers of the Union, based on the argument of 'executive federalism'. This implies that the EU law, lacking a federal arm for its execution, becomes applicable automatically in Member States' territories.[172] The Member States' organs act as *de facto* organs of the Union when executing Union law; for any wrongful conduct in this course, the Union is to be held responsible in terms of WTO law and international law in general.[173] The justification of the Union to

[169]Cases C-104/81 *Hauptzollamt Mainz v Kupferberg*, [1982] ECR I-3641, para. 13 and C-12/86 *Demirel v Stadt Schwäbisch Gmünd*, [1987] ECR I-3719, paras. 9 and 11. It is to be noted that the ECJ in the *Demirel* Case was dealing with an association agreement pursuant to Article 217 TFEU. See further Neframi (2012), p. 326.

[170]Neframi (2002), p. 202.

[171]Neframi (2002), p. 201.

[172]Kuijper (2010), pp. 213–214.

[173]*EC – Trademarks and Geographical Indications* (WT/DS174/R), Report of the Panel of 15 March 2005, paras. 7.98 and 7.725.

assume answerability for actions of Member States in areas falling within the exclusive Union powers (customs tariffs) is based on the fact that the organs of the Member States were acting functionally as EU organs in applying EU law, given that the original schedules of concessions were withdrawn from the Member States to the benefit of the EU ones.[174] The transfer of powers from Member States to the Union level entails transfer of sovereignty, and this justifies the substitution (succession) of the Member States from the Union in terms of their WTO obligations. Obviously, answerability is the preceding step of responsibility to comply with the DSB rulings and recommendations. The Union, being offered answerable for any measures of the Member States, is very likely to be held responsible for the same measures, should they be found inconsistent with the WTO disciplines. The problem of the fallacy of joint responsibility regime becomes a concern, in that the practice of attributing the wrongful acts of Member States to the Union, without distinguishing the ownership of relevant competence, risks holding the Union responsible for wrongful acts falling within the areas of non-conferred competences.

From this course of arguments, it can be inferred that the Union should not claim answerability for matters falling within the residual powers of the Member States. The reason for this is the missing functional action of the Member States under the auspices of EU law. In light of this discourse, the fundamental question to be addressed is to understand the reasons that explain the Union's assumption of answerability for measures instituted from Member States in execution of their residual competences. Presumably, the Union assumes joint responsibility in the context of DSP in the name of Member States by virtue of the inextricable linkage of powers.

The joint participation of the EU and its Member States in mixed agreements reveals several challenges, and requires a proper justification, at least from a theoretical perspective. The joint participation of the EU and its Member States in mixed agreements, when considering the legal threats that it may cause for the international legal order, cannot be considered 'simply optional'. Any pragmatic behavior of a political character should be set aside to the benefit of a more appraised legal certainty. The justification of joint participation in international agreements becomes particularly relevant in cases of shared competences, given that by their nature, their exercise at the Union level may cease within the lifetime of mixed agreement, and this would lead to an increased level of uncertainty.[175] Indeed, the progressive expansion of treaty-making powers of the EU, as well as the dynamic path and the spill-over effect of the European legal integration, which has continuously expanded the powers of the Union institutions, constitute a clear concern for the legal uncertainty of third parties in international agreements. This is particularly related with the questions of membership of the EU and its Member

---

[174] *EC – Computer Equipment*, (WT/DS62, 67, 68/R), Report of the Panel of 05 February 1998, paras. 4.9–4.11, 4.15. See also Kuijper (2010), p. 214.

[175] See also Eeckhout (2011), pp. 216–217.

States in the decision-making institutions of treaties, voting rights, and the participation in the dispute settlement mechanisms.[176] As a result, third countries may not be certain as to the proper entity bearing international responsibility for breach of obligations established in a mixed agreement.[177] Hence, the missing declaration of powers, as a guide for the third parties on the responsibility of EU and its Member States, may be considered a handicap that is compensated from the joint responsibility regime.

Difficulties may however arise even in cases of mixed agreements with declaration of powers, insofar as the discourse of powers cannot be limited in the formal distribution of powers, but should take into account also their operation. These concerns are related with the principle of conferral, as a fundamental premise for the Union's internal and external action. This principle, as will be further discussed in the following Chapters, restricts the ability of the Union to take international obligations autonomously. Furthermore, the exercise of competences conferred to the Union can be indispensably related with the residual powers of the Member States. Similarly, certain non-conferred powers may hinder the accomplishment of conferred powers, and this leads to a vertical clash of authority claims. Hence, areas initially claimed to fall within the authority of the Union, may have their practical extension within the authority of the Member States. This could amount to the Union becoming practically unable to observe international obligations arising out of the mixed agreements.

The *EC – Asbestos* scenario evidenced that, even in an exclusive area of powers, such as GATT, there exist certain powers resting with the Member States. The *EC – Asbestos* concerned trade in goods, an area that is covered *in abstracto* from the exclusive competences of the Union. However, the imposition of a health measure, which amounted to a ban of trade with asbestos, was not enacted in the framework of any EU measure, but rather it resulted from the exercise of residual powers of France. Furthermore, even the health measures *per se*, cannot be easily construed within the category of shared or residual powers, given that they are included both in the list of Article 4 TEU (shared powers), and in Article 6 TEU (residual powers of Member States). Obviously, the determination of the ultimate authority which is competent to legislate in this area would be one of the main challenges for pursuing a legitimate solution on the matter. In light of this, one could pose several theoretical questions in relation with the contentious distribution of powers and the implications for the joint responsibility regime, and *vice versa*. Accordingly, to what extent could the responsibility of the EU in relation with a disputed measure (e.g. the French Decree) be *sufficiently* determined from the 'quantity' of EU legislation in a particular area (e.g. the number of measures regulating asbestos)? How likely is that the criterion of the 'quality' of legislation (measured by the causal link between the disputed measure and the EU legislation on asbestos) be disregarded in the assessment of competences? To what extent could the quantity of

[176]See also Eeckhout (2011), p. 218 and Simmonds (1989), pp. 108–109.

[177]Eeckhout (2011), p. 265.

measures be decisive for the unionization of particular areas, hence leading to the expansion of Union's competences toward non-conferred areas? Is this constellation able to produce legitimate consequences in terms of responsibility, if this is assessed in light of the law of international responsibility of states and international organizations?

With reference to jurisprudence, it is maintained that the ECJ has endorsed several assertions on these issues, which go beyond an extensive approach for interpretative jurisdiction.[178] The ECJ has maintained that Member States may not invoke their discretion for the exercise of residual powers on intellectual property rights in relation with obligations deriving from a mixed agreement, where the Union law covers *by large* the subject matter of the agreement.[179] The fact that a field may be covered 'by large' by the Union competence, although the competence is not effectively exercised from the Union, may suffice to preclude the discretion of Member States on the matter. This is so, even in case that the residual powers provide for the exclusive jurisdiction of a Member State over a matter in dispute. As a result, a Member State may be presumed in breach of obligations of the Union flowing from a mixed agreement, even if the subject matter in dispute falls within its residual powers, but is covered by large from the Union law.[180] As a remedy, infringement proceedings may be instituted before the ECJ against a Member State for breach of international obligations corresponding to areas falling within the residual powers of Member States, in order to prevent the Union from becoming internationally responsible for such wrongful acts.[181]

This construction amounts to the Union expanding its effective powers over areas that are residual with Member States. Hence, following the wide interpretation of the ECJ, the element of quantity of legislation (e.g. measures regulating asbestos in general) could prevail over the element of quality (i.e. the missing causal link between the disputed measure, namely the ban of asbestos from France, with the Union legislation in the same area of dispute). As to the quest for legitimacy, obviously this interpretation could be criticized based on the predictions of the general law of responsibility. Accordingly, the overriding of the quality criterion from the quantity one hinders the principle of attribution of conduct as a proposition of the *legi generali* of international responsibility. Hence, the consequences of this exercise cannot be legitimated by virtue of political motives, but have to find the relevant remedies within the Union, in order to ensure that the responsibility for the wrongful act is attributed to the proper subject that has committed that act. Only in this way, could the joint responsibility regime accomplish a certain degree of legitimacy and handle the systemic deficiencies of the distribution of powers.

---

[178] See also Neframi (2012), p. 328.

[179] Case C-13/00 *Commission v Ireland*, [2002] ECR I-2943, paras. 16–20 [*Berne Convention* Case].

[180] Case C-239/03 *Commission v France*, [2004] ECR I-598, paras. 27–31.

[181] *Ibid*, paras. 26, 29–30.

As much as the consequences of breach of WTO obligations are concerned, an overview of the material aspects of responsibility is also important, particularly in relation with the legitimacy of the allocation of burden. The breach of WTO obligations can be associated with a certain degree of material damages that are suffered mainly from the economic entities that operate in the international trade domain. These damages can typically consist of forgone advantages due to the withdrawal of trade concessions from contracting parties. In case that the Union, or any of its Member States, impose trade measures against a contracting party in violation with the regime of concessions, the cross border trade between the Union and the contracting party will be impaired. The trade privileges will obviously not be enjoyed any further from the trade operators, which may subsequently suffer loss of profits and other damages due to the decrease in trade volumes, as well as other negative effects from the competition. In these circumstances, any prudent business entity would endeavor to recover its damages, and the claim for non-contractual liability would be the conventional legal instrument remedying the injured rights.

The question to be addressed in this regard concerns the prospect of the non-contractual liability of the EU for non-compliance with the WTO Agreement for succeeding in the EU legal order. The EU law provides that the Union institutions are, in principle, obliged to make good any damage caused by its servants in the course of performance of their duties (Article 340(2) TFEU), while a similar obligation is presumably true also for the institutions of all the Member States. The ECJ has conceived the main cumulative conditions for establishing the regime of non-contractual liability for wrongful conduct. These conditions require that the infringed rule of law must be intended to confer rights; the breach must be sufficiently serious, in that the alleged wrongful action manifestly and gravely disregards the limits in discretion of the institutions; and that there must be established a causal link between the breach of obligations and the damages sustained by the injured party.[182] The denied direct effect of the WTO Agreement and the non-conferral of rights on individuals would, in principle, suffice to preclude the EU and its Member States to incur liability on the ground of violation of obligations.[183] Indeed, the jurisprudence has so far not succeeded in conceiving non-contractual liability in light of the WTO Agreement in relation to an unlawful conduct. This is due to the missing conferred rights of the Agreement, the lack of an expressed intention of the EU institutions in implementing particular obligations, or lack of an expressed reference in any particular provisions.[184] It remains uncertain

[182]Joined Cases C-46/93 and C-48/93 *Brasserie du Pêcheur and Factortame*, [1996] ECR I-1029, paras. 51, 55. The same practice was reaffirmed in Case C-352/98 P, *Bergaderm and Goupil v Commission*, [2000] ECR I-5291, paras. 42, 43.

[183]See for example Joined Cases C-120/06 and C-121/06 *FIAMM and Fedon v Council and Commission*, [2008] ECR I-6513, para. 176.

[184]Cases C-70/87 *Fediol v Commission*, [1989] ECR I-1781, para. 19 and C-149/96 *Portugal v Council*, [1999] ECR I-8395, para. 49. See also Joined Cases C-120/06 and C-121/06 *FIAMM and Fedon v Council and Commission*, [2008] ECR I-6513, para. 112. See also Case C-377/02 *Van Parys*, [2005] ECR I-1465, para. 40.

whether these conditions would suffice for triggering international responsibility of the wrongdoers, as long as the ECJ is quite restrictive in terms of discretionary powers of the Union or Member States institutions.

Since the non-contractual liability for wrongful acts is not established in the WTO context, from the judicial policy perspective, it could hardly be expected from the ECJ to establish non-contractual liability for lawful conduct. Therefore, the possibility of individuals incurring damages due to actions of institutions, which are not deemed unlawful, remains quite theoretical. Although the conditions of an actual damage, a causal link between the damage and the conduct of the institution, and the unusual and special nature of the damage would *ex hipothesi* be satisfied,[185] the ECJ could fail to establish any liability under the WTO Agreement due to the nature of damages. The latter are deemed quite usual in the course of international trade, and particularly in terms of the WTO Agreement, which is designed as a forum of political negotiations between trading partners.[186]

Notwithstanding any systemic limitations with regard to the consequences of international responsibility under the WTO Agreement for individuals, it should be emphasized, that this Agreement constitutes a binding instrument for the EU and its Member States. With this respect, it can be maintained that the regime of joint responsibility cannot be affected from the internal contest of powers. This could be sustained from the public international law perspective, as long as the question of the division of powers may be construed in light of the internal affairs of a polity. Accordingly, the internal law of states and the rules of organizations cannot be invoked as a justification for their failure to perform the treaties' obligations (Article 27 VCLT and Article 27 Vienna Convention on the Law of Treaties between States and International Organizations or between International Organizations (1986) (VCLTSIO)). In the context of WTO Agreement, this would imply that, as long as no specific indication is made, the EU and its Member States, in their quality as parties, cannot claim their internal distribution of powers for observing their WTO obligations. To ensure the legal certainty in relation with the third parties in this Agreement, both the EU and its Member States shall be held jointly responsible for honoring their obligations.[187]

However, even in this level of the analysis, it is useful to recall the central fallacy permeating the relationship between the joint responsibility regime and the internal division of powers in the Union polity, consisting in the formal-substantive gap of the WTO membership. Accordingly, both the Union and its Member States have entered the WTO Agreement with their individual powers, with the Union exercising its conferred powers, and the Member States exercising their residual powers.

[185]Case C-237/98 *Dorsch v Council*, [2000] ECR I-4549, para. 19. See also Joined Cases C-120/06 and C-121/06 *FIAMM and Fedon v Council and Commission*, [2008] ECR I-6513, para. 52, and Case C-81/86 - *De Boer Buizen v Council and Commission*, [1987] ECR I-3677, para. 17.

[186]See also Joined Cases C-120/06 and C-121/06 *FIAMM and Fedon v Council and Commission*, [2008] ECR I-6513, paras. 55, 56.

[187]See for general considerations on the matter Neframi (2002), p. 199. See also Heliskoski (2001), pp. 121–155.

This is a valid normative argument for entering a mixed agreement such as the WTO one.[188] Although from the international law perspective this fallacy does not influence the quality of a joint responsibility regime, from the EU law perspective, the division of powers deserves attention, inasmuch as the implementation of the WTO Agreement is concerned.[189]

## V. Conclusions

The question of international responsibility of the EU and its Member States in the context of WTO Agreement remains very complex and entails various fallacies, particularly in terms of the distribution of burden from the violation of WTO disciplines. This Chapter aimed to elaborate particular facets of these fallacies, as well as to establish a theoretical framework for the analysis of the premises and conditions of the participation of the EU and its Member States in the DSP, as well as for the management of fallacies of the joint responsibility regime.

An inquiry on the structure of powers in the Union polity revealed that, from an overview of the vertical distribution of competences in the Union polity, it is not possible to draw a clear and static separation of powers between the Member States and the Union. Rather, the scheme of powers is characterized of a dynamic nature caused from a continuous contest of powers from the participants in the polity. This entails the joint participation of the Union in the WTO Agreement, as a measure for mitigating the negative effects in the changing scheme of powers, and furthermore as a premise for the joint responsibility regime.

From an analysis of the claim that the reconceptualization of the common commercial policy, by including the areas of TRIPS and GATS within the scope of this policy, would resolve the problem of representation of the entire polity in the WTO, it became clear that the grounds for critics persist even after the constitutional changes brought by the Treaty of Lisbon. The designation of the EU as a sole representative of the Union polity, besides its practical advantages, cannot resolve the problem of protection of residual powers of the Member States, as a premise for the constitutional balance in the Union polity. Indeed, the designation of the common commercial policy so as to include the remaining areas covered from WTO, made the EU virtually competent to formally represent the entire Union polity, but not effectively able to conform with its formal aspects of the WTO membership, inasmuch as the Union does not hold the ultimate authority over all of these areas. Rather, the Member States uphold their residual powers, which are inextricably linked with the conferred powers included in the common commercial policy. As such, the Union cannot succeed the membership of Member States in the WTO Agreement.

[188]See also Neframi (2002), p. 201.

[189]See also Neframi (2002), p. 200.

In light of these observations, it became clear that the joint membership of the Union and its Member States in the WTO Agreement remains a guarantee for the constitutional balance between the conferred and residual powers. Hence, due to the inextricable linkage of powers in the Union polity, the joint membership in the WTO agreement remains the most convincing normative argument for avoiding any vertical frictions in the polity. This is in line with viewing mixed agreements as instruments for an inclusive approach toward contradicting interests, which serves as a premise for the constitutional balance in the Union polity, as opposed to an exclusive one.[190] Obviously, the inability to distinguish beforehand the ownership of competences, favors pragmatic solutions, such as the joint membership regime, which, although missing a compelling legal logic, remains plausible in terms of legal certainty.

Besides the internal constitutional factors supporting the joint membership regime, the constitutional nature of the WTO Agreement constitutes an addition argument in favor of this regime. The practice has proven that the WTO Agreement lacks direct effect in the legal orders of the EU and its Member States. As a consequence, the internal actions in the EU polity for attributing the responsibility, particularly inasmuch as liability is concerned, are in principle biased and, as such, have resulted unsuccessful. This has resulted in a restricted approach of the legality review of the Union's conduct; namely only in terms of the direct implementation of the WTO Agreement. This argument is grounded on the constitutional nature of the WTO Agreement, which is mainly based on the principle of negotiations of reciprocal concessions. It is particularly this argument that endorses the necessity for both the Union and its Member States to participate jointly in the WTO Agreement and to act jointly in the course of its implementation. This reflects an inclusive approach in terms of the participation of both the Union and its Member States in political-decisional and normative-judicial processes in the interest of their constitutional balance, and as a guarantee for the legal certainty for the implementation of the WTO Agreement.

The joint responsibility regime is not a mere outcome of the missing declaration of powers in the WTO membership, but rather results from a combination of internal and external constitutional factors. These factors have favored the prevalence of the pragmatic decision of the EU to represent its Member States in the DSP under the thesis of joint responsibility. This decision is cultivated gradually by means of the increasingly integrative forces within the EU polity. This process has also defined the dominant role of the Union in the international economic relations, hence resulting in an ever increasing eagerness of the Union to assume responsibility of the entire Union polity. Such behavior is qualified as pragmatic, not only due to a missing adequate normative framework, but also because the Union appears to be indifferent as to the fact that the assumption of responsibility could result in exercising the prerogatives of Member States, which derive from their residual powers. Obviously, this constitutes one of the crucial fallacies of the joint

[190] Heliskoski (2001), p. 27.

responsibility regime, which remains a concern, although so far has not caused any detrimental effects on the vertical relationship EU and its Member States.

The *EC – Asbestos* scenario illustrate the way in which these theoretical allegations may become a case for internal disputes in the future. The fallacies of the joint responsibility regime could particularly result in the unionization of residual powers of the Member States. The most obvious domain where the frictions may emerge due to these fallacies is the DSM. The participation in the DSP is an indication for the answerability of the Union, and the latter is a premise for responsibility. As such, the Union may become subject to retaliatory or cross-retaliatory measures for non-conforming with the DSB rules and recommendations in relation with WTO inconsistent measures instituted from Member States within the scope of their residual powers. The fallacy continues with the transposition of this problem into an internal issue, inasmuch as the respective Member State may refuse to comply with DSB rulings. Such refusal would essentially attribute to the Union the duty to remedy the injured WTO obligations, although the normative infrastructure at the EU level for obliging Member States to comply with their own WTO obligations is missing.

While explaining the facets of the joint responsibility regime and its fallacies, these arguments reveal also the question whether there exist any ways to ensure that the Union and its unrelated Member States remain unaffected from the consequences of this fallacy. Furthermore, would there be a way to allocate the burden of responsibility to the Member States to whom the wrongful act is attributed? These concerns are addressed by taking a closer look at the internal constitutional principles of the Union polity. These principles could assist in elaborating a model for the participation of the Union in the DSP, and at the same time, they could suggest relevant propositions for distributing the burden of responsibility on a normative basis.

## References

Antoniadis, Antonis. 2004. The Participation of the European Community in the World Trade Organization: An External Look at European Union Constitution-Building. In *European Union Law for the Twenty-First Century: Rethinking the New Legal Order*. Vol. 1: Constitutional and Public Law: External Relations, ed. Takis Tridimas and Paolisa Nebbia, 321–344. Oxford: Hart.

Bogdandy, Armin von. 2005. Legal Effects of World Trade Organization Decision Within European Union Law: A Contribution to the Theory of the Legal Acts of Damages Under Article 288(2) EC. *Journal of World Trade* 39: 45.

Bourgeois, Jacques H.J. 1997. Mixed Agreements: A New Aproach? In *La Communauté Europé enne et les Accords Mixtes: Quelles Perspectives?*, ed. Jacques H.J. Bourgeois, Jean-Louis Dewost, and Marie-Ange Gaiffe, 83–91. Conférences de Bruges, vol. 11. Bruxelles: Presses interuniversitaires européennes.

Cremona, Marise. 1982. The Doctrine of Exclusivity and the Position of Mixed Agreements in the External Relations of the European Community. *Oxford Journal of Legal Studies* 2: 393–428.

———. 2008. Defining Competence in EU External Relations: Lessons from the Treaty Reform Process. In *Law and Practice of EU External Relations: Salient Features of a Changing Landscape*, ed. Alan Dashwood and Marc Maresceau, 34–69. Cambridge: Cambridge University Press.

———. 2012. Member States Agreements as Union Law. In *International Law as Law of the European Union*, ed. Enzo Cannizzaro, Paolo Palchetti, and Ramses A. Wessel, 288–324. Studies in EU external relations, vol. 5. Boston: Martinus Nijhoff.

Dani, Marco. 2010. Remedying European Legal Pluralism: The FIAMM and Fedon Litigation and the Judicial Protection of International Trade Bystanders. *European Journal of International Law* 21 (2): 303–340. doi:10.1093/ejil/chq026.

Dashwood, Alan. 1997. Why Continue to Have Mixed Agreements at All? In *La Communauté Européenne et les Accords Mixtes: Quelles Perspectives?*, ed. Jacques H.J. Bourgeois, Jean-Louis Dewost, and Marie-Ange Gaiffe, 93–98. Conférences de Bruges, vol. 11. Bruxelles: Presses interuniversitaires européennes.

Dowrick, F.E. 1983. A Model of the European Communities' Legal System. *Yearbook of European Law* 3 (1): 169–237. doi:10.1093/yel/3.1.169.

Eeckhout, Piet. 1997. The Domestic Legal Status of the WTO Agreement: Interconnecting Legal Systems. *Common Market Law Review* 34: 11.

———. 2011. *EU External Relations Law*. 2nd ed. Oxford EU law library. Oxford, New York: Oxford University Press.

Geiger, Rudolf, Daniel-Erasmus Khan, and Markus Kotzur. 2015. *European Union Treaties. Treaty on European Union, Treaty on the Functioning of the European Union*. München; Oxford: Beck; Hart.

Heliskoski, Joni. 2001. *Mixed Agreements as a Technique for Organizing the International Relations of the European Community and Its Member States*. The Hague, New York: Kluwer Law International.

Hilf, Meinhard. 1995. The ECJ's Opinion 1/94 on the WTO: - No Surprise, but Wise?. *European Journal of International Law* 6 (1): 245–259. doi:10.1093/ejil/6.1.245.

Hirsch, Moshe. 1995. *The Responsibility of International Organizations Toward Third Parties. Some Basic Principles*. Dordrecht, Boston: Martinus Nijhoff.

Jacobs, Francis G. 2008. Direct Effect and Interpretation of International Agreements in the Recent Case Law of the European Court of Justice. In *Law and Practice of EU External Relations: Salient Features of a Changing Landscape*, ed. Alan Dashwood and Marc Maresceau, 13–33. Cambridge: Cambridge University Press.

Kuijper, Pieter. 1995a. The Conclusion and Implementation of the Uruguay Round Results by the European Community. *EJIL* 6: 222–244.

Kuijper, Pieter-Jan. 1995b. The New WTO Dispute Settlement System: The Impact on the Community. In *The Uruguay Round Results: A European Lawyers' Perspective*, ed. Jacques H.J. Bourgeois, Frédérique Berrod, and Eric Gippini Fournier, 87–114. Bruges conferences, vol. 8. Brussels: European Interuniversity Press.

Kuijper, Pieter Jan. 2010. International Responsibility for EU Mixed Agreements. In *Mixed Agreements Revisited: The EU and Its Member States in the World*, ed. Christophe Hillion and Panos Koutrakos, 208–227. Modern studies in European law, vol. 21. Oxford [England], Portland, OR: Hart.

MacLeod, I., I.D. Hendry, and Stephen Hyett. 1996. *The External Relations of the European Communities. A Manual of Law and Practice*. Oxford, New York: Clarendon Press; Oxford University Press.

Maduro, Miguel Poiares. 2009. Courts and Pluralism: Essay on a Theory of Judicial Adjudication in the Context of Legal and Constitutional Pluralism. In *Ruling the World?: Constituetionalism, International Law, and Global Governance*, ed. Jeffrey L. Dunoff, 365–379. Cambridge: Cambridge University Press.

Neframi, Eleftheria. 2002. International Responsibility of the European Community and of the Member States Under Mixed Agreements. In *The European Union as an Actor in International Relations*, ed. Enzo Cannizzaro, 193–205. The Hague, New York: Kluwer Law International.

———. 2012. Mixed Agreements as a Source of European Union Law. In *International Law as Law of the European Union*, ed. Enzo Cannizzaro, Paolo Palchetti, and Ramses A. Wessel, 325–349. Studies in EU external relations, vol. 5. Boston: Martinus Nijhoff.

Noyes, John E., and Brian D. Smith. 1988. State Responsibility and the Principle of Joint and Several Liability. *Yale Journal of International Law* 13: 225.

Petersmann, Ernst-Ulrich. 1986. The EEC as a GATT Member - Legal Conflicts Between GATT Law and European Community Law. In *The European Community and GATT*, ed. Meinhard Hilf, Francis Geoffrey Jacobs, and Ernst-Ulrich Petersmann, 23–72. Studies in transnational economic law, vol. 4. Deventer, The Netherlands, Boston: Kluwer.

Rossi, Lucia Serena. 2012. Does the Lisbon Treaty Provide a Clearer Separation of Competences Between EU and Member States? In *EU Law After Lisbon*, ed. Andrea Biondi, Piet Eeckhout, and Stefanie Ripley, 85–106. Oxford [England], New York: Oxford University Press.

Sack, Jörn. 1995. The European Community's Membership of International Organizations. *Common Market Law Review* 32 (5): 1227–1256.

Salles, Luiz Eduardo. 2014. *Forum Shopping in International Adjudication: The Role of Preliminary Objections*. Cambridge: Cambridge University Press.

Schermers, Henry G. 1983. International Organizations as Members of Other International Organizations. In *Völkerrecht als Rechtsordnung, Internationale Gerichtsbarkeit, Menschenrechte: Festschrift für Hermann Mosler*, ed. Hermann Mosler and Rudolf Bernhardt, 823–838. Beiträge zum ausländischen öffentlichen Recht und Völkerrecht, vol. 81. Berlin, New York: Springer.

Simmonds, Kenneth R. 1989. The European Economic Community and the New Law of the Sea. In *Recueil des cours: Collected Courses of the Hague Academy of International Law*, VI, 9–166. Collection, Tome 218. Dordrecht: Martinus Nijhoff.

Tancredi, Antonello. 2012. On the Absence of Direct Effect of the WTO Dispute Settlement Body's Decisions in the EU Legal Order. In *International Law as Law of the European Union*, ed. Enzo Cannizzaro, Paolo Palchetti, and Ramses A. Wessel, 249–268. Studies in EU external relations, vol. 5. Boston: Martinus Nijhoff.

Thies, Anne. 2006. Cases T-69/00, *FIAMM and FIAMM Technologies*, T-151/00, *Le Laboratoire du Bain*, T-301/00, *Fremaux*, T-320/00, *CD Cartondruck*, AG, T-383/00, *Beamglow Ltd* and T-135/01 *Giorgio Fedon &(and) Figli S.p.A., Fedon S.r.l. and Fedon America USA Inc.*, Judgments of 14 December 2005, Grand Chamber of the Court of First Insurance. *Common Market Law Review* 43 (2): 1145–1168.

———. 2013. *International Trade Disputes and EU Liability*. Cambridge studies in European law and policy. New York.

Timmermans, C.W.A. 1981. Division of External Powers Between Community and Member States in the Field of Harmonization of National Law. A Case Study. In *Division of Powers Between the European Communities and Their Member States in the Field of External Relations: Colloquium, 30 and 31 May 1980, Amsterdam*, 15–28. Deventer, Netherlands: Kluwer.

Timmermans, Christiaan. 2000. Organising Joint Participation of E.C. and Member States. In *The General Law of E.C. External Relations*, ed. Alan Dashwood and Christophe Hillion, 239–247. London: Sweet & Maxwell.

Tomuschat, Christian. 2002. The International Responsibility of the European Union. In *The European Union as an Actor in International Relations*, ed. Enzo Cannizzaro, 177–191. The Hague, New York: Kluwer Law International.

Weiler, Joseph H.H. 1999. *The Constitution of Europe: "Do the New Clothes Have an Emperor?" and Other Essays on European Integration*. Cambridge: Cambridge University Press.

Wessel, Ramses A. 2008. The EU as a Party to International Agreements: Shared Competences, Mixed Responsibilities. In *Law and Practice of EU External Relations: Salient Features of a Changing Landscape*, ed. Alan Dashwood and Marc Maresceau, 152–187. Cambridge: Cambridge University Press.

# Chapter 4
# The Responsibility of the Union Polity in the WTO in Light of the Constitutional Framework of Principles

## I. Introduction

The analysis of the international responsibility of the EU and its Member States in the context of their WTO membership endorsed the thesis that the joint responsibility regime is an answer for the systemic challenges within the constitutional infrastructure of the Union polity. The EU legal order is a creation of public international law, and its supranational features define it as "a developed form of international organization which displays characteristics of an embryonic federation".[1] These considerations reaffirm the highly disputed nature of the Union polity, which is based on a legal order that accommodates various conflicting interests and tensions. In view of this, the EU and its Member States constitute a polity that combines the actions of supranational and intergovernmental institutions. This intertwined nature of governmental actions, which results in a fusion of mixed powers of all participants, constitutes a systemic premise that triggers joint responsibility in terms of other areas of international law.

This state of tension is reflected also in the case of the WTO membership, where the Union cannot participate as a sole representative of the Member States, although the common commercial policy constitutes an exclusive competence of the Union. In particular, the vertical distribution of powers and the internal political-decisional practices in the Union could be regarded as ultimate reasons for the mixed participation of the EU and its Member States in the WTO Agreement and for the joint responsibility regime.[2] The internal constitutional arrangements of the Union polity may provide relevant normative predictions for addressing the fallacies of the joint responsibility regime. This is based on the assumption that the EU legal order accommodates the main premises on which the fallacies of the joint responsibility

[1] Arnull and Wyatt (2006), p. 132. See further Witte et al. (2011), p. 53.
[2] See also Eeckhout (2011), p. 221 and Ehlermann (1983), p. 6.



P. Ruka, *The International Legal Responsibility of the European Union in the Context of the World Trade Organization in Areas of Non-Conferred Competences*,
DOI 10.1007/978-3-319-57177-5_4

regime occur. These premises are anchored in the federal relationship of the Union polity, and are explained from the structure of powers in the polity.

The central thesis underlying this Chapter presumes that the joint responsibility regime has a systemic character, which is rooted in the EU legal order, and as such, it can be explored by analyzing its constitutional principles. This highlights the main constitutional premises for conceiving a normative model for the EU participation in the DSP, as a precondition for preventing the fallacies of the joint responsibility regime, as well as for managing the consequences of this participation. A framework of selected constitutional principles is proposed for the analysis of particular aspects of the responsibility of the EU and its Member States in the WTO.

From a methodological point of view, the framework of principles shall be used as a tool for criticizing the state of the law and practice in relation with the joint responsibility regime, as well as a dogmatic instrument for elaborating a normative framework for addressing the fallacies of this regime from a constitutional perspective.[3] By means of the constitutional framework of principles, it is possible to elaborate further on certain factors that explain the joint responsibility regime and its fallacies. Obviously, this framework cannot be detached from the legal traditions of the Member States, which could occasionally contribute in the analysis.[4] All these premises assist in elaborating a model of participation of the EU in the DSP, which answers the challenges of the current state of the law and practice with more realistic predictions.

This framework consists of a three-pillar model, where each of the pillars is seen as an extension of the principle of the rule of law in the EU legal order. The framework of principles regards the principle of the rule of law as the central premise for the construction of all legal relationships in the polity, which is addressed at the outset of this Chapter. The first pillar to be considered is the thesis of the unity of the EU legal order as an expression of the rule of law, which is realized through the principle of effectiveness. The second pillar addresses the principle of the rule of law and the principles of political organization in the polity. The third pillar refers to the rule of law and the principles of political processes. All these pillars maintain the institutional federal balance, which is a premise for addressing the fallacies of the joint responsibility regime by means of the normative model of the Union participation in the DSP.

[3]According to Bogdandy, the "[p]rinciples form the epicentre of a legal scholarship striving for autonomy and searching for a disciplinary proprium behind the multifariousness of norms and judgments." Bogdandy (2010), p. 12.

[4]This is based on the idea that the constitutional principles can evolve even from a minority of Member States, as long as they meet the requirements of the EU legal order. Joined Cases C-120/06 and C-121/06 *FIAMM and Fedon v Council and Commission*, [2008] ECR I-6513, Opinion of the AG Poiares Maduro, para. 55.

## II. The Principle of the Rule of Law as a Premise for Justice and Unity in the Union

The principle of the rule of law permeates all the legal relationships in the Union polity.[5] This principle is essential for the normative value of the EU legal order and for its unity and effectiveness. The central idea of a 'community of law' is based on the assumption that the constellation of legal propositions ensures the exercise of public authority and the transactions of all actors by means of legal rules.[6] In the EU, the rule of law constitutes a common denominator for the Union and the Member States, and is regarded as a fundamental value of the Union, which is guaranteed from the EU institutions.[7] Further to its function for protecting individuals from the governing authority, the principle of the rule of law implies that in EU matters, the EU law rules in an effective way, autonomously from the will of political and administrative actors.[8]

The EU law may rule effectively by overcoming the challenging effects that emerge from municipal legal orders of the Member States in the form of federal tensions, and from the external fragments of international law where the EU and its Member States participate. Obviously, these tensions represent the diverging interests of the Member States, which occasionally collide with the interests of the Union. The Member States, as primary stakeholders of the Union, have endowed the polity with their trust and sovereignty in order to pursue the interests of the Union as a whole and to deliver benefits of a public nature for all the participants. The principle of the rule of law serves as the principal guarantee for this trust by ensuring cooperative behavior of all the parties and by preventing or compensating for any potential defections. In view of this, one of the primary effects of the rule of law is to guarantee the legal certainty in a polity where the federal tensions emerge as a manifestation of the authority claims of the participating legal orders.

In the absence of a hierarchy between the three sets of legal orders of the Member States, the EU and international law, the function of the EU legal system is to smoothly accommodate the various and contradicting claims of authority without nevertheless hindering the effectiveness of other legal orders, or by compensating for any potential cleavages among conflicting claims. In this way, the EU legal order can be seen as a hub that ensures the unity of the legal orders by

---

[5]The principle of the rule of law, sometimes interpreted either as a philosophy or political theory, is defined as "the supremacy of law", as distinguished from moral norms of the society. Barnet (2006), p. 67.

[6]This understanding of the 'rule of law', which is coined by Professor Dicey as of 1885, suggests for the absolute predominance of regular law by means of constraining governmental arbitrary authority against citizens; the equal subjection of all subjects to the law; and that the personal freedoms are formulated by ordinary law rather than by abstract constitutional declarations. Martin (2002), p. 441. See also Dicey (1885), p. 175 et seq.

[7]Articles 2, 7 TEU and Article 263 TFEU.

[8]Bogdandy and Ioannidis (2014), p. 5.

accommodating the tensions in a pluralistic manner, and by solving conflicts through the prioritization of interests based on normative rules, principles, and values. Similarly to federal entities, the Union also "presents a tension between the whole and the parts, centrifugal and centripetal forces, central [Union] organs and Member States".[9] The coherence between these legal orders is responsible for the state of unity that dominates the EU legal system, and ensures that different systems are treated equally; this being a significant premise for justice in the polity. In this sense, the "unity is constitutive for diversity" within the Union polity.[10] This relationship between diverse legal orders, is a feature of the European integration, and explains how very diverse economies, social structures, national identities, traditions and cultures are to a great extent structured in harmony with each other, even in the absence of a formal federative constitutional document.

However, without ignoring the incidental federative effects that the Treaties create for the constitutional structure of the EU, the absence of a formal constitution denotes the dominance of diversity in the EU polity. Various authors argue that the process of constitutionalization requires the constitution to 'permeate' all legal relationships in the polity.[11] In view of this, the absence of a formal constitution does not reject the conduct of certain constitutionalization processes, which essentially suggests that constitutional processes in the unity lead to the creation of laws with constitutional value.[12] The unity of the EU legal order constitutes an important consequence of the constitutionalization processes that have taken place continuously in the Union polity. The principles have assisted the jurisprudence in conceiving and shaping the constitutional law in the EU. On a parallel level, the legislative activity has ensured the harmonization of the legal systems of Member States. The combination of the constitutionalization and harmonization processes makes the EU legal system very dynamic, but able to preclude internal fragmentation concerns.

The joint responsibility regime is a prime example of the potential tensions that the fragmentation of international law could bring for the Union polity. The fallacious effects of this regime in relation with the distribution and devolution of responsibility from the WTO membership contrary to the rules of attribution constitute a case for internal constitutional tensions in the Union polity. The constitutionalization processes in the Union polity constitute a premise for conceiving an adequate infrastructure for addressing the fallacies of the joint responsibility regime. Hence, the institutional framework of the Union polity is able to conduct processes of a constitutional character that address the issue of the EU participation in the DSP, as well as the fallacies of the joint responsibility regime.

---

[9]Weiler (1981), p. 268.

[10]Bogdandy (2010), pp. 26, 28, referring also to Hegel, GWF, Wissenschaft der Logik I, 1932, originally 1832, ed Lasson, 59.

[11]Bogdandy (2010), p. 16, referring also to Hegel, GFW, Rechtsphilosophie, (1821; edited by Moldenhauer and Michel from 1970), § 274.

[12]Peters (2006), p. 36.

This is ensured by managing the problems of mixity of the WTO Agreement in relation with the distribution of responsibility within the polity.

The relevance of the principle of the rule of law for addressing the fallacies of the joint responsibility regime is however rather abstract, inasmuch as this principle would predict for the constitutional processes too general propositions. Other subprinciples of the rule of law are more adequate for these processes. These principles are analyzed in relation with different facets of the responsibility of the Union polity from the WTO membership. For systematic purposes, these principles are grouped in three different pillars, which address, respectively, the unity and effectiveness of the EU legal order (through the principles of primacy and autonomous legal order, direct effect and direct applicability, comprehensive legal protection, and state liability), the principles of the political organization (including the principles of dual legitimacy, structural compatibility, constitutional tolerance, and loyalty), and the principles of political processes (which include the principles of constitutional legality, conferral, the implied powers doctrine, and the principles pursuing the federal balance in the Union, such as subsidiarity and proportionality).

## III. The Unity of the EU Legal Order Through the Principle of Effectiveness and the Predictions for the Joint Participation in the DSP

The effectiveness of the EU legal order is an extension of the principle of rule of law, and consists of a number of principles that serve to the unity of the legal order, such as the principles of primacy, autonomy of the EU legal order, the direct effect and direct applicability, the comprehensive legal protection, and the principle of liability. The thesis of unity under the principle of effectiveness shall be addressed as a cognitive process for exploring its relevance for the fallacies of the joint responsibility regime and for the model of participation in the DSP.

The principle of effectiveness refers to the effectiveness of legal norms. It constitutes a 'creation' of the jurisprudence, and has assisted the ECJ in its way of expanding its constitutional role for structuring the relationship between the legal orders of the EU and its Member States.[13] As such, it has backed-up the policy of legal integration by enhancing the effectiveness of EU law and implanting it into the national legal orders.[14] Its content primarily "includes an obligation on national courts to ensure [that] they give adequate effect to EU law in cases arising before them".[15] The principle of effectiveness ensures the *output legitimacy* of the Union,

[13] Bogdandy (2010), p. 29.

[14] See also Graig and de Búrca (2011), p. 65.

[15] Graig and de Búrca (2011), p. 218.

and at the same time, it allows for the *uniform application of EU law*, which is fundamental for achieving legal equality.[16] The principle of equality is another precondition for the protection of diversity and the enhancement of unity within the Union.[17] The concept of unity of the legal order rests on the idea of uniformity.[18] Only through the uniform application of EU law can the EU legal order be effective, and as such, it would be able to deliver the expected legitimacy. The latter is one of the normative criteria of democratic legitimacy, which is judged in terms of the EU policy outcomes for the people.[19]

The principle of effectiveness, if perceived as an encompassing concept for the implementation, enforcement, and compliance of the EU legal order, is achieved through the cooperation of the EU institutions with the national institutions that perform the indirect administration of EU norms.[20] The Member States are required to interpret the EU legal norms in an effective way in order to preserve the effectiveness of the EU legal order, which in turn is a precondition for the validity of the EU constitutional norms.[21] A valid EU constitutional framework is able to produce legitimate legal norms. With these predictions in mind, it might be possible to construe a normative standard for assessing the systemic fallacies of the joint responsibility regime of the WTO membership, and to suggest a legitimate model

[16]Bogdandy (2010), p. 30. By asserting the need for uniformity, the ECJ has affirmed that for the purpose of determining the meaning and scope of EU norms, it should be given an independent and uniform interpretation throughout the EU; an interpretation that must consider the context of the provision and the purpose of the relevant regulations. See for example Cases C-327/82 *Ekro BV Vee- en Vleeshandel v Produktschap voor Vee en Vlees*, [1984] ECR I-107, para. 11; C-287/98 *Grand Duchy of Luxemburg v Berthe Linster, Aloyse Linster and Yvonne Linster*, [2000] ECR I-6917, para. 43; C-357/98 *The Queen v Secretary of State for the Home Department, ex parte Nana Yaa Konadu Yiadom*, [2000] ECR I-9265, para. 26; C-170/03 *Staatssecretaris van Financiën v J. H. M. Feron*, [2005] ECR I-2299, para. 26; C-316/05 *Nokia Corp. v Joacim Wärdell*, [2006] ECR I-12083, para. 21; and C-195/06 *Kommunikationsbehörde Austria (KommAustria) v Österreichischer Rundfunk (ORF)*, [2007] ECR I-8817, para. 24.

[17]*Ibid.*

[18]Chalmers et al. (2010), p. 160.

[19]On the normative criteria of democratic legitimacy see further Schmidt (2013), p. 2.

[20]Accetto and Zleptnig (2005), p. 381.

[21]This proposition is based on a strictly positivist approach, according to which, *the supposition that the constitution is a valid norm is only true if the legal order that is established on its basis pursuant to the principle of legitimacy, is effective*, in so far as it is actually applied and obeyed. The principle of effectiveness is considered an essential precondition for a legal order to exist, because the effectiveness is regarded as a *conditio sine qua non*, rather than as a rationale for the validity of its constituent norms. Therefore, the norms are valid not because the total legal order is effective, but because they are established in conformity with the constitution, which is valid only if the total legal order is effective. Hence, the principle of effectiveness can be defined as a fundamental norm of the positive international law, which restricts the principle of legitimacy by defining its limits, in that an ineffective legal order ceases to be legitimate because the constitution is no longer effective, and as such it is unable to produce a valid legal order. In this way, it is argued that the principles of effectiveness and legitimacy are different but dependent on each other as regards the validity of norms. See further on this analysis, Kelsen and Tucker (1966), pp. 560–561.

for the EU participation in the DSP. In practical terms, this would mean that the decision of the Union to participate in the DSP for matters falling outside its areas of competences should comply with the normative framework of the EU legal order in order to produce legitimate outcomes. The Member States should make this decision effective, so as to allow for its actual application and obedience.

If built on the premises of *EC – Asbestos* Case, these predictions would mean that a decision of the DSB that obliges the Union to withdraw the trade measure enacted by France should be made effective from the Member States. In principle, pursuant to Article 216(2) TFEU, France would be obliged to comply with the DSB ruling, as an indirect result of the EU decision to participate in the DSP. From an internal constitutional perspective, the refusal of France to comply with the DSB rulings would amount to an EU norm being ineffective, and as such, it can be regarded as a violation of the Treaty provisions, namely Articles 2 and 4(3) TEU, i.e. the rule of law and the duty to cooperate. From the perspective of the WTO obligations, the refusal of France to comply with the DSB rulings and recommendations amounts to a breach of (formal) obligations from the EU. As a result, the Union may become subject to retaliatory or cross-retaliatory measures, which subsequently may be devolved to unrelated Member States. These measures are a direct result of the EU decision to participate in the DSP, and as such, they are binding for the entire polity.

As much as the enforcement of DSB rulings is concerned, the refusal of France to comply with the DSB decision, may entitle the Commission to initiate infringement proceedings pursuant to Articles 258, 260 TFEU in relation with the material violation of Articles 2, 4(3) TEU and Article 216(2) TFEU, namely the principles of rule of law, loyalty and the duty to comply with the international obligations of the Union. The other Member States and their individuals incurring welfare loss due to the Canadian retaliatory measures do not have significant remedies in their disposal. As already maintained in jurisprudence, the victims of a trade measure that results from the Union's actions lack the *ratione materiae* for claiming damages against the Union.[22] This is in line with the Council Decision concluding the WTO Agreement, which converges with the position endorsed in jurisprudence that, by its nature, the WTO Agreement is not susceptible to being directly invoked in the Union or Member States' courts.[23] In this regard, the principle of effectiveness could support cessation actions or political processes against France to comply with the DSB, but fails to redress the fallacies of the joint responsibility regime in terms of the damage compensation. However, the principle of effectiveness remains the basis for construing a number of subprinciples, which provide important predictions for the question of joint responsibility.

---

[22]Joined Cases C-120/06 and C-121/06 *FIAMM and Fedon v Council and Commission*, [2008] ECR I-6513, paras. 49–56, 132–133, 176–188. See further Chalmers et al. (2010), p. 655.

[23]Council Decision 94/800/EC (of 22 December 1994) concerning the conclusion on behalf of the European Community, as regards matters within its competence, of the agreements reached in the Uruguay Round multilateral negotiations (1986–1994) [1994] OJ L336/1, 2, last recital.

## *1. The Relevance of the Principles of Primacy and Autonomous Legal Order for the Joint Membership of the EU and Its Member States in the WTO Agreement*

The thesis that the EU legal order must be effective in order to be valid and to produce legitimate results, is materialized by means of other principles, such as the principles of primacy and autonomous legal order. The fallacies of the joint membership regime of the EU and its Member States challenge the thesis of validity, inasmuch as the achievement of legitimate outcomes is concerned. This regime could lead to illegitimate consequences, such as the wrongful devolution of burden from retaliatory measures that disregard the rules of attribution of wrongful conduct. This Section addresses the predictions of the principles of primacy and autonomous legal order with regard to the fallacious model of the joint responsibility regime, as a premise for preserving the effectiveness and validity of the EU legal order.

The principles of autonomous legal order and primacy are the forerunner of the EU constitutionalization processes, in that they have served as stepping-stones for conceiving the EU Treaties as a 'new legal order' of public international law.[24] In order to overcome the weakness of the public international law model of intergovernmental consensus, it became obvious that the EU legal order had to claim a different kind of authority, an autonomous one, which would be binding upon the Member States, but at the same time, would not supersede their universal sovereignty. The Member States have attributed to this domain a certain degree of autonomy, which in turn is curtailed to them.[25] This is achieved through the constitutionalization of treaties, a process that has exceeded the conventional treaty interpretations of international law, whose canons reject the thesis of 'sovereignty loss'.[26] In this way, the ECJ immunized the autonomy of the EU legal order by claiming that subsequent unilateral domestic provisions cannot override the EU law.[27] It follows that, the valid adoption of new national legislation incompatible with EU law is precluded, while any existing conflicting national norm is rendered inapplicable. This 'negative' way of determining the autonomy was the basis for conceiving the primacy of the EU legal order as a regime of precedence over the conflicting national laws. In addition to this functional approach, the ECJ employed a 'contractarian' (or more 'positivistic') argument to affirm that Member States agreed to give primacy to EU law by creating a specific legal order, which became

[24]Case C-26/62 *Van Gend en Loos v Administratie der Belastingen*, [1963] ECR I-001, 12, para. 4 and Case C-6/64 *Flaminio Costa v E.N.E.L.*, [1964] ECR I-585, 594.

[25]Amtenbrink (2012), p. 54. Referring also to Timmermans (2008a), p. 78.

[26]Weiler (1981), p. 270.

[27]Case C-6/64 *Costa v E.N.E.L.*, [1964] ECR I-585, 594 and Case C-106/77 *Amministrazione delle Finanze dello Stato v Simmenthal SpA.*, [1978] ECR I-629, para. 17.

an integral part of their national legal systems, and by limiting their sovereignty in order to empower the Union institutions with rights to legislate.[28] Furthermore, they have acknowledged the normative value of the primacy by affirming that the Treaties and their consequent legislation have precedence over the laws of the Member States under the conditions settled by case law.[29] The regime of primacy does not suggest, however, any voidance of municipal laws, but rather provides for the inability of the latter to make the EU law ineffective.

The current constellation of norms in the EU legal order has opted in favor of the principle of primacy of EU law, which in turn "does not succeed in creating complete unity by establishing a strict hierarchy; rather, at the center of the constitutional interplay one finds an 'unregulated' relationship due to the competing jurisdictional claims".[30] In the absence of a formal hierarchy, the principle of primacy illustrates the advancement of the EU legal order into a 'like-supranational' one, which has gained many features of a federation without having a formal constitution that subordinates the legal orders of the Member States to the EU legal order. This thesis is based on the prediction that the positive harmonization of legal orders under the initiative of the Commission, combined with the negative integration under the auspices of the ECJ, has established a form of "*normative supranationalism*".[31] This concept represents the relationship and hierarchy between Union policies and legal measures with competing policies and legal measures of Member States that led to a deepening process of the EU integration.

The principle of primacy plays an instrumental role for the effectiveness of the EU legal order, in that it serves as a conflict rule in cases of competition between EU norms and national norms.[32] Its main function is to 'neutralize' the conflicting national norms that would challenge the effects of the EU norms in a unilateral way. The way in which this function is accomplished constitutes the conceptual differentiation of the principle of primacy from supremacy.[33] The prevalence of EU law toward conflicting national norms by means of inapplicability rather than voidance suggests for a pluralist approach of conflict resolution between the EU and Member

[28]Graig and de Búrca (2011), p. 258, commenting on Case C-6/64 *Costa v E.N.E.L.*, [1964] ECR I-585.

[29]Declaration No. 17 annexed to the Final Act of the Intergovernmental Conference which adopted the Treaty of Lisbon, dated on 13 December 2007 (Declaration No. 17 annexed to the ToL).

[30]Bogdandy (2010), p. 32.

[31]Accetto and Zleptnig (2005), p. 380. Referring also to Weiler (1981), p. 271 *et seq.*

[32]See also Neframi (2010), pp. 325–326.

[33]The differentiation of the concepts of 'primacy' and 'supremacy' is made at a theoretical level only by some authors, such as Bogdandy, although the majority of legal scholarship does not distinguish between these terms. Without nevertheless ignoring the relevance of this debate, the author of this work adopts the concept of primacy in line with Declaration No. 17 annexed to the Treaty of Lisbon. See further on this matter Dashwood (2011), p. 270 *et seq.*, Graig and de Búrca (2011), p. 256 *et seq.*, Martin (2002), p. 487, Chalmers et al. (2010), p. 203 *et seq.*, Bogdandy (2010), p. 32.

States.[34] Hence, the effects of a conflicting national norm are apportioned, and consequently only those that restrict the effects of EU law are precluded, while the other part remains in force.

The ECJ has asserted the absolute prevalence of EU law against conflicting national norms, including the constitutional ones, despite the way in which the constitutional courts of Member States have received it.[35] However, the principle of primacy is subject to limitations, such as the principles of legal certainty, *res judicata*, protection of public interest, and the principle of legitimate expectations.[36] National legal systems may put certain limitations on the principle of primacy, either through subsequent changes of ordinary or constitutional laws that award primacy to EU norms, or through reserves on constitutional review of EU norms based on fundamental rights, *ultra vires*, or constitutional identity criteria.[37] These challenges manifest the multi-jurisdictional claims in the polity, and reject the thesis of unconditional primacy of EU law.

The autonomy of the EU legal order constitutes a strong premise for the unity of the EU legal order by rendering the legal sources autonomous and independent from the domestic legal orders of Member States or the international legal order. Being regarded as a reaction of the ECJ for protecting the EU integration from political and administrative actors,[38] the thesis of the 'autonomous legal order' was not merely conceived as an answer to the question of what the EU is if it is not an international or a federal legal order, but rather it served as a basis for the development of other revolutionary doctrines, such as primacy and direct effect.[39] This constellation of principles constitutes a premise for the autonomous and effective exercise of attributed powers at the EU level. The principle of autonomous legal order predicts that the decisions of the EU institutions, which are taken within the scope of the Union powers, constitute autonomous commands of the EU legal order. They are immune from the reservations of particular Member States. As such, they deserve effective and uniform application of EU law throughout the polity, and are able to produce legitimate consequences. In this way, the principles of autonomy and primacy ensure the validity of the EU legal order and enhance its

[34]Bogdandy (2010), p. 32.

[35]Case C-11/70 *Internationale Handelsgesellschaft mbH v Einfuhr- und Vorratsstelle für Getreide und Futtermittel, Frankfurt-am-Main*, [1970] ECR I-1125, para. 3.

[36]Dashwood (2011), pp. 272–273.

[37]Such examples could typically come from the English, German, or French legal systems, which by means of their integration policies have exercised pressure against the unconditional primacy of the EU legal order. See further on this subject Graig and de Búrca (2011), pp. 273–280, 285–286 and Dashwood (2011), pp. 273–277. For the constitutional jurisprudence of the German Constitutional Court see these Decisions: BVerfGE 37, 271 2 BvL 52/71 (*Solange I*); *Brunner v The European Union Treaty* (*Maastricht Judgment*) Cases 2 BvR 2134/92 & 2159/92; *Lisbon Treaty Judgment* BVerfG, 2 BvE 2/08 of 30.6.2009; and *Honeywell*, BVerfG, 2 BvR 2661/06 of 06.07.2010.

[38]See also Bogdandy (2010), pp. 28–29.

[39]Dashwood (2011), p. 61.

authority, independence, and reputation. From these general considerations, it can be inferred that the decisions of the EU that are taken in the context of WTO membership, if exercising attributed powers, can be defined and be given effect as commands of the EU legal order. As such, these decisions should produce legitimate consequences and be regarded with due level of effectiveness. In its quality of a conflict rule, the principle of primacy, suggests that the DSB decision, being regarded as a consequence of the EU decision to participate in the DSP, should prevail over the national measure that conflicts with the WTO. This is so, given that a DSB decision would amount to an international obligation for the EU, and as such, binding upon the Member States (Article 216(2) TFEU). To what extent could this proposition suggest that the Union participation in the DSP for matters of non-conferred competences may be construed as an invalid command of the EU legal order, and as such, it may not be entitled to effectiveness? Following a strict interpretation, the adoption of decisions outside the scope of conferred powers, would make the decision *ultra vires*, hence, invalid to produce legitimate outcomes. As a result of this, and pursuant to the legal maxim *jus ex injuria non oritur*, the consequences of the Union participation in the DSP for matters of non-conferred competences should not enjoy primacy over conflicting conduct of the Member States.

In practical terms, this discourse can be applied to the premises of the *EC – Asbestos*. From the normative perspective, given that the ban of asbestos from France, being a health policy measure, amounts to a residual competence of the Member States, the Union should not defend this measure. The decision of the Union to participate in the DSP can be considered from two different angles. From one perspective, this decision can be regarded as resulting from an encroachment of powers, hence an *ultra vires* act. As such, the effectiveness of its consequences should be denied. From another perspective, this participation can be regarded as lacking *ratione materiae* but *necessary* to honor the formal aspect of the WTO membership. In this context, the consequences could be construed as an autonomous manifestation of the Union's external policy, and as such, be regarded with the full authority that an EU norm deserves. The formal-substantive gap becomes then a paradox, to the extent that an illegitimate act, such as the EU decision to defend a national act enacted out of the scope of EU powers, could lead to a valid solution, such as the regard of the consequences of this act with due level of effectiveness. This paradox can be explained by the element of 'necessity'. This thesis justifies the EU participation in the DSP, as a duty to perform its formal obligations in the course of DSP, despite the missing *ratione materiae*. This element is rooted in the regime of joint responsibility, which has been preferred against that of several responsibility, precisely because it is rather impossible to construe a clear and definite vertical division of powers in the EU polity.[40]

---

[40]This thesis is adopted in the following Sections in order to construe the element of necessity in the context of other constitutional principles addressing the fallacies of the joint responsibility regime.

One of the consequences of the EU participation in the DSP would be a DSB decision that obliges France to withdraw its Decree banning asbestos. In case that France would not comply with this decision, both the EU and France would be regarded in violation of the WTO obligations. In order to avoid retaliatory measures, the EU could choose to comply with the DSB decision by its own initiative and institute a legislative act in accordance with Article 288 TFEU, either with a general or individual scope of application. Absent a material competence, the EU would lack the power to institute such a measure. However, insofar as this measure would be considered an international obligation, it would amount to a binding joint obligation for the EU and France (Article 216(2) TFEU). By means of this mechanism, pursuant to the principle of primacy, the EU would be able to claim authority over a dissenting position of France, and render its measure inapplicable insofar as it would conflict with the EU measure complying with the DSB decision.

As a concluding remark, it can be suggested that the principles of primacy and the autonomous legal order can address certain systemic issues triggered by the joint WTO membership of the EU and its Member States. While the principle of autonomy strengthens the claim of authority of the EU law in general, the principle of primacy neutralizes the conflicting effects of the national norms. In this way, the consequences of the EU participation in the DSP for matters of non-conferred competences may gain a binding character for the concerned Member State. In relation with this aspect of the joint responsibility regime, it can be maintained that the principles of primacy and autonomous legal order are instrumental for addressing the fallacies, but they fail to resolve its consequences effectively. Hence, it is the necessity of the Union to comply with its formal WTO obligations rather than the principles of autonomous legal order and primacy *per se*, that could the EU decision to participate in the DSP for matters of non-conferred powers.

## *2. The Decision of the EU to Participate in the DSP in Light of the Principles of Direct Effect and Direct Applicability*

The principles of direct effect and direct applicability are instrumental for the effectiveness of the EU norms. Considering that the effectiveness of the EU legal order constitutes a premise for the validity of the legal order, it is useful to explore the extent to which the principles of direct effect and direct applicability can address the fallacies of the joint responsibility regime and the formal-substantive gap of the EU membership in the WTO Agreement. In order to explore any relevant implications for the model of EU participation in the DSP, the decision of the EU to participate in the DSP and its consequences shall be construed in light of the doctrines of direct effect and direct applicability.

Public international law requires active actions from the states to make international agreements effective in their domestic legal order, mainly based on monist or dualist lines. This does not require states to provide to international agreements direct effect and direct applicability within their legal orders. It is even more exceptional for the decisions of international organizations to have direct effect within the territories of the contracting parties without first enabling certain transposing instruments. Contrary to this practice, the primary or secondary norms of the EU legal order are attributed direct applicability and direct effect within the territory of the Member States without being always subject to transposition; hence they have a self-executing power. Because the majority of the EU norms have direct applicability, they are also able to be invoked directly before the national courts whenever they confer rights to individuals, which the courts are bound to protect, thus producing direct effect in the subjective sense.[41] In a broad sense, the doctrine of direct effect can be defined as "the obligation of a court or another authority to apply the relevant provisions of [Union] law, either as a norm which governs the case or as a standard of review".[42] Jurisprudence indicates that the main criteria for a provision to have direct effect are that it should be *sufficiently clear, precise* and *unconditional*, in that it is not subject to discretionary measures of the Union institutions or Member States for its application or effects, and it is sufficiently precise to be relied upon unequivocally from individuals in courts.[43]

The norms that lack direct applicability may still have direct effect under certain conditions. Certain norms, such as the directives, may become applicable after being transposed from the Member States into their legal orders. They are free to choose the form and method of implementation, but not the result to be achieved, because the latter is prescribed by the EU legislator and is precluded to hinder the result that the directive prescribes.[44] The autonomy of transposition is subject to restrictions and is monitored by the Commission, which tracks the implementation process pursuant to Article 17(1) TEU, and may start infringement procedures under Article 258 TFEU in case of default. The non-transposed directives might hinder conferred rights to individuals, who can claim them directly in national courts subject to certain conditions. Accordingly, should Member States fail to transpose the directives in due time, or should they implement them incorrectly, individuals are entitled to claim remedies on the basis of the content of these directives, subject to the criteria that this content is unconditional and sufficiently precise.[45] In this way, the principle of effectiveness is developed in parallel with the doctrine of direct applicability and supplements the latter in various circumstances.

The principle of primacy depends on the principles of direct applicability and direct effect. This relationship can be constructed according to the 'primacy' and the 'trigger' models; two approaches that bring different results. The 'primacy' model regards primacy as a constitutional fundamental principle of the EU, and

---

[41]Case C-26/62 *Van Gend en Loos v Administratie der Belastingen*, [1963] ECR I-001, 12, para. 4 and 13 para. 1, 6.

[42]Kapteyn et al. (2008), p. 517.

[43]Kapteyn et al. (2008), pp. 515–516 and Graig and de Búrca (2011), p. 180 *et seq*.

[44]Article 288, para. 3 TFEU.

[45]Kapteyn et al. (2008), p. 525.

does not subject its application to any threshold criteria. Hence, the principle of primacy,

> is capable, in itself, of producing *exclusionary effects* within the domestic legal order – understood as the mere setting aside of national rules which are incompatible with a hierarchically superior norm of Union law, and thus amounting to judicial review of the validity of domestic rules judged against the obligations imposed upon the Member States under the Treaties.[46]

Because the discussion at this level is not about the applicability of the norm, but deals with the prevalence of the EU norm over national conflicting norms, the theory has distinguished this dimension of primacy from its "*substitutionary effects* – understood as the direct and immediate application of Union law, so as to create new rights or obligations derived from the Treaties which do not already exist within the national legal system".[47] The second theory has developed the 'trigger' model, which subjects the application of primacy, as a remedy to resolve the conflict between the EU and national norms, to the threshold criteria of the principle of direct effect. This is made with the argument that primacy takes its value only after the EU norm has been rendered cognizable before the national court.[48] This line of arguments considers the direct effect as an indispensable tool for the applicability of the principle of primacy.

As a conflict rule, the principle of primacy suggests that, in order for any retaliatory measures to be precluded, the EU could comply with the DSB decision by enacting a legislative act of general or individual character, by means of which, it obliges the concerned Member State to comply with the DSB ruling. Pursuant to the principle of primacy, the defecting measure would become inapplicable. In the premises of *EC – Asbestos*, the principle of direct applicability suggests that, if the EU, by means of a directly applicable act, would require France to comply with a DSB ruling that declares France in violation of the WTO Agreement, the respective EU decision would have effective consequences for France. If the EU would not employ a directly applicable act, its effectiveness would rely on conditions of the principle of direct effect, namely that the provisions should be sufficiently clear, precise, and unconditional.[49]

With respect to the model of participation of the EU in the DSP, the 'primacy' model provides that, no matter whether such a decision would be directly effective or not, it would have exclusionary effects against a conflicting French measure that does not comply with the DSB ruling and the relevant EU measure enforcing it in the Union. Contrary to this, the 'trigger' model would award to the EU decision primacy only to the extent that it would be cognizable for France, hence it should

[46]Dougan (2007), pp. 932–934 and Dashwood (2011), p. 279.

[47]Dashwood (2011), p. 279.

[48]Dougan (2007), p. 934 and Dashwood (2011), p. 279.

[49]Here again, one could note that the EU act obliging France to comply with a DSB ruling or recommendation has to be construed in light of the necessity of the EU to comply with its formal obligations of the WTO membership, in order not to be regarded as an *ultra vires* act.

gain the qualities of an act with direct effect. Note should be made to the fact that the 'primacy' model is not concerned about the applicability of the norm and its exclusionary effects are distinguished from the substitutionary effects of EU norms. In the conditions where the Union may participate in the DSP also for matters falling within the non-conferred areas of powers, the EU participation in the DSP could be qualified within the category of substitutionary effects, in that it creates new obligations for the Member States outside the scope of the Treaties. The 'primacy' model would be then only partially applied in this context, and, as such, it would leave the fallacies of the joint responsibility regime unaddressed. In light of these observations, the 'trigger' model seems to be more plausible for addressing the fallacious model of joint responsibility, in that it is concerned more about the direct effect of the EU norm, which in this case is related with the DSP participation of the Union. Hence, taking into account the *modus operandi* of the 'trigger' model, in order to ensure that the participation of the Union in the DSP for matters of non-conferred powers produces legitimate consequences for the participants, the Union has to produce, preferably beforehand, an act which either is directly applicable, or satisfies the conditions of the direct effect. This act should be able to ensure that the participation of the Union in the DSP follows the principle of legitimacy, and as such, it can be effective. In this way, the participation of the Union in the DSP allows for the principle of primacy to outplay the WTO incompliant national measures in accordance with the DSB rulings, without having to justify the participation of the Union in the DSP on the basis of the joint membership clause.

To conclude, it can be emphasized that the principles of direct applicability and direct effect strongly support the effectiveness and unity of the EU legal order. The predictions of theoretical models that construe the relationship between the principles of primacy and the doctrines of direct applicability and direct effect suggest that the decision of the EU addressing the fallacies of joint responsibility regime should comply with the criteria of direct effect, in order to guarantee the prevalence of such decisions against conflicting national norms.

### 3. The Predictions of the Principles of Comprehensive Legal Protection and State Liability for the Breach of WTO Obligations from the Union Polity

Unlike the rules of international law, the EU norm does not depend on the acceptance of the addressee for complying with it.[50] The EU legal order has a specific system of enforcement that ensures the effective application of EU norms. The principles of comprehensive legal protection and state liability are part of this system, and can provide useful predictions in terms of redressing the distribution of

[50] Bogdandy (2010), p. 30.

burden of retaliatory measures among participants, as part of the fallacies of the joint responsibility regime. Accordingly, the victims of retaliation may look for relevant instruments to redress their damages. It would thus be useful to elaborate on the prospect of the principles of comprehensive legal protection and state liability for breach of WTO obligations from the Union and its Member States, particularly for measures falling within the residual areas of powers.

The principle of comprehensive legal protection is another application of the principle of effectiveness and serves as a guarantee for the rule of law in the EU legal order. It protects the rights that may be violated by the unlawful exercise of public authority, and provides for a comprehensive tool of legal remedies, such as the judicial review. The principle of state liability, on the other hand, provides for the relevant remedies for the injured rights. The main subjects of these principles are nationals, including economic operators, who can plead before the national courts the obligations of the Member States arising out of the Treaties, in order to ensure in due time and in an effective manner the direct legal protection of their individual rights.[51] The vigilance of nationals constitutes an effective supervision of legality, in addition to the diligence of the Commission and Member States through the infringement procedures provided in Articles 258 and 259 TFEU.[52]Any restrictive measures taken against these subjects, should be based on clear and distinct criteria for the purpose of respecting fundamental rights and freedoms, with a particular attention to the protection and observance of the due process of law.[53]

Instruments ensuring the comprehensive legal protection include the preliminary ruling proceedings of the ECJ on the interpretation of the Treaties, and the judicial review of legal acts of the Union. The ECJ is competent to judge on actions related to the legality of secondary legislation, and on the failure of Member States to fulfill the obligations of the Treaties (Articles 19(3) TEU, and 258, 260 TFEU). The Member States are obliged to provide sufficient remedies for ensuring *effective legal protection* in the areas covered by EU law (Article 19(1) TEU). In this way, the element of coerciveness, which is missing at the EU level, is compensated at the national level by means of national instruments of law enforcement.

While the instruments of comprehensive legal protection provide the infrastructure for the protection of rights, the principle of state liability provides a crucial remedy for the breach of EU law. With the provisos that the effectiveness of the Union law would be impaired, and that the protection of rights conferred to individuals would be weakened, the ECJ has conceived a system of remedies that ensures that the Member States are held liable for failing to observe their obligations.[54] The responsibility of the Member States for compliance with EU law is an inherent principle of the EU legal order, and may lead to state liability for damages

[51]Case C-26/62 *Van Gend en Loos v Administratie der Belastingen*, [1963] ECR I-001, 13, paras. 3, 4.

[52]*Ibid*, para. 5.

[53]Declaration on Articles 75 and 215 TFEU, Official Journal of the EU C 326/348, 26.10.2012.

[54]Joined Cases C-6/90 and C-9/90 *Francovich et al. v Italy*, [1991] ECR I-5357, para. 33.

incurred by individuals as a result of breaches of Union law.[55]As to the damages, it is maintained that the injured party has to prove that those are actual and sufficiently certain in order to be redressed.[56] The concept of damage in the context of Union liability covers both the material loss in the form of a reduction in a person's assets (*damnum emergens*) and the loss of an increase in those assets which would have occurred had the wrongful act not taken place (*lucrum cessans*).[57] The assets of persons adversely affected due to the infringement of a rule of law protecting a personal right trigger the Union's non-contractual liability.[58]

The principle of state liability is understood as an obligation for the defaulting state to redress, i.e. to make good, losses and damages incurred by individuals as a result of the breach of EU obligations from Member States in the execution of Union law; an obligation that corresponds to a right of reparation in the disposition of the injured party. The state liability cannot however be limited to the directives only, because it is part of the system of application and enforcement of Union law.[59] As such, it ensures the effectiveness of Treaty provisions, which are directly effective, by entailing the right of individuals to claim before national courts their compliance and the relevant remedies.[60] The state liability may be established for breach of Treaty obligations which are not directly applicable, such as in the case of the non-transposed directives, subject to the conditions that (1) the results prescribed by the directive are able to confer rights to individuals; (2) the content of the conferred rights is identifiable; and (3) there exists a causal link between the failure of the state to timely transpose the directive (the breach of obligation) and the loss and damage suffered by the injured parties.[61]

The principle of state liability may extend its application beyond the mere transposition of directives, by addressing the infringement of other sources of Union law, such as the Treaties and the secondary legislation, as long as they relate to conferred rights on individuals and the content of these rights can be established solely on the basis of these provisions. As already addressed in the previous Chapters, the Union law confers a right to reparation where three conditions are met: (1) the rule of law infringed must be intended to confer rights on individuals; (2) the breach must be sufficiently serious; and (3) there must be a direct causal link

---

[55]*Ibid*, para. 35.

[56]Case C-308/87 *Alfredo Grifoni v European Atomic Energy Community*, [1994] ECR I-341, para. 40, Joined Cases C-104/89 and 37/90 *Mulder et al. v Council and Commission*, [2000] ECR I-203, paras. 51, 63.

[57]Case C-238/78, *Ireks-Arkady GmbH v European Economic Community*, [1979] ECR I-203, Opinion of AG Capotorti, para. 9.

[58]*Ibid.*

[59]Joined Cases C-6/90 and C-9/90 *Francovich et al. v Italy*, [1991] ECR I-5357, para. 36. See also Joined Cases C-46/93 and C-48/93 *Brasserie du Pêcheur and Factortame*, [1996] ECR I-1029, para. 39.

[60]Joined Cases C-46/93 and C-48/93 *Brasserie du Pêcheur and Factortame*, [1996] ECR I-1029, paras. 20, 22.

[61]Joined Cases C-6/90 and C-9/90 *Francovich et al. v Italy*, [1991] ECR I-5357, para. 40.

between the breach of the obligation resting on the state and the damage sustained by the injured parties.[62] While the first and the third conditions are of a concrete nature, the second condition requires further elaboration due to the risk of abstract interpretations.

In order to assess whether the breach of Union law is sufficiently serious, first it should be established whether the Member State or the Union institution to which a violation is attributed, has *manifestly* and *gravely* disregarded the limits at its discretion. This is particularly so where the Member State or the Union institutions are exercising wide discretionary powers, given that in other cases, where a very limited or no margin of discretion is available, the failure to transpose a directive would constitute a serious breach of the Union law in itself.[63] The condition of sufficient serious breach is determined by taking account of the following factors:

> the clarity and precision of the rule infringed; the extent of the margin of discretion which the rule infringed allowed to national or [Union] bodies; the question whether the infringement was committed intentionally, or damage caused intentionally; whether an error of law was excusable or inexcusable; the fact that the [behavior] of a [Union] Institution may have contributed to the infringement; whether or not the national measures or practices which are contrary to [Union] law are being maintained.[64]

These elements aim to reduce uncertainties in establishing the due level of responsibility for breach of Union law, which subsequently would lead to state liability.

With a view to *EC – Asbestos*, the EU decision to participate in the DSP in defense of a French measure might trigger retaliatory/cross-retaliatory measures against goods and services originating not only in France but also in other Member States. The nationals (including economic actors) of the latter might in turn incur damages of a trade character by means of increased tariffs or other barriers. Considering the nature of international trade, it is very unlikely that Member States of the EU would incur direct damages from retaliatory measures. The principles of comprehensive legal protection and state liability do not offer any significant results with regard to the distribution of burden.

In order for the French Decree to trigger the state liability of France, the cumulative criteria of the principle of state liability have to be satisfied. Accordingly, the right to reparation is awarded to victims of a breach, if the infringed rule of law, i.e. the WTO Agreement, intends to confer rights, if the breach is sufficiently serious, and if there is established a causal link between the breach and the damages. The first condition, whether the infringed act is able to prescribe results that confer rights to subjects of Union law, can be answered in the negative. A DSB ruling authorizing Canada to institute retaliatory measures against the EU and its

---

[62] Joined Cases C-46/93 and C-48/93 *Brasserie du Pêcheur and Factortame*, [1996] ECR I-1029, para. 51.

[63] *Ibid*, paras. 45, 47. See further Graig and de Búrca (2011), p. 250 and Kapteyn et al. (2008), pp. 478, 559–560.

[64] Kapteyn et al. (2008), p. 561.

Member States in a particular trade area is an indirect consequence of the EU participation in DSP and the EU joint responsibility from WTO Agreement. As much as the conditions of liability are concerned, it remains quite difficult to construe the decision of the EU to participate in the DSP as a sufficiently serious breach that manifestly disregards the limits of institutional discretion.[65] The EU answerability in the DSP could be regarded as an act of representation of France, or even as a manifestation of formal obligations of the Union as a jointly responsible WTO member, but could hardly be construed as an act conferring rights to individuals.

With regard to the second condition, namely the factors that lead to a sufficiently serious breach of the WTO obligations, the first and foremost element to be considered is whether the rules infringed are clear and precise. Insofar as the DSB ruling amounts to a joint obligation for the EU and its Member State, it has to be regarded as a mandatory rule to be observed from the concerned Member State. In general, it can be assumed that DSB rulings aim to achieve quite precise effects in terms of the trade measure, and as such, they should be regarded as prescribing clear obligations for the concerned Member State. In addition, the fact that such obligations do not leave to the defecting WTO Members too much discretionary power to choose their compliance with the WTO formal obligations, the incompliance with the DSB rulings could amount to an intentional infringement of such obligations. In addition, it can be expected for this incompliance not to be qualified as an excusable error of law, as long as the subjective choice of the Member State for not complying with a DSB ruling can be regarded as manifesting an intentional strategy. The maintenance of this measure in force, even in the presence of an EU legislative act obliging the Member State to comply with the DSB ruling, reaffirms the breach of the Member State in terms of both the WTO Agreement and EU law.

The third condition, namely the causal link between the damages that the injured parties have incurred and the breach of the Member State, proves difficult to be established. The incurred damages are caused by lawful retaliatory barriers, which are an indirect consequence of the wrongful measures imposed by Member States. As such, the EU should not be held liable insofar as the internationally wrongful act is attributed to the Member States due to measures instituted within their residual areas of powers. This condition supports the thesis that the burden of incompliance with the WTO obligations should be borne from the Member State that has instituted the measure.

To conclude, it can be maintained that the regime of state liability for breach of Union obligations as conceived in jurisprudence, could hardly be applied by analogy in the context of compliance with DSB rulings.[66] The ECJ has denied the direct effect of the WTO Agreement and DSB rulings in the EU legal order. The provisions of the WTO Agreement, and particularly the DSU, could hardly be

[65] Thies (2013), p. 112.

[66] See further on this discussion Thies (2006), pp. 1160–1162.

construed to intend the conferral of rights upon the victims of retaliation.[67] As a result, the non-contractual liability for failure to enforce DSB rulings for any wrongful measures of the Union or its Member States cannot be successfully invoked from the injured parties.[68] In this way, the principles of comprehensive legal protection and state liability are not able alone to address the fallacies in terms of the welfare distribution, and to redress the real victims of the cross-retaliatory measures.

## IV. The Predictions of the Principles of Political Organization for the Normative Model of the Union Participation in the DSP

Having considered the fallacies of the joint responsibility regime and the consequences of the EU participation in the DSP in view of the principles that ensure the unity of the EU legal order through the thesis of effectiveness, it is now turned to the second pillar of constitutional principles, which addresses these concerns in light of the political organization of the polity. The principles of political organization construe the relationship between the constituent Member States and the institutional framework of the polity. The EU polity is regarded as a '*Staatenverbund*', a compound or a composite of states (intergovernmental view) and constitutions (federal view), that is autonomous from its constituent Member States, which in turn remain sovereign even after having transferred certain powers to the polity.[69] This view reaffirms the thesis that the Union is neither an international organization, nor a federal state. Although from a functional point of view, the Union polity is framed in a symmetrical way with a federal polity, so far any formal recognition of the federal form of governance is essentially rejected.

Under the spirit of the principle of the rule of law, the principles of political organization have construed the relations between the Union institutions and Member States in a pluralistic way. These relationships have managed to mitigate the systemic perplexities that emerge out of the competing claims of power and sovereignty, which result in different claims of authority in the polity. This has been reflected in a quasi-federal system of execution of powers, which is characterized of a blurred and evolving nature of the division of competences. Furthermore, the decentralized system of enforcement of Union law depends on the Member States' conformity. In view of these constitutional problems, the question is, what keeps the polity united and to what extent would these forces manage the fallacies of the joint responsibility regime from a systemic perspective? The principles of political organization in the Union polity have the merit for this, and as such, they could also

[67]Thies (2013), p. 118.

[68]Thies (2006), p. 1160.

[69]Bogdandy (2010), pp. 38–39 and Wessel (2014), p. 132, referring also to Lisbon Treaty Judgment BVerfG, 2 BvE 2/08 of 30.6.2009.

prove useful for construing a model for the Union participation in the DSP. The following offers an overview of the constitutional principles dealing with the authority, legitimacy, constitutional tolerance, and structural compatibility, and particularly the principle of loyalty, as a premise for explaining the central perplexities of the political organization in the Union.

## *1. The Claim of Authority and the Principle of Dual Legitimacy*

The constitutional framework in the Union polity maintains an institutional equilibrium that accommodates contradicting claims of authority. These claims come from two opposite directions, namely the Member States, which claim to be the ultimate holders of power, and the Union, which is endowed with conferred powers from the Member States in order to pursue the common interest. The claims are thus different in nature; those of the Union lacking a validated adoption from the European constitutional *demos*, and those of the Member States manifesting this constitutional advantage in any possible event.[70] The parallel claims of authority constitute an inherent source of conflict in the Union. However, the constitutional principles of the political organization have limited these different claims of authority pursuant to a system of vertical division of powers, which maintains a sound level of legitimacy.

Obviously, the legitimacy in the Union polity, which has been subject to critics, depends significantly on the legitimacy organized by the national constitutions.[71] The critic on democratic deficit of the Union was somehow corrected with the empowerment of the European Parliament, which is elected with direct suffrage. Pursuant to Article 289 TFEU, the Parliament obtained an equivalent power to the Council, which represents the original line of legitimacy in the Union through representatives of Member States' governments. Thus, the exercise of power in the Union level is based on the principle of dual legitimacy.[72] In view of this unique solution, one can speak of a 'European way of federalism', which is "constructed with a top-to-bottom hierarchy of norms, but with a bottom-to-top hierarchy of authority and real power".[73] This view of explaining the political organization of the Union polity suggests that the Union cannot be seen as disconnected from its Member States.

---

[70]As one authority puts it, "Europe's constitutional architecture has never been validated by a process of constitutional adoption by a European constitutional *demos* and, hence, as a matter of both normative political principles and empirical social observation, the European constitutional discipline does not enjoy the same kind of authority that may be found in federal states where their federalism is rooted in a classic constitutional order". Weiler (2002), p. 567.

[71]See also Bogdandy (2010), p. 39.

[72]See also Bogdandy (2010), p. 50.

[73]Weiler (2002), p. 568.

From the above observations, it can be inferred that the principle of dual legitimacy explains the equilibrium between the different claims of authority. The conflicting claims could be present even in a case like *EC – Asbestos*, where the EU assumption of responsibility reflects the centralist idea of the external Union action, while the Member States keep exercising their authority over the residual power, such as trade with asbestos. Obviously, an unsuccessful DSB ruling would have revealed the conflict. In light of this, and in order to prevent such theoretical conflicts from happening, it can be suggested that the relevant political-decisional proceedings in the Union address beforehand the question of participation of the Union in the DSP by establishing the relevant normative framework of representation.

## *2. The Structural Compatibility and the Rejection of the Constitutional Homogeneity*

The competition of authority claims can be seen in terms of the relation between the Union's and Member States' constitutional orders. Through the lenses of the social, political, and cultural frameworks, the EU polity is characterized by a pronounced diversity and pluralism. The Treaties aim to achieve the social cohesion and economic convergence, as well as to create an ever-closer union among peoples of Europe based on the market economy and the liberal values of freedom, democracy, rule of law, respect for human rights and human dignity.[74] The unity in the EU polity is the result of the integration processes, which rely on a certain degree of structural compatibility among Member States.[75] The spill-over effects of the EU integration have increasingly emphasized the autonomy of the EU legal order and reinforced its claim of authority. However, a constitutional homogeneity has not been ascertained yet,[76] mainly due to the missing constitutional validation from a European *demos*. Hence, it is the constitutional cohesion between the national and EU legal orders, which permeates the pluralist nature of the constitutional sources in the polity.

## *3. The Principle of Constitutional Tolerance*

According to a pluralistic view, the EU legal order can be seen as a set of constitutional legal orders that are not necessarily in competition with each other,

[74]Preamble, Articles 1 and 2 TEU.

[75]Bogdandy (2010), p. 40.

[76]Bogdandy (2010), p. 40.

but rather intertwined and complementary.[77] The EU constitutional order is understood as a fusion of nationally organized areas of life into the European domain.[78] This construction indicates for an organizational function, but falls short in terms of the integrative function, when it comes to the integration of plural national identities into a larger polity.[79] This deficit, which makes the social acceptance of EU authority subject to the will of national constitutional orders, is nevertheless compensated by a highly dynamic interplay of legal principles and values, which constitute the basis for the relationship between diverse legal orders within the multilevel EU constitutional order. The principle of the rule of law governs these relationships by construing a federal-like order of compliance that rejects any hierarchy between constitutional norms.[80]

The principle of "more unity – more Europe", which promotes an "ever closer union among the peoples of Europe",[81] would not suffice to absorb the federal tensions in a structurally diverse Union due to the missing normative value. Both the national courts and the ECJ have shown a certain level of deference respectively toward the EU and national legal orders. This suggests for a certain degree of institutional tolerance toward diversity. The principle of diversity, which accommodates the constitutional tolerance in it,[82] has been confirmed in the Treaties.[83] The deference to the national identities constitutes a strong premise for acknowledging the constitutional diversity of the Member States. In turn, they have also accepted the Union authority, notwithstanding their declared reserves toward the ultimate claim of sovereignty, lately in terms of the national constitutional identities.[84]

Amid this mutual acceptance, one finds the pluralistic construction of the EU constitutional order, which is organized upon the values of diversity, and is substantiated from the principle of constitutional tolerance.[85] This principle is part of a federal constitutional discipline, which rejects a statist-type constitution. National constitutional actors accept the European constitutional discipline "as an autonomous voluntary act, endlessly renewed on each occasion, of subordination,

[77]Amtenbrink (2012), p. 43.

[78]Bogdandy (2010), p. 38.

[79]Amtenbrink (2012), pp. 43, 44, referring also to Bauböck (2002), p. 127.

[80]See on the concept of 'European rule of law' Amtenbrink (2012), p. 54.

[81]Preamble TEU, recital 13. See also Bogdandy (2010), p. 38.

[82]Bogdandy (2010), p. 38.

[83]See for example Article 3(3) para. 4 TEU, Articles 152, 165, 167 TFEU, recital 3 of the Preamble and Article 22 of the Charter of Fundamental Rights of the EU, which recognize the cultural, linguistic, social and religious diversities in Member States. In particular, Article 4(2) TEU provides for the obligation of the Union to respect the national identities of Member States, which are inherent in their fundamental political and constitutional structures, inclusive of regional and local self-government.

[84]Amtenbrink (2012), pp. 47–52. See further the Lisbon Treaty Judgment of the German Federal Constitutional Court BVerfG, 2 BvE 2/08 of 30.6.2009.

[85]See also Bogdandy (2010), p. 38.

in the discrete areas governed by Europe, to a norm which is the aggregate expression of other wills, other political identities, other political communities".[86] The principle of constitutional tolerance remains very abstract and lacks the normative value. However, it explains from a functional perspective the way in which the entire constitutional order could be re-dimensioned to the EU reality. The principle of constitutional tolerance could compensate for the absent integrative function in the EU constitutional legal order, by means of acknowledging the identity of others and accepting their 'alienship', rather than demarcating the borders.

From these observations, it can be inferred that the conflicting claims of authority are mitigated within a system which is oriented from functionalism, and is based on the mutual tolerance and deference to other claims to the benefit of coexistence in diversity. This explains the inadequacy of demarcation of powers in the vertical dimension of the polity. The principle of constitutional tolerance could be regarded too abstract for addressing the fallacies of the joint responsibility regime. Nevertheless, it predicts that the model of the Union participation in the DSP can overcome the obstacles of the vertical distribution of powers to the extent that it is based on constitutional processes that result in decisions that are an aggregate of the best interests. It is on these decisions, that the legitimacy of the Union participation for matters falling within non-conferred areas of powers could be based.

## *4. The Principle of Loyalty as a Premise for Managing the Fallacies of the Joint Responsibility Regime*

The conflicting claims of authority in the Union polity trigger a latent mistrust in the constitutional relationship between the participants of the polity. This has led to a decentralized system of enforcement, which makes the EU law dependent on the cooperation of Member States. The theses that address the opposing claims of authority through the pluralistic approaches of structural compatibility and constitutional tolerance offer only a functionally oriented approach for describing the political organization of the Union polity. The principle of loyalty substantiates the normative content that is necessary for construing the model of the political organization in the polity. This principle has the merit to compensate for the divergences and fragmentation tendencies in the EU constitutional order, by absorbing the opposing claims of authority, and by ensuring effectiveness, uniformity, and unity. In view of these predictions, the principle of loyalty is employed to analyze certain general aspects of the formal-substantive gap of the WTO membership of the EU and its Member States, and the fallacies of the joint responsibility regime. The analysis of the principle of loyalty casts its content and predictions in different lights. First, a doctrinal perspective on the principle of loyalty is offered.

[86]Weiler (2003), p. 21 and Weiler (2002), p. 568.

This is followed by an analysis of the legal framework and some jurisprudential aspects on the content of the principle. The analysis concludes with an application of the principle of loyalty on open questions of the fallacies of the joint responsibility regime based on the premises of *EC – Asbestos*. This is made with the aim of highlighting relevant predictions for the normative model of the EU participation in the DSP for matters of non-conferred competences.

## a. Doctrinal Perspectives on the Principle of Loyalty

The principle of loyalty is designated by the EU Treaties and jurisprudence as an essential principle of the EU legal order.[87] Being conceived in the constitutional practice of the German Empire, this principle entails a federative character in that it "clearly stands for a *mutual consideration of interests* and neither favors the federation nor the constituent states unilaterally".[88] It continues to be elaborated in the modern German constitutional tradition along the same line.[89] According to the German Federal Constitutional Court, this principle provides that "both the federation and the *Länder* are obliged to cooperate pursuant to the nature of the constitutional 'pact' between them and have to contribute to its consolidation as well as to the maintenance of the well-understood interests of the federation and the constituent states".[90] In the language of the Austrian Constitutional Court, "the "mutual consideration of interests" prohibits the "excessive disavowal of the other tier's interests" and that the consideration of one's own interests must not "torpedo" the other's interests".[91]

The federalist doctrine has conceived the concept of 'federal loyalty', also referred to as *pactum foederis*, as a tool for ensuring the cooperation between the federal institutions and the constituencies of the federation by means of the mutual consideration of interests. The federal loyalty is further distinguished from the 'constitutional loyalty', which is described in the constitutional practice as a legal institution that ensures absolute and unconditional obedience of individuals and organs of a state to the constitutional provisions. This manifests the goals of the social contract, a *pactum unionis* between the people, as the sovereign holder of the constituent power on the one hand, and the state organs on the other.[92] Both these

[87]In doctrine and jurisprudence, the principle of loyalty is also referred to as the principle of 'sincere cooperation', 'loyal cooperation', 'fidelity' (mainly in the United States) or 'good faith'.

[88]Gamper (2010), p. 160. Emphasis added.

[89]This principle is spread in other constitutional traditions worldwide, while in the EU legal order it is advocated from Germany. Countries that have imported the principle of loyalty include Austria, Switzerland, Belgium, Italy, Spain and South Africa. See further Gamper (2010), pp. 160–161 and Mortelmans (1998), pp. 84–85.

[90]Gamper (2010), p. 160, referring also to BVerfGE 6, 309, 361.

[91]Gamper (2010), p. 165, referring in particular to VfSlg 10.292/1984, 15.281/1998, 17.497/2005, 17.854/2006.

[92]See further Gamper (2010), p. 161.

perceptions of loyalty manifest its relevance for construing the political organization of the polity.

The mutual consideration of interests manifests the *element of reciprocity* between the participants of the *pactum foederis*, namely the constituent units and the federal institutions. This element remains present also in the *pactum unionis*, where the *reciprocal agreement* of the people to empower the public authority with governing powers is continuously maintained through the constitutional loyalty.[93] The element of reciprocity is another characteristic of the political organization in the Union polity. It permeates the vertical relationships between the Union institutions and its Member States and their citizens, by endorsing in this way their constitutional loyalty to the Union law.

In addition to the element of reciprocity, the principle of loyalty shares common attributes with the principle of *bona fide*, which essentially aims "to create a spirit of respect for the legal order and hence legal, political, and economical stability as progress for all mankind".[94] Either as a prerequisite, or as a consequence thereof, the principle of loyalty entails the spirit of the principle of *pacta sunt servanda* among the participants in the Union by means of general obligations that underpin the content of the *bona fide* principle and the element of reciprocity.[95] Furthermore, the principle of *pacta sunt servanda* is acknowledged as "a fundamental principle of any legal order and, in particular, the international legal order" and "requires that every treaty be binding upon the parties to it and be performed by them in good faith".[96] In light of this constellation of principles, the normative value of the principle of loyalty permeates both the one-sided and the two-sided EU obligations of the Member States.[97] The elements of reciprocity and *bona fide* do not however imply that the principle of loyalty is subject to the voluntary appreciation of the participants. Loyalty entails obligatory propositions that discipline the subjective attitudes of 'sincerity' and 'loyalty' on objective terms of a norm. However, as put by one authority, because the entire "European legal order ultimately rests on the *voluntary obedience* of its Member States, and therefore on their loyalty, the principle of loyalty has a key role in generating solutions to open questions and thus [moderating] conflicts that may arise in a polycentric and diverse polity".[98] As such, the principle of loyalty compensates for the missing means of coercion in the EU level by predicting the voluntary enforcement of EU norms.

[93]Gamper (2010), p. 161.

[94]Kotzur (2012), p. 509, para. 4, referring also to Kolb (2000), pp. 86–92.

[95]See also Edward and Lane (2012), pp. 45, 318.

[96]Case C-162/96 *A. Racke GmbH & Co. v Hauptzollamt Mainz*, [1998] ECR I-3655, para. 49, referring also to Article 26 VCLT.

[97]Examples of one-sided obligations (provision of information) and two-sided obligations (cooperation, participations of EU officials in national court hearings) are provided in Mortelmans (1998), p. 79 *et seq*.

[98]Bogdandy (2010), p. 42. Emphasis added.

The concept of 'voluntary obedience' needs to be further considered in light of the principle of loyalty. The 'voluntary obedience' in the EU polity has a controversial nature, if considered in terms of the concepts of *pactum foederis* and *pactum unionis*. The element of 'obedience' of Member States toward the Union's claim of authority conveys the constitutional loyalty, which is an argument in favor of the *pactum unionis*. However, the fact that loyalty in the Union polity is not unconditional, as the concept of constitutional loyalty would predict, disqualifies the Union polity from being a *pactum unionis* in the strict sense. Further, the European way of federalism rejects the thesis of the EU as a *pactum foederis* in the conventional sense, insofar as it lacks a constitutional pact in the Union, which would require a 'top-to-bottom' hierarchy of real authority and power.[99] However, the role of the *pactum foederis* as a tool for the mutual consideration of the interests of Member States and the Union is still accomplished in the Union due to the voluntary obedience that permeates political relationships in it. In view of this, the concept of voluntary obedience constitutes an aggregate of both functions of the federal and the constitutional loyalty, which are embodied in a '*pactum fidelis*' between participants. This thesis predicts that the political relationships in the Union polity are organized upon a superstructure that allows for the reciprocal deference to interests in a cumulative manner, rather than in an exclusionary one. This precludes the disavowal of the other interests, and ensures the compensation of coercive functions of a constitutional pact with the voluntary obedience. The *pactum fidelis* in the Union, based on the principle of loyalty, incorporates the principles of reciprocity, *bona fide* and *pacta sunt servanda*.

The principle of loyalty, with its ability to *generate solutions* to open questions, could reduce the externalities emerging out of the fragmentation tendencies in the EU legal order, which lead to federal tensions between the participants. Hence, it pursues the rule of law by shaping the manifold relationships between public authorities in the EU polity, by absorbing the diverging claims of authority, and by pursuing the effectiveness, uniformity, and unity of the EU legal order.[100] It is nevertheless useful to emphasize that the principle of loyalty may not prove adequate to ensure the viability of the polity, as long as the normative value of the principle depends on the voluntary acceptance of the Member States.[101] However, this principle plays a supplementary role for the division of powers in the polity, which is the main superstructure governing the competition of claims of authority between the Union institutions and the Member States. The principle of loyalty assists the principle of checks and balance to ensure that the power in the EU is exercised in compliance with the horizontal and vertical division of powers. A further relationship can be drawn between loyalty and other principles that ensure the effectiveness of EU law. While in relation with the principle of primacy, which is considered a 'conflict rule', loyalty plays a subsidiary role by reinforcing the

[99]Weiler (2002), p. 568.

[100]See also Bogdandy (2010), p. 41.

[101]See also Antoniadis (2004), 337.

obligation not to apply the conflicting national norms against the EU norms, in terms of the principle of effectiveness, the principle of loyalty requires its subjects to make the EU law effective.[102]

The principle of loyalty predicts an internal self-restricting conduct for the actors when exercising their powers, by takeing into consideration the interests of other participants, so that the allocation of powers operates as smoothly and harmoniously as possible.[103] In order to strike a proper balance during the application of the principle of loyalty, the principle of proportionality may be employed as an instrument for weighing between the conflicting interests of the participants, and their legitimate expectations in the implementation of EU law. The system of law enforcement in the Union is based on the premises of the 'missing means of coercion at the EU level'. By expanding the outreach of EU law, the principle of loyalty has manifested a significant normative value with this regard, without nevertheless changing the structure of powers. Accordingly, with the proviso that EU law should be provided with full effectiveness and primacy, the principle of loyalty obliges the Member States to accord national law an *interprétation conforme* with EU law, by requiring their institutions to provide indirect enforcement of rights that are not directly effective, as well as a right to reparation based on the principle of liability.[104] In this way, the principle of loyalty has been interpreted so as to expand the liability for breach of directly effective Union law also to other legislation of this body, by providing in this way a strong premise for the uniform application of EU law.

Nevertheless, the principle of loyalty should not be interpreted as a mechanism that triggers the absolute and unconditional obedience of Member States to the Union law. Although the principle of loyalty does not constitute a coercive means for the execution of the Treaty obligations, it is employed to compensate for the decentralized system of enforcement, which remains with the Member States. This is ensured by means of contractual tools inherent in the nature of the principle of loyalty, such as the principles of *bona fide*, *pacta sunt servanda*, and reciprocity. Hence, with all the constructive perspectives that rely on the duty of loyalty as a tool for achieving normative solutions in the Union, an overestimation of the principle would still be dangerous. The positioning of the duty of loyalty as an instrument to mitigate conflicting interests might not always prove successful inasmuch as the principle suggests for a duty to make best endeavors to agree on a common interest, which might not be the cumulative of all interests of the parties, but could also result in a lower common denominator.[105] The Member States may potentially make use, at any time, of their sovereign rights over the retained powers in a mixed agreement. Such divergent trends would circumvent the unity of the EU

[102]Neframi (2010), pp. 326–327.

[103]Gamper (2010), pp. 164–165.

[104]Edward and Lane (2012), p. 320 *et seq*, 353–354.

[105]See on this discussion MacLeod et al. (1996), pp. 149–150.

legal order and could result in a constitutional crisis of the Union.[106] In view of this, the duty of loyalty could arguably resolve the conflicting interests only by means of a 'best-endeavors' approach. The missing guidance from the ECJ as to the proper application of the duty of loyalty may shade off the real normative power that this principle could have for addressing the fallacious joint responsibility.

### b. The Legal Framework of the Principle of Loyalty

The normative framework of the principle of loyalty is mainly provided in Article 4 (3) TEU, which stipulates that,

> [p]ursuant to the principle of sincere cooperation, the Union and the Member States *shall*, in *full mutual respect*, assist each other in carrying out tasks which flow from the Treaties.
>
> The Member States *shall take any appropriate measure*, general or particular, to ensure fulfillment of the obligations arising out of the Treaties or resulting from the acts of the institutions of the Union.
>
> The Member States *shall facilitate* the achievement of the Union's tasks and *refrain* from any measure which could [jeopardize] the attainment of the Union's objectives.[107]

One of the central elements of this provision is the association of the principle of loyalty with the pursuit of the Union's interests through the attainment of the Union's tasks and objectives. The Member States have a duty to abstain from measures that could frustrate the achievement of common objectives once they are indicated as such from the EU.[108] This provision could imply that the interests of individual Member States are realized only to the extent that the common interests proclaimed by the Treaty objectives are achieved. This is ensured from the cumulative consideration of the interests of participants, so that a due level of deference is provided.

The first paragraph provides a general obligation for both the Union institutions and Member States to assist each other in performing the obligations arising out of the Treaties. This general obligation is established in reciprocal terms (full mutual respect), and entails both the predictions of the principles of *bona fide* and *pacta sunt servanda*. The cooperation mentioned in this paragraph consists in mutual assistance for implementing the Treaties. In the second and third paragraphs of the provision, the parity among the Union and the Member States and the 'soft' nature of the obligation for assistance is transformed into a differentiated relationship between the parties. The Member States are submitted to the authority of the Union institutions by means of more explicit, yet general, obligations, which are ensured

[106]MacLeod et al. (1996), p. 150.

[107]Emphasis added.

[108]Chalmers et al. (2010), p. 224.

through 'specific-result' and 'best efforts' obligations.[109] The content of these obligations can be classified in the categories of positive and negative obligations. Accordingly, the duty of the Member States to *take any appropriate measures* and the duty to *facilitate the achievement of the Union's tasks* are identified as positive obligations, while the Member States' duty to *refrain from any measures* jeopardizing the attainment of the Union's objectives can be regarded as a negative obligation.[110]

The group of positive obligations, for methodological purposes, can be organized in three subcategories, which are mostly elaborated in jurisprudence. In the first group, it can be mentioned the *obligation to take all appropriate measures*, general or particular, that are necessary to ensure the effective application of Union law.[111] This implies an obligation for the Member States to take the necessary legal, administrative, or constitutional measures in order to provide EU law with internal effects, notwithstanding the internal division of powers between centralized or decentralized bodies, or between the legislative, executive or judiciary branches of government.[112] Here the principle of loyalty plays an instrumental role for the principles of primacy, adequacy and effectiveness, given that it provides for the Member States an obligation to take all measures necessary to ensure the implementation of EU law.[113] In the second place, the principle of loyalty can be seen as an *obligation to ensure the protection of rights* stemming from the primary and secondary law. This is particularly relevant for the judicial observance of the principles of direct applicability and direct effect of the Union law.[114] In the third place, it can be mentioned the *obligation to act in order to achieve the objectives of the Treaties*, which is a powerful tool for ensuring a closer level of integration in the polity.[115] In view of this, in addition to pursuing the Union interests, this provision strengthens the autonomy of the EU legal order.[116]

The category of negative duties can similarly be analyzed in light of a threefold framework, by highlighting different perspectives on the obligation of Member States to refrain from measures jeopardizing the attainment of the Union's objective. Firstly, the Member States have the obligation to abstain from measures which could impede the effectiveness of Union law, such as by encouraging certain actors (particularly in the area of competition) to act against the Union law.[117] Secondly,

109See further Neframi (2010), p. 325.

110Kapteyn et al. (2008), p. 147 *et seq*. See also Edward and Lane (2012), p. 45.

111Kapteyn et al. (2008), p. 148.

112Kapteyn et al. (2008), pp. 148–149.

113Graig and de Búrca (2011), p. 219, Neframi (2010), p. 324 and Edward and Lane (2012), pp. 318–319. See further Case C-68/88 *Commission of the European Communities v Hellenic Republic*, [1989] ECR I-2965, para. 23.

114Kapteyn et al. (2008), p. 150.

115Kapteyn et al. (2008), p. 151.

116Neframi (2010), p. 324 and Cremona (2008), p. 125.

117Kapteyn et al. (2008), pp. 151–152.

one could mention the obligation of the Member States to abstain from measures that could hinder the internal functioning of the Union institutions, in particular in terms of their internal organization, which could impede their independence and autonomy.[118] Thirdly, the Member States are obliged to abstain from measures that hinder the development of EU integration, such as by concluding agreements with third countries, or by employing national measures that hinder the realization of a result prescribed by a directive.[119]

The positive and negative obligations that the duty of loyalty entails allow for the dominance of Union's objectives over the individual ones. However, these obligations are often combined with other principles and Treaty provisions. Hence, the duty of loyalty cannot be enforced as an obligation *per se*, but could rather be employed as a mechanism for enforcing other obligations referred to in the Treaties in the form of obligations, tasks, or objectives. In this context, it should be emphasized that the ability of the principle of loyalty to be invoked in courts has been questioned in various occasions. The duty of sincere cooperation is usually associated with the infringement of particular substantive provisions, and as such, it cannot prove sufficient to sustain a claim for infringement of the Union law before the ECJ.[120] Hence, the loyalty principle ensures that other substantive and procedural disciplines are duly achieved. The jurisprudence has regarded the failure to ensure effectiveness of EU law as a breach of the principle of loyalty *per se*.[121] In this way, in case that other Treaty provisions anchored to the principle of loyalty are violated, the duty of loyalty can also be considered as breached.

### c. The Principle of Loyalty in the ECJ Jurisprudence

With the proviso that the principles manifest their real value in courts, it is useful to consider the normative value of the principle of loyalty in terms of preventing or solving conflicts between various actors in the EU polity. As already observed in the ECJ jurisprudence, the principle of loyalty "is no piece of empty political rhetoric: it has provided the basis, in whole or in part, for the development of an entire series of much more specific, legally binding obligations incumbent upon the Member States, aimed at securing the effectiveness of Union law and policy".[122] In addition, this principle is also relevant for the Union institutions. The following analysis addresses four modes of relationship between the Union institutions and

---

[118]Kapteyn et al. (2008), p. 152.

[119]Kapteyn et al. (2008), p. 153.

[120]Case C-192/84 *Commission of the European Communities v Hellenic Republic*, ECR [1985] I-3967, para. 20.

[121]See for example Case C-68/88 *Commission of the European Communities v Hellenic Republic*, [1989] ECR I-2965, para. 4 of the *dispositif* in relation to para. 23 of the decision. See for further examples Edward and Lane (2012), p. 319.

[122]Dashwood (2011), p. 25.

Member States from an internal perspective. In the first mode of relationship, the principle of loyalty provides for the obligation of Member States to cooperate *bona fide* with the Union institutions in order to ensure the application of the Treaties.[123] Accordingly, the national authorities have the duty to furnish the Commission with the necessary information that can be required for the achievement of Treaty obligations and to consult it before adopting measures that could affect the Union law.[124] The consultations with the Commission during the implementation of EU law assist in finding adequate ways for overcoming obstacles without challenging the Treaty provisions.[125]

In the second mode of relationship, the principle of loyalty provides for the duty of EU institutions to assist national authorities of Member States to enforce EU law. The Union institutions are under the duty of loyalty toward the judicial authorities of Member States, and should furnish them with all the relevant information acquired in the course of observation of EU law.[126] These two modes of relationship alone show the two-way direction of the principle of loyalty. They reinforce the thesis that the principle of loyalty has a vertical character, and mainly operates in the national domain due to the decentralized system of enforcement of EU law.

In the third mode, the duty of loyalty requires from the Member States to facilitate the application of EU law between each other on a priority basis, as opposed to their individual or bilateral interests. Even when such interests are not directly related to EU law, but could only have marginal implications on it, the Member States should take into consideration the expectations of third Member States and as such, they are precluded to hinder the effects of EU law against the latter. Therefore, in their bilateral relations, Member States cannot, directly or indirectly, violate rights of citizens pursuant to the Treaties through any prior or subsequent agreements, even when they operate outside the scope of the Treaties.[127] This mode of relationship shows the principle of loyalty being employed to implicitly justify the outreach of EU law against the residual powers of Member States.

In the fourth mode of relationship, the principle of loyalty can be invoked between the EU institutions themselves. Accordingly, the dialogue between the

---

[123]Case C-192/84 *Commission of the European Communities v Hellenic Republic*, ECR [1985] I-3967, para. 19.

[124]See for example, Case C-186/85 *Commission of the European Communities v Kingdom of Belgium*, ECR. [1987] I-2029, paras. 39–40, Case C-141/78 *French Republic v United Kingdom of Great Britain and Northern Ireland*, ECR [1979] I-2923, paras. 9, 11, Case C-459/03 *Commission v Ireland* (MOX Plant), [2006] ECR I-4635, paras. 179, 182. See also Kapteyn et al. (2008), p. 154.

[125]Case C-94/87 *Commission of the European Communities v Federal Republic of Germany*, ECR [1989] I-175, para. 9.

[126]Case C-2/88 *J. J. Zwartveld et al.* (Order of the Court), ECR [1990] I-4405, para. 10. See also Kapteyn et al. (2008), p. 155 and Dashwood (2011), p. 323.

[127]Case C-235/87 *Annunziata Matteucci v Communauté française of Belgium and Commissariat général aux relations internationales of the Communauté française of Belgium*, [1988] ECR I-5589, para. 19.

institutions of the Union is subject to the same mutual duties that govern the relationship between the Member States and the Union, in that they should not ignore the rule of law and exercise their discretionary powers in a manifestly wrong or arbitrary way.[128] In this way, all the relationships between participants in the EU polity are subjected to the principle of loyalty. In all these modes of relationship, the individuals and private entities are not directly subjects of the principle of loyalty. However, they can benefit indirectly from the enforcement of EU law due to this principle.[129] Similarly, third countries can also benefit from the principle of loyalty in an indirect way, but this can only be ensured through a particular legal basis.[130]

In addition to the internal implications in the EU polity, the principle of loyalty influences the external action of Member States and Union institutions in a direct and an indirect manner. International agreements concluded by the Union on an exclusive basis, or jointly with the Member States, serve as a basis for achieving the Union's common objectives in the area of external relations. Pursuant to Article 216(2) TFEU, such agreements are binding upon the EU institutions and Member States. The principle of loyalty is inherent in this obligation, and becomes more evident in the process of the conclusion and execution of international agreements. Here, the principle of loyalty comes into play with its 'competence-regulatory' function, which is conceived in the context of the principle of effectiveness. Accordingly, by considering the international agreements, particularly the mixed ones, as part of the EU legal order, Article 216(2) TFEU makes their provisions subject to the positive and negative duties provided in Article 4(3) TEU. This is particularly ensured by awarding these agreements effective implementation. This obligation is subject to preliminary proceedings before the ECJ, which ensures their uniform interpretation in the EU polity.[131] This process, under the effects of the principle of primacy, can further lead to a prioritization of the international agreements against the conflicting national legal systems. In this way, the principle of primacy addresses the vertical competition of powers to the expense of the Member States' residual powers and their autonomy.

Further to this direct influence on the external action of the EU, Article 4(3) TEU may indirectly restrain the Member States' residual competences. The negative duty prescribed in the third paragraph of Article 4(3) TEU, requires Member States to *refrain* from any measure that could jeopardize the attainment of the Union's objectives. One example is the obligation of Member States not to enter into international agreements with third parties, in case that their content would interfere with the Union's powers and their full effectiveness. Pursuant to Article 3(2) TFEU, the Union has exclusive competence for concluding an international agreement,

---

[128]Case C-204/86 *Hellenic Republic v Council of the European Communities*, [1988] ECR I-5323, paras. 16, 17, and Case C-65/93 *European Parliament v Council of the European Union*, [1995] ECR I-643, para. 23.

[129]See also Mortelmans (1998), p. 76 *et seq.*

[130]Mortelmans (1998), p. 79.

[131]Neframi (2010), pp. 334–335.

when it is necessary for the Union to be able to exercise an internal competence, or in so far as its conclusion may affect common rules or alter their scope. From this provision, it can be inferred that the Member States are not competent to enter into international obligations that limit the capacity of the Union to act within the conferred areas of powers. This provision has a preemptive character, in that it does not require the Union to have exercised its competence in concluding international agreements. The exclusive nature of this power is recognized *ipso lege* for those international obligations that may affect or alter the scope of common rules, thus excluding the possibility for the Member States to exercise any of their residual powers that fall under the scope of this abstract provision.[132] The exercise from the Member States of competences to enter international obligations is subjected to the compatibility with the Union law in order to prevent any conflict of binding norms and to provide full effectiveness of the Union law in the internal dimension, as well as to ensure the unity of the EU polity in the external relations. In this regard, the duty of loyalty is central.

Additionally, Article 351(2) TFEU requires in a hypothetical manner that, pursuant to the principle of loyalty, Member States yield to Union law, either by not entering the new agreements that could interfere with the scope of the EU powers, or by eliminating any incompatibility established thereto.[133] The principle of loyalty is therefore responsible for limiting the external action of the Member States to the extent that this action is conflicting with the common rules or the achievement of the Treaty objectives, either in actual or potential circumstances.

Due to its correlation with other legal principles and institutions, the principle of loyalty may be subject to limitations which are not directly related with this principle *per se*, but with its particular applications, such as for example the principle of effectiveness. Accordingly, the limitation of the principle of effectiveness due to the exercise of the principle of procedural autonomy amounts to indirect limitations to the principle of loyalty. The duty to provide effectiveness of EU law pursuant to the principle of loyalty is balanced against the principles of national judicial systems, such as the protection of the rights of defense, the principle of legal certainty, the principle of legitimate expectations, and the proper conduct of procedure.[134] However, these limitations, which make the application of Union law virtually impossible or excessively difficult, should not, pursuant to the principle of equivalence, jeopardize the application of Union law, in the sense of being treated less favorably than the domestic law. This serves as a guarantee against disguised limitations. As a result of this balance, the principle of loyalty can only be limited when its application would distort national procedural rules.

---

[132]See also Neframi (2010), p. 341.

[133]See also Neframi (2010), p. 344.

[134]Cases C-312/93 *Peterbroeck, Van Campenhout & Cie SCS v Belgian State*, [1995] ECR I-4599, para. 14 and C-455/06 *Heemskerk BV and Firma Schaap v Productschap Vee en Vlees*, [2008] ECR I-8763, paras. 46–48.

The balance of principles presented above leads to a more principled discussion that takes into consideration also the fact that the duty to yield to the EU norms should be proportional with that which is necessary to be achieved, and should take into consideration the principle of subsidiarity in its broadest sense.[135] The principle of proportionality applied in this regard would predict that showing deference to EU norms, should not exceed what is necessary to achieve by "unduly [subverting] established principles underlying the legal systems of the Member States".[136] Furthermore, the principle of subsidiarity, as a general rule, limits the Union to act in the areas that do not fall within its exclusive competences, and it only operates subject to the condition that the objectives pursued by the action cannot be sufficiently achieved by Member States (Article 5(3) TEU). These principles, also in combination with the principle of conferral, preserve the vertical balance of powers within the Union polity, and could serve as virtual barriers to the principles of effectiveness and loyalty. Hence, the action of the Union in areas falling within non-conferred powers depends on the willingness of the Member States to empower the Union or not. As a result, the principle of loyalty is applicable only to the extent that the balance of powers is construed in respect of the principles of conferral, subsidiarity, and proportionality.

### d. The Relevance of the Principle of Loyalty for the Fallacies of the Joint Responsibility Regime

Having analyzed the principle of loyalty, it is now turned to the relevance of this principle for the formal-substantive gap and for the fallacies of the joint responsibility regime, and particularly for the consequences of the Union participation in the DSP. To reiterate, the fallacies related to the WTO membership of the EU and its Member States are rooted in the blurred nature of the distribution of powers in the polity. On the one hand, the Member States enjoy all the substantive benefits from their WTO membership. On the other hand, the EU devolves its substantive benefits to its Member States, collectively or individually, given that the polity is regarded as a Union of Member States and not as a separate entity. The satisfaction of the formal WTO obligations faces a gap, considering that the effective control over all WTO disciplines is shared in a blurred way between the EU and its Member States. This gap is formally resolved by the joint responsibility regime, which presumes the EU and its Member States jointly responsible for all the WTO obligations. The model of joint responsibility is fallacious, in that it considers the Union as a 'black-box', and disregards the nature of powers within the polity. Consequently, this model allows for the retaliatory measures to be imposed against the EU for trade measures instituted by any of its Member States in violation of the WTO

[135] Joined Cases C-430/93 and C-431/93 *Van Schijndel* and *Van Veen v SPF*, [1995] ECR I-4705, Opinion of AG Jacobs of 15 June 1995, para. 27.

[136] *Ibid.*

disciplines, despite the fact that such defective measures fall outside the scope of the EU powers. In this way, the devolution of liabilities to other unrelated Member States leads to a misallocation of burden with depressing consequences for their welfare.

In this theoretical scenario, the principle of loyalty would predict that the mutual consideration of interests should permeate all relationships between the Member States as such, and with the Union institutions, and that the Member States should manifest voluntary obedience toward the EU legal order. Such interests consist in trade benefits that can be accrued due to the imposition of trade barriers against other WTO trading partners. The principle of loyalty is applicable in this scenario to the extent that its predictions should serve the attainment of the Treaty objectives. Obviously, the EU participation in the DSP to defend a trade measure imposed from a Member State within its residual powers against another WTO Member, has no direct relationship with the Treaty objectives. It could be in view of this challenge that the principle of loyalty is allegedly considered insufficient to address alone the fallacies of the EU participation in the DSP for matters falling outside the Treaties' objectives.[137]

The concerns raised with regard to the normative value of the principle of loyalty in this scenario can be addressed in terms of the content of this principle. The *pactum fidelis* in the EU polity triggers the functions of voluntary obedience and the mutual consideration of interests, although an absolute and unconditional obedience is in principle excluded. In a situation of diverging interests between the Member States and the Union, the principle of loyalty would provide for the parties the duty to coordinate their interests, if it would be necessary to ensure the unity of actions.[138] This would imply for a Member State to align its trade measures against the WTO Members also with the interests of the Union and other Member States. The dynamic nature of international trade and the natural (or post-colonial) connections of some EU Member States with third countries in the world do not always allow for a smooth alignment of these interests. Hence, the principle of loyalty would restrict the Member States to pursue their diverging interests to the detriment of the Union. This is manifested in their obligation not to deny the interests of the Union and other states. The Member States might claim their authority over residual powers and disregard any restrictions in their exercise. However, they have the duty to consult the Commission in order to overcome any obstacles that might emerge in exercising their powers, inasmuch as they could lead to potential conflicts that would challenge the Union law.

The normative predictions of the principle of loyalty cannot however lead to a change of structure of powers within the polity. This principle reaffirms the residual powers of the Member States and the conferred powers of the Union, by inviting the parties to coordinate their interests for attaining the Treaties' tasks and objectives, an obligation that flows from the requirement of unity in the international

[137]See also Antoniadis (2004), p. 328 and Eeckhout (2006), pp. 463–464.

[138]Opinion 1/94 of the Court of Justice *re WTO Agreement*, [1994] ECR I-5267, para. 107.

representation of the Union.[139] In this way, the principle of loyalty does not target the unionization of powers, but it rather allows the participants to engage for the Union's objectives their individual powers in a constructive way. This reasoning would imply that the principle of loyalty requires Member States to align their interests with the Union and other Member States, and to exercise their powers in a coordinated way in order to comply with the formal obligations of their WTO membership. Hence, the Member States would be precluded from infringing the interests of other participants by exercising their residual powers, when this would amount to a violation of the WTO disciplines, and would in turn trigger joint responsibility.

This thesis entails a self-restricting attitude, which is particularly based on the principles of reciprocity, *bona fide* and *pacta sunt servanda*. Given that the Union and its Member States are *ipso lege* jointly responsible for their WTO obligations, the Member States are also responsible, on a reciprocity basis, for observing their part of obligations. Accordingly, when the exercise of residual powers may trigger joint responsibility, the Member States should exercise such powers in consultation with other jointly responsible parties. This allows the interests of other participants to be considered cumulatively in the decision-making process. Consequently, the decisions on trade measures, which lead to joint responsibility, would gain legitimacy. The EU institutional framework offers an adequate setting for ensuring this function.

From a formal point of view, it can be maintained that the EU assumes international responsibility *ipso lege* by means of participation in the DSP. Pursuant to Article 216(2) TFEU, the EU, being bound by this Agreement, cannot reject its participation in the DSP on a unilateral basis, with the argument that it is not responsible for the disputed measures. The internal distribution of powers is not a reason for absolving the EU from its responsibilities from the WTO membership. Hence, the consequences of the Union participation in the DSP, in light of Article 216(2) TFEU, are binding upon the EU and its Member States. As such, a test for justifying the need for cooperation in addressing the consequences of the EU participation pursuant to the objectives or tasks flowing from the Treaties would be satisfied from this Article alone.

Additionally, it can be suggested that the objectives of the Treaties can be construed in a pluralistic manner, in that they may be seen as cumulatively representing the objectives of the constituent Member States. According to this view, and also in line with the thesis of unity of the EU polity, the Union constitutes a common pool of Member States' interests. The Treaties require the institutional framework to serve to the interests of the Member States and their citizens (e.g. Article 13(1) TEU). Furthermore, the objectives of the Treaties are defined

[139]Opinion 1/94 of the Court of Justice *re WTO Agreement*, [1994] ECR I-5267, para. 108 and Ruling 1/78 of the Court of Justice, [1978] ECR I-2151, paras. 34–36 and Opinion 2/91 of the Court of Justice, [1993] ECR I-1061, *Opinion delivered pursuant to the second subparagraph of Article 228 (1) of the EEC Treaty – 'Convention N° 170 of the International Labour Organization concerning safety in the use of chemicals at work'*, para. 36.

so widely that it may hardly be found a residual power of the Member States that would not, by means of a broad interpretation, be construed in light of the Union objectives. In this perspective, there is a significant promise for the principle of loyalty to be qualified as a normative principle for addressing the fallacies related with the joint responsibility regime.

Following these observations, it is now turned to the premises of the *EC – Asbestos* in order to address the relevance of the principle of loyalty for the fallacies of the joint responsibility regime. First, the decision of the EU to participate in the DSP is not only a formal obligation flowing from Article 216(2) TFEU. Obviously, more than a decision to join France in the proceedings on a solidarity basis, the EU has the duty to cooperate with its Member States by assisting them in enforcing EU law. Given that the WTO Agreement is part of the EU legal order, its enforcement is a joint obligation for both the Union and France. This construction suggests, nevertheless, that the Union should join the DSP as a co-defendant, and not substitute France by representation.

Following the above, the consequences of the EU participation in the DSP are addressed in different stages of the *EC – Asbestos* scenario. In the first stage, it is assumed that the DSB finds the French measure in violation of the WTO disciplines. Consequently, this measure should be withdrawn, and the competence for this belongs exclusively to France. Should France refuse to comply with such a ruling, the EU, in its quality of a (co)participant in the DSP, has to find a way to comply with it. This task for the EU is quite abstract, given that the measure represents a public health policy, for which the EU cannot become exclusively competent. The EU competence is limited to its capacity of exercising powers for the coordination, support, or the supplement of the Member States. This may not suffice to address the concern in a thorough manner.[140] Therefore, the parties at this stage of DSP have to foresee the possibility of facing retaliatory or cross-retaliatory measures from Canada.

From a theoretical perspective, it is quite unrealistic to speculate whether, at this stage, France would have the intrinsic reasons to comply or not with the DSB ruling. The refusal of France to withdraw the measure triggers the EU responsibility as a sole participant to comply with the DSB ruling. In terms of the principle of loyalty, this stage posits the interest of France to keep the trade measure in power and to accrue the corresponding benefits to the detriment of Canada, against the interest of the Union not to become responsible for a measure that does not result from its legislative acts, and moreover, falls beyond its conferred powers. The Union's interest represents the interest of other Member States, which would prefer to avoid any indirect retaliatory or cross-retaliatory measures. In this tension, the principle of loyalty predicts the duty of France to take its decision for withdrawing the measure by considering, instead of disavowing, the interest of the Union and other Member States. Obviously, this decision rests on the voluntary obedience of France to continue or not its course to the detriment of the Union's interests.

---

[140] Article 6(a) TFEU.

In the second stage, the assumption persists with France not complying with the DSB ruling, which entitles Canada to require authorization for retaliatory or cross-retaliatory measures against France and the EU. Possibly, these measures might suffice against France alone, but as the practice has shown, the trade flows are very dynamic, and so are the retaliatory measures. At this stage, being confronted with trade loss, either France or the EU might decide to comply with the DSB decision. In case that France refuses to comply, the EU might enact an individual or general legislative measure obliging France to comply with the DSB ruling, or transposing the latter within the EU legal order. At this point, an external relation matter would be transformed into an internal issue. The principle of loyalty at this stage would be more promising for succeeding with its normative power, in that it could oblige France to take appropriate measures to ensure the fulfillment of the Treaties (such as the compliance with international obligations) and the act of the institutions of the Union.[141] Furthermore, the act of the Union complying with the DSB ruling is a premise for starting infringement procedures pursuant to Articles 258 *et seq*. TFEU and the corresponding penalties. Accordingly, France may face proceedings before the ECJ should it continue refusing compliance with the legislative act transposing the DSB ruling.

Obviously, France could disregard these obligations and claim a certain degree of autonomy in defending its measure against Canada. It could argue that a competence not conferred to the Union remains with the Member States, and that the principle of loyalty cannot be interpreted to amount to a change of the structure of powers in the polity.[142] Hence, this course of arguments challenges the normative outreach of the principle of loyalty. Pursuant to Article 4(3) TEU, the Member States have the (positive and negative) duty of loyalty toward the Union and other Member States. In view of this, the claim of authority over residual powers should be aligned in compliance with these duties. This argument confronts a number of principles and limitations. It follows that, the duty of France to comply with the DSB ruling, either defined as a duty to take appropriate measures of compliance, or as a duty to abstain from measures hindering the effectiveness of EU law, does not take over the power of France to exercise its power. France remains ultimately competent to withdraw its trade measure at any case. However, the obligation to comply, either from an international law perspective, or from the EU law perspective, hinders somehow the autonomy of France in regulating freely this area of governance. Nevertheless, this hindrance is not caused by the EU legal order *per se*, but rather by the formal WTO obligations of France and the EU. Therefore, the principle of loyalty would be interpreted only as a tool for restricting the scope of France in disavowing the interests of the Union by diverting the welfare loss toward other Member States unrelated with this matter.

[141] Article 4(3) TEU also in relation with Article 216(2) TFEU.

[142] Article 4(1) TEU and Opinion 1/94 of the Court of Justice *re WTO Agreement*, [1994] ECR I-5267, para. 107.

Insofar as the claim of authority of France is directed against the consequences of the EU participation in the DSB, this would restrict their effect in the EU legal order. Based on the positive duties of loyalty, France has to take appropriate measures, general or particular, to provide effective application of EU law. In terms of the negative duties, France is obliged to abstain from measures impeding the effectiveness of EU law. Therefore, France would be obliged to comply with a DSB ruling on the withdrawal of measures in light of the principles of loyalty and effectiveness. This combination would be even more justified in terms of an EU legislative act complying with the DSB ruling. This category of positive duties is triggered despite the division of powers, and serves as an instrument for ensuring the primacy and effectiveness of EU law.

In addition, the positive duty amounts to an obligation for the Member State to facilitate the attainment of the Union tasks by enhancing the EU integration and autonomy. As long as the Union participation in the DSP is construed as an obligation to comply with the formal obligations of the WTO membership, hence to fulfil its international obligations (Article 216(2) TFEU), France is also obliged to facilitate this task of the Union, and to comply with the consequences arising out of this participation. International agreements are part of the EU legal order, and as such, they entitle the Union to develop its autonomous profile. Accordingly, the Union institutions should not be conditioned from unilateral actions of Member States, when taking decisions to observe the Union's international obligations. The refusal of France to comply with the DSB ruling may challenge this expression of the Union's autonomy.

Despite its limitations, the principle of loyalty constitutes a strong premise for construing a normative model for the EU participation in the DSP. According to the ECJ, the need for unity in implementing the WTO Agreement triggers the duty of cooperation, under which, cross-retaliatory measures against WTO Members are instituted in order to compensate for the actual distribution of powers between the EU and its Member States.[143] This mechanism has been conceived for those cases where the EU and its Member States act as active litigants in the DSP, but cannot be denied for other configurations as well. Hence, the EU and its Member States might need to coordinate their efforts to retrieve the trade benefits against defecting trade partners. One can identify two explanatory variables employed from the ECJ, such as *the need for unity* in international representation, and the fact that *the mixed nature of powers* in the polity precludes the EU and its Member States from instituting individually effective cross-retaliatory measures that would force defecting WTO Members to terminate their trade measures. These variables enabled the ECJ to the need for cooperation in instituting cross-retaliatory measures in order for the EU and its Member States to retrieve the desired trade benefits from the WTO Agreement. The principle of loyalty is thus conceived as a duty that prevails over the claims of authority of Member States over their residual powers.

[143]Opinion 1/94 of the Court of Justice *re WTO Agreement*, [1994] ECR I-5267, paras. 107–109.

The same variables could hold true for the *EC – Asbestos* scenario, where the EU appeared as passive litigant in the DSP. Accordingly, the EU could be faced in these proceedings with cross-retaliatory measures, which would lead to welfare loss, despite the fact that the EU is not competent to withdraw the defecting trade measures. In these conditions, it could be suggested that the Union and France would have to cooperate in order to address the consequences of the EU participation in the DSP. This participation could lead to an obligation for France to withdraw the measure and comply with the WTO obligations, in order to avoid any damages for the EU. Presumably, the duty of loyalty would solve the competition between the claim of authority over residual powers and the consequences of the EU participation in DSP in favor of the Union interests. This is based on the necessity to preserve the unity in the international representation and to comply with the obligations emerging out of the international treaties. The principle of loyalty entails the idea of 'mutual respect', which is the basis for the countervailing (compensatory) principle. This principle implies for the institutions of the EU and its Member States the duty to cooperate with each other by not transgressing the powers of each other, but by assisting each other in maintaining the authority within these powers.[144]

As a conclusion, it can be suggested that the principle of loyalty is entrusted from the jurisprudence with the normative function of addressing the fallacies of the joint responsibility regime in the context of the WTO membership.[145] Nevertheless, its normative value is questioned insofar as the internal distribution of powers could be prejudiced. Accordingly, Member States may not, in principle, be inclined to surrender their prerogatives based on the duty of loyalty, particularly when this would imply to allow an international body, over which the Member States have no influence, to regulate the provision of services in certain areas such as health, education, or tourism. Therefore, the duty of loyalty manifests its value in the procedural aspects of the interaction of the Member States' residual powers with the Union's virtual competences in the context of WTO Agreement. In light of this, the duty of loyalty may be seen as a 'process-oriented' obligation, which obliges the Member States to coordinate their policies and efforts until a common position is found, and until the Union is designated as a sole representative of the interests of the polity.[146] The duty of loyalty may be limited to the efforts for achieving a common position without prejudicing the outcome.[147] In the context of WTO membership, this is particularly obvious in the process of negotiation and conclusion of new agreements. As much as the unified representation is concerned, the practice that the Commission represents the entire polity in the decision-making bodies as well as the dispute settlement proceedings has, so far, never questioned

[144]Chalmers et al. (2010), p. 223.

[145]Opinion 1/94 of the Court of Justice *re WTO Agreement*, [1994] ECR I-5267, paras. 107–109.

[146]MacLeod et al. (1996), pp. 148–149 and Antoniadis (2004), p. 328.

[147]Antoniadis (2004), p. 328.

the outreach of the duty of loyalty.[148] In light of these remarks, the duty of loyalty may be deemed relevant if construed as an obligation of conduct. The construction of the duty of loyalty as an obligation of result would provide the principle with a higher normative value, but in any case, this value should not be overestimated. The principle of loyalty has not been justiciable alone, and as such, it could hardly be used as a specific legal basis for invoking before the ECJ the cooperation of the Member States.

The principle of loyalty, more than an end, is used as a means for accomplishing other goals and principles. With its instrumental nature, it serves as the main driving factor for the self-regulatory mechanism conceived by the ECJ for compensating the externalities of the formal-substantive gap. It obliges the Member States to avoid the consequences of the EU participation in the DSP, by cooperating with the Union and avoiding defective measures that trigger responsibility. In this way, the principle of loyalty can offer relevant predictions in terms of construing a normative model for the Union participation in the DSP. Particular applications of the principle of loyalty, such as the duty to consult the Union when taking decisions that affect the enforcement of EU law, or to provide information on these matters, would help in overcoming the fallacies of the joint responsibility regime, by enabling the Union and other Member States to defend their interests in advance. Hence, the conception of the ECJ for the duty of loyalty as a tool for ensuring compliance with the WTO obligations can be constitutionalized in a model that addresses the fallacies of the joint responsibility regime in an institutionalized manner.

## V. The Political Processes Under the Rule of Law Principle and the Predictions for the Fallacies of the Joint Responsibility Regime

The perplexities arising out of the conflict of authority between the Union institutions and the Member States, as well as the conflicts that emerge from the evolving nature of the distribution of powers, are particularly manifested in the political processes in the polity. The question of blurred competences in the Union polity, as a factor for the federal tensions between the Union and its Member States, constitutes a decisive factor for the joint responsibility of the EU and its Member States in the context of WTO Agreement. In light of this assumption, the fallacies of the formal-substantive gap and the joint responsibility regime can be analyzed by employing the principles that enable the rule of law in the conduct of political processes. These principles include the principle of the constitutional legality, the principle of conferral, the doctrine of implied powers, the principles of the federal balance, including the doctrine of the vertical division of powers, and the principles

[148] See also Antoniadis (2004), p. 329.

of subsidiarity and proportionality. These principles are employed for analyzing the fallacies of the joint responsibility regime, and for elaborating on relevant predictions for the model of the Union participation in the DSP.

## *1. The Principle of Constitutional Legality as a General Limitation for the EU and Its Member States*

The principle of constitutional legality is central for the political processes, in that it manifests the positivist, yet non-hierarchical character of the Union law. Although a doctrinal creation, the principle of constitutional legality proves relevant in terms of the fallacies of the joint responsibility regime. The principle of constitutional legality suggests for a strict adherence of the legislative, executive, and judicial activity to the legal propositions of a constitutional nature that establish the institutions and governmental apparatus, define the scope of their sovereign powers, and guarantee the individual civil rights and liberties.[149] These propositions are part of the EU legal superstructure in the form of rules of recognition that allow the institutions to enact rules of change. The political processes produce an infrastructure of legal propositions at the Union level, which results from the application of the rules of change by the Union institutions and the Member States. This body of law is only valid if some conditions are satisfied, and in this way, it is able to produce legitimate outcomes.

Although the hierarchy of propositions of the superstructure and infrastructure in the formal sense is missing, certain priorities can be inferred from the Treaties, such as the indispensable conformity of the secondary EU legislation and the national legislation with the primary EU legislation.[150] Accordingly, the principle of constitutional legality predicts that the relation between the Treaties and the secondary legislation is construed in terms of the negative and the positive sense of legality. In the negative sense, the Treaties have *primacy* over the secondary legislation, in that every secondary act of the Union has to respect higher-ranking norms, while in the positive sense, the acts of secondary legislation must have a legal basis that can be traced back to the primary legislation, which is better expressed in the principles of *conferral* and *limited powers*.[151] Hence, an act of secondary legislation, in order to have binding effects, should state reasons and its legal basis.[152]

From these general observations on the principle of constitutional legality, it could be inferred that the EU, in the course of its DSP participation, is obliged to

---

[149]For a definition of terms 'constitutional' and 'legality' see Garner and Black (2010), pp. 283, 770.

[150]Dowrick (1983), pp. 226–228.

[151]Bogdandy (2010), pp. 33, 35.

[152]Case C-370/07 *Commission of the European Communities v Council of the European Union*, [2009] ECR I-8917, para. 45. See further Cremona (2012), pp. 314–315.

comply with the Treaties when representing the Member States. This prediction would be valid not only for the decision of the EU to participate in the DSP, but also for any legislative act that would oblige the Member States to comply with the subsequent DSB rulings. In the premises of *EC – Asbestos*, this prediction would pose two main questions for consideration. First, to what extent would the decision of the EU to assume representation of the French measure be based in the Treaties, and secondly, on what normative grounds could the EU oblige France to comply with a DSB ruling requiring the EU to withdraw the French measure banning asbestos? The EU lacks conferred competences in the area of public health, as they rest with the Member States (Article 6(a) TEU). The French measure banning asbestos was not transposing any EU measures on the prohibition of exports, imports, or the use of these materials. Therefore, the EU acting in defense of the French measure is not justified in terms of the principle of constitutional legality. As a result, an EU legislative act obliging France to comply with a DSB ruling would hardly comply with this principle.

To conclude, it can be suggested that the principle of constitutional legality puts essential restrictions on the EU participation in the DSP. The EU decision to defend a Member State measure exercising its residual powers could hardly be compatible with the Treaties. The model of the EU participation in the DSP should consider the predictions of the principle of constitutional legality, by establishing adequate processes that ensure the compliance of the Union actions with the Treaties in the negative and positive senses of legality. In this way, it is possible to observe the constitutional limitations that determine the validity of the legal infrastructure of the Union, and prevent the encroachment of the powers of the Member States.

## *2. The Principle of Conferral and the Implied Powers Doctrine*

The principle of conferral and the implied powers doctrine can be seen as instruments for ensuring the principle of constitutional legality, insofar as they allow the Union to exercise its power in a legitimate way. These principles could be employed as standards for justifying the participation of the Union in the DSP. Furthermore, they may be construed in line with the rules of attribution, inasmuch as they could be used to determine whether the WTO wrongful conduct could be attributed to the Union in terms of the principle of conferral and the implied powers doctrine. As such, they may assist with their predictions for construing a model for the Union participation in the DSP, which complies with the principle of constitutional legality.

Otherwise recognized as the principle of attributed or limited powers,[153] the principle of conferral provides for the Union the authorization to act only within the limits of the competences conferred in the Treaties, in order to attain the objectives

[153]Bogdandy (2010), p. 35.

set out therein (Article 5(1, 2) TFEU). Furthermore, Article 13(2) TEU provides for the institutions the duty to act within the limits of the conferred powers and in conformity with the procedures, conditions and objectives set out in the Treaties, and the duty to practice the mutual sincere cooperation in this regard. The principle of conferral constitutes for the Union institutions both an empowerment and a limitation clause for acting within the boundaries, and in this regard, this principle plays the role of the rule of recognition. Hence, the Treaties serve as the constitutional charter that determines the subject matter in which the Union institutions can enact secondary legislation.[154]

The fact that the EU institutions are dependent only on powers conferred on them by Member States, is confirmed in the Treaties as well as in the jurisprudence.[155] The principle of conferral reveals the thesis that the Member States are the ultimate holders of sovereignty, and that the governing powers are conferred upon the Union on a limited basis; hence, they retain the residual (non-conferred) powers (Articles 4(1) and 5(2) TFEU).[156] The regime of conferred powers rejects any kind of 'omnipotence' of the Union institutions, in that they lack a general law-making capacity that would allow its institutions to determine autonomously the limits of their action.[157] The powers of the EU shall not be extended to the expense of Member States, without their prior consent as provided through the Treaty amendments pursuant to Article 48 TEU.[158] In this way, by defining the powers of institutions, the Treaties acknowledge the residual powers of Member States, and protect them from being encroached by the Union legislation. The limitation function of the principle of conferral reduces uncertainties created by the blurred lines in the vertical distribution of powers, which are created from the lack of an enumerated list of conferred or residual powers, the employment of teleological interpretation from ECJ, the application of the competence on the approximation of laws (Article 114 TFEU), the application of the '*Passerelle*' (flexibility) clause (Article 352 TFEU), and the implied powers doctrine.[159]

In addition to the transfer of powers in an enumerated or explicit manner, the EU legal order has recognized the doctrine of implied powers, which is initially

---

[154]Schütze (2012), p. 153.

[155]Opinion 2/00 of the Court of Justice, *Competence of the Community to conclude Cartagena Protocol*, [2001] ECR I-9713, para. 5, 30/33 and Case C-370/07 *Commission v Council*, [2009] ECR I-8917, para. 47.

[156]This implies that the Member States remain the ultimate holders of the competences, although the concept of conferral refers to a process of transferring powers, rather than bestowing them in the sense of lending. This prediction is however an abstract simplification of the EU – Member States relationship, given that in practice the conferred powers may not be exercised from the Member States as long as they are conferred upon the Union.

[157]Kaczorowska (2013), p. 167. See also Schütze (2012), pp. 153–154.

[158]See also Kaczorowska (2013), p. 163.

[159]Schütze (2012), p. 153.

conceived in the jurisprudence of the ECJ,[160] and is subsequently constitutionalized in Articles 3(2) and 216(1) TFEU. This doctrine provides that the Union is authorized to enter into international agreements with third countries or international organizations not only when the Treaties explicitly so provide, but also where the conclusion of the agreement is 'necessary' to achieve, within the sphere of the Union policies, the objectives of the Treaties, or is provided for in a legally binding Union act, or is likely to affect common rules or their scope. The wording and the context of this provision suggest that the doctrine of implied powers is mainly concerned with the extension of EU action in the external dimension, without expanding the competences in substantive terms. However, the potential application of the implied powers doctrine in the internal dimension is recognized in the jurisprudence, where allegedly it is accepted that, in order to ensure the effectiveness of the EU legal norms, the Treaties confer to the institutions also those powers that are indispensable to carry out the tasks flowing from the Treaties.[161] The exercise of the implied powers in the internal context is conditioned from the necessity to ensure the effectiveness of conferred powers, and only exceptionally is used in the jurisprudence.[162]

The implied powers doctrine supplements the principle of conferral, and is derived as a result of, allegedly, not a wide, but rather an accepted interpretation of rules laid down in a law or in an international treaty, which supposedly contain also those rules without which that law or treaty would be meaningless or unreasonably and uselessly applied.[163] The rationale behind the implied powers doctrine is the principle of effectiveness, which, with its claim of the '*effet utile*' of the Union norms, serves as a utilitarian method for achieving the unity and uniformity of the EU legal order.[164] The necessity to enter into international agreements despite the absence of an expressly conferred competence is justified as a corollary complement of the internal competences.[165] The implied powers doctrine, as a corollary of the principle of conferral, is construed by employing a negative way of reasoning, according to which, a specific power explicitly conferred in the Treaties

[160] Case C-22/70 *Commission v Council* (ERTA), [1971] ECR I-263. See also Joined Cases C-3/76, 4/76, 6/76 *Cornelis Kramer et al.*, [1976] ECR I-1279, para. 19/20 and Opinion 1/76 of the ECJ, [1977] ECR I-741, *Opinion given pursuant to Article 228 (1) of the EEC Treaty – 'Draft Agreement establishing a European laying-up fund for inland waterway vessels'*, paras. 3, 4.

[161] Joined Cases C-281/85, 283/85, 284/85, 285/85, 287/85 *Federal Republic of Germany et al. v Commission of the European Communities*, [1987] ECR I-3203, para. 28 and Case C-478/93 *Kingdom of the Netherlands v Commission of the European Communities*, [1995] ECR I-3081, para. 32.

[162] This is confirmed in Case T-240/04 *French Republic v Commission of the European Communities*, [2007] ECR I-4035, para. 37.

[163] Case C-8/55 *Fédération Charbonnière de Belgique v High Authority of the European Coal and Steel Community*, [1956] ECR I-291, 299.

[164] Case C-22/70 *Commission v Council* (ERTA), [1971] ECR I-263, paras. 25–27, 31. See also Dashwood (2011), pp. 914, 916 and Lauwaars (2008), p. 225.

[165] See further on the 'complementarity' or 'parallelism' principle Dashwood (2011), pp. 912, 914–918.

"either would not make any sense or would not permit a reasonable application", if not deemed to include the derived powers which are "necessary to attain the objectives for which the main specific power is intended".[166] Obviously, the principle of conferral remains a normative condition for both the exercise of internal and external action given that the implied powers doctrine is related exclusively with the existing powers, and as such, it requires that the actions of the Union's institutions be justified on the basis of the Treaties.[167] In addition to the practical effect of the EU law provisions, the criterion of necessity to attain a conferred competence, task, or objective is essential for triggering the implied powers doctrine.[168] In this way, this doctrine includes the principle of conferral as part of its construction.

Having emphasized the main predictions of the principle of conferred powers and the implied powers doctrine, the relevance of these principles for the EU participation in the DSP is now discussed based on the premises of *EC – Asbestos*. The central question in this regard, is the extent to which the decision of the EU to represent Member States can be justified in light of the conferred or implied powers, as a premise for enabling the EU to oblige Member States to comply with the DSB rulings. This question concerns the decision of the EU to participate in the DSP for measures falling outside the conferred powers of the EU. During the compliance with the DSB ruling, the Union may transgress the conferred powers. Hence, the question is how to justify the status of the EU as a passive litigant in the DSP based on the Treaties' scheme of powers.

With its empowerment and limitation function, the principle of conferral provides that the action of the Union is limited within the powers conferred in the Treaties for the attainment of the objectives set out therein. In light of this, the decision of the EU to participate in a DSP for matters falling out of the conferred powers constitutes a violation of the principle of conferral. Based on the premises of *EC – Asbestos*, this conclusion would qualify the defense of the French measure from the EU as a violation of the principle of conferral, inasmuch as the disputed measure is issued on the basis of public health policy. The absence of a conferred power in this area makes it impossible for the EU to construe its action in light of the objectives of the Treaty.

The decision of the EU to participate in the DSP may be further considered in light of the implied powers doctrine. This doctrine is reserved for the capacity of the Union to enter into new agreements for matters that are not provided in the Treaties. Given that the EU participation in the DSP, in no plausible circumstances, could be construed as a new international agreement, the doctrine of implied powers is not relevant for addressing the questions of the joint responsibility regime. Furthermore, an essential condition for applying this doctrine is the attainment of treaty

---

[166]Lauwaars (2008), p. 225.

[167]See further Lauwaars (2008), p. 225.

[168]Case C-478/93 *Netherlands v Commission*, [1995] ECR I-3081, para. 32 and Case T-240/04 *France v Commission*, [2007] ECR I-4035, para. 37.

objectives by executing the conferred powers.[169] This condition cannot be proven in the context of *EC – Asbestos*, because the measure represents a public health policy, for which the Union lacks the conferred powers and the relevant objectives. Hence, the participation of the Union in the DSP is not justified from the logic of the implied powers doctrine either.

As a conclusion, the participation of the EU in the DSP for non-conferred powers is defined as a violation of the principle of conferral in the strict sense of interpretation, inasmuch as the procedural position of the EU cannot be associated with a conferred power serving the attainment of Union's objectives. Furthermore, this participation could hardly be justified upon the predictions of the implied powers doctrine, given that this participation is not considered as a new agreement in the meaning of Article 216(1) TFEU. As a result of these observations, the implied powers doctrine proves scarce in addressing the fallacies of the joint responsibility regime. Therefore, the model of participation in the DSP should take account of the principle of conferral for a proper attribution of responsibility.

## *3. The Federal Balance in the Union and Its Relevance for the Membership of the EU and Its Member States in the WTO*

The federal balance in the Union polity represents an overarching concept that includes the vertical distribution of powers between the Union and the Member States, the processes through which these powers are exercised, and the relevant limitations that maintain the balance in the polity. In addition to the principles of constitutional legality and conferral, the principles of federal balance provide relevant perspectives on the Union polity in terms of the substantive aspects of the WTO membership. The predictions and limitations of the division of powers doctrine play an instrumental role in determining whether the DSP participation is able to produce legitimate consequences. The following offers a brief overview of the distribution of powers and the principles of subsidiarity and proportionality, which preserve the vertical equilibrium of powers.

---

[169]Only the attainment of the objectives of the Treaties does not suffice to justify the implied powers doctrine. This conclusion has been emphasized with regard to the legal capacity of the Union to conclude international agreements, whereby the ECJ has conceived the pertinent condition that a conferred competence needs nevertheless to be identified, due to its constitutional importance for protecting the vertical division of powers. See Opinion 2/00 of the ECJ *re Cartagena Protocol*, [2001] ECR I-9713, para. 5 and Case C-370/07 *Commission v Council*, [2009] ECR I-8917, para. 46. See also Dashwood (2011), pp. 911–912.

### a. The Vertical Division of Powers

The vertical division of powers in the EU polity was discussed in Chap. 3 in light of the mixed nature of the WTO Agreement. This model is further important for the federal balance in the Union polity, inasmuch as the issues of sovereignty and legitimacy are concerned. The doctrine of national sovereignty limits the accomplishment of a federal Union, and the vertical division of powers is the central concern in this doctrine. The balance of powers in the multi-centered EU polity struggles between the federative and confederative trends, and to a certain extent, inflicts on the relationship with third parties.[170] The multilevel governance in the EU polity is continuously associated with the phenomena of competence overlapping and competence creep, the tension between the centralization and decentralization in the same policy area, as well as with an interdependence among different levels of government and their structural failure to interact effectively.[171] This Section elaborates on the relevance of the vertical division of powers' model for the membership of EU and its Member States in the WTO.

The EU Treaties have constitutionalized the exercise of powers in the polity. Article 3(6) TEU requires the Union to pursue the Treaty objectives in a commensurable extent with the conferred powers, a limit which is reaffirmed in Article 5 (1, 2) TEU. However, the main concern related to the distribution of powers consists in their material definition and the inability to establish boundaries. Accordingly, certain powers, such as the common commercial policy or the internal market, could hardly have a delimited scope. For this reason, there is an inherent competition for authority between the Member States and the Union, which affects various adjacent (neighboring) areas. Additionally, other powers, qualified as shared competences, have general limitations in terms of their preemptive effects, such as those determined in Article 4(3) TFEU. This scheme might lead to the creation of grey areas in the distribution of powers.[172] These areas could become object of conflicting claims of authority, which subsequently could harm the vertical balance in the polity. In order to pursue a certain legitimacy, the participants could be inclined to adopt a constructive approach of interpretation, which considers the competition for authority in an inclusive rather than exclusive manner, given that both the Union and its Member States are part of the same constitutional framework.

The vertical distribution of powers can be analyzed from a static or dynamic perspective. According to a static view, political processes in the Union should comply with the current scheme of powers in place at the time when the action occurs, based also on the principle *tempus regit actum*. Article 5(2) TEU connects the attainment of the Treaties' objectives with the conferred competences listed in the catalogue, suggesting for a static state of powers distribution. However, the

[170]See further on the federal discussions in the EU Howse and Nicolaidis (2001), p. 2 *et seq*.

[171]Howse and Nicolaidis (2001), p. 3.

[172]Rossi (2012), p. 102.

catalogue is non-exhaustive, inasmuch as the category of shared competences can change due to their preemptive nature, while the objectives of the Union are wide enough to escape a strict interpretation. Hence, the system of attribution of powers is quite hybrid, in that it allows for the scheme of powers to change over time.[173] The changing nature of powers in the Union polity makes these schemes quite dynamic and unpredictable. This view is supported from the lack of a distinct delimitation of powers, the grey areas of powers in the category of shared competences, their non-exhaustive numbering, and the degree of preemption, which determines the extent to which a shared competence is still available to be exercised at the Member State level.[174] Indeed, the lack of a formal constitution has been viewed as a threat to the stability of the distribution of powers in the material sense, by exposing Member States to continuous limitation of their fields of competences to the benefit of the Union.[175] The primordial schemes of the distribution of powers adopted in the Treaties have evolved, under the influence of the ECJ, into a sophisticated system of distribution of powers, which includes more guarantees and limitations to the deference of the Member States' sovereignty.

Obviously, this dynamic scheme of distribution of powers in the Union polity preserves a certain level of sovereignty for the Member States by excluding *a priori* any complete federalization of the EU. This might lead to challenging situations for the legitimacy in the Union polity, mainly due to the competence creep at the EU level. The federal division of powers may become subject to legislative or judicial processes, which respectively aim to remedy these concerns in order to bring the legitimacy in place. These constitutional processes are not without implications for the external relations of the EU polity. Accordingly, as a result of the changing scheme of internal powers, the structure and levels of representation in international organizations, such as the WTO, might also change from Member States to the EU or *vice versa*.

The dynamic nature of the distribution of powers in the EU polity is significant for the joint responsibility regime in the context of WTO membership. The scheme of powers is relevant for determining the legitimation of the Union participation in the DSP, inasmuch as they could lead to a deadlock scenario. Accordingly, based on the premises of *EC – Asbestos*, in case that the EU assumes answerability for a measure falling within the non-conferred areas of powers, the Union may not be able to comply with the DSB ruling due to lack of adequate competence. The temporal dimension of the scheme of powers plays an important role for the substantial dimension of the membership of the EU and its Member States in the WTO, given that it defines the authority that is entitled to legislate in a certain area at a certain point of time. The unionization of a shared competence that has been initially exercised by the Member States will have immediate effects in the vertical distribution of powers, in that the Member States will not be able to legislate

[173] See also Rossi (2012), p. 90.

[174] Rossi (2012), p. 102.

[175] Weiler (2001), p. 59.

anymore in this area in an autonomous way. Furthermore, the repatriation of competences may still be possible in case that the Union ceases to exercise the shared powers (Article 2(2) TFEU). Hence, the claims of authority can alter from the Member States to the Union and back.

To conclude, the challenges posed by the dynamic scheme of the distribution of powers constitute a crucial factor for the uncertainty of responsibility in the context of WTO Agreement. In order to preclude potential fallacies of the joint responsibility regime, the constitutional processes in the Union should consider the scheme of powers as a relevant factor for addressing the Union's responsibility from WTO membership. In this way, it could be ensured a legitimate devolution of responsibility among Member States, as a premise for preventing challenges for the EU way of federalism.

### b. Principles of Subsidiarity and Proportionality

Having considered the implications of the division of powers between the EU and its Member States for their membership in the WTO, it is now turned to the main predictions of the principles of subsidiarity and proportionality for this membership and for the fallacies of the joint responsibility regime. While the principle of conferral governs the limits of powers in the Union polity by restricting their scope, the principles of subsidiarity and proportionality govern the restrictions on the use of powers (Article 5(1) TEU). The WTO membership and the participation of the EU in the DSP can be analyzed in light of the restrictions and limitations of the principles of subsidiarity and proportionality, which could prove useful for the model of this participation.

The principle of subsidiarity provides for one of the main restrictions in the political processes. By rejecting any propositions that the centralized state planning can control the relationship between the state and the individual, the primary understanding of the subsidiarity principle remains that the decisions influencing the individuals should be taken as closely as possible to them.[176] In the political and constitutional dimension, the normative function of the principle of subsidiarity is to allocate the power between the center and periphery by striking a balance that takes into account the interests of all participants.[177] These predictions are particularly relevant for the federal balance in the Union polity.

[176]Before making its way in the political and constitutional framework of modern states, the principle of subsidiarity was coined in the religious doctrine of the Roman Church based on the Catholic doctrine of Thomas Aquinas. Kaczorowska (2013), p. 181. This doctrine conceives the principle of subsidiarity as a social order of a multiplicity of communities (families, corporations, localities) that mediates the relationship between the individual and the state, by recognizing the diversity and integrity due to the plurality of human nature. Lovin (2007), p. 97 referring in particular to the encyclical *Rerum Novarum* issued by Pope Leo XIII in 1891.

[177]See further Kaczorowska (2013), p. 181.

Article 5(3) TEU provides that, under the principle of subsidiarity, the Union shall act, in non-exclusive areas, *only if* and *in so far as* the objectives of the proposed action cannot be sufficiently achieved by the Member States' central, regional or local institutions, but rather can, by reason of the *scale* or *effects* of the proposed action, be better achieved at Union level. This principle addresses the question whether a measure can be better achieved at the Union or at the Member State level. As such, the principle of subsidiarity can be formulated as a test, which would justify the unionization of the shared powers only in case that, from an assessment of the intended consequences of a given decision, it results that the aimed objectives of this decision can be made better off.[178] This assessment is not only quantitative (sufficient achievement of objectives by reason of scale), but also qualitative (sufficient achievement of objectives by reason of the effects of the proposed action). The standard of comparison may potentially lead also to arbitrary assessments on the issue of what is 'better' for the achievement of the objectives. The objective assessment of this question rests on the decision-making system of the Union, where the Member States are directly involved.[179]

The principle of proportionality serves as an additional guarantee for observing the proper use of the Union powers. Pursuant to Article 5(4) TEU, the content and the form of the Union action shall not exceed what is necessary for achieving the objective of the Treaties. The principle of proportionality represents a deontological assessment of the Union action in accordance with the Treaties' objectives, in that the emphasis is put on the means to be used for the achievement of these objectives, which should be proportional.[180]

Although the principle of subsidiarity establishes a structural order by means of the duty of the institutions in the center to justify their actions upon the most *optimal* achievement of the objectives, it still does not inform any preference among the different levels of hierarchy in the polity.[181] The principle of subsidiarity entails a *duty of care* for the central authority to observe the powers of the lower level of government. This is not because the latter are more legitimate than the former; this would rather be the function of other principles, such as the legality and

[178]See further Bogdandy and Bast (2010), pp. 302–303, where it is suggested that a two-tier test is required pursuant to Article 5(3) TEU: in the first step it is required the determination of an insufficiency at the national, regional or local level to deal with the problem, while in a second step it is required the Union's capacity for solving the problem. However, the Union's capacity can only pass the second tier of the test if the objectives of the Treaties can be 'better' achieved by means of a unionized power. In this way, although it might be perceived an insufficiency of achievement of the Union's objectives at the national, regional or local level, the Union's action is not justified unless it can better achieve its objectives, by reason of scale or effects.

[179]The Member States are represented in the legislative organ of the Union, the Council. Additionally, Article 5(3) TEU and the Protocol No. 2 on the Application of the Principles of Subsidiarity and Proportionality entitle the national parliaments of the Member States to ensure the compliance with the principle of subsidiarity.

[180]As in the case of the principle of subsidiarity, the National Parliaments are equipped with the procedural tools to ensure the observance of the principle.

[181]Montgomery (2002), p. 51.

conferral. Through the lenses of subsidiarity, the desired level of legitimacy can be achieved by exercising the powers at *the proper (most efficient) level of governance*. The 'optimality' and 'efficiency' concepts employed in this regard are economical in nature, but in the context of the principle of subsidiarity, they provide a standard of reference. These concepts ensure that the EU decision-makers determine properly the level of their action, by deciding whether the objectives of the Treaties can be better achieved at the Union level or not. The optimality level of decision-making is developed as a theory in international economics but shares a similar logic to the principle of subsidiarity. Accordingly, by mitigating externalities of the decision-making, the doctrine of optimality predicts the maximization of the social well-being in the polity through optimal (better) results.[182]

This theory is found compatible with the system of concurrent powers between the German Federation and its constituent States (*Länder*), which, pursuant to Article 72(2) of the German Basic Law (*Grundgesetz*) in power until the amendments of 27 October 1994, provided that the Federation had the right to legislate, when the regulation by a *Land* prejudiced the interests of other *Länder*, or the country as a whole.[183] The relevant prediction in this provision with regard to the optimality doctrine was the maximization of the welfare of the Federation as a whole or the protection of interests of other *Länder* from the defecting *Länder*,[184] a thesis that had a strong federal character and kept the interventions from the Federal legislator immune from judicial review.[185] Although it might not be expected for

[182]According to Tinbergen, the optimum order in terms of the social well-being, when the decision-making affects third parties or has external effects in general, can be achieved if the "decisions will be taken at a sufficiently high level that the external effects outside the sphere of legal competence of the decision-makers can be neglected". Montgomery (2002), p. 52 and Timmermans (2008b), p. 142, referring to Tinbergen (1964), p. 57, Tinbergen (1959), and Tinbergen et al. (1976), p. 86. Tinbergen has developed the theory of the optimum economic policy in terms of qualitative and quantitative changes through policy instruments and aims to achieve the "optimum order" that maximizes the national or social well-being not only by combining various policy instruments, but also by selecting the relevant instruments in a centralized or decentralized dimension. This dimension is defined in the geographical (central or local authorities) and functional (specialized private organs) sense. Furthermore, Tinbergen has classified the instruments employed in a country in four categories based on the effects that they exercise in other countries, namely as *supporting*, *conflicting*, *neutral*, or *mixed*. See further Tinbergen (1964), pp. 57–60.

[183]Timmermans (2008b), p. 142, referring also to Kapteyn (1993), p. 44.

[184]This variation of subsidiarity is still comparable to the principle of subsidiarity in the EU polity, although the premises are slightly different.

[185]See further Rau (2003), p. 227 *et seq*. According to this author, after the constitutional amendments of 15 November 1994, this standing has essentially changed and as a result, Article 72(2) became more open to judicial review. The new formulation of Article 72(2) of the German Basic Law, which is in force after the amendments of 1 November 2006 provides that in order to ensure legal and economic unity among States and the national interests with regard to particular concurrent powers, the Federation can legislate on a priority basis in comparison to the *Länder*, if and to the extent that the establishment of equivalent living conditions throughout the federal territory or the maintenance of legal or economic unity renders federal regulation necessary in the national interest.

the principles of subsidiarity and proportionality to entail a significant judicial relevance, they may still induce a political influence over the legislative processes by making the institutional conduct more accountable.[186]

These general observations on the principles of subsidiarity and proportionality may be relevant for the Union participation in the DSP. It was evoked that the principle of subsidiarity proves useful in determining whether the measures in a particular area of non-exclusive competences should be taken at the Union level or could be better achieved at the Member States level, and the duty of care could serve as an instrument for achieving the highest level of optimality. The principle of proportionality, which concerns all kinds of competences, predicts that the content and the form of actions proposed at the Union level should not exceed what is necessary for achieving the objectives. The main predictions of these principles, as provided in the Treaties, combined with the predictions on the optimal decision-making theory, offer a relevant framework for addressing the question of the EU participation in the DSP. This analysis considers, firstly, the relevance of the principles of subsidiarity and proportionality for the EU participation in the DSP, with a view to the premises of *EC – Asbestos*. Subsequently, the doctrine on the optimal decision-making and the concept of the duty of care are combined to analyze the premises of the principles of subsidiarity and proportionality for the decision of the EU to defend its Member States in the DSP for questions of non-conferred competences.

The decision of the EU to participate in the DSP constitutes an action that may trigger responsibility for the Union. This decision should be assessed based on the legality criteria in general, and particularly on the predictions of the principles of subsidiarity and proportionality, as long as this decision could amount to a *de facto* unionization of the Member States' residual competences. This decision could be construed in light of the principle of subsidiarity, as long as it determines the level of representation, which for a measure at dispute, should be raised from the Member State level, as the primary competent entity, to the EU level, which is the subsidiary entity. With the proviso that the disputed measure does not constitute an exclusive competence of the Union, it can be proposed that, for measures for which the unionization of powers is allowed, the defense can be raised at the EU level. This is only to the extent that the objectives of the Treaties cannot be achieved at a level of Member State representation, but rather can be better achieved at the Union level by reason of scale or effects. Before taking the decision to participate in the DSP for a measure falling within the non-conferred areas of powers (hence, un-unionized areas), the EU should assess the premises of the principles of subsidiarity and proportionality. In this application, certain elements of the optimal decision-making should be taken into account, such as any actual or potential cost for the stakeholders, the probability of success of the DSP, the probability of retaliatory measures, and any guarantees that the concerned Member State shall

[186]On the skepticism with regard to the judicial success of the principles of subsidiarity and proportionality, see Rossi (2012), p. 96 and Timmermans (2008b), p. 141.

comply with these measures based on the principles of loyalty and primacy. Pursuant to the principle of proportionality, this assessment should also take into account the fact whether the increase of the participation in the DSP at the Union level would exceed what is necessary for achieving the objectives of the Treaties.

The primary function of the optimal decision-making in this case is to avoid any burden that the Union polity might face as a result of the EU participation in the DSP, or to make this burden easy to be neglected. This can serve as the first premise of an optimal decision-making. A second premise is related with the duty of care, which is vested in the Union institutions, and which essentially aims to increase optimality by reducing any probability of burden. In these preliminary phases, the burden can be calculated as a product of two factors; the *probability of retaliatory measures*, which is directly related to the probability that the case will be lost, and the *gravity of loss*. The gravity of loss includes the actual damages created by the disputed trade measure and the potential damages. The latter category refers to the direct damages that the related industries incur until the DSB ruling shall be enforced, as well as the enforcement costs. Given that the DSU does not recognize the concept of damage-compensation, but only allows for retaliatory measures, the value of the total damages might reach at most the double amount of actual damages.[187] The gravity of loss should be taken into account because, in case of an imposition of any retaliatory measures from the claimant, the domain of retaliation might be diverted to the EU level and, as a result, the burden may devolve to its Member States, which in this scenario are to be considered as third parties. Based on these premises, the optimal decision-making can be achieved to the extent that the probability of burden either is neglected, or otherwise its probable effects for the third parties are inconsiderable. In case that the impacts of the Union participation in the DSP would be considerably high, the participation would not be justified based on the optimum decision-making doctrine.

The assumption of burden from the Union, which exceeds what is necessary for the attainment of the Treaty objectives, makes the Union participation in the DSP unproportional in comparison with the sole participation of the concerned Member State. The eagerness of the Union to assume answerability has a price, which is only justified in case that the principles allow it. Otherwise, this conduct is not legitimate, inasmuch as it is not construed in compliance with the commands of the Union law; hence, it produces invalid consequences.

The application of the principles of subsidiarity and proportionality and the doctrine of optimal decision-making are limited in the case of the WTO membership of the Union polity, given that the EU is not competent for all the WTO areas. These doctrines prove scarce for those areas falling within the residual competences of the Member States, unless the latter decide to unionize them by means of

[187]This is because the concept of 'retaliatory measures' consists in the imposition of additional obstacles to trade in the counter direction by creating new damages that amount to the old ones. For this reason, the total loss amounts to the double of the actual and potential damages in addition to enforcement costs of the DSB decision.

legislative procedures. Hence, these doctrines cannot serve as normative grounds for the unionization of powers *per se*, but rather as justification for these decisions. Accordingly, the decision to increase the level of DSP participation at the EU level is legitimate not to the extent that this would make the parties better off, but rather on the basis that the parties have taken a decision that makes them better off, and that the third parties agree with the consequences of this decision. In more concrete terms, this would mean that by applying the predictions of the principle of subsidiarity, the decision of the EU to participate in the DSP is justified in case that it ensures a reduction of the overall burden from the measures, or the effects of burden are neglectable for third parties. Should the effects of burden be considerably high for the third parties, according to the doctrine of optimal decision-making, the determination of the level of participation at the Union level would not be justified, unless the Member State that has instituted the disputed measure would provide the relevant guarantees for making the burden neglectable. Hence, the relevant Member State should comply with the DSB ruling in order to avoid retaliatory measures. This proposition is in line with the predictions of the principle of proportionality, inasmuch as the content of action proposed at the Union level does not exceed the expectations of the third parties in terms of their interests.

In the premises of the *EC – Asbestos*, the principles of subsidiarity and proportionality would essentially prove adequate for justifying the EU decision to represent France. This is mainly due to the fact that there was no cost from retaliation in this proceeding. Nevertheless, in case that the French measure would have been found in violation of the WTO disciplines, the EU would have been faced with retaliatory and cross-retaliatory measures. The burden of these measures would be devolved to other Member States if France would not comply with a DSB ruling requiring the withdrawal of the WTO incompliant measures. Assuming that the cost of participation would exceed any benefits for the Union polity, the principles of subsidiarity and proportionality would predict for the EU not to participate in the DSP. Accordingly, these principles can predict two completely different regimes on the EU participation in the DSP, depending on the outcomes of the proceedings. These principles need to clarify beforehand the probability that the case will succeed or not, in order to predict the adequacy of the decision.

As a conclusion, it can be maintained that the principles of subsidiarity and proportionality could assist in reaching a plausible decision for the Union participation in the DSP, inasmuch as, in combination with the doctrine of optimal decision-making, the fallacies of the joint responsibility regime would be mitigated or precluded. In order to ensure the justification of this decision, an adequate decision-making process should be established. This would allow all the interested parties to represent their interests in the process of justifying their participation, and to provide the relevant approval for all the consequences of this participation. The proceedings comply with the principles of subsidiarity and proportionality, as long as the Union's decision to participate in the DSP ensures that the objectives of the Treaties are better achieved, and that this decision is proportional, in that its content and form do not exceed what it is necessary to achieve.

## VI. Concluding Remarks: The Principle of Institutional Balance as a Premise for the Membership of the EU and Its Member States in the WTO

This Chapter aimed to address the participation of the Union polity in the WTO Agreement, and particularly the participation of the Union in the DSP in light of the framework of the constitutional principles of the EU legal order. These principles, deriving from the general principle of the rule of law, ensure the unity of the EU legal order, and provide for the political organization of the participants in the Union, and for the political processes between them. The result of the interaction of these principles is a state of institutional balance, which is able to absorb the tensions between the conflicting claims of authority. The question to be addressed in this concluding Section is to consider whether the principle of institutional balance would be able to accommodate the fallacies of the joint responsibility regime and the consequent tensions that they may cause for the polity. This Section considers the issues that endanger the federal relationship between the EU and its Member States in general. It continues with some insights on the extent to which the decision of the EU to participate in the DSP could impair the federal balance in the Union, and the predictions that the principle of institutional balance could provide for the EU participation in the DSP. Although of a legal-political character, the issue of federal tensions is relevant for exploring another aspect of the WTO membership of the Union polity.

According to a pluralistic approach, the Union and the Member States can be seen as a unified body with many centers of governance that are integrated and interrelated with each other in a complementary way. The Union polity is seen as 'a constitutional order of states', and the EU is considered.

> as part of a complex system of multi-level governance, whereby governmental power is dispersed across different types of public authorities, operating at different levels (the supranational, the national and also the regional), but each [characterized] by mutual interdependence in their activities.[188]

The underlying idea of this system is the protection of the federal balance between the various constituencies and the central organs. From an observation of the political processes in the Union, it is obvious that the distribution of powers between the EU and its Member States resembles to that of.

> traditional confederations of States and federal States in that the distribution of governmental powers and functions as between the central governmental organs has varied over the decades, and the powers of the central organs *vis à vis* Member States have been subject to centripetal as well as centrifugal political forces, with consequent shifts in power.[189]

These institutions operate in accordance with the principle of checks and balance, mainly perceived in the horizontal relationship of the central institutions,

[188] Dashwood (2011), p. 66.

[189] Dowrick (1983), p. 207. See further Weiler (1981), p. 268.

namely the Commission, the Council, the Parliament, and the Court. The institutional framework in the EU polity is designed to accommodate tensions arising out of the conflicting interests of the participants, and serves as a forum where these interests are pursued or accommodated (arbitrated) in line with the general interest.[190]

The federal tensions in the EU polity occur between two opposing tendencies. On the one hand, the supranational tendencies aim at achieving more governing power in the center by means of the process of '*approfondisement*', namely by deepening and expanding the areas of integration, which lead to *normative supranationalism.*[191] On the other hand, national instruments conduct a process of *diminution* through the *decisional supranationalism*, which is observed by the intergovernmental guard.[192] Such national tendencies aim at preserving the decisive power at the discretion of the Member State, even in those cases where the integration is inevitable. In this constellation, there exists a default tension between the central and the peripheral governmental entities, which employ the legal and institutional framework as a catalyst for achieving a balanced distribution of power. Therefore, both the processes of *deepening* and *diminution* are part of a formula that accommodates the cyclical interaction of the judicial-normative process and the political-decisional process. These processes aim at achieving an equilibrium, which is responsible for the overall stability of the system and its resilience against the recurring crises generated within or outside the polity.[193] In addition, they allow the Member States to 'digest' the constitutionalization effects of the Treaties, which, in the course of integration, have experienced a certain normative evolution unprecedented in other international organizations.[194] This formula can be symbolically vested upon the principle of institutional balance, which represents the combination of the relevant principles and institutions that ensure the federal balance by pursuing the desired equilibrium. This principle can be seen as a procedural tool which observes the balance of powers between participants, by highlighting the duty of each institution to exercise its powers with due regard for the powers of other institutions, without nevertheless setting preferences among them.[195] The principal content and function of the principle of institutional balance can be described as pursuing the accommodation of all interests in the shaping of political decisions, by encouraging a higher degree of democracy in the polity.[196]

---

[190]Case C-57/72 *Westzucker GmbH v Einfuhr- und Vorratsstelle für Zucker*, [1973] ECR I-321, para. 17. See further Bogdandy (2010), pp. 36–37.

[191]Weiler (1981), p. 292.

[192]Weiler (1981), p. 292.

[193]Weiler (1981), p. 292.

[194]Weiler (1981), pp. 292–293.

[195]Case C-70/88 *European Parliament v Council of the European Communities* [1990] ECR I-2041, paras. 22 *et seq*, and Case C-133/06 *European Parliament v Council of the European Union*, [2008] ECR I-3189, para. 57. See further Bogdandy (2010), p. 36.

[196]Tancredi (2012), p. 261.

The factors that endanger most the federal relationship between the EU and its Member States can be explained with the tensions inherent in the constitutional structure of the Union polity. These tensions may emerge from the horizontal relationship of the Union's institutions, their internal organizational and operational rules, as well as from the vertical relationship of the Union's institutional framework with the Member States. Indeed, the EU constitutional model is adapted to the polycentric and horizontal character of the Union political system.[197] By producing a sustainable equilibrium of forces and interests, it mitigates the tensions in an institutionalized way. This equilibrium reveals the principle of institutional balance in the EU polity, which is a merit of the Union's constitutional construct and a fundamental guarantee that the Treaties have granted to all the stakeholders in the polity.[198] In terms of the political processes, this principle is able to produce "not only a surprisingly salutary normative effect but also a surprisingly stable political polity".[199] Such normative effects are ensured from the principles of conferral, subsidiarity, and proportionality, which serve as normative safeguards for the structure of power in the Union polity, and can be regarded as the central operational tools of the principle of institutional balance.

At the EU level, the political processes can be portrayed from the *decisional supranationalism*, which "relates to the institutional framework and decision-making processes by which Community policies and measures are, in the first place, initiated, debated and formulated, then promulgated and finally executed".[200] The political processes in this course rely on the integration of Member States into the supranational infrastructure of the Union polity as well as on the principles of political organization, unity, and effectiveness. The thesis of decisional supranationalism inherits some features of the traditional intergovernmentalism that exercise a diminutive pressure toward centralization tendencies, which alone would reduce the role of the Member States in the decision-making processes.[201]

The institutional balance can potentially fluctuate due to contradictions in the perception of the claims of authority from the Union or Member States. These claims can be perceived from the counterparties based on two different standards of expectations. The expectations on the claim of authority can be normative, if they are based on a non-derogative power, in that the party claims exclusive authority on that power, or they can be regarded as cognitive, in case that the party adapts its

[197]Bogdandy (2010), p. 36.

[198]Case C-9/56 *Meroni & Co., Industrie Metallurgiche, SpA v High Authority of the European Coal and Steel Community*, [1958] ECR I-011, 152, para. 8.

[199]Weiler (2001), p. 57.

[200]Weiler (1981), p. 271.

[201]See for further insights on *decisional supranationalism* and *diminution* tendencies, Weiler (1981), pp. 273, 280–292.

position and expectations pursuant to the new changed circumstances.[202] The course of integration affects often the normative and cognitive expectations of the parties. Hence, the perceptions based on these expectations might lead to federal tensions. However, the expectations might vary in the course of integration, which means that it may happen for a power not to be perceived any longer on normative but rather on cognitive standards; a change which leads to a more lenient reaction of the actors in such situations. As a result, the federal tensions based on cognitive standards can be absorbed more easily from the institutional framework than those emerging in the context of the normative non-derogative expectations.

Either of a cognitive or of a normative nature, the expectations are mostly raised at the Member State level, and often in two main settings. Illustrative is the principle of primacy and the way in which it is perceived in two different legal orders. The primary effect of the principle of primacy, as an instrument for neutralizing the effects of contradicting national law, makes the national institutions not very enthusiastic about this principle. As such, they threaten to deny the primacy of the EU law over the municipal constitutional orders with regard to certain particular areas, for example the cultural identity. This perception can be manifested through the sovereign claim arising out of a legislature (like in the UK), or through the claim of authority from the national constitutional courts (e.g. the German Federal Constitutional Court) to review the EU acts from a constitutional law perspective. In both these cases, the tensions are related to the question of competences and as such, they have a federal character. In essence, these tensions question the actual 'unconditional nature'[203] of the principle of primacy, which is based on the very assumption that the preference of the EU law over the conflicting national norms, cannot depend on the unilateral acceptance of the authority, which would impair the uniform application of EU law. However, the principle of primacy triggers questions of constitutional importance in the Member States, and as such, the level of normative expectations is very high. As a result, the claim of authority from the EU is hardly grasped at the Member State level without any significant reactions from the national institutional framework. The federal relationships are more sensitive against changes of expectations that have normative grounds rather than those anchored in the cognitive domain.

Having considered the relationship between the federal tensions and the changes of normative expectations that fluctuate the institutional balance, it is now turned to some insights about the effects that the EU decision to participate in the DSP could have for the federal balance in the Union, and the predictions that the principle of institutional balance could offer for the WTO membership. Before considering these issues, it is important to emphasize that the WTO membership constitutes a prime opportunity for the Member States to become "subject to conflicting

[202]See further Bogdandy and Ioannidis (2014), p. 15, referring to Luhmann (1981), pp. 115–116.

[203]See further on the discussion on the unconditional authority of the EU law, Chalmers et al. (2010), pp. 188–197.

obligations with no means of resolving them".[204] Accordingly, the fact that the Member States do not have effective means against the Union's measures in the context of their WTO membership, deprives them of the vertical checks and balances, and stimulates institutional imbalances to the detriment of the Member States' authority over residual powers.[205] In this way, the Member States do not have any means to express their views on the participation of the Union in the DSB, and furthermore, they have no instruments to stop the Union from such a representation when they consider it to be in violation of their residual powers.

The decision of the EU to participate in the DSP is formally relevant for the institutional balance in the polity. The doctrine of federal balance is strongly related with the formal premises predicted by the principle of institutional balance as a procedural tool. This implies that, in order to preserve the federal balance, the decision-making process should be conducted pursuant to procedural rules that allow the affected stakeholders to participate in the political-decisional and judicial-normative processes. Hence, when the EU participates in the DSP through the Commission, it is assumed that the EU exercises a power which is conferred by the Treaties, such as the external representation of the Union in the area of common commercial policy (Article 17(1) TEU in relation with Article 3(1)(d) TFEU). In exercising this power, the Member States should participate and represent their interests in the decision-making process.

Although the Union participation in the DSP does not constitute a Union measure *per se*, it could nevertheless create equivalent effects, given that this participation exposes the EU against retaliatory measures from the trading partners. In view of this, it can be suggested that the Commission needs to take a decision on a case-to-case basis whenever it is called to represent the Union or its Member States in the DSP. The internal formalization of the process of participation in the DSP is an argument against the autonomy of the Union to conduct its external representation in the area of common commercial policy. Given that the latter constitutes an exclusive competence of the Union, any limits have to be justified. Accordingly, the fact that retaliatory measures can be imposed in relation to a trade measure that falls outside the conferred powers of the Union, constitutes a strong normative ground for subjecting the external representation of the Union to the political-decisional procedures, which could be also subject to judicial-normative processes. Such processes and procedures allow the Union to conduct its policies within the conferred powers and the conferred consent of the Member States, and prevent any *ultra vires* action.

The political-decisional processes allow the Member States to accomplish their interests only by participating in the political processes that influence their rights and obligations. Obviously, the default position of the joint responsibility regime

---

[204]Case C-377/98 *Kingdom of the Netherlands v European Parliament and Council of the European Union*, [2001] ECR I-7079, Opinion of the Advocate General Jacobs of 14 June 2001, para. 147.

[205]Tancredi (2012), p. 268.

would dictate the status of joint answerability in the DSP, and as such, this prediction would prejudice the result of a formal decision. Nevertheless, in light of the thesis of decisional supranationalism, the decision of the EU to participate in the DSP would have to follow the procedural steps of initiation, debate, formulation, promulgation, and execution. Furthermore, these phases could be subject to judicial-normative processes in order to ensure the affected parties that their normative expectations and interests are duly observed. These formalities address the fallacies of the joint responsibility regime by endowing the EU participation in the DSP with a greater level of legitimacy.

From the premises of *EC – Asbestos* it is clear that the decision of the EU to participate in the DSP by assuming answerability for a French measure, does not follow a typical legislative procedure.[206] The DSB proceedings failed to discover the legal grounds of the French representation from the EU, or any other justification of the procedural standing of the EU in this case. Presumably, the Commission should have considered during the internal preparatory phases the claims of Canada with reference to the French measure, and consequently it should have been aware that France was not implementing EU law when instituting the measure. Nevertheless, the EU participation in the DSP confirms that the Commission has assumed the risks that would emerge if the French measure would have been found WTO-inconsistent and unjustified. Hence, had the proceedings been unsuccessful, the EU participation in the DSP in the name of France would doubtfully have resisted to any judicial scrutiny, given that the EU was acting in an area of residual powers of Member States.

Having considered the relevance of the decision-making procedure for the participation in the DSP, it is now turned to the relevance of this discussion for the federal tensions, and the role that the principle of institutional balance could play for absorbing the federal tensions in relation to the fallacies of the joint responsibility regime. Obviously, the failure of the EU to base its decision to participate in the DSP in the normative framework amounts to a lack of legitimacy of the EU participation in the DSP. Had the *EC – Asbestos* been unsuccessful and resulted in retaliatory measures against the EU, this lack of legitimacy could have become a constitutional issue in the polity. A speculation that the EU participation in the DSP could have been considered null or void goes beyond the limits of a hypothetical scenario. Nevertheless, the message that this case provides is quite relevant for the issue of the internal federal balance of the Union. The political-decisional process, as a manifestation of the decisional supranationalism thesis, is able to produce legitimate outcomes if and to the extent that the participants respect the powers of other participants, and take a cumulative account of all the interests, also pursuant to the principles of loyalty, subsidiarity, and proportionality. In the *EC – Asbestos*, this proposition could have led to a decision not to step in the DSP instead of France, because the latter is responsible for its own measures. Only in this

[206]Note that the lack of publicity of the decision does not exclude the conduct of any internal administrative decision-making procedure within the Commission.

way, the principle of institutional balance could have been able to satisfy the normative expectations of the Member States.

The predictions of the decisional supranationalism thesis may be particularly relevant for the legitimacy of the EU participation in the DSP. Based on the premises of *EC – Asbestos*, the French measures relate to public health policies, which, under the current state of the Treaties, can be regarded as measures falling either under the shared competences (Article 4(2)(k) TFEU), or under the residual competences of the Member States, usually excluded from harmonization, but subject to coordination. This means that the normative expectation of the Member States would be for the EU to limit itself within its powers. A decision-making procedure that ignores these expectations could be regarded as *ultra vires*. However, whether the *EC – Asbestos* would still cause a tension of a federal character, this remains also doubtful, given that the action of the EU in coordinating and supporting the Member States' actions in the areas of public health policy could still be admitted from them. In this case, the EU claim of authority could be construed upon cognitive standards. In such circumstances, the probability of a federal crisis would be neglectable or insignificant; hence, easily absorbable within the constitutional processes in the Union. Consequently, should the decision of the EU to participate in the DSP be subject to the standard decision-making proceedings, where the Member States also participate, very probably they would support it. In this way, the consequences of the EU participation in the DSP would obtain the desired level of legitimacy. The advantage of the formula of decisional supranationalism stands on the fact that it is able not only to criticize the processes that inflict on the institutional balance of the polity, but also allows the participants to avoid any frictions or tensions on matters that can still be digested at the national level.

## References


Accetto, Matej, and Stefan Zleptnig. 2005. The Principle of Effectiveness: Rethinking its Role in Community Law. *European Public Law* 11 (3): 375–403.

Amtenbrink, Fabian. 2012. The European Court of Justice's Approach to Primacy and European Constitutionalism - Preserving the European Constitutional Order? In *The European Court of Justice and the Autonomy of the Member States*, ed. Hans-W Micklitz and Bruno de Witte. Cambridge, Antwerp, Portland: Intersentia.

Antoniadis, Antonis. 2004. The Participation of the European Community in the World Trade Organization: An External Look at European Union Constitution-Building. In *European Union Law for the Twenty-First Century: Rethinking the New Legal Order*. Vol. 1: Constitutional and Public Law: External Relations, ed. Takis Tridimas and Paolisa Nebbia, 321–344. Oxford: Hart.

Arnull, Anthony, and Derrick Wyatt. 2006. *Wyatt and Dashwood's European Union Law*. 5th ed. London: Sweet & Maxwell.

Barnet, Hilaire. 2006. *Constitutional & Administrative Law*. UK, US, Canada: Routledge-Cavendish.

Bauböck, Rainer. 2002. Political Community Beyond the Sovereign State, Supranational Nationalism and Transnational Minorities. In *Conceiving Cosmopolitanism: Theory, Context and Practice*, ed. Steven Vertovec and Robin Cohen. New York: Oxford University Press.

Bogdandy, Armin von. 2010. Founding Principles. In *Principles of European Constitutional Law*, ed. Armin von Bogdandy and Jürgen Bast, 2nd ed., 11–54. Oxford, Portland, OR; München, Germany: Hart; CH Beck.

Bogdandy, Armin von, and Jürgen Bast. 2010. The Federal Order of Competences. In *Principles of European Constitutional Law*, ed. Armin von Bogdandy and Jürgen Bast, 2nd ed., 275–307. Oxford, Portland, OR; München, Germany: Hart; CH Beck.

Bogdandy, Armin von, and Michael Ioannidis. 2014. Systemic Deficiency in the Rule of Law. What It Is, What Has Been Done, What Could Be Done. *Common Market Law Review* 51: 1–38.

Chalmers, Damian, G.T. Davies, and Giorgio Monti. 2010. *European Union Law. Cases and Materials*. 2nd ed. Cambridge: Cambridge University Press.

Cremona, Marise. 2008. Defending the Community Interest: The Duties of Cooperation and Compliance. In *EU Foreign Relations Law: Constitutional Fundamentals*, ed. Marise Cremona and Bruno de Witte. Oxford, Portland, OR: Hart.

———. 2012. Member States Agreements as Union Law. In *International Law as Law of the European Union*, ed. Enzo Cannizzaro, Paolo Palchetti, and Ramses A. Wessel, 288–324. Studies in EU external relations, vol. 5. Boston: Martinus Nijhoff.

Dashwood, Alan. 2011. *Wyatt and Dashwood's European Union Law*. 6th ed. Oxford, Portland, OR: Hart.

Dicey, Albert Venn. 1885. *Lectures Introductory to the Study of the Law of the Constitution*. London: Macmillan.

Dougan, Michael. 2007. When Worlds Collide! Competing Visions of the Relationship Between Direct Effect and Supremacy. *Common Market Law Review* 44 (4): 931–963.

Dowrick, F.E. 1983. A Model of the European Communities' Legal System. *Yearbook of European Law* 3 (1): 169–237. doi:10.1093/yel/3.1.169.

Edward, David A.O., and Robert C. Lane. 2012. *Edward and Lane on European Union Law*. Cheltenham: Edward Elgar.

Eeckhout, Piet. 2006. The EU and its Member States in the WTO - Issues of Responsibility. In *Regional Trade Agreements and the WTO Legal System*, ed. Lorand Bartels and Federico Ortino, 449–464. International economic law series. Oxford: Oxford University Press.

———. 2011. *EU External Relations Law*. 2nd ed. Oxford EU law library. Oxford, New York: Oxford University Press.

Ehlermann, C.-D. 1983. Mixed Agreements: A List of Problems. In *Mixed Agreements*, ed. David O'Keeffe and Henry G. Schermers, 3–21. Deventer, Boston: Kluwer Law and Taxation Publishers.

Gamper, Anna. 2010. On Loyalty and the (Federal) Constitution. *Vienna Online Journal on International Constitutional Law* 4: 157.

Garner, Bryan A., and Henry Campbell Black. 2010. *Black's Law Dictionary*. 9th ed. St. Paul, MN: West.

Graig, Paul, and Gráinne de Búrca. 2011. *EU Law. Text, Cases, and Materials*. 5th ed. Oxford: Oxford University Press.

Howse, Robert, and Kalypso Nicolaidis. 2001. Introduction: The Federal Vision, Levels of Governance, and Legitimacy. In *The Federal Vision: Legitimacy and Levels of Governance in the United States and the European Union*, ed. Kalypso Nicolaidis and Robert Howse, 1–27. Oxford [etc.]: Oxford University Press.

Kaczorowska, Alina. 2013. *European Union Law*. Abingdon, Oxon, London: Routledge.

Kapteyn, P.J.G. 1993. De Coraplexe Rechtsorde van het Unieverdrag: Subsidiariteitsbeginsel en Nieuwe Bevoegdheden. In *Europa in de Steigers: van Gemeenschap tot Unie*, ed. K. Hellingman and P. van Dijk, 41–52. Europese monografieën, vol. 40. Deventer: Kluwer.

Kapteyn, P.J.G., A.M. McDonnell, K.J.M. Mortelmans, C.W.A. Timmermans, and L.A. Geelhoed, eds. 2008. *The Law of the European Union and the European Communities. With Reference to Changes to be Made by the Lisbon Treaty*. 4th ed. Alphen Aan Den Rijn, Frederick, MD: Kluwer Law International; Sold and distributed in North, Central and South America by Aspen Pub.

Kelsen, Hans, and Robert W. Tucker. 1966. *Principles of International Law*. 2nd ed. New York: Holt Rinehart and Winston, Inc..

Kolb, Robert. 2000. *La Bonne Foi en Droit International Public. Contribution à l'Étude des Principes Généraux de Droit*. 1st ed. Publications de l'Institut universitaire de hautes études internationales, Genève. Paris: Presses universitaires de France.

Kotzur, Markus. 2012. Good Faith (Bona Fide). In *The Max Planck Encyclopedia of Public International Law*, ed. Rüdiger Wolfrum, VII. New York, NY: Oxford University Press.

Lauwaars, R.H. 2008. Institutional Structure. In *The Law of the European Union and the European Communities: With Reference to Changes to be Made by the Lisbon Treaty*, ed. P.J.G. Kapteyn, A.M. McDonnell, K.J.M. Mortelmans, C.W.A. Timmermans, and L.A. Geelhoed, 4th ed., 175–272. Alphen Aan Den Rijn, Frederick, MD: Kluwer Law International; Sold and distributed in North, Central and South America by Aspen Pub.

Lovin, Robin W. 2007. Religion and Political Pluralism. *Mississippi College Law Review* 27: 97.

Luhmann, Niklas. 1981. *Ausdifferenzierung des Rechts. Beiträge zur Rechtssoziologie und Rechtstheorie*. 1st ed. Frankfurt am Main: Suhrkamp.

MacLeod, I., I.D. Hendry, and Stephen Hyett. 1996. *The External Relations of the European Communities. A Manual of Law and Practice*. Oxford, New York: Clarendon Press; Oxford University Press.

Martin, E.A. 2002. *A Dictionary of Law*. 5th ed. Oxford [England], New York: Oxford University Press.

Montgomery, John Warwick. 2002. Subsidiarity as a Jurisprudential and Canonical Theory. *Law & Justice The Christian Law Review* 148: 46.

Mortelmans, Kamiel. 1998. The Principle of Loyalty to the Community (Article 5 EC) and the Obligations of the Community Institutions. *Maastricht Journal of European and Comparative Law* 5: 67.

Neframi, Eleftheria. 2010. The Duty of Loyalty: Rethinking its Scope through its Application in the Field of EU External Relations. *Common Market Law Review* 47 (2): 323–359.

Peters, Anne. 2006. The Constitutionalisation of the European Union – Without the Constitutional Treaty. In *The Making of a European Constitution: Dynamics and Limits of the Convention Experience*, ed. Sonja Puntscher Riekmann and Wolfgang Wessels, 1st ed., 35–67. Wiesbaden: VS Verlag für Sozialwissenschaften.

Rau, Markus. 2003. Subsidiarity and Judicial Review in German Federalism: The Decision of the Federal Constitutional Court in the Geriatric Nursing Act Case. *German Law Journal* 04 (03): 223–236.

Rossi, Lucia Serena. 2012. Does the Lisbon Treaty Provide a Clearer Separation of Competences Between EU and Member States? In *EU Law After Lisbon*, ed. Andrea Biondi, Piet Eeckhout, and Stefanie Ripley, 85–106. Oxford [England], New York: Oxford University Press.

Schmidt, Vivien A. 2013. Democracy and Legitimacy in the European Union Revisited: Input, Output and 'Throughput'. *Political Studies* 61 (1): 2–22. doi:10.1111/j.1467-9248.2012.00962.x.

Schütze, Robert. 2012. *European Constitutional Law*. Cambridge, UK, New York: Cambridge University Press.

Tancredi, Antonello. 2012. On the Absence of Direct Effect of the WTO Dispute Settlement Body's Decisions in the EU Legal Order. In *International Law as Law of the European Union*, ed. Enzo Cannizzaro, Paolo Palchetti, and Ramses A. Wessel, 249–268. Studies in EU external relations, vol. 5. Boston: Martinus Nijhoff.

Thies, Anne. 2006. Cases T-69/00, *FIAMM and FIAMM Technologies*, T-151/00, *Le Laboratoire du Bain*, T-301/00, *Fremaux*, T-320/00, *CD Cartondruck*, AG, T-383/00, *Beamglow Ltd* and T-135/01 *Giorgio Fedon &(and) Figli S.p.A., Fedon S.r.l. and Fedon America USA Inc.*,

Judgments of 14 December 2005, Grand Chamber of the Court of First Insurance. *Common Market Law Review* 43 (2): 1145–1168.

———. 2013. *International Trade Disputes and EU Liability*. Cambridge studies in European law and policy. New York: Cambridge University Press.

Timmermans, C.W.A. 2008a. General Aspects of the European Union and the European Communities. In *The Law of the European Union and the European Communities: With Reference to Changes to be Made by the Lisbon Treaty*, ed. P.J.G. Kapteyn, A.M. McDonnell, K.J.M. Mortelmans, C.W.A. Timmermans, and L.A. Geelhoed. 4th ed. Alphen Aan Den Rijn, Frederick, MD: Kluwer Law International; Sold and distributed in North, Central and South America by Aspen Pub.

———. 2008b. The Basic Principles. In *The Law of the European Union and the European Communities: With Reference to Changes to be Made by the Lisbon Treaty*, ed. P.J.G. Kapteyn, A.M. McDonnell, K.J.M. Mortelmans, C.W.A. Timmermans, and L.A. Geelhoed, 4th ed., 115–174. Alphen Aan Den Rijn, Frederick, MD: Kluwer Law International; Sold and distributed in North, Central and South America by Aspen Pub.

Tinbergen, Jan. 1959. The Theory of the Optimum Regime. In *Selected Papers.: Edited by L. H. Klaassen [and others], etc. [With a Portrait and a Bibliography.]*, 264–304. Amsterdam: North-Holland.

———. 1964. *International Economic Integration*. 2nd ed. Amsterdam [u.a.]: Elsevier.

Tinbergen, Jan, Antony J. Dolman, and Jan van Ettinger. 1976. *Reshaping the International Order. A Report to the Club of Rome*. 1st ed. New York: Dutton.

Weiler, Joseph H.H. 1981. The Community System: The Dual Character of Supranationalism. *Yearbook of European Law* 1 (1): 267–306. doi:10.1093/yel/1.1.267.

———. 2001. Federalism Without Constitutionalism: Europe's *Sonderweg*. In *The Federal Vision: Legitimacy and Levels of Governance in the United States and the European Union*, ed. Kalypso Nicolaidis and Robert Howse, 54–70. Oxford [etc.]: Oxford University Press.

———. 2002. A Constitution for Europe? Some Hard Choices. *JCMS: Journal of Common Market Studies* 40 (4): 563–580. doi:10.1111/1468-5965.00388.

———. 2003. In Defence of the Status Quo: Europe's Constitutional *Sonderweg*. In *European Constitutionalism Beyond the State*, ed. Joseph Weiler and Marlene Wind, 7–23. Cambridge, UK: Cambridge University Press.

Wessel, Ramses A. 2014. Can the EU replace its member states in international affairs? An International law perspective. In *The European union in the world: Essays in honour of Marc Maresceau*, ed. Inge Govaere, Erwan Lannon, Peter van Elsuwege, Stanislas Adam, and Marc Maresceau, 129–147. Leiden, Boston: Martinus Nijhoff.

Witte, Bruno de, Grainne de Burca, and J.H.H. Weiler. 2011. The European Union as an International Legal Experiment. In *The Worlds of European Constitutionalism*, ed. Grainne de Burca and J.H.H. Weiler, 19–56. Cambridge: Cambridge University Press.

# Chapter 5
# A Model for the Union Participation in the DSP and the Management of the Responsibility Concerns

## I. Introduction

The participation of the Union polity in the DSP bears theoretical and practical implications of a legal, economic, and political nature. As already underlined in the previous Chapters, the Union participation in the DSP in relation with matters of non-conferred competences proves fallacious, inasmuch as the Union may be found responsible for measures attributed to the Member States. Considering that the Union may not be able to redress the wrongful act in due course, the burden of responsibility from retaliatory or cross-retaliatory measures is very likely to be devolved to other unrelated Member States of the Union. Although the withdrawal of concessions in the context of retaliation is temporary, the restrictions resulting in increased trade barriers make all the parties worse off, and are, as such, undesired. Against this background, this Chapter addresses the questions whether the regulation of the participation of the Union in the DSP can resolve the fallacies of the joint responsibility regime, and the extent to which a model of participation can manage the consequences of the participation in the DSP. These questions are elaborated by developing a normative model of participation of the Union in the DSP, which accommodates the normative and cognitive expectations raised from the participants, based on the international law of responsibility, the WTO Agreement, and the normative predictions of the constitutional framework of principles of the EU. The underlying thesis of this Chapter endorses the proposition that the fallacies of the joint responsibility regime resulting from the constitutional nature of the Union polity and the WTO Agreement, can be resolved from the EU constitutional infrastructure by taking account of the international obligations of the EU and its Member States.



P. Ruka, *The International Legal Responsibility of the European Union in the Context of the World Trade Organization in Areas of Non-Conferred Competences*,
DOI 10.1007/978-3-319-57177-5_5

## II. The Management of the Problems of Mixity: A Focus on the Consequences of the Joint Responsibility Regime

The fallacies of the joint responsibility regime from the WTO membership result mainly from the false mixity, which is caused from the vertical distribution of powers in the Union polity. This makes the Union virtually competent to participate in the WTO decision-making and judicial-normative processes also for areas remaining within the residual powers of the Member States. The missing procedural arrangements in the Union polity could be identified among the systemic deficiencies that influence the management of the problems of mixity in the context of WTO Agreement. Part of the problem is the fact that the Union participation in the DSP does not follow a particular procedural path for accommodating the interests of the Member States.

In light of these observations, it is maintained that the proceduralization of the Union participation in the DSP could be organized on the basis of a mediating strategy, which balances the Union's aims for the necessary autonomy in exercising its conferred powers, the concerns of the Member States for observation of the residual powers, and the quest of third parties for legal certainty in the trade relationship with these actors.[1] This strategy would succeed the informal arrangements used in the institutional practice of the Union polity, consisting of mechanisms for ensuring a single or coordinated representation of the Union and its Member State, or for achieving a common position in the negotiation of mixed agreements.[2] These arrangements reflect the principle of loyalty as a premise for the unity of international representation of the EU polity.[3] Although having achieved a certain degree of stability in the conduct of the formal WTO obligations of the EU and its Member States, these arrangements have not been formalized upon reliable procedural instruments with predictable effect for the parties.

The Uruguay Round and the subsequent Opinion of the ECJ for the conclusion of the WTO Agreement brought a new reality in terms of emphasizing particular facets of the vertical division of powers in the Union polity.[4] After these processes, it became obvious for the EU that the exercise of the competences in areas such as the GATS and TRIPS would confuse the administration and implementation of the covered disciplines of the WTO Agreement, in case that the parties would not

---

[1]Heliskoski (2001), p. 157.

[2]Among these mechanisms can be mentioned the 'Rome formula', which was used in Rome for the 1967 cereal negotiations following multilateral trade negotiations of the Kennedy Round, as well as in the Paris Conference on International Economic Cooperation (1957–1977). Another instrument has been the 'PROBA 20' (Council Decision of 30 March 1981), a procedural compromise for cases where Member States did not accept Union's exclusive powers. See further Frid (1995), p. 197 and Timmermans (2000), p. 243.

[3]Timmermans (2000), p. 244 and Antoniadis (2004), p. 328. See also Heliskoski (1996), p. 81.

[4]Opinion 1/94 of the Court of Justice *re WTO Agreement*, [1994] ECR I-5267.

conform to their reciprocal duty of loyalty.[5] This could hinder the unitary representation of the Union polity in the WTO proceedings, which would depend on the discretion of the Member States.[6] In these circumstances, a total succession of the Member States in the WTO would be inconceivable, whereas a formal declaration of powers would be inadequate from the perspective of the constitutional nature of powers. Instead, a Code of Conduct has been considered as a salvage of this problem of mixity.[7] Not only in the doctrine, but also in certain institutional processes, there have been attempts to formalize the Union participation in the DSP based on a model that would impose clear rules in this regard.[8] As to the compliance with the DSB rulings and recommendations, only partial regulations have been provided, which cover the areas of anti-dumping and anti-subsidy measures.[9]

The draft of a Code of Conduct on the WTO membership became object of discussions in 1995–1996. This draft was initiated by the Commission as a novelty concept to address the mixity problems of the WTO membership, particularly in the course of negotiation of financial services in the context of GATS.[10] The Intergovernmental Conference preparing the Amsterdam Treaty aimed at introducing a provision in the Treaty as a legal basis for the Council decisions in this regard, but again with no success.[11] The issue of the Code of Conduct returned in the agenda of the Intergovernmental Conference of 2000 preparing the Treaty of Nice, mainly based on the existing contributions of the Commission on a Code of Conduct in relation with the GATS negotiations on financial services.[12] The Presidency of the Conference of Representatives of the Governments of the EU Member States proposed a draft for the current Article 207 TFEU on the Common Commercial Policy and a draft of the new Protocol on detailed rules for participation by the European Union (European Communities and Member States) in WTO

---

[5] Heliskoski (1996), p. 79.

[6] Hilf (1995), p. 258.

[7] See also Antoniadis (2004), pp. 337–338.

[8] See for the contributions from the doctrine in particular Timmermans (2000), Cremona (2001), Antoniadis (2004). See for the institutional processes Presidency Note of the Conference of the Representatives of the Governments of the Member States on the Intergovernmental Conference (IGC 2000)—Extension of the Qualified Majority Voting, Document CONFER 4789/00 of 26 October 2000, 3–9; Summary of the Progress Report in the Intergovernmental Conference on Institutional Reform, Document CONFER 4790/00 of 3 November 2000, 23–28.

[9] Council Regulation (EC) No 1515/2001 of 23 July 2001, on the measures that may be taken by the Community following a report adopted by the WTO Dispute Settlement Body concerning anti-dumping and anti-subsidy matters, Official Journal L 201, 26/07/2001 10–11, repealed from the Regulation (EU) 2015/476 of the European Parliament and of the Council of 11 March 2015 on the measures that the Union may take following a report adopted by the WTO Dispute Settlement Body concerning anti-dumping and anti-subsidy matters, OJ L 83, 27.3.2015, 6–10.

[10] Commission of the European Communities (1996), p. 281, paras. 718, 720. See also Cremona (2001), p. 65.

[11] Timmermans (2000), p. 244. See also Cremona (2001), p. 65.

[12] Cremona (2001), p. 65.

proceedings ("draft Code of Conduct" or "dCoC").[13] These proposals were not included in the text of the Treaty and no Code of Conduct came into being. The following highlights some aspects of the dCoC as it appeared in its latest versions before the Intergovernmental Conference 2000. This draft is useful for the current challenges of the joint responsibility regime and particularly for the issue of the Union participation in the DSP.

The dCoC addresses the participation of the EU in all WTO proceedings for the negotiations (Article 3(1)), decision-making proceedings (Article 4(1)), and the dispute settlement proceedings (Articles 7–8). It aims to establish a single procedure for the exercise of all kinds of competences in the Union polity (Article 2 dCoC). In this way, the Council formulates a common position for all the WTO areas falling within the exclusive powers of the Union, shared powers, or powers residual with the Member States. This position is articulated from the Commission (Articles 3–5 dCoC). The common position constitutes for the Commission the mandate of representation. The Member States exercise their residual powers through their participation in the Council acting by a qualified majority (Article 5 dCoC). Their participation in the WTO meetings, either directly, or through the Presidency of the Council, should not prejudice the mandate of the Commission (Article 4(1) dCoC). The Commission ensures that the Member States are consulted for positions to be stated on their behalf (Article 4(4) dCoC). All these proceedings ensure the unity of representation of the Union polity.

The upholding of the unity in the Union's representation in the DSP remains the ultimate goal (Article 7(1) dCoC). The Commission represents the Union and its Member States in all proceedings initiated against them (respondent proceedings), in spite of the fact whether the Union or the Member States are competent for the disputed measures. The draft Code of Conduct does not provide for a common position in the case of DSP representation. Rather, the unified representation consists of a defense position, which, pursuant to Article 7(2) dCoC, is jointly formulated from the Commission, the concerned Member States, the Council and the Trade and Policy Committee of the Council provided in Article 207(3) TFEU (Article 207 Committee). The duty of loyalty permeates this procedure. The proceedings initiated by the Union or its Member States against third states (claimant proceedings), are based on mandates (common positions) approved by the Article 207 Committee acting by qualified majority (Article 8(1, 2) dCoC). The Member States may pursue their own DSP for measures falling within their residual powers in cases where no common position is achieved, and as long as the Council has decided by a qualified majority against such a request (Article 8(3) dCoC).

Two aspects are particularly relevant with respect to the Union participation in the DSP. First, the Council, acting by a qualified majority, may deny the right of a

[13]Presidency Note of the Conference of the Representatives of the Governments of the Member States on the Intergovernmental Conference (IGC 2000)—Extension of the Qualified Majority Voting, Document CONFER 4789/00 of 26 October 2000, 3–9, and Summary of the Progress Report in the Intergovernmental Conference on Institutional Reform, Document CONFER 4790/00 of 3 November 2000, 23–28.

Member State to pursue the DSP for matters falling within the residual powers. Obviously, by precluding the Member States from its autonomous action in the context of DSP, this instrument confirms the monopoly of the unified representation in the hands of the Union. This constitutes a clear case where the Union impedes the allocation of powers by assuming obligations in relation with the residual powers of Member States. This argument triggers the issue of legitimacy, inasmuch as the Union has to base its decision on conferred (internal) powers. This decision would be valid and able to produce legitimate outcomes only to the extent that it follows the predictions of the principle of constitutional legality. This action at the Union level would be criticized on the basis of the analogy with Article 207(5) TFEU, which provides certain limitations on the qualified majority voting in particular areas of the GATS and TRIPS. Moreover, Article 2(5) TEU precludes any harmonization in the areas of residual powers of the Member States.

Second, pursuant to Article 7(3) dCoC the concerned Member States "*shall make every effort to ensure that the WTO procedures do not result in the calling into question of advantages enjoyed by the [Union] or by other Member States.*"[14] This provision reveals the Union's concern about the joint responsibility regime. The Member States are under an obligation to make their best efforts to ensure that the consequences of the DSP initiated as a result of their measures do not result in retaliatory measures against the Union or its Member States. In this way, the concerns related with the joint responsibility regime are addressed by means of an obligation of conduct, in that it provides for a 'best efforts' approach to strive for achieving a particular result. Any connotations of flexibility in this regard should be taken with reserves, as long as the 'best efforts' approach, inherent in the obligation of conduct, is not linked with the result *per se*, but rather with the means for achieving the result, hence, without prejudicing the outcome of the DSP. The EU and its Member States involved in the DSP have to demonstrate that they did strive to achieve the prescribed result, namely that their actions or omissions in the course of the DSP should not result in hindering the Union's substantive trade benefits of WTO membership.

The upholding from the defaulting Member State of the WTO inconsistent measure, even after a DSB ruling or recommendation requires its withdrawal, results in the hindrance of trade benefits for the concerned WTO Member to the benefit of the individual interest of the wrongdoer. From the WTO law perspective, this establishes a negative status quo, which keeps in place a system that hinders the substantive rights of the WTO membership. This status quo may be reversed only through the compliance with the DSB ruling. The non-compliance gives rise to the authorization of the injured state with the right to suspend the concessions against the EU, hence affecting the other unrelated Member States of the EU. This action would expand the negative effects of the status quo to other Member States. In this way, the conduct of the Commission and the concerned Member State may be deemed as hindering the common interests of the Union. Obviously, this could not

[14] Emphasis added.

be regarded as a best effort in the meaning of Article 7(3) dCoC, insofar as this obligation of conduct aims precisely at the termination of the state of wrongfulness.

This regulation limits the flexibility of the Union with regard to the compliance with DSB rulings and recommendations. A DSB ruling or recommendation does not leave too much room for maneuver for the wrongdoer. The 'best efforts' approach may imply that the institutions of the Union or the Member States may not postpone the compliance with DSB rulings to extremes. Accordingly, they should not manifestly and gravely disregard the limits in discretion to the detriment of their obligation (of conduct), in order to ensure that the third Member States are not affected from retaliatory measures. This would constitute an infringement of Article 7(3) dCoC.

However, the Union may assume a wider scope of discretion when it comes to the compliance with the DSB rulings and recommendations. As it is already established with the Regulation 2015/476, the Commission has the discretion to repeal, amend, or adopt other special implementing measures deemed appropriate under the circumstances, in order to bring the Union in conformity with the recommendations and rulings contained in the report.[15] The established procedure provides for the review of the Union's conduct in the anti-dumping or anti-subsidies areas for disputed or non-disputed measures, as well as for the duty of the interested parties to provide the relevant information needed for enacting measures in these areas.[16] Additionally, it is provided that the measures in the areas of anti-dumping or anti-subsidies procedures shall take effect from the date of entry into force and shall not serve as a basis for the reimbursement of the duties collected prior to that date, unless otherwise provided for.[17] This regulation is an art of proceduralization, but its scope is very limited as it addresses mainly areas for which the Union is competent, such as competition and state aid.

Another area where proceduralization attempts have been successfully concluded is the management of problems of mixity in international investment agreements, where the Union and its Member States may incur financial responsibility in relation with investor-to-state disputes. Regulation (EU) 912/2014[18] applies only to investor-to-state dispute settlement where the Union or its concerned Member States participate as respondents (Article 1) in the course of

[15] Article 1(1) of the Regulation 2015/476. The same was provided in the Article 1(1) of the repealed Council Regulation (EC) No 1515/2001. The difference between these acts is that, in the repealed Regulation (1515/2001), the competent body for enacting measures in compliance with the DSB rulings was the Council, while with the new Regulation (2015/476) this competence is vested on the Commission.

[16] Articles 1(2, 3), 2 of the Regulation 2015/476. Cf. Articles 1(2, 3), 2 of the Regulation 1515/2001.

[17] Article 3 of the Regulation 2015/476. Cf. Article 3 of the Regulation 1515/2001.

[18] Regulation (EU) 912/2014 of the European Parliament and of the Council of 23 July 2014 establishing a framework for managing financial responsibility linked to investor-to-state dispute settlement tribunals established by international agreements to which the European Union is party, OJ L 257, 28.8.2014, 121–134.

Union or mixed agreements on international investments. This Regulation is a prime example of the management of problems of mixity, and could have a theoretical relevance for the model of the Union participation in the DSP, inasmuch as it addresses the damages that the Union may incur by virtue of wrongful measures attributed to Member States. To the extent that such damages are considered 'inequitable', the Regulation provides that the international responsibility for violation of international investment agreements follows the vertical division of competences, and that the financial responsibility be allocated, as a matter of Union law, between the Union and the concerned Member State pursuant to predetermined criteria.[19] Accordingly, whereas the Union should defend all measures falling within its exclusive powers, the attribution of financial burden follows the rules of attribution of conduct. The Union bears responsibility for measures attributed to the Union or to Member States acting under the control of the Union (by virtue of Union law).[20] The representation in the dispute settlement proceedings is subject to alternation, in case that the measure in dispute does not exclusively concern a Union measure.[21] However, this alternation does not prejudice the division of competences or the financial responsibility of the wrongdoer.[22]

The Regulation (EU) 912/2014 is a significant step toward formalization, and manifests the concerns of the Union in terms of the burden of responsibility from the joint participation in DSPs. Unlike the draft Code of Conduct, which remained a project, this Regulation became reality due to the budgetary burden that the investment arbitral awards may have for the Union. The DSP rulings and recommendations do not pose such imperatives, insofar as the burden of retaliation is distributed in the society. However, this Regulation endorses some valuable lessons with respect to the normative model of the Union participation in the DSP. First, it reaffirms the relevance of the distribution of powers for the attribution and reallocation of burden for breach of international obligations. The allocation of burden of responsibility is made pursuant to the rules of attribution of the international responsibility, and this follows the allocation of powers.[23] Second, it suggests the flexible decision-making as an instrument for maintaining a sound equilibrium between the Union and the Member States with reference to the observance of

[19]Recitals 3, 5 of the Regulation (EU) 912/2014.

[20]Recital 7 of the Regulation (EU) 912/2014.

[21]However, pursuant to Recital 11 and Article 9(2, 3) of the Regulation (EU) 912/2014, the Union decides to assume a respondent role in cases attributed to Member States "where the dispute also involves treatment afforded by the Union, where it appears that the treatment afforded by a Member State is required by Union law and where similar treatment is being challenged in a related claim against the Union in the [WTO], where a panel has been established and the claim concerns the same specific legal issue and where it is necessary to ensure a consistent argumentation in the WTO case." Furthermore, the respondent status of the Union is necessary in case that "the Union would bear all or at least part of the potential financial responsibility arising from the dispute".

[22]Recitals 10, 17 and Article 1 of the Regulation (EU) 912/2014.

[23]Recital 3 and Article 3 of the Regulation (EU) 912/2014.

powers. The decisions whether the Union or a Member State should act as a respondent are taken as implementing acts on the basis of "full and balanced factual analysis and legal reasoning".[24] Third, the Union and the Member States have to practice the duty of loyalty in the course of participation in the DSP, and should observe their reciprocal interests.[25] In particular, the duty of loyalty includes "the prompt notification of any significant procedural steps, the provision of relevant documents, frequent consultations and participation in the delegation to the proceedings".[26] Fourth, the Regulation (EU) 912/2014 provides for the possibility that an award which is paid from the Union by virtue of its procedural position as respondent, be transposed to the responsible Member State through an individual decision of the Commission, which subsequently may become subject to legality review pursuant to Article 263 TFEU.[27] Lastly, it can be highlighted the role of the Commission as a guardian of the unity in the polity, by vesting it with implementing powers of the Regulation (EU) 912/2014. The Regulation only marginally connects with the WTO proceedings, in those cases where the investment claims are related with claims against the Union in the WTO.[28] This aims to ensure a unified representation in the interrelated proceedings. However, it can be maintained that this Regulation, although not directly applicable for the participation of the Union polity in the DSP, still offers useful insights on the capability of the Union infrastructure to constitutionalize processes that can manage the fallacies of the joint responsibility regime in terms of participation in the DSP, and can manage the burden of responsibility in an appropriate and equitable manner.

Following these normative considerations, it is now turned to the examination of some more general facets of the draft Code of Conduct, which, although remaining an 'attempt of formalization' of the Union participation in the DSP, still prove relevant for construing a normative model. These facets elaborate on the background of the draft Code of Conduct, the reasons that caused these attempts to fail, and the message one can receive from this failure. As much as the first aspect is concerned, the formalization of the representation has been linked with the need to enhance the legal certainty of the third parties, as to the conduct of the procedure for the Union participation in the DSP. More than a broad aim, these attempts of formalization have escorted an ever-increasing dimension of the international trade, materialized through an increase of the WTO disciplines and the expansion of the membership in the WTO Agreement. These external reasons have significant implications for the vertical distribution of powers in the Union polity. In light of this, the Member States have looked for a solution between two inconvenient alternatives: either to withdraw from the WTO and leave the EU as a sole representative of the polity, a politically and strategically undesired solution, or to make

[24]Recital 13 and Article 9(2) of the Regulation (EU) 912/2014.

[25]Recital 14 and Articles 6, 9(4) of the Regulation (EU) 912/2014.

[26]Recital 15 of the Regulation (EU) 912/2014.

[27]Recital 20 of the Regulation (EU) 912/2014.

[28]Article 9(3) of the Regulation (EU) 912/2014.

a declaration of powers, which could virtually resolve the problems of mixity.[29] In the background of the attempts for formalization, the main aim has been therefore to address the internal constitutional challenges by means of regulatory instruments that ensure the unitary representation of the Union and its Member States in the WTO proceedings, being political-decisional and judicial-normative. These concerns permeate the draft Code of Conduct, insofar as it emphasizes the procedural arrangements for achieving a common position of the EU and its Member States and the appointment of the EU as a sole negotiator and representative for the entire Union polity.

The attempts for establishing a Code of Conduct reaffirm the relevance of the distribution of powers for the problems of mixity in the WTO Agreement. The residual powers of the Member States are reaffirmed as an incontestable constitutional imperative. It remains disputable whether this approach remains actual after the confirmation of the common commercial policy as an exclusive competence and its encompassing effects over the trade in services and commercial aspects of intellectual property, particularly in light of the discourse on the virtually conferred powers *versus* the actual powers of the Member States.

As to the second issue, it can be maintained that the reasons for the failure of the establishment of a Code of Conduct could have been quite formal. By reflecting the current state of the law and practice on the matter, the draft Code of Conduct mainly aimed to formalize the participation in the DSP, rather than to address the fallacies of the joint responsibility regime. The idea of formalizing the participation in the WTO proceedings was an alternative for the expansion of the common commercial policy to include the areas of the GATS and TRIPS. Since the latter alternative prevailed in the negotiations of the Treaty of Nice, the former became redundant.[30] Obviously, this argument overestimates the significance of the exclusive nature of the competence on common commercial policy. Whether the proposed alternative on the formalization of the EU participation in WTO proceedings would have resolved the problems of mixity, this is another question, which does not invalidate the theoretical relevance of the formalization attempts for the Union participation in the DSP.

With respect to the third issue, it can be held that the message of the failure of formalization can be construed as a normative argument in favor of the model of the Union participation in the DSP. Accordingly, behind the failure of the draft Code of Conduct, one can see the vertical competition of powers in the Union polity and the inextricable linkage of their exercise. The Union participation in the DSP, being reduced to the arguments of the distribution powers, could not have a different end, other than entering another spill-over process of deepening and expanding the areas of integration following the functionalist model. Indeed, since the Court announced with its Opinion 1/94, that the residual powers of the Member States in the areas of GATS and TRIPS are the main argument for concluding WTO Agreement in a

[29]See also Antoniadis (2004), p. 337.

[30]Cremona (2001), pp. 65–67. See also Antoniadis (2004), p. 338.

mixed way, it took less than one decade to articulate the political decision to eliminate the 'last obstacle' of the unified representation. This argument, endorsed formally with the Treaty of Lisbon, cannot resolve the fallacies of the joint responsibility regime in a substantive manner. In case that the ECJ, in the current configuration of the Treaties, would be required to issue another Opinion on the conclusion (or continuation) of the WTO Agreement, probably it could choose to follow its formal path by sticking on the mere interpretation of distribution of powers. However, no preliminary judicial observation could conceive *ex ante* the limits of powers conferred to the Union by the Member States, as ultimate holders of sovereign rights. Indeed, the current scheme of distribution of powers, with its limitations in terms of harmonization, as well as under the effect of the substantive restrictions on their exercise, could well lead the Court to pursue a more substantial approach for the analysis of the limits of conferral and their implications on the regime of mixity. Accordingly, the current limitations, as a reaffirmation of the residual powers of the Member States, serve the thesis that the EU and its Member States should keep acting jointly in the course of the WTO membership, as long as they hold competences that are inextricably linked.

To conclude, the underlying idea of the draft Code of Conduct is to construe the conditions for ensuring the unity of representation of the Union polity in the DSP, as one of the aspects of the joint responsibility regime. The concrete meaning of the obligation of conduct (Article 7(3) dCoC) is to ensure that the DSP is pursued with a view to protecting also the common interest of the Union in terms of trade benefits. The unity of representation in this context is of particular relevance. Being aware of the potential effects of cross-retaliatory measures, the Intergovernmental Conference conditioned the participation of the Union as a representative of the concerned Member States with their obligation to comply with the DSB rulings and recommendations. The Union or the concerned Member State may choose to comply with the ruling, or may postpone this compliance to the extremes by means of negotiation processes or compensations. The 'best efforts' approach in this respect predicts for the cumulative consideration of the common interest of the Union and unrelated Member States, in order to protect them from negative effects of the DSP. The element of consideration of interests reveals the predictions of the principle of loyalty and endorses the Union as a *pactum fidelis*. In this context, the principle of loyalty and the need for a uniform representation could resolve the fallacies of the joint responsibility regime by synchronizing at the Union level the conflicting interests of the Member States and the Union in relation with their participation in the DSP. The proceduralization of the decision-making is a plausible premise in this regard. A procedure for resolving the questions of responsibility could be a better premise than the partition of treaty obligations.[31]

[31] Schermers (1983), p. 830.

## III. Formalization Versus Flexibility of the Union Participation in the DSP

The failure of the efforts to formalize the Union participation in the DSP by means of a Code of Conduct may be considered as a missed opportunity in terms of addressing the fallacies of the joint responsibility regime. In the current state of the law, the Union has in place no formalized procedures for the management of problems of mixity in terms of the participation in the DSP, either as a complainant, or as a respondent. This results in the Union representing the Member States also for matters falling within their residual areas of powers. As already observed in the previous Chapters, such observations do not aim to prejudice this art of participation of the Union in the DSP, but rather to establish relevant procedures that ensure an adequate level of legitimacy in this context. In light of the above, the question is about elaborating the possible alternatives for conceiving a formalization of the Union participation in the DSP.

At the outset, it should be emphasized that the formalization of the decision of the Union to participate in the DSP should not prejudice the format of representation, which is construed in accordance with the strategic interests of the participants. Accordingly, the Union may enact a legislative act of a general character, which addresses in an exhaustive manner the conditions for the Union participation in the DSP (the 'prior' or 'formalized' procedure). Alternatively, the Union may enact a general 'framework regulation', which determines the conditions for the Union institutions to decide on a case-by-case basis on the participation in the DSP, and to address the consequences of this participation (the 'flexible' procedure). In any case, it is important that the participation of the Union in the DSP is regulated, and the consequences of this participation are determined in a predictable manner.

In view of that, one could highlight some advantages and disadvantages of both these alternatives. The procedure of formalization has a significant disadvantage in terms of the ability of the legislator to predict beforehand all the situations for which the questions of responsibility are triggered. Therefore, the model of the participation has to be construed at a rather general level, so as to include all the situations where the participation of the Union in the DSP would be questioned. Such a regulation could provide, for instance, the obligation of the Union to participate in all the DSP for matters of non-conferred competences with the status of joint/optional participant or principal/mandatory representative.[32] Other formats of participation are also possible, such as the designation of the Union, based on a principal-agent relationship, as a principal representative of the concerned Member State, which may optionally participate as a subsidiary representative.[33] For the

[32]See further *infra* Section V(2)(a)(iv) in this Chapter ("The format of the Union participation and representation in the DSP").

[33]It should be noted that the joint responsibility regime in the case of principal-agent relationship is not incurred by virtue of a special agreement, but rather by virtue of the joint membership in the WTO Agreement.

formalized type of procedure, it is important to ensure that the consequences of the participation are duly regulated beforehand, so that the parties are aware of their responsibilities. The flexibility procedure appears more advantageous in this regard, as long as it ensures the adaptability of the format of representation in the DSP in accordance with the adequate needs of the entire polity. This is particularly guaranteed by not prejudicing the distribution of powers *in abstracto*, but instead pursuing a dynamic equilibrium that evolves and grows naturally under the spill-over effects of the EU integration.[34] Furthermore, the flexibility procedure may respond more adequately to the concerns of autonomy.

However, the flexibility procedure entails higher transaction costs, inasmuch as it requires the coordination of a high (and ever increasing) number of participants. Their interests are also unpredictably divergent due to their constitutional differences in cultural identity, their natural connections with particular WTO Members, their changes in geo-political and security interests, as well as the dynamics of their trade interests. The inability of coordination would increase the risk of incurring joint responsibility to the extent that the Union and the concerned Member States may not make use of their bargaining power in the DSP. Therefore, as put by one author, a sort of a more formalized procedure could "be preferred to reduce the transaction costs of *ad-hoc* co-ordination", which could require the "[delegation] of power to supranational institutions".[35] Hence, the formalization procedure presents clear advantages in this regard, considering that a general regulation is immune from pragmatic decisions of the participants.

The formalized procedure ensures a higher degree of transparency on the way the Union polity deals with the consequences of the participation in the DSP. This may also serve as a guarantee for the public, which might be affected from possible countervailing measures when purporting to predict adequately the consequences of these proceedings. Additionally, the Member States, which are not related with the disputed measure, could enjoy from formalized procedures a higher level of protection of their interests, because a normative framework creates more predictable obligations on the wrongdoers to observe the interests of the other Member States (similarly to Article 7(3) dCoC). Another reason in favor of the formalization is the interest of every affected stakeholder to review the legality of the Union's action. This would allow the interested parties to make use of their judicial standing for invoking the legality of the Union's decision for representation based on the specific propositions of the framework, rather than struggling with the missing direct effect of the WTO Agreement.

It is then concluded that, notwithstanding the disadvantages of each of these alternatives, the regulation of the Union participation in the DSP represents a constitutional imperative that could address the fallacies of the joint responsibility regime. Each of these procedures is able to construe normative frameworks for the concerned Member State or the Commission to observe the cumulative

[34] See also Heliskoski (2001), p. 244.

[35] Graig (2012), p. 27.

considerations of interests from the wrongdoers. Additionally, these frameworks could provide the normative basis for complying with the DSB rulings in the course of the DSP. Hence, these instruments could ensure the observance of the international obligations of the Union in view of Article 216(2) TFEU. In this way, the obligation of the Member States and the Commission to provide deference to the interests of the Member States from their substantive aspects of the WTO membership (based on the model of Article 7(3) dCoC) could become justiciable by means of infringement proceedings pursuant to Articles 258 *et seq.* TFEU. This possibility has its own limitations, considering that the 'best efforts' approach of compliance with the DSB rulings and recommendations would not be justiciable as to the result, but rather as to the means. Therefore, the respondents could be answerable before the ECJ with regard to their role in the DSP for doing all they can within their powers to avoid the incurrence of any countervailing measures. This implies that the Commission and the concerned Member State(s) cannot be held responsible for breach of their obligation of conduct in relation with the defense strategy applied in the DSP. However, once a DSB ruling with final effects has found the measure inconsistent with the WTO disciplines, the wrongdoer is under the obligation to comply with this ruling, and the formalization procedure would be a significant guarantee in this regard.

## IV. The Premises of the Normative Model of the Union Participation in the DSP

The above observations endorse the need to reconsider the issue of formalization of the Union participation in the DSP from a different angle. This builds on the current constitutional structure of the Union and reflects the good practice of the WTO relationship of the EU and Member States. Yet, it employs the existing constitutional principles of the Union polity as an answer to the fallacies of the joint responsibility regime in a more constructive way, which is in line also with the predictions of the international law of responsibility. The ultimate aim is to pursue a normative model in which the constitutional values of the Union polity permeate the EU participation in the DSP.

Before elaborating the relevant propositions on the management of the problems of mixity concerning responsibility, it is useful to recall the main premises where the model and its normative elements could be based. These premises are mainly rooted in the constitutional framework of principles, namely the unity of the EU legal order, the principles of political organization, and the principles of political processes, which are presented as sub-values of the rule of law. Additionally, two other groups of premises, address, on the one hand, the premises suggested from the *legi generali* on the international responsibility as much as the responsibility of the EU from the WTO is concerned, and on the other hand, the premises of the law of the mixed agreements, with a view to the WTO law.

## *1. The Premises Related with the International Law of Responsibility*

The patterning of the normative model should take into consideration the role of international rules of legal responsibility for breach of international agreements. As already pointed out in Chap. 2, the rules of international responsibility aim to prevent or minimize the breach of obligations by deterrence, or to provide the relevant remedies for the breach.[36] In light of this, the model of participation of the Union polity in the DSP should aim at accomplishing these aims of the responsibility regime, as prerogatives for the effectiveness of the legal orders of the WTO and the EU. The effectiveness is influenced from the ability to remedy the invaded rights. The regime of responsibility is triggered from the invasion of rights,[37] which in the relationship between the Union polity and the WTO Members is quite complex. Obviously, the WTO Agreement constitutes the primary source of normative rules for determining the state of invasion of rights. This could imply that the determination from the DSB of inconsistent measures that violate the WTO disciplines should be considered as an invasion of legal interests, despite the missing direct effect of the WTO Agreement and DSB decisions in the legal orders of the EU and its Member States. Based on this reference, the model of responsibility should be able to prevent or remedy the violated legal interests of the participants.

These predictions are in line with the view of international responsibility as a regulatory mechanism for the protection of the authority of states over their legal interests as a corollary of their sovereignty.[38] It is in light of this that the participation of the Union and Member States should be construed, i.e. as a guarantee of rights and obligations of states. This participation is not a mere pragmatic decision, but represents the opportunity for other Member States to defend their prerogatives. Similarly, the active participation of the Union should be limited to its own prerogatives, as a guarantee for those Member States of the Union that have no direct relation with the disputed measure. Following the thesis of effective responsibility, the model of participation in the DSP should pursue the ultimate aim of effective responsibility, which fulfills the sovereignty claims of all participating states. Accordingly, the system of responsibility should ensure that the Member States that have instituted wrongful measures should maintain a direct affiliation with all the stages of the DSP, i.e. from answerability to full responsibility.

The direct participation of the concerned Member States in the DSP is in line with their WTO obligations corresponding to their residual powers. This constitutes a premise for the system of responsibility, considering that only the direct answerability ensures the effective compliance with the predictions of the principles of

[36]Hirsch (1995), p. 8. See also Dupuy (1989), pp. 105–106.

[37]Brownlie (1998), p. 435.

[38]Pellet (2010), pp. 4–5, referring also to ILC Commentaries to Draft ARSIWA, Commentary to Article 2 ARSIWA, paras. 2, 177.

*pacta sunt servanda* and *bona fide*. The concept of answerability entails the obligation to be called into account and to legally respond for the wrongful conduct, and this is crucial for the procedural standing in the DSP.[39] The establishment of breach of international obligations triggers the accountability of the wrongdoer, which remains the ultimate subject capable to comply with the regime of accountability, namely to ensure the cessation and the restitution of the injured legal order to the greatest possible extent.[40] In light of this, the Union should not be held accountable for wrongful acts of Member States falling within their residual powers. This suggests that the attribution of responsibility should follow the attribution of conduct, which is construed pursuant to the ownership of competences. Considering that the Union and the Member States cannot control each other for their respective powers, it is suggested that the Union's responsibility should be limited to the conferred powers. This is in line with the prediction that the principle of the attribution of conduct entails the unity between the wrongful conduct and the wrongdoer.

These rules do not exclude the attribution of responsibility to the Union *ex relatione*,[41] thus in the absence of any form of complicity. Following the doctrine of the reciprocal indetermination of legal orders,[42] the Union cannot invoke its internal structure of powers, or even the *ultra vires* nature of the measure, or its missing relationship with the disputed measure, to escape responsibility. Once the Union participates in the DSP, it has to defend the measure as if it was committed from its own organs. This art of responsibility could hardly be construed in light of the doctrine of substitution, given that the Member States cannot absolve their obligations falling within the residual powers, and the Union cannot succeed their rights and obligations in this domain due to constraints from the limited powers doctrine.[43] This is another premise to be taken into account for the normative model of participation in the DSP.

The above observations sit, however, uneasily with the joint responsibility regime, which entails the relational type of the Union's responsibility. In this respect, the responsibility of the Union and the concerned Member State could follow the scheme of the invocation of primary and subsidiary responsibility, which can be combined further with the scheme of powers. Accordingly, the primary responsibility is vested on the subject that owns the competences for enacting the wrongful measure. In case that this subject does not comply with this obligation, the subsidiary responsibility comes into play, as an alternative mode of reparation of the injured legal order.[44] Only subsequently, it could be possible to engage the internal institutional framework of the Union polity to ensure the compliance with

[39] See generally, Crawford and Watkins (2010), p. 283.

[40] Crawford and Watkins (2010), p. 286.

[41] See also Dominicé (2010), pp. 281–282.

[42] See generally, Dupuy (2010), p. 174 *et seq.*

[43] See generally, Hirsch (1995), pp. 53–54.

[44] See also Orakhelashvili (2010), p. 662.

the regime of responsibility. This is in line with the premise that the allocation of subsidiary responsibility is followed by a reallocation of remedial duties between jointly responsible entities.[45] This entitles the Union to issue a legislative act for obliging the defaulting Member State to comply with its own obligations. The two-steps operation of the principle of attribution could assist in designating the proper alignment of responsibility. Accordingly, in the first step, it is determined the primary relationship between the wrongful conduct and the primarily responsible subject. In the second step, the influential role of the co-participant is considered, as a premise for attributing the due level of responsibility, whether it has to be a *joint*, or a *subsidiary* one. This complies with the thesis that the responsibility for the wrongful act lies with the subject to whom the act is attributed, and this follows the holder of the relevant competence.[46]

The normative model should prevent the vicarious responsibility of the Union for measures of Member States enacted within their residual powers.[47] This is because the vicarious responsibility shifts the burden from the Member State to the Union, while the joint responsibility regime entails joint (namely shared) responsibility, which is triggered *ex relatione*.[48] The model of vicarious responsibility could particularly be incurred in case that the Union represents the Member State in the DSP. This format of participation in the DSP would constitute a diversion from the joint participation in the DSP, as a corollary of the joint responsibility regime and the duty of answerability.

The Member States are bound by their own WTO obligations, which should be observed within the auspices of their residual powers. Any breach of these obligations, involves an obligation to make reparations.[49] The breach of the WTO obligations constitutes an internationally wrongful act. The imposition of measures in violation of WTO disciplines is prohibited, and this constitutes the legal reason triggering the international responsibility of the wrongdoer.[50] The cessation of wrongful measures in a timely manner constitutes the main remedy in the WTO legal system, which aims at bringing the state of illegality to an end. Non-compliance with this obligation triggers the imposition of retaliatory measures, which amounts to a trade burden upon the wrongdoer. This form of liability constitutes a constraining tool against the wrongdoer for disregarding the DSB ruling, and not a compensation for the injured state.

The joint responsibility regime entails an obligation for both the Union and the Member States to exercise the duty of care when performing actions that could

---

[45]See also Orakhelashvili (2010), pp. 647–665.

[46]See generally, Hirsch (1995), p. 24.

[47]See generally on vicarious responsibility, Quigley (1987), p. 80.

[48]*Affaire des biens britanniques au Maroc espagnol, Great Britain v. Spain*, (1925) 2 R.I.A.A. 615, 648–649. See further Crawford (2008), p. 553.

[49]*The Factory at Chorzów*, Merits, 1928, 29, and *The Factory at Chorzów*, Jurisdiction, 1927, 21.

[50]See generally Crawford and Watkins (2010), p. 286.

trigger the responsibility of the partner.[51] This can be observed also in the course of participation in the DSP, where the Union and the concerned Member State have to show a certain level of deference to the normative expectations of each other. This allows the construction of a model of participation in the DSP that is based on a pluralist approach of integration of the premises of other legal orders, which in turn could assist in establishing an adequate level of normativity.

The law of responsibility predicts the ability of the legal order to trigger foreseeable consequences from the internationally wrongful conduct. Hence, the thesis that where there is responsibility, there is justice (*ubi responsibilitas, ubi ius*), can serve as a premise for the legal certainty for all participants. The international law of responsibility seeks to prevent the dominance of the interests of the group over the individuals.[52] The assumption of responsibility from the Union may be construed as a domination of the collective interests over the unrelated Member States, which could incur the burden of responsibility by means of devolution from the responsibility assumed by the Union in the DSP. This concern can be addressed from the model of responsibility, which should build on the premise that the system of responsibility precludes the incurrence of burden from the collective action, unless this action is legitimate, and considers the individual interests in a cumulative way.

## 2. *The Premises Related with Mixed Agreements and Particularly the WTO Agreement*

The mixed agreements are binding upon the Union (Article 216(2) TFEU) not only for the category of the conferred powers covered by the agreement, but also for the entire agreement.[53] The Member States derive their obligations toward third states in a mixed agreement not only by virtue of their direct membership, but also by virtue of their membership in the Union. Therefore, even when exercising their residual powers in relation with WTO obligations, they are not merely observing their individual obligations to the WTO Member, but they are, also in light of the unity of external representation, exercising an EU law obligation.[54] Indeed, the unitary representation of the Union in external relations depends on the Member States reaffirming continuously their sovereign rights over residual powers.[55]

[51] See generally on the duty of care, Quigley (1987), pp. 119–120.

[52] Eagleton (1928), p. 228.

[53] Cases C-104/81 *Hauptzollamt Mainz v Kupferberg*, [1982] ECR I-3641, para. 13 and C-12/86 *Demirel v Stadt Schwäbisch Gmünd*, [1987] ECR I-3719, paras. 9 and 11. It is to be noted that the ECJ in the *Demirel* Case was dealing with an association agreement pursuant to Article 217 TFEU. See further Neframi (2012), p. 326.

[54] See also Timmermans (2000), p. 245.

[55] See also Hilf (1995), p. 258.

However, from the thesis of the unitary representation, it can be inferred that the Member States are obliged under the Union law to comply with their own obligations from mixed agreements.

With respect to the WTO Agreement, its mixed nature suggests some further premises that would enhance to a certain extent the normative character of the model of the Union participation in the DSP. The EU participation in the DSP is not only a matter of WTO law, but also a matter of Union law, and the consequences of this participation, such as the compliance with the DSB rulings and recommendations shall be construed within the context of Union law.[56] The EU legal order should interact as smoothly as possible with the WTO legal order, in order to prevent any possible subordination of the former to the latter.[57] This can be ensured by putting into place the necessary procedural safeguards that prevent the Member States to be isolated in the DSP, and which could preclude the Union's regulatory authority.[58] The defense of major interests of the Union and Member States in the DSP from the Commission, such as the development and health policies, enhances the chances for a better protection of the regulatory autonomy.[59] Moreover, the continuous denial of direct effect of the WTO Agreement could be a further guarantee to the benefit of this insulation,[60] although not in the cases where the Union implements particular obligations of the Agreement, or its secondary acts refer to specific WTO law provisions (the principle of implementation pursuant to the '*Nakajima/Fediol*' exceptions).[61]

The structure of powers in the Union polity qualifies the WTO Agreement as a mixed agreement. The Union is virtually competent for the entire scope of the Agreement, due to the qualification of the common commercial policy as an exclusive EU competence. However, particular facets of this competence have their extensions in the domain of the residual powers of the Member States. This makes the case for a *false* or *quasi* mixity,[62] a concern that the normative model of the Union participation in the DSP should consider. Accordingly, the rules of attribution of conduct will sit uneasily along with the unclear separation of powers in the Union. In case that it would be possible to distinguish the ownership of powers of the Union and the Member States, the joint responsibility regime could be supplemented with a regime of several responsibility, whereby the owner of separated powers should be deemed responsible for its wrongful acts. This is in line with the concepts of primary and subsidiary responsibility, and reaffirms the thesis

---

[56]See also Thies (2013), p. 134.

[57]Antoniadis (2004), p. 343.

[58]Antoniadis (2004), p. 343.

[59]Antoniadis (2004), p. 344.

[60]Antoniadis (2004), p. 343.

[61]Cases C-70/87 *Fediol v Commission*, [1989] ECR I-1781, paras. 19–22; C-69/89 *Nakajima v Council*, [1991] ECR I-2069, para. 31; and C-149/96 *Portugal v Council*, [1999] ECR I-8395, para. 49. See also Case C-280/93 *Germany v Council* (Bananas), [1994] ECR I-4973, para. 111.

[62]Timmermans (2000), p. 241.

that the joint responsibility regime is an ultimate solution for overcoming the uncertainty of competences.

These problems may become particularly obvious in the course of compliance with the DSB rulings or recommendations, considering that the Union may be unable to identify an internal competence for obliging the Member State to comply. Similarly, the Union may be unable to institute countermeasures in areas falling within the residual powers of the Member States.[63] This issue suggests that, in order to address the concerns from the cross-mixity, the Union may be co-defendant with the Member States, rather than substitute them in the DSP. By precluding the expansionary effect of the mixed agreement, this mode of participation ensures the immunity of the residual powers from the harmonization and reaffirms the plausibility of the joint responsibility regime as a guarantee for the legal certainty.[64]

The lessons from the mixed agreements and the international law of responsibility suggest that the rights and obligations arising out of international agreements should not be stretched to other states. Similarly, in the case of the WTO Agreement, the Union has to ensure that the joint responsibility regime does not result with additional obligations of other Member States in relation with attributes falling within their residual powers. This follows the example of the UNCLOS, which prevents the EU from conferring rights under the Convention to those Member States which are not state parties (Article 4(5) UNCLOS). It is for the EU to ensure that neither its rights, nor its obligations, are stretched to its unrelated Member States. However, this premise can only be used by analogy in the case of the WTO Agreement, inasmuch as the Member States are jointly responsible for the formal aspects of the WTO membership by virtue of their joint membership.

The quest for legal certainty in mixed international agreements demands safeguarding the interests of the third parties, as a significant premise of the very existence of the mixed agreement. Accordingly, the process of attribution of responsibility in the Union polity should not circumvent the interests of the third parties. This is based on the assumption that the internal rules of organization should not serve as an instrument for shifting or denying the international responsibility of the Union or its Member States (Articles 27 VCLT and 27 VCLTSIO).

## *3. The Premises of the Constitutional Framework of Principles*

This group of premises manifests the predictions of the constitutional principles of the EU legal order. These principles permeate the thesis of the unity of the EU legal order and guide the political organization and political processes. With respect to the normativity of the model, the main proposition suggests that the framework that determines the conditions of the Union participation in the DSP should ensure the

[63]See also Heliskoski (2001), p. 215.

[64]See further on this discussion, Heliskoski (2001), pp. 189–190.

effectiveness of the regime of responsibility. Furthermore, this model should take into account the predictions of the principle of constitutional legality and the principle of conferral. They serve as preconditions for the validity of the model, its legitimacy, and its deference to the rule of law, which permeates all legal relationships in the Union. In this way, the decision of the EU to participate in the DSP should constitute a valid command of the EU legal order, in order to produce legitimate outcomes and become effective.

The model has to take into account the limitations that the lack of direct effect of the WTO Agreement poses on the issue of responsibility. In view of this, it can be suggested that the normative model considers the predictions of the 'trigger' model in terms of the effectiveness of the consequences of the participation in the DSP, in order to overcome any obstacles from the 'primacy model', which conditions the primacy of EU norm with its cognition in the Member State's legal order (direct effect). Accordingly, the Union has to adopt beforehand, either a general formalized arrangement, or a flexible one, which provides the conditions of the participation of the Union in the DSP, and as such, it ensures the recognition of this decision within the EU legal order.[65] In this way, in case that the consequences of this decision would mean for the Union an obligation to comply with a DSB ruling requiring the withdrawal of inconsistent national measures falling within the residual powers of the Member States, then the Union shall have the relevant normative instrument to oblige the defaulting Member State to comply. This is ensured by the principle of primacy, which outplays any inconsistent national measure by neutralizing its challenging effects. This scheme can be employed alone, without having to justify the decision to participate in the DSP by virtue of the joint responsibility regime.

Another premise to be considered is that the Union and the Member States have to act jointly due to the inextricable linkage of their competences.[66] Accordingly, the Union is subject to virtually conferred competences in certain areas covered by the WTO Agreement, and the action of the Union in the conferred areas depends on the discretionary action of the Member States. This premise is permeated also from various principles of the political organization and political processes, which cast their origin, content, or application in the thesis of the unity of the EU legal order. In light of this, the mixity of competences, and particularly their inextricable linkage, serve as a major premise for the joint representation in the DSP. The internal division of powers should remain an internal issue of the Union, and as such, it should not become a matter for the DSB.[67]

An essential premise that manifests another aspect of the unity is the principle of loyalty, which serves as a basis for organizing the political relationships in the Union polity. Indeed, a binding cooperation procedure at the Union level can be an effective premise to organize the political relationships in a fragmented polity in

[65] See further on the recognition of the decisions Dougan (2007), p. 934 and Dashwood (2011), p. 279.

[66] Timmermans (2000), p. 245.

[67] Timmermans (2000), p. 246.

order to ensure the unitary representation.[68] From a normative perspective, the principle of loyalty provides that the Member States should strive to reach a common position and to express it with a single voice, and this is particularly so in the context of exclusive powers.[69] As much as the non-conferred powers are concerned, the normative value of the principle of loyalty is reduced, given that the Member States are only under the obligation to make their best efforts to reach a common position.[70] However, the principle of loyalty is the best evidence of a *pactum fidelis* in the Union polity, which entails the voluntary obedience of the participants. This substantiates the political relationships in the Union, and organizes them upon a superstructure that allows for the reciprocal deference to other's interests in a cumulative manner, rather than in an exclusionary one. The tension between the pursuance of individual interests and the self-restricting attitude in terms of not disavowing the interests of the others could be subject to the principle of proportionality.[71] This attitude is particularly based on the principles of *pacta sunt servanda* and *bona fide*, which the principle of loyalty conveys.

In spite of the limitations in relation to different categories of powers, the principle of loyalty brings the focus on another premise for the normative model, namely the need for a common position of the Union and Member States. In addition to the exclusive or shared competences of the Union, the common position is particularly necessary for unifying the voices of the Member States in the context of residual competences of the Member States, which are either shared (but not exercised at the Union level), or not conferred at all. This process consists in deciding as to whether the participation in the DSP should be made at the Union level, or better left with the concerned Member State. The principles of subsidiarity and proportionality could serve as important premises for coming to an adequate decision on the optimal and efficient level of participation in the DSP, in accordance with the predictions of the duty of care.

The normative premises emphasize further the role of the ECJ in enforcing any procedural arrangements for a coordinated exercise of mixed competences of the Union and Member States.[72] This role is based on the constitutional nature of these arrangements, which should be embodied in legislative acts of the Union. Furthermore, these acts should acknowledge the role of the ECJ, which by means of the judicial review, allows the Union and the Member States to defend their interests with reference to the Treaties. The predictions of the duty of loyalty can be among the premises that should be observed in the course of the judicial review.[73]

[68]See also Bourgeois (1995), p. 19, where a binding coordination procedure within the Union polity is regarded as a premise for precluding the TRIPS and GATS from becoming a source of uncertainty in terms of the responsibility for their compliance.

[69]MacLeod et al. (1996), pp. 148–149. Antoniadis (2004), p. 328.

[70]MacLeod et al. (1996), p. 149.

[71]Gamper (2010), pp. 164–165.

[72]Timmermans (2000), p. 246.

[73]Timmermans (2000), p. 246.

Additionally, the model should take account of the interests of all participants, by ensuring adequate protection in the course of political-decisional processes, and by providing a comprehensive legal protection for the victims of retaliation, including the state liability for wrongful acts.

The complexities of the WTO disciplines and the breadth of its ambit need an institutional memory for the entire Union and the consolidation of the institutional competencies, which can well be embodied within the Commission.[74] This function constitutes a significant premise also for the role of the Commission as a representative of the Union and its Member States in the WTO proceedings. This role fits well with the executive and the independent nature of the Commission, as the representative of the Union's interest. The function of institutional memory can be further combined with the high level of expertise within the Commission, which is utilized in different parallel processes, such as the negotiation and the management of the mixed agreements in the area of common commercial policy. Furthermore, the Commission ensures the interaction of the Union with the industry, which, also with the help of lobbies and the relevant expertise, may facilitate the decision-making in terms of protecting the interests of the European economy worldwide, also in the context of DSP.[75] In a multi-centered system of governance, this process would be very difficult, if not centralized at the institutional framework of the Union.

To conclude, it can be maintained that the said premises go beyond the traditional approaches of addressing problems of mixity in the context of WTO membership. Obviously, the Union and its Member States should address the consequences of international responsibility from the WTO membership for questions of non-conferred competences based on their internal constitutional framework. The relevant constitutional principles should be part of this model. This, however, should not prejudice the fact that the responsibility from the WTO membership is part of the general category of international responsibility. This set of rules, as observed in the second Chapter, aims to maintain the peace between sovereign states and international organizations, and predict the normative propositions of international responsibility. The rules of international responsibility should be included in the model for ensuring the deference to the normative expectations of third states in terms of legal certainty. Further, they could be a significant tool for addressing the problems of mixity in terms of responsibility, and particularly the fallacies of the joint responsibility regime. In this way, this model could re-conceptualize the attempts of formalization, which, being focused exclusively on internal rules, and being particularly concerned about the participation rather than about the issues of responsibility, have neglected the value that could be derived from the adoption of general rules on international responsibility.

Being based on the cumulative consideration of normative premises, the proposed normative model manifests the predictions of the principle of constitutional

[74] Antoniadis (2004), p. 338.

[75] See also Antoniadis (2004), pp. 338–339.

tolerance. This constitutes a premise for the pluralist construction of the constitutional legal orders that are not in competition with each other. This approach could compensate for the deficiencies of the individual legal orders in addressing alone the fallacies of the joint responsibility regime. Hence, the proposed premises endorse the thesis that the question of responsibility for matters of non-conferred competences can be addressed beyond the limitations raised from the individual legal orders. Therefore, a pluralist approach on the matter would offer more normative arguments for the Union participation in the DSP.

## V. The Modelling of a Normative Construction for the EU Participation in the DSP

The participation of the Union polity in the DSP, as it stands in the current state of the law and practice, represents a fallacious model, which can be criticized from the perspectives of the international law of responsibility, the law of mixed agreements, and notably the WTO Agreement, and the EU constitutional principles. In light of this criticism, and considering the prospect of the highlighted premises in terms of addressing the fallacies of the joint responsibility regime, it is now turned to the modelling of the conditions of the Union participation in the DSP. The current practice and the attempts of formalization of this participation, such as the draft Code of Conduct, assist in patterning an adequate model that answers at best to the normative and cognitive expectations of the participants.

The normative model concerns mainly the participation of the Union as respondent in the proceedings for matters that involve non-conferred powers of the Union, or blurred areas of powers, where the ownership of competences is unclear or their exercise is inextricably linked with the participation of both the Union and the concerned Member State. The normative model does not, in principle, distinguish between the participation and the representation of the Union polity in the DSP as a defendant, or as a claimant in terms of construction of the relevant configurations. However, as to the consequences of this participation, the main attention is drawn to the participation as respondent, as this procedural position may trigger the joint responsibility regime. Furthermore, the normative model may address the conferred powers of the Union, but this issue is only marginally considered in this work.

The following addresses initially some general considerations on the normative model, such as the legal form and the competences for adopting the normative model, the normative choice, the need for a reconceptualization of the joint responsibility regime, and the constitutional value of the model. It then follows with the content of the model, by focusing in particular aspects such as the formulation of a common position, the format of representation, the mandate of the Commission, and the issues of attribution of responsibility in the course of compliance with the DSB rulings and recommendations.

## *1. General Remarks on the Normative Model*

### a. The Formal Aspects of the Normative Model

The formal aspects of the normative model aim to address two main questions: Firstly, what type of legal act could be suitable for accommodating the normative model in the legal order? Secondly, where are the competences for adopting the respective act dealing with the normative model?

#### i. The Legal Form of the Normative Model

The normative model of the Union participation in the DSP shall consist of a system of rules, which governs the conditions and the processes for the participation of the EU and its Member States in the DSP, and manages the consequences of this participation. As to the normative aspects, the model could be construed in the normative framework of the Union law by means of a legislative instrument enacted by the Council and the European Parliament.[76] The legal infrastructure may be embodied in a regulation, which either regulates beforehand the content of the model by formalizing it in an exhaustive manner, or establishes a general framework for the Union to determine the conditions of the Union participation in the DSP on a case-by-case basis. Presumably, the form of such an infrastructure is irrelevant for the following analysis. This is to the extent that the content of the respective alternatives leads to comparable results in terms of the regulation of the Union participation and representation in the DSP.

#### ii. The Competence for Adopting the Normative Model

The pleading for a normative model addressing the participation of the Union polity in the DSP inherits the same constitutional limitations that permeate the joint responsibility regime, as revealed in the *EC – Asbestos* case. The virtual competence of the Union to cover the entire spectrum of disciplines of the WTO Agreement, particularly due to the designation of the common commercial policy as an exclusive one, recasts the issue of the formal-substantive gap also in the formal aspects of the normative model, as much as the competence for adopting the legislative framework is concerned. While the regulation of the Union participation in the DSP represents a constitutional imperative for addressing the fallacies of the joint responsibility regime, the main question to be addressed in terms of the normative character of the model is the identification of the relevant competence for its adoption. This formal aspect is significant for ensuring the adequate level of legitimacy, in terms of the Union participation in the DSP.

---

[76] See for similar considerations Heliskoski (2001), p. 247.

As an expression of the constitutional legality, the principle of conferral could be depicted as one of the main premises of the normative model, as long as it determines the boundaries of a legitimate participation of the Union in the DSP. In light of the unstable and dynamic scheme of vertical distribution of powers in the Union polity, the principle of conferral calls for a cautious approach in determining the relevant competence for adopting the normative model. This operation should tackle the issue of legitimacy in the course of the Union participation in the DSP, not only for exclusive and shared areas of EU competences, but also for the residual powers of the Member States. In this way, the normative model should be able to deconstruct the thesis of false mixity inherent in the Union's membership in the WTO, and terminate the state of dependency of the Union participation and representation in the DSP from the discretionary conduct of the Member States, which is a factor for increased uncertainty.

With these predictions in mind, it could be expected that the quest of an adequate competence for adopting the normative model may vary among different alternatives, depending on their ability to gain the relevant constitutional momentum. The first and foremost alternative would be to search for a relevant competence among the competences conferred on the Union. Obviously, the common commercial policy, which it is claimed to accommodate the entire areas of WTO disciplines, could be proposed as the default competence of the Union with regard to the participation in the DSP. In this way, based on Articles 3(1)(e) and 207 TFEU, the Union institutions should be allegedly competent to adopt the normative model. Pursuant to Article 207(2) TFEU, the European Parliament and the Council may enact regulations in accordance with the ordinary procedure, in order to adopt measures defining the framework for implementing the common commercial policy. The normative model could be construed as a set of measures that operationalizes an important aspect of the common commercial policy in relation with the Union participation in the DSP. As a matter of analogy, the Union has used Article 207 TFEU to adopt the Regulation (EU) 912/2014, although the subject matter—namely the international responsibility in the context of foreign investment disputes—could well be subject to the residual powers of the Member States.

However, considering that the spectrum of WTO disciplines includes not only conferred powers, but also residual powers of the Member States (Articles 5–6 TFEU), the question is then how to deal with this category of powers which cannot be casted within the Union's exclusive powers? The qualified majority voting would not comply with the complete picture of Article 207 TFEU, which, in its paragraph 4, provides for the Council to act unanimously for the negotiation and conclusion of agreements in the field of trade in cultural and audiovisual services, as well as in the field of trade in social, education, and health services. These parallel areas of the residual powers listed in Article 6 TFEU would require unanimous decision-making. This formula would serve as a lower common denominator for the entire spectrum of competences provided in Articles 3–6 TFEU. Obviously, since the normative model does not constitute an agreement *per se*, the adoption of the model with unanimous procedure in the Council would apply only by means of a wide interpretation of Article 207 TFEU.

A unanimous adoption of the normative model could be a proof for its wide acceptance from the Member States, but it could nonetheless insulate the normative model against any objections. The Member States may claim residual powers, which cannot be hindered from an abstract designation of the common commercial policy as an exclusive competence covering the entire spectrum of WTO disciplines. If this would be the case, then it would be necessary to search for other solutions to address the fallacies related with this virtual character of the common commercial policy. In order to satisfy to the greatest extent the predictions of the positive and negative legality, it could be suggested that the normative model be adopted based on Article 352 TFEU (the flexibility clause). This clause compensates for the missing conferred powers in the Treaties, as it serves as an exception to Articles 3(6) and 5(1, 2) TEU. Hence, the adoption of the normative model pursuant to Article 352 TFEU is bound to function as an alternative for the failure of the EU institutions to adopt the model based on the common commercial policy powers.

The main premises for the application of the flexibility clause are that the action at the Union level is necessary, and that the Treaties have not provided the necessary powers to attain one of the objectives set out in the Treaties (Article 352(1) TFEU). The latter implies that the flexibility clause is applicable in case that the institutions fail to identify the relevant powers for adopting the model in the context of common commercial policy. Indeed, on the one hand the common commercial policy requires the Union to act in the course of the DSP also for areas covered from residual powers of the Member States. On the other hand, the spectrum of competences provided in Articles 3–6 TFEU fails to provide full powers to the Union for conducting this policy. This is because the Union has only ancillary powers in certain areas for which Member States retain sovereignty, hence excluded from unionization and harmonization (Article 2(5) and 207 (6) TFEU). Here comes into play the former criterion for the application of the flexibility clause, namely that the action of the Union should be necessary in order to achieve the objectives of the Union. The participation of the Union in the DSP, also for matters residual with the Member State powers, is part of the common commercial policy, which, although designated as an exclusive competence, implicates matters for which the Member States are competent, or are inextricably linked with their retained powers.

According to Article 352(1) TFEU, the normative model could be adopted from the Council, acting unanimously on a proposal from the Commission and after obtaining the consent of the European Parliament. Furthermore, paragraph 2 requires the involvement of national parliaments through the relevant procedure for monitoring the subsidiarity principle referred to in Article 5(3) TEU. Indeed, this is only one of the downsides related with the application of the flexibility clause. At the national level, the parliaments are increasingly inclined to restrict the application of flexibility clause in the Council. For instance, the German law on the Exercise by the Bundestag and by the Bundesrat of their Responsibility for Integration in Matters concerning the European Union, in its Section 8, provides that the German representative in the Council meetings may vote in favor of measures pursuant to Article 352 TFEU only if so authorized by law.[77] This provision indicates that the application of the flexibility clause may be subject to extensive procedural limitations in the Member States' national legal systems. Although such procedural limitations are no easy hurdles for the normative model, Article 352 TFEU remains the safest path for adopting a regulation dealing with the model, as long as the residual powers of the Member States are better observed in this way. One of the advantages of the application of Article 352 TFEU is that it fills the lacunae of the Treaties without requiring significant changes of a constitutional character.

In case that the flexibility clause would not prove successful, the establishment of a normative model could require the amendment of the Treaties. Obviously, this is no easy exercise, given that the amendment of the Treaties requires particular constitutional moments, where the Member States pursue political-decisional processes that aim a substantial change in the constitutional superstructure of the Union polity. However, in case that the adoption of a regulation establishing the normative model fails for constitutional grounds, the amendment of the superstructure to this end remains the ultimate alternative. The Member States may decide to complement the superstructure of the EU legal order with a relevant proposition that empowers the Union institutions to adopt the necessary legal infrastructure for the normative model. The Treaty instrument for achieving this is provided in Article 48 TEU. This instrument requires the ratification of amendments from the Member States pursuant to their constitutional provisions.

The provision of the Treaties with the relevant proposition for adopting the normative model could follow the same path pursued for the draft Code of Conduct during the Intergovernmental Conferences preparing the Treaty of Amsterdam (1995–1996), and later the Treaty of Nice (2000). However, the probability that the normative model succeeds in highly intensive political agendas permeating these processes is quite low. The failure of the draft Code of Conduct, or its simplification with the current variant of Article 207 TFEU, is the best example for this.

To conclude, after confronting these alternatives, it is suggested that the employment of the current treaty mechanisms, and most prominently, Article 352 TFEU, could prove more adequate for adopting the normative model. Although subject to procedural limitations, the flexibility clause constitutes a safe path in terms of ensuring an adequate level of legal certainty. It does so by precluding any theoretical possibility for claims of sovereignty of the Member States regarding their residual powers in the course of the Union participation in the DSP. The principle of loyalty (Article 4(3) TEU) could prove relevant in this operation. As an

[77]Gesetz über die Wahrnehmung der Integrationsverantwortung des Bundestages und des Bundesrates in Angelegenheiten der Europäischen Union (Integrationsverantwortungsgesetz - IntVG) of 2 September 2009 (BGBl. I S. 3022), amended through the Article 1 of the Law of 1 December 2009 (BGBl. I S. 3822). Own translation.

expression of the *pactum fidelis*, this principle unfolds its normative capacity by facilitating the political-decisional processes for the adoption of the normative model. The positive and negative duties of the Member States are strong premises for aligning their interests with the Union, and exercising their powers in compliance with the international obligations of the Union pursuant to Article 216 (2) TFEU.[78]

### b. The Normative Choice of the Model

The normative model provides for the principles and other propositions that allow or limit the Union or its Member States to participate in the DSP, and defines their procedural status in the proceedings, e.g. as joint or as sole participants with principal or subsidiary representation powers. Furthermore, the model addresses the consequences of this participation for the concerned parties and other Member States. As to the instruments of the model, it could be suggested that they consist of political-decisional processes accommodated in the constitutional infrastructure of the Union, and should ensure that the parties take the relevant decisions for the participation of the Union in the DSP. The processes should observe the principles and propositions that provide for adequate representation in the DSP, and should be able to accommodate the consequences of the Union participation in the DSP in accordance with the normative expectations of the participants.

The logic of the model could be based on a mediating strategy, which integrates divergent claims of authority in an inclusive way. This is based on the mechanism of *alternated competences*,[79] which targets particularly shared powers and those powers that are inextricably linked with each other. Accordingly, the Union and the Member States can decide on their responsibilities for the performance of joint obligations by avoiding any concurrent exercise of powers.[80] While in many mixed agreements this method could prove useful, in the case of the WTO Agreement it may sit uneasily. This method cannot be implanted in the *formalized* model, given that the ownership of substantive obligations cannot be easily predicted due to the dynamic scheme of powers. However, the parties may agree on the allocation of formal obligations of the WTO membership, particularly in terms of compliance with the DSB rulings and recommendations. The *alternated competences* method could be more compatible with the *flexibility* model of participation in the DSP, given that the decisions on the participation in the DSP are taken on a case-by-case basis. The effects of this approach are the same with that of a declaration of responsibilities in the mixed agreements, with the distinction that the former does

[78] See *supra* Section IV(4)(c, d) in Chap. 4 ("The principle of loyalty in the course of the ECJ jurisprudence" and "The relevance of the principle of loyalty for the fallacies of the joint responsibility regime").

[79] Heliskoski (2001), pp. 157–158.

[80] Heliskoski (2001), pp. 135–136.

not consist in an *a priori* declaration of powers, but rather constitutes an internal arrangement for compensating for the missing declaration of powers.

The method of alternation of competences compensates for the internal structural deficiencies in the Union and reduces uncertainties in relation with the ownership of powers. Absent of this instrument, the attribution of wrongful conduct could follow the process of apportion of the obligations referring to the respective competences of each of the joint participants.[81] However, this method could fail in cases of inextricably linked competences, which make the allocation of powers virtual, and as such, are unable to explain the formal ownership of the WTO obligation. Therefore, by avoiding the internal rules of the organization, the approach of the allocation of responsibility pursuant to the rules of attribution of conduct compensates for the uncertainties of the distribution of powers.[82]

### c. The Reconceptualization of the Joint Responsibility Regime

The joint responsibility regime, as a default regime in the WTO Agreement, is a fallacious model inasmuch as the responsibility is attributed to the Union for measures of non-conferred powers. This model could be combined with a joint and several regime of responsibility, as long as the normative premises do not exclude this option. In light of this, the joint responsibility regime could be supplemented with an appendix, which addresses more adequately the consequences of the Union responsibility resulting from the breach of WTO obligations from the Member States. The underlying idea of this regime is to conceive a model of responsibility that presumes the parties as jointly responsible for their joint formal obligations, but only as a transitory stage, which terminates with the ultimate allocation of responsibility to the wrongdoer.

### d. The Constitutional Value of the Model

The model of participation conveys a constitutional value by containing clear and unequivocal rules.[83] These features enhance the normative efficacy of the model. The constitutional value of the model would ensure its ability to preclude the fallacies of the joint responsibility regime in the context of WTO from leading to constitutional conflicts in the Union polity. Considering that the Union participation in the DSP may trigger consequences for the federal relationship as well as for the individuals, this participation should be organized on the basis of constitutional

---

[81] ILC, Second Report on Responsibility of International Organizations, UN Document A/CN.4/545 *re* Comments and observations received from international organizations, 26, para. 5. See also Eeckhout (2011), p. 263.

[82] See also Eeckhout (2011), pp. 263–264.

[83] Antoniadis (2004), pp. 338, 339.

rules of the Union polity. This may imply that the conduct of the Union in the context of DSP may be subject to judicial review from the ECJ, pursuant to the applicable law and the general principles of the Union law; no international agreement could prevent the role of the Court in this regard.[84] Indeed, international agreements are part of the EU legal order, and following a monistic view, based on Article 216(2) TFEU, they cannot enjoy a supra-constitutional status.[85] The ECJ has affirmed its jurisdiction to interpret mixed agreements, including the provisions under the competences of the Member States. The judicial scrutiny would guarantee that the outcome of the proceedings complies with the constitutional order of the Union.

The constitutional value is a precondition for the unconditional acceptance of the model from all the parties. As such, it can serve as a basis for organizing the entire mechanism of participation of the Union and its Member States in the DSP, as well as for ensuring the compliance with the DSP rulings and recommendations pursuant to the principle of constitutional legality, as a strict adherence of the legislative, judicial, and executive activity to the constitutional propositions. The constitutional nature makes the model a source for valid and legitimate EU norms, which are able to be effectively enforced within the legal orders of the Union and the Member States. In this way, the model can be conceived in the context of the normative supranationalism of the Union, inasmuch as it establishes a priority-based relationship between the Union and the Member States on their joint participation in the DSP. The model, by preserving the autonomy of the EU legal order and its unity in the external relations, provides the Union's claims of authority with more prevalence, as long as they result from a normative framework approved with unanimity. In this way, the acts of the Union for the participation and representation in the DSP, and for the compliance with the DSB rulings and recommendations, can be perceived as commands of the EU legal order and as such, they enjoy the attributes of primacy. These acts should be able to neutralize conflicting effects of national norms that challenge the EU norms in a unilateral way.

One of the effects of the constitutional value of the model is that it fills a normative gap in terms of the consequences of the Union participation in the DSP for matters of non-conferred competences. In this respect, the model precludes the 'substitutionary' effects of this participation, in that it does not create new rights and obligations for the Member States in relation with their residual powers not provided in the Treaties. Additionally, the acts of the Union complying with the DSB rulings could have direct applicability and direct effect, in case that they would be designated as individual decisions pursuant to Article 288, para. 4 TFEU. In this way, pursuant to the predictions of the 'trigger' model of primacy, the principle of primacy is not compromised from the recognition of the DSB rulings in the national legal order.

---

[84] Thies (2013), p. 134.

[85] See for an analogue view Case C-402/05P *Kadi and Al Barakaat International Foundation v Council and Commission*, [2008] ECR I-6351, Opinion of the AG Poiares Maduro, para. 28.

### e. The Relation of the Model with the Current Practice

The current practice of the representation in the DSP is characterized of an intense cooperation between the Commission, the concerned Member States, and the representatives of the industry affected from the proceedings.[86] The model of participation should be built upon the current practice of the Union participation in the DSP. This practice, far from being formalized and legitimated, has achieved a certain degree of legal stability, and has so far not produced hard cases with implications for the attribution of responsibility. The DSB has already accepted the mixed nature of the WTO Agreement from the EU perspective and the preponderance of the Union's dominant role in the areas of exclusive powers.[87] Indeed, the Union has represented France in *EC – Asbestos* for a French measure; neither the panels, nor the claimant questioned the procedural capacity of the Commission. The DSB practice has shown that the EU may become respondent, irrespective of the fact whether it has enacted the disputed measures or not. The EU has stepped in the proceedings when the Member States have been called solely answerable for their national measures.[88] The EU has subsequently assumed the respondent position in these proceedings, in spite of its role in the wrongful conduct, and even in cases where the competence belonged to the Member States.[89] Certainly, the EU and its Member States have been jointly respondents for trade measures resulting from their joint action.[90] Hence, the role of the Union as a representative of all Member States jointly or severally, constitutes a consolidated practice.

An advantage of this practice is related with the third states being accustomed to the unified representation of the Union from the Commission.[91] However, the lack of formalization remains fallacious in terms of the legitimacy of the DSP's outcomes. The missing procedures within the Union for taking a decision on the participation in the DSP have left unregulated many issues, such as the formulation of a common position, or the mandate of participation. Therefore, the model should trace the current practice in relation with the format of representation, and

---

[86]Kuijper (2010), p. 224.

[87]Kuijper (2010), p. 226.

[88]See for example *Portugal – Patent Protection under the Industrial Property Act* (WT/DS37), settled on 8 October 1996; *Belgium – Measures Affecting Commercial Telephone Services* (WT/DS80); *Ireland – Measures Affecting the Grant of Copyright and Neighbouring Rights* (WT/DS82); and *European Communities - Measures Affecting the Grant of Copyright and Neighbouring Rights* (WT/DS115).

[89]See in particular *European Communities – Patent Protection for Pharmaceutical and Agricultural Chemical Products* (WT/DS153).

[90]*European Communities – Measures Relating to the Development of a Flight Management System* (WT/DS172) and *France – Measures Relating to the Development of a Flight Management System* (WT/DS173). These two requests for consultations are identical and addressed from the United States respectively to the EU and France. See also EC – *Computer Equipment*, Report of the Panel (WT/DS62, 67, 68/R), where the EU participated in the DSP as a representative for the Union and the concerned Member States, namely United Kingdom and Ireland.

[91]Timmermans (2000), p. 246.

formalize it in legal instruments, while also focusing more on the consequences of this participation.

## *2. The Content of the Normative Model*

Either a general framework or a legislative act would be adequate to regulate in detail the two main aspects of the Union participation in the DSP, namely, the conditions of the participation and its consequences. Both these elements are interrelated and have effects on each other. The content of the normative model consists of selected principles and processes that could be followed from the participants, in order to address the fallacies of the joint responsibility regime. Many of the processes, such as the formulation of a common position for the DSP, the conditions of unified representation, the formulation of the mandate of representation or the format of participation in the DSP, could be part of a single political-decisional process. The second group addresses the management of the consequences of the participation in the DSP, and includes the compliance with the DSB rulings and recommendations, the allocation of burden of responsibility in the Union polity and its enforcement, and the prospect of the victim compensation. Considering the complexity of these issues, the following considers the elements separately.

### a. The Conditions and the Processes of the Union Participation in the DSP

#### i. The Formulation of a Common Position

The formulation of a common position constitutes the primary goal of the normative model. From a chronological point of view, the common position is the result of a new DSP initiated against the Union and its Member States. Whereas for the cases falling within the conferred powers of the Union, the common position may be desirable, for the matters falling within the residual powers, a common position is indispensable. The common position should result from a political-decisional process, where the Member States utilize the institutional infrastructure of the Union in order to align their positions in a single document. This is not new in the institutional practice. The Union already established practices for achieving the common position on behalf of negotiation and conclusion of mixed agreements (Article 218 TFEU). The common position was also part of the draft Code of Conduct (Articles 5, 6, 8(3)). Similarly, the normative model of participation in the DSP could provide for the Council, or the Article 207 Committee, to establish a common position related with the participation in the DSP. The political-decisional processes in the Council, in addition to bringing the Union proceedings and the intergovernmental interests together in the same route, have the advantages of endowing the common position with an intergovernmental authority.[92] Additionally, the involvement of the Member States in these proceedings by means of their participation in the Council, ensures that they show due diligence over the activities of the Union, as a separate obligation of the Member State in relation with the international obligations of the polity. In this way, these processes legitimize the operation of the Union for areas falling within the residual powers of the Member States.

The content of the common position is an aggregate of the interests of the Union and the Member States, which claim their residual powers in relation with the subject matter in dispute. This act does not have to address the defense strategy in the proceedings, but rather the general lines of participation therein. The concept of the common position should not be equated with the concepts of 'standing' or 'defense' in the DSP. Rather, it should be limited to the careful assessment of the relevance of the division of powers for the matter in question, and the consideration of all possible consequences that the DSP might have for the EU and its Member States.[93] After identifying the best strategy of defense, the Commission proposes the general guidelines on the defense and the required actions in the course of the proceedings, including the compliance with the DSB ruling and recommendations.

The attainment of a common position should not be understood as an easy procedural task, considering that it has to address the concerns of the Member States in relation with their trade interests, which influence areas of their residual powers.[94] The challenge in this process consists in the fact that the Union may hinder Member States from the exercise of their residual powers. However, in the course of the DSP, the cooperation between the Union and the concerned Member States may become problematic and hinder, as such, a professional representation.[95] This fact could be another argument in favor of ascertaining the common position beforehand. The current practice has ignored this concern in an arbitrary way, or has overestimated the outreach of the designation of the GATS and TRIPS areas as part of the common commercial policy. The vertical competition of powers permeates this process. The common position could become subject to political negotiations and as such, it may end up as the lowest common denominator. For this reason, the common position should represent a general document rather than a draft of submissions to the DSB. The decision-making should be confined to a limited range of general issues, such as the management of the problems of mixity in terms of the residual powers of the Member States. Any involvement of all

[92]For a similar suggestion in the context of the conclusion of mixed agreements, see Hyett (2000), p. 251 and Heliskoski (2001), p. 248.

[93]See also Kuijper (2010), p. 225.

[94]On difficulties of attainment of common positions in mixed agreements see Koutrakos (2006), p. 164.

[95]Kuijper (1995), p. 114.

Member States and the Commission in the details of submissions would hinder the successful representation in the DSP.[96]

The process of formulation of the common position should be guided by principles that ensure a more legally oriented result, rather than a political statement. Such principles ensure an adequate defense of common commercial interests of the Union polity and avoid the declarations of powers, which, by manifesting the internal tensions, may hinder the authority of the Union as a unified actor.[97] The unity of representation is ensured to the extent that the Union and the Member States shall formulate a common position, and designate a unified representative, by precluding any opportunity of the DSM or third parties to take account of the internal distribution of powers in the EU polity.[98] Although the unified representation has a great practical relevance, it still cannot resolve the problem of the protection of residual powers of the Member States, as a premise for the constitutional balance in the polity. Hence, the thesis of the unity of representation should be complemented with considerations of the negative impacts on residual powers.

In light of these concerns, the Member States are generally required to adopt a common position as a block, in order to preserve the autonomy of the EU legal order.[99] The question of the internal division of powers should remain an internal matter of the Union polity, and in no circumstances should become a matter for the third states in the WTO Agreement, and neither for the DSB.[100] The common position could be established by a qualified majority. In the doctrine, one can find alternative views suggesting that the common position and the mandate of representation could be controlled from the unanimity procedures, which weaken the supranational element in the vertical clash between the Union interests and the interests of the Member States.[101] This is in line with the scheme of the decision-making in the context of Article 207(4) TFEU, which reserves the unanimity voting for the negotiation and conclusion of particular situations related with the areas of GATS and TRIPS.

One could maintain that the qualified majority is not appropriate inasmuch as it could unionize areas of residual powers, and this is prohibited from the Treaties (Article 2(5) TEU). On the other hand, the unanimity requirement would lead to a lower common denominator in terms of the common position and the mandate of representation. However, given that the Member States are the masters of the Treaties, their attributes have to be respected. Amid these two opposing arguments, it could be proposed that the model provides as a standard procedure, that the decisions are reached with the consensus of all Member States. In case of failure, the qualified majority could be applied as a default procedure. However,

[96]Kuijper (2010), pp. 224–225.

[97]See also Timmermans (2000), p. 246.

[98]Timmermans (2000), p. 246.

[99]Eeckhout (2011), p. 224.

[100]See also Timmermans (2000), p. 246.

[101]Timmermans (2010), pp. 7–8.

considering that the residual powers are at stake, the model should provide substantial guarantees for precluding that the Union participation as a unified representative in the DSP results in the harmonization of residual areas. The powers of the concerned Member State in these areas should not be prejudiced. Indeed, this is the default limit of the Union action imposed by Treaties. The qualified majority voting should not be seen as an instrument that unionizes the residual powers of the Member States.

This scheme is a way-out from an institutional impasse that would otherwise prove fallacious, whereby the Union becomes responsible by virtue of the joint responsibility regime. The qualified majority voting with substantial guarantees offers a mediating strategy, a process oriented solution which invites the parties to show their loyal cooperation, and *exercise their residual rights in deference to the others' interests*. This is in line with the voluntary obedience predicted by the *pactum fidelis*, which permeates the political organization of the Union polity.

As to the legitimacy concerns related to the qualified majority voting, it can be maintained that the normative model and its operative instruments are the legal basis for the decisions. Once the model is approved (following the unanimity procedure) in accordance with the Treaties, it is valid, and as such, it is able to produce legitimate outcomes. Nevertheless, it should be highlighted that, whereas this scheme could prove efficient in terms of the regulation of the Union participation in the DSP, it could sit uneasily with the issue of compliance with the DSB rulings and recommendations.[102] Accordingly, the Union may be required to oblige the Member States to withdraw national measures enacted in exercise of their residual powers. In the absence of a material competence, this obligation of the Union may remain unsatisfied. The normative model could address this concern by designating the concerned Member State as a principal of the obligation, and the Union as an agent defending its interests. This construction, which entrusts the Union with the exercise of the Member States competences, reaffirms the residual powers of the Member States, and at the same time preserves the unity of the legal order in terms of the external competences.[103]

The normative model should also consider the cases where the common position may not be achieved. This may be possible in cases where the intensity of the Member States' interests is so strongly affiliated with their residual powers, that the action at the Union level is not defensible. In case that even the qualified majority of the Member States does not agree to formulate a common position for the entire Union, the joint participation should not be hindered. Indeed, the lack of a common position implies that the concerned Member States should be answerable alone in the DSP, and the Union should represent its own position. This impedes a successful joint participation, and serves as a premise for incurring joint responsibility in the course of the DSP. The model should be able to address this situation in accordance with the constitutional principles.

---

[102]This issue shall be discussed in Section (b) below.

[103]Heliskoski (2001), pp. 247–248.

The draft Code of Conduct resolved this conflict by allowing the Council to prohibit the participation of the Member State in the DSP by a qualified majority voting (Article 8(3) dCoC). This radical approach would be criticized on the grounds of federal balance, inasmuch as this decision would amount to a *de facto* assumption of powers of the Member States. Although this decision would be legally valid, as long as the normative model allowing for this option would be approved by unanimity, it still does not represent a mediating strategy for the cumulative deference to the interests of Member States. The failure of a qualified majority voting speaks for the existence of a blocking minority, which should not be neglected. In order to increase its moral acceptance, and to meet the normative expectation of the Member States, the model could choose to establish common positions, with the condition that the concerned Member State takes the principal role of representation and coordinates its position with the Union, which is designated as a subsidiary representative. Such a role would be particularly desired in those cases where, by following the principles of subsidiarity and proportionality, it results that the polity may become better off if the representation would be left with the Member State. This format is further reflected in the format of participation.

The duty of loyalty represents a significant instrument for ensuring the attainment of a common position. The political-decisional processes should ensure the parties to make their best efforts to reach a common position.[104] The failure to reach a common position reveals the conflicting claims of authority. In such cases, the conflict may be referred to the ECJ, which may oblige the parties to coordinate their actions in deference to their reciprocal interests. In this way, the process of formulation of a common position serves as a preliminary stage for synchronizing the opposing claims among participants. Strategically, it is better to pursue the synchronization in this phase, rather than in the later stages, where the cross-retaliatory measures are involved.

ii. The Conditions for the Unified Representation from the Commission

The common position constitutes a premise for the unified representation of the Union polity. The designation of a unified representation of the Union and the concerned Member States constitutes another normative element recommended to be included in the model of participation in the DSP.[105] This constitutes a procedural arrangement with significant relevance given that the Member States may remain reluctant in delegating their responsibility wholeheartedly to the Commission.[106] The constitutional principles could facilitate this process and provide the relevant guarantees for the parties to maintain the unity in representation. Accordingly, any reluctance of the Member States to mandate the Commission for their

[104]MacLeod et al. (1996), p. 149.

[105]Antoniadis (2004), p. 339 and Timmermans (2000), pp. 246–247.

[106]Antoniadis (2004), p. 340.

representation in the DSP for matters falling within their residual powers, should be compensated with substantial guarantees from the Union to pursue their interests in the DSP in the spirit of loyalty. The principle of loyalty, as the best evidence of a *pactum fidelis* in the Union polity, entails the voluntary obedience of the participants. This permeates the political relationships in the Union. The duty of loyalty would restrict the Member States to pursue their conflicting interests to the detriment of those of the Union. The normative model could allow for the reciprocal deference to others' interests in a cumulative manner, rather than in an exclusionary one. The unified representation should comply with these propositions. The political-decisional processes ensure that the participants consult the Commission and other Member States about the exercise of their attributes in the DSP, and at the same time, show their duty of care—an obligation entrusted on any entity, whose complicit actions may lead to a wrongful act that triggers joint responsibility.

In order to uphold the unity representation, the model should preclude any parallel representation of the Union and the Member States in the DSP.[107] The common position avoids this art of representation. However, in cases where the common position is not reached, or is much disputed from the Member States due to their high intensity of interests on the matter in the DSP, the representation could be adopted on the basis of a principal-agent relationship. Unlike the conventional understanding of this concept, the principal-agent relationship in the context of the normative model results from the legislative framework, rather than from a bilateral agreement between the concerned Member State and the Union. Based on this understanding, the Union, although jointly responsible with the Member States, acts on behalf of the interests of the concerned Member State as an agent.[108] This constitutes an alternative for those cases where the Member States fail to formulate a common position. The idea of the unified representation should not preclude the concerned Member States from participating as joint representatives in the proceedings. However, the common position or the designation of the Commission as their agent, hence as a primary representative, would shade off their procedural role. In these conditions, it could be maintained that the joint representation does not compromise the unified representation.

The common position and the mandate of representation should provide for the quality of the participant as primary or subsidiary representative, given that it triggers particular consequences in terms of the devolution of responsibility. This differs from the cognitive forms of agency, where the concerned Member State is designated as an agent not by virtue of empowerment from the respondent, but rather by virtue of choice of the decision-making body.

The management of the problems of mixity in the context of WTO membership represents an economic calculus. As such, it follows the logic of the optimal and effective decision-making in terms of deciding the participation in the DSP at the Union or the Member State level. This logic conveys the political-decisional

[107]This would be in line with the Article 7 dCoC.

[108]See also Antoniadis (2004), p. 339.

processes for deciding whether there should be a sole or a joint representation in the DSP. Obviously, the action at the Union level represents a collective action, which is associated with some loss of autonomy, particularly in those cases where the decision-making follows the majority voting.[109] The designation of the Commission as a sole representative of the Union and the Member States could be inspired from the following idea:

> The group will often be more powerful than any individual; it will bring together expertise; it will spread the workload; it will normally have greater resources than any individual; and it can facilitate attainment of goals that could not have been otherwise achieved.[110]

Furthermore, the designation of the Commission as a sole representative serves to the consolidation of the institutional memory, which is necessary for the successful defense of the Union's interests. In light of these advantages, the Council, or the Article 207 Committee could be more inclined to trust the Commission with the role of the sole representative.

The Commission, as an independent institution of the Union, has the relevant attributes for ensuring this function. In the course of the representation in the DSP for non-conferred powers, the Commission should preserve a certain equilibrium between two parallel interests. Firstly, the Commission represents the interests of the Union by virtue of its constitutional functions, and secondly, it represents the interests of the concerned Member State by virtue of the Union's act establishing the common position. This double role would be challenged in case that the Council, or the Article 207 Committee would fail to formulate a clear and unconditional mandate, which would provide the Commission with the relevant space for construing the most adequate defense strategy before the DSP. In addition, this mandate is also necessary for ensuring that the Commission pursues all the necessary steps for the enforcement of the system of responsibility, inasmuch as this constitutes a guarantee for the sovereignty claims of all participants. Indeed, this function is well vested in the Commission, as a body with a pronounced independence in the Union polity.

### iii. The Mandate of Representation in the DSP

The mandate of representation reflects the common position of the Union and its Member States in relation with the DSP. The mandate of representation regulates the position of the Commission and the concerned Member States in the proceedings, the conditions of their participation, and any limitations in this regard. In cases of designation of the Union as a principal representative, the mandate constitutes a formal approval for this role, and empowers the Commission to undertake the answerability on behalf of the concerned Member State. Considering that the

---

[109]Graig (2012), p. 26 (with further reference).

[110]Graig (2012), p. 26.

answerability may lead to responsibility to comply with the DSB rulings or recommendations, the mandate should cover also the consequences of this participation; hence the entire cycle of the DSP. A clear and unconditional mandate of representation ensures and guides the Commission to develop the most optimal strategy of defense.

The mandate of representation should reflect the equilibrium between the diverging interests of the Union and the concerned Member States, which are embodied in their respective claims of authority pursuant to the scheme of powers. The mandate can be construed as an art of 'cross-sector' mixity, which endows the Union with the mandate to represent the Member States for measures falling within their residual powers, without executing these powers, and by preserving the vertical balance of powers. This model does not preclude the concerned Member States to participate jointly as subsidiary representatives and to observe closely their interests, as well as to contribute to the proceedings.

The mandate should ensure that the unity of representation is accomplished without transferring internal powers to the Union. The normative model may provide the unconditional cooperation of the parties to the benefit of a successful participation in the DSP. This substantiates the action of the Union and the Member States as a single bloc on the basis of the *pactum fidelis*. The principle of loyalty is among the essential instruments permeating the process of resolution of conflicts. This can be embodied in a binding cooperation procedure,[111] based on the model of conciliation committees provided in Article 294 TFEU. These committees aim to resolve the differences between EU institutions in the legislative process. Similarly, in case that any conflicts of interests in the representation of the Union and its concerned Member State would hinder the common position and the mandate of the unified representation, a conciliation committee composed of representatives of the Commission, the concerned Member State, and the Council, or the Article 207 Committee, shall convene to resolve the impasse in the representation. This may reaffirm the mandate of representation, or may renew it with different conditions. This procedure serves as a fast-track mechanism for resolving conflicts of a constitutional nature.[112]

### iv. The Format of the Union Participation and Representation in the DSP

The format of the Union participation and representation in the DSP is a corollary of the process of formulation of the common position and the conditions for the unified representation of the Union polity. The notion of the unified representation seems to compromise the relevance of the format of the Union participation and representation in the DSP, inasmuch as it connotes an art of sole participation and representation. Indeed, the format of participation and representation substantiates

---

[111] Bourgeois (1995), p. 19.

[112] See also Antoniadis (2004), p. 339.

the unified representation by providing adequate configurations that convey this thesis. It serves as a premise for enhancing the unity and effectiveness of the EU legal order, as an encompassing idea for the implementation, enforcement and compliance. The thesis of the unified representation does not exclude the joint participation and representation of the Union and its Member States in the DSP. However, considering the intensity of the interconnection of the respective powers of the parties, and the consequences that different formats of representation could have in a particular DSP, the Council, or the Article 207 Committee, may select the most optimal configuration and endorse it in the relevant act.

The reason why the relevance of the format of representation is compromised is that the proposition of the unified representation of the Union entails the idea that the EU should be the sole participant in the DSP, and that the Commission should be the sole representative. Indeed, the Commission has very rarely been a sole participant in the proceedings (e.g. in *EC – Asbestos*). In the majority of cases, two or more co-participants, namely the Commission, and the concerned Member State (s), represented the Union polity in the proceedings. The thesis of the unified representation is not compromised by the format of the joint participation, or even from the joint representatives (namely, the co-defendants), as long as they obey to a common position approved by the Council, or the Article 207 Committee, and execute in a synchronized manner the mandate of representation. To the extent that the Union may be unable to institute countermeasures in areas falling within the residual powers of the Member States,[113] the Union may be co-defendant (jointly representative) with the Member States, rather than substitute them in the DSP, in order to address the concerns of cross-mixity. This is in line with the thesis that the doctrine of substitution is not sustained in the WTO membership of the Union polity.

In light of these observations, and before considering the Union's procedural standing in the DSP, it is first necessary to distinguish between the 'participation' and the 'representation' in the DSP. Each of these concepts can be found in the form of 'sole' or 'joint' participation/representation. Obviously, the representation in the DSP should be always unified, but this does not exclude the possibility that two (joint) representatives are designated on behalf of the Union, with the condition that they express a unified (common) position. The format of representation conveys the central decision on the designation of the Union or the concerned Member State as a principal representative, subsidiary representative or principal co-representative. This decision transforms the default format of representation, which is determined on the basis of the ownership of competences or the authorship of the wrongful act, into an 'alternated' one, where the Union takes the place of the Member State in the DSP. In addition, one could distinguish between the conditions of participation in the DSP, which could be combined as 'mandatory'/'optional' for the Union and the Member State. Furthermore, it could be distinguished between three categories of powers: powers 'conferred' on the Union; 'non-conferred' (residual) powers of the

[113] See also Heliskoski (2001), p. 215.

Union; and powers which are either conferred, or non-conferred, but, being not easily distinguished or inextricably linked to each other, they are designated as 'blurred' powers. The ownership of competences in relation with the disputed matter has a decisive value for the selection of an adequate configuration of the Union participation and representation in the DSP.

The patterning of the format of representation constitutes a significant step for establishing the answerability (as accountability) of the parties, which serves as a preliminary step for the regime of responsibility. This format should be able to ensure the necessary premises that oblige the wrongdoer to comply with its formal WTO obligations, and cease the wrongful conduct in due time. In this way, the system of accountability could prove efficient. Additionally, the format of representation should be able to convey the thesis of the attribution of responsibility based on the ownership of powers (when possible), or alternatively, based on the authorship of the wrongful conduct. This reaffirms the idea that the wrongful act should be affiliated to the wrongdoer as a premise for the principle of attribution of responsibility.

The selection of the format of participation and representation in the DSP is based on the model of 'optional standing'. This is defined as "a normative procedural framework within which the [Union] and the Member States may themselves determine which of them, in the final analysis, is the correct party to a particular relationship under a mixed agreement".[114] This constitutes an essential procedural moment for addressing in advance the fallacies of the joint responsibility regime. The formats of participation and representation in the DSP are proposed in three configurations, namely, the *ordinary* format, the *alternated (competence)* format, and the *alternated (authorship)* format.

(a) The *ordinary* format refers to those DSPs that concern trade measures, which are instituted either from the EU, or from the concerned Member State under the legislative requirements of the EU legal order. The label 'ordinary' is explained by the fact that this category includes most of the DSPs, given that the majority of the WTO disciplines falls within the conferred areas of the Union. For this reason, the Commission is designated as a mandatorily sole representative of the Union polity, while the Member States can exercise an optional joint participation. The latter means that the participation of the Member State is possible and preferable, but not necessary to distinguish it from the Commission's participation, which is mandatory.
(b) The *alternated (competence)* format could be designated for those DSPs, where the residual (non-conferred) powers of the Member States are at stake. Presumably, the 'default' participant and representative in these proceedings should be the concerned Member State, which is the principally answerable and responsible subject for the measure. In principle, the Commission's participation in these cases could be optional, but considering that the Union may incur

[114] Heliskoski (2001), p. 245.

subsidiary responsibility pursuant to the joint responsibility regime (*ex relatione*), it would be preferable that the Union participates jointly with the concerned Member State. The decision-making body may reverse this format by designating the Commission as a principal representative, and the Member State as a subsidiary representative, hence alternating their roles by following a principal-agent model of relationship. If this would be the case, the concerned Member State and the Commission should participate mandatorily jointly in the DSP, given that the joint participation is a safe alternative for ensuring the execution of the DSP rulings and recommendations. As to the labeling, the concept of *alternated (competence)* is explained by the facts that the format provides for the possibility of alternating between the *principally* and *subsidiary* default representatives, and that the default status is determined from the *ownership of competences*. Hence, the *competence* criterion proves relevant for the default configuration of the principal and subsidiary representatives.

(c) The *alternated (authorship)* format slightly deviates from the *alternated (competence)* one. This format is conditioned from the blurred category of powers that are at stake in the DSP, which could include both the conferred (shared or exclusive) as well as non-conferred (residual) categories of powers. Whereas the logic of alternating the roles between the participants remains the same, the system of reference differs. The 'default' format in this category of cases cannot follow the logic of the ownership of powers, because it proves irrelevant for explaining the affiliation of the wrongful conduct with the answerability. Accordingly, in case that the ownership of powers would be the decisive criterion for the default configuration, then the scheme could be biased due to the fact that principal representative could be designated the virtual owner of the 'blurred' competence, while the wrongdoer could be designated as subsidiary representative. As a result, the consequences of this configuration would be compromised and the fallacies of the joint responsibility regime would still persist.

In order to avoid this fallacious scheme, the 'default' configuration does not follow the competence criterion, but the *authorship* one, which establishes a direct connection of the wrongdoer with its status as a principal representative; hence labeled *alternated (authorship)* format. With respect to the default configuration, the ownership of competence is irrelevant. This matter remains irrelevant for the entire proceedings in the DSB, because it constitutes an internal issue of the Union. In this way, the *author of the disputed measure* is designated by default as the principal representative of the polity, and the other subject as the subsidiary one. Accordingly, in case that the wrongful measure is instituted from the Member State, the default configuration shall designate it as a principal, and the Commission as a subsidiary representative. The Council, or the Article 207 Committee, may reverse this scheme and alternate the roles between parties, by designating the Commission as the principal representative, and the concerned Member State as the subsidiary one. In case that the measure is instituted from the Union, the decision-making body may leave the default configuration unchanged. Alternatively, the Council, or the Article

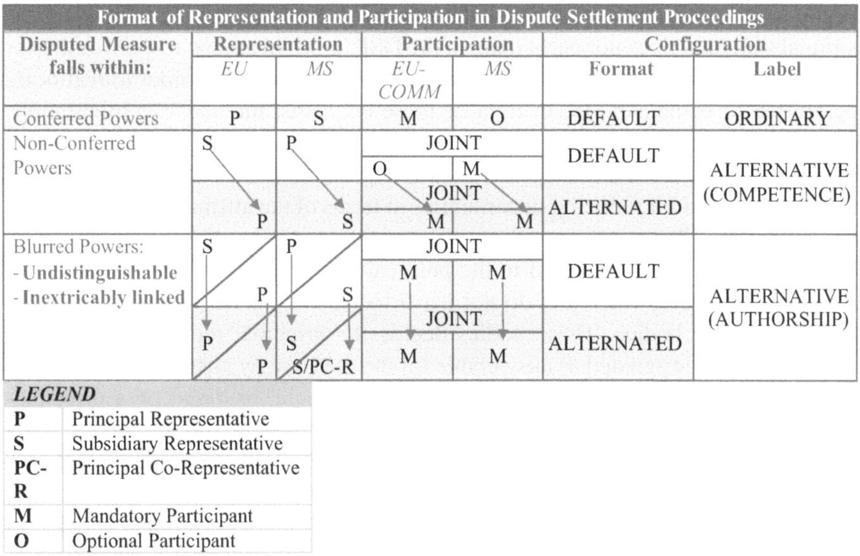


**Fig. 5.1** Format of representation and participation in dispute settlement proceedings

> 207 Committee may choose to designate the concerned Member State as principal co-representative in case that this configuration would be appraised as beneficial. If this would be the case, the coordination shall be indispensable in order to avoid unproductive parallel representation that could hinder the unified representation imperative. Preferably, the Commission should remain the principal representative in all these configurations, while the Member State may optionally be as such. The participation in any of these configurations should be mandatorily joint, considering that the parallel claims of the same powers may be at stake. These configurations can be illustrated in the Fig. 5.1.

This figure is built on the premise that the joint responsibility regime is the default one. The primary function of these configurations is to deconstruct the abstract regime of the joint responsibility, and to establish the basis for engaging a several responsibility regime at a second stage. The formats of representation show only the most adequate relationship between the disputed measure in the DSP, the competence that covers its subject matter, or the author of the measure, and the procedural position of the Commission or the Member State in the DSP. As it appears, the joint participation of the Union and the concerned Member States in the DSP is either a default or a preferred option. As a prerequisite for the joint responsibility regime, this format precludes the overruling of interests of the participants.[115] The participation of the wrongdoer in the proceedings is a premise

[115]Heliskoski (2001), p. 194.

for the application of the rules of attribution. In case that the wrongdoer, using the optional standing, does not participate in the DSP, it might escape responsibility for the act. In such cases, other instruments have to be employed in order to reallocate the burden of responsibility. In light of these concerns, the above configurations regard the mandatory joint participation of the Union and the Member States in all the DSP, as a procedural strategy for addressing the fallacies of the joint responsibility regime, and for reducing uncertainties in terms of the attribution of conduct to the wrongdoer.[116]

This strategy is substantiated in the political-decisional processes in the Union based on predictable rules that do not leave too much discretionary power to the decision-making bodies. These bodies decide the principal representative of the Union, which is designated as answerable for the measure by virtue of ownership of the relevant competence, the authorship of the measure, or based on a principal-agent relationship. When selecting the proper configuration, the decision-making body has to establish the adequate level of representation, which could be attributed to the Union, or to the Member State. The decision should follow an objective analysis, which is oriented from the guiding thesis that the ultimate holder of responsibility should be the entity to whom the wrongful conduct is attributed, or the one that can remedy the injured legal order. The selected configuration should serve this aim at best.

In this respect, the principles of conferral and attribution of conduct could help by designating a delimitation of the Union action from the Member States, or by affiliating the wrongful conduct with the wrongdoer. Additionally, the analysis should consider the predictions of the principles of subsidiarity and proportionality, combined with the doctrines of optimal and efficient decision-making, in order to determine the adequate level of representation. Accordingly, to the extent that the participation at the Union level could be regarded as a unionization of the external action in the disputed area, provided that the condition of conferral is satisfied, the Council, or the Article 207 Committee, may designate the Commission as a principally answerable subject. This is as long as the representation of the Union would become better off in terms of the maximization of the social well-being of the polity. This decision can nevertheless be justified to the extent that the negative externalities of the Union participation in the DSP are *neglected*, or they are *absorbed* from the wrongdoer in the course of compliance with the DSB rulings and recommendations. The designation of the Commission as a principally answerable subject in the DSP may not satisfy the criterion of proportionality, in case that the subsidiary role suffices for the attainment of the same outcomes. This analysis is justified from the fact that the unionization of residual powers is at stake. Additionally, the analysis has to consider the prospect of success of the proceedings. With this respect, it is necessary to assess the probability that the initiated DSP could lead to responsibility, hence that the case will be lost, and the gravity of loss.

---

[116] Heliskoski (2001), p. 197.

The possible consequences and the prospect of reallocation of burden should be considered cumulatively in this calculus.

There are however some procedural limitations in relation with this aspect of the normative model. The procedural position of the Union polity as a respondent in the DSP does not depend exclusively on the will of the EU institutions or the Member States. The joint responsibility regime suggests for a plurality of responsible entities. Generally, the victim has the discretionary freedom to invoke the responsibility of each entity in relation to the wrongful act (Articles 47 ARSIWA and 48 DARIO).[117] However, in practice this option is not widely employed due to the complicated internal structure of the Union, which induces the WTO Members to invoke the responsibility of both the Union and the concerned Member State. From a formal perspective, the Union and its Member States may resolve any doubts in relation with this concern, by submitting a declaration of responsibilities pursuant to this scheme. This declaration would preclude individual claims against the Union and the concerned Member State.

### b. The Management of the Consequences of the Union Participation in the DSP

The management of the consequences of the Union participation in the DSP for matters of non-conferred competences or for blurred areas of competences, constitutes another objective of the normative model. The fallacious model of the joint responsibility regime could serve as a political justification for establishing an instrument to steer the Council, or the Article 207 Committee, into conferring a clear mandate to the Commission concerning its position in relation with the DSB decisions.[118] By endorsing the principle of constitutional legality, the normative framework or the general act would create the necessary legal basis for pursuing the compliance with the DSB rulings and recommendations, as premises for avoiding possible cross-retaliatory measures.

This part of the normative model should be based on the constitutional framework of principles, but at the same time, it should be guided from the predictions of the international law of responsibility. In order to meet the normative expectations raised upon the WTO Agreement, the normative model has to find a balance between the expectation that the responsibility shall be affiliated with the wrongdoer, and the designation of the Union as a principally responsible subject in the context of alternated configurations.

---

[117]See also *The Corfu Channel Case* (merits) (*UK v Albania*), 1949, Dissenting Opinion by Judge Azevedo, 78, 92.

[118]Bogdandy (2005), p. 64.

i. The Compliance with the DSB Rulings and Recommendations

The compliance of the Union and the concerned Member State with the DSB rulings and recommendations for areas of non-conferred competences reveals another facet of the fallacies of the joint responsibility regime. The central constitutional challenge related with the issue of compliance, is to find the relevant legal instruments that ensure that the Union, if found responsible for the Member State measures, complies with the DSB ruling or recommendation without becoming subject to retaliatory or cross-retaliatory measures, and without violating the limitations of the Treaties with respect to the distribution of powers.[119] This question is intentionally construed in light of the formal obligations of the Union and its Member States in the context of their WTO membership, by avoiding a question that would put in the first place the Union's incapability to oblige a Member State to withdraw a measure that falls within its residual powers. The question is not misconstrued, given that it takes account of the virtual nature of the Union's competences. The emphasis is however put on the primary cause of the cross-retaliation, which is the inducement for compliance with formal obligations.

Obviously, the virtual nature of the competences in the disputed area, makes the obligation arising out of the DSB ruling or recommendation also virtual for the Union. The fact that the Commission participated in the DSP as a principal or a subsidiary representative of the Union, does not alter the ownership of the obligation; the principle of the reciprocal indetermination of the legal orders precludes the change of vertical competences or their definition by virtue of the WTO membership. The Union and its Member States are under their joint obligation to comply with international agreements binding on them (Articles 216(2) TFEU and 4 (3) TEU). The duty of loyalty entails various forms of positive and negative obligations for the Member States to cooperate for ensuring the fulfillment of the obligations arising out of the Treaties or resulting from the acts of the Union's institutions. However, the limitations from the principle of conferral are also of a normative nature for the Union. Hence, any construction that would change the nature of powers would be invalid.

In light of these observations, the normative model construes the legislative act or the general framework for the participation of the Union in the DSP for matters of non-conferred competences, as an instrument for filling the normative gap. This complies with the principle of constitutional legality. However, the main challenge of the model is to draw a compromise between the predictions of the rules of attribution, and the general limitation of the Union not to change the internal structure of powers by means of its participation in the DSP. This concern can be addressed by empowering the Union to enact an individual decision for complying

[119] It should be recalled that, as marked out in the previous Chapters, the principle of constitutional legality, in combination with the principle of conferral put limits on the Union's exercise of powers. Furthermore, the Union is precluded from measures that would change the structure of powers appointed in the Treaties.

with the DSB rulings or recommendations. This decision transposes the virtual obligation of the Union into a real obligation for the concerned Member State. In this way, the model reallocates the responsibility following the rules of attribution, and at the same time, precludes the Union to legislate on a non-conferred or an unclear area of powers. Pursuant to the principle of loyalty, the Member State is under the obligation to take any appropriate measures, general or particular, to ensure the fulfillment of the obligations arising out of the Treaties or resulting from the acts of the institutions of the Union. The general acts entitling the Union to participate in the DSP and the individual act of the Union transposing to the Member State the virtual obligation incurred from the DSB ruling, could be regarded as acts of the Union in the meaning of Article 4(3) TEU. This would amount to an obligation for the concerned Member State to withdraw the measure that is inconsistent with the WTO Agreement. In this way, the burden of responsibility, i.e. the cessation of the wrongful act, is reallocated to the primarily responsible subject pursuant to the default configuration. This is in line with the premises suggested from the international law of responsibility, which allows for the subject incurring subsidiary responsibility to reallocate the remedial duties with other jointly responsible entities.[120]

### ii. The Allocation and Enforcement of Responsibility from the Union Participation in the DSP

The issue of compliance with the DSB rulings and recommendations involves also the allocation of burden to the wrongdoer. The political-decisional processes in the context of the normative model engage the internal constitutional infrastructure of the Union to address the fallacies of the joint responsibility regime. This ensures the reallocation of responsibility and allows the Union to discharge the burden to the wrongdoer. The Union, when obliging the wrongdoer to comply with the DSB rulings, does not institute measures in the areas related with these rulings, but rather transposes its virtual obligation into a real one. This right of recourse for ensuring the cessation of the wrongful act is in line with the predictions of the international law of responsibility,[121] and constitutes a substantial guarantee of the normative model for the residual powers of the Member States. The concerned Member States maintain the ultimate right to comply with the DSB rulings.

The model should provide relevant normative propositions for addressing the allocation of responsibility from the participation in the DSP between the EU and its concerned Member States. The inclusion of specific rules for the allocation of responsibility, providing clear instructions on the division of responsibility in cases of breaches of WTO obligations, constitutes a necessary complementation of the

---

[120] See also Orakhelashvili (2010), pp. 647–665.

[121] Articles 47(2)(b) ARSIWA and 48(3)(b) DARIO.

missing norms in this regard.[122] These propositions may follow the logic endorsed from the configurations of representation, given that they are built on the considerations on the vertical distribution of powers, and the rules of attribution.

(a) The responsibility for complying with the DSB rulings in cases where an *ordinary* configuration of participation and representation is followed, is primarily borne from the Union. The concerned Member State becomes responsible in this scenario only in a subsidiary way. This complies with the rules of attribution, inasmuch as the wrongful measure is instituted from the Union, or the Member State acting under the control of the Union. The Union is potentially capable to redress the wrongful measure through cessation, and to incur the burden of retaliation in case of non-compliance. Therefore, the joint responsibility regime in these cases does not result fallacious in terms of the allocation of burden.

(b) In the *alternated (competence)* configuration, the default procedural position, which designates the concerned Member States as the primary answerable and responsible subject, is reversed from the Council, or the Article 207 Committee, by replacing it with the Commission. In case that the measure is found inconsistent with the WTO law and a DSB ruling requires its withdrawal, the Union should follow the procedure of transposition of burden to the wrongdoer. Obviously, the Union should follow this step in case that the circumstances convince the decision-making bodies to comply with the DSB rulings or recommendations. If this would be the case, the Council or the Article 207 Committee could enact individual decisions requiring the wrongdoer to comply with its formal WTO obligations. This is in line with the joint and several responsibility regime, which provides to the subsidiary responsible entity the right of recourse against the principally responsible one.

    In case that the concerned Member State fails to comply, the Commission may start the infringement proceedings in the ECJ pursuant to Articles 258 *et seq*. TFEU. This obligation can be construed based on Article 216(2) TFEU and Article 4(3) TEU, inasmuch as the non-compliance with DSB rulings violates the Treaty obligations of the Member States to comply with the WTO Agreements. However, considering that the case concerns a residual power of the Union, the non-compliance can be construed also as an infringement of the act transposing the virtual obligation of the Union for complying with the DSB ruling to the real wrongdoer. Hence, the international obligation of the Union is transposed into an internal obligation of the concerned Member State to comply with the Union acts.

(c) As to the *alternated (authorship)* configurations, the same proposition as for the *alternated (competence)* formats can be maintained. The difference in this scenario is that the Union and the Member States cannot exercise the

[122] See also Kuijper (2010), p. 225.

competence autonomously. Therefore, in case that the Union would be designated as a principally responsible subject for a wrongful conduct attributed to the Member State, and in case that the Union decides to comply with the DSB ruling, then it can oblige the concerned Member State, by means of an individual act, to withdraw the wrongful measure. Similar to the *alternated (competence)* configuration, the right of recourse aims to transpose an obligation that is borne virtually by virtue of the 'forced' joint membership, to the default configuration. In this case, the wrongdoer should comply with the DSB ruling due to its own international obligations, as well as due to the internal obligation from the Union law.

However, the blurred or inextricably linked nature of competences may complicate the process of compliance. In case that the powers are inextricably linked and a separate identification is impossible, the rule of preponderance could be proposed as an alternative solution for the inability of the allocation responsibility on a several basis.[123] According to this rule, the duty to comply with the DSB rulings may be attributed to the entity that has the superiority in power or influence in relation with this compliance. Even in this format, the Commission may initiate infringement proceedings against the wrongdoer for violation of Treaty obligations and infringement of the Union acts. In this scenario, it could be suggested that the Union and the concerned Member States decide jointly on the transposition or allocation of the burden of responsibility. The main criteria for this should remain the authorship of the measure or the rule of preponderance. In this way, the fallacy of the joint responsibility regime is deconstructed by means of extraordinary instruments, which regard the jointly responsible entities as jointly capable for pursuing a normative solution. As to the content of the solution, although it remains essentially difficult to predict the allocation of responsibility among the primarily or subsidiarily responsible parties, the responsible body could come close to the default position, if it follows the relevant criteria, i.e. the authorship or the rules of preponderance.

The above alternatives are illustrated in the Fig. 5.2.

The compliance with the DSB rulings, by virtue of an act of the Union transposing its virtual obligation to the concerned Member States, internalizes (absorbs) the international obligation into the Union polity. The refusal of the concerned Member State to comply would make the Union norm ineffective, and as such, could be regarded as a violation of the Treaties (Articles 2 and 4(3) TEU). This would entitle the Commission to institute infringement proceedings pursuant to Articles 258 *et seq.* TFEU in relation with the material violation of the rule of law, the principle of loyalty, and the duty to comply with the international obligations of the Union (Article 216(2) TFEU). In this way, the principle of effectiveness is

[123] Kuijper (2010), p. 225.

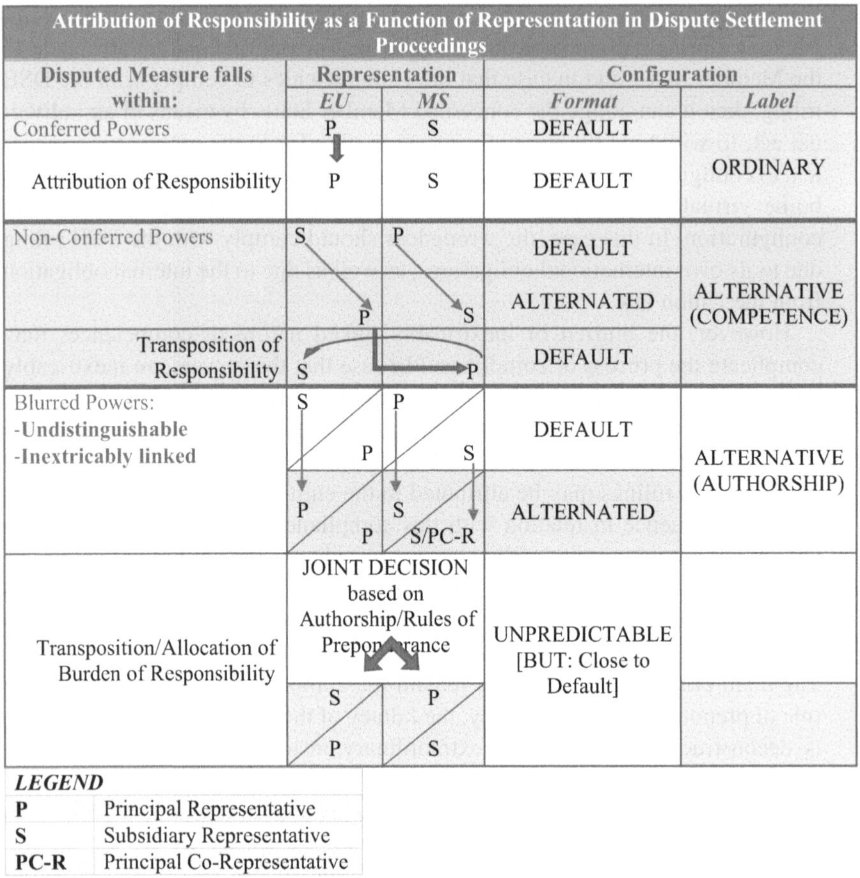


**Fig. 5.2** Attribution of responsibility as a function of representation in dispute settlement proceedings

accommodated in the normative model as a premise for supporting the cessation of the wrongful act.

By precluding the invasion of legal interests of other participants from the wrongdoer, the allocation of the burden of responsibility and its adequate enforcement convey the aims of the international law of responsibility.[124] These instruments can be construed as a general obligation of the Union and its Member States to take account of their reciprocal interests in view of the Union as *pactum fidelis*. The Member States are obliged to ensure that the DSP does not result in calling into question the advantages enjoyed by the Union and the third Member States. This obligation is based on the duty of loyalty and its inherent values, namely the principles of reciprocity, *bona fide* and *pacta sunt servanda*.

[124]Brownlie (1998), p. 435.

Furthermore, the normative model serves as a significant premise for precluding the damages of individuals due to retaliation. In view of this, the EU and its concerned Member State should make their best efforts to ensure that the selected format of representation does not result in hindering the other Member States from trade benefits of their WTO membership. Failure of the Member State to comply with the DSB rulings would make the incurrence of damages from the individuals certain, and this could increase the incidence of compensation claims against the Union or its Member States. Also for this reason, the Union and the entire society would become better off, in case that the wrongdoer would comply with the DSB rulings and recommendations.

The lack of direct effect of the WTO Agreement and the DSB rulings should not preclude the adoption of an act from the Union institutions complying with these rulings. These acts result from the normative model of the Union participation in the DSP. The internal Union acts may be subject to legality review from the ECJ, inasmuch as they implement the normative predictions of the model of the Union participation in the DSP. This art of enforcement actions could produce *ex nunc* effects, and as such, would be able to concentrate on the cessation of the wrongful act.

The allocation of responsibility should be able to convey the objectives of the international law of responsibility for preventing the breach of international obligations by means of the deterrent effects on the wrongdoer. The WTO system of responsibility is centered on the cessation of the wrongful measures, inasmuch as no right to compensation is granted to the victims; rather retaliation is the only means for inducing the wrongdoer toward cessation. In view of this, the normative model cannot go beyond this remedy. The joint responsibility regime of the Union and its Member States diminishes the material effects of cross-retaliation. Furthermore, the assumption of responsibility from the EU in the DSP also for non-conferred competences discourages any deterrent effects on the real wrongdoers. The normative model mitigates these systemic concerns by reallocating the burden to the wrongdoer, and by precluding the possibility of cumulative responsibility of both the Union and the concerned Member State.

### iii. The Prospect of the Victim Compensation According to EU Law

The normative model has to be complied with, in order to accomplish its aim, namely to prevent the fallacies of the joint responsibility regime. The failure of the wrongdoer to comply with the DSB rulings or recommendations may lead to the institution of countermeasures against the Union. As already highlighted earlier, the economic operators are the ultimate victims of cross-retaliation. The question is whether the normative model could provide any normative reference for the comprehensive legal protection of the victims of retaliation.[125]

---

[125]This obligation can be construed in light of the obligation of the Member States to provide effective legal protection to their individuals in areas covered by EU law (Article 19(1) TEU).

The prospect of compensation of the victims is already addressed in the jurisprudence. This has denied such a right by virtue of the missing direct effect of the WTO Agreement in the EU legal order. The lack of direct effect, and sometimes the lack of standing of economic operators before the ECJ pursuant to Article 263 (4) TFEU for invoking unlawfulness of Union acts, have been among the reasons for the unsuccessful prospect of compensation of the victims.[126] The need to maintain a certain scope for maneuver for the political negotiations, as an answer to the political character of the DSU and the WTO Agreement in general, has caused the ECJ to restraint the judicial review of the Union's action in relation with the WTO negotiations. The financial burden on the Union following the judicial review would create deterrent effects on the political institutions and put them in significant disadvantages toward other trading partners. This abstract reasoning has prioritized the general interest of the Union over the individual interests of economic operators, which incur damages from bargaining strategies of the political institutions in the course of compliance with the DSB rulings. In other words, the ECJ has excluded the judicial course as an alternative for shifting to the Union the economic burden of countermeasures. This issue is not exclusively related with the fallacies of the joint responsibility regime, but results from the nature of the WTO Agreement. In light of these concerns, it would be useful to consider the implications of the normative model for the legal protection of individuals and the prospect of their compensation.

Whereas it is often suggested that the lack of remedies is allegedly regarded as a deficiency of legal protection, it should also be emphasized that this concern would be true only to the extent that an individual right exists.[127] The argument that the WTO Agreement and the DSB rulings do not confer rights on individuals is decisive for denying compensation due to retaliatory measures, but this does not make the EU legal order deficient in terms of the legal protection of individuals. The legal order of the EU should be able to pursue a sound balance between the contradictory ends of equal treatment, as a premise for justice, the general interest of the Union, and the legal certainty.[128] In view of this, the need to balance the political scope for maneuver of the Commission should be balanced against the standard of the judicial protection provided from a complete system of legal remedies.[129] The normative model could employ a mediating strategy for balancing these objectives.

---

[126]See also Thies (2013), pp. 71, 74, 93, 192.

[127]Bogdandy (2005), p. 53.

[128]This formulation is only a symbolic reduction of Radbruch's conception of the legal system as striving "through its organs and doctrine to achieve three related, interdependent but ultimately contradictory ends: - justice, i.e. the perennial axiom of equal treatment; - particular doctrines or sub-values of justice, in their individualist, socialist, utilitarian or other formulations; and - legal certainty". See further Dowrick (1983), p. 230. Referring also to Wolf and Radbruch (1963) and Radbruch and Lask (1950).

[129]Thies (2013), p. 73.

In principle, the compensation could be considered legally justified also for the unlawful conduct of the Union in the course of the DSP, to the extent that the relevant provisions confer rights or benefits on individuals.[130] Indeed, it is already suggested that,

> a [Union] legislative measure whose application leads to restrictions of the right to property and the freedom to pursue a trade or profession that impair the very substance of those rights in a *disproportionate* and *intolerable* manner, perhaps *precisely because no provision has been made for compensation* calculated to avoid or remedy that impairment, could give rise to non-contractual liability on the part of the [Union].[131]

From this *dictum*, it can be inferred that the lack of direct effect does not preclude the right to compensation for non-contractual liability in the context of WTO obligations of the Union and its Member States. With reference to the EU legal order, the concept of direct effect is not an absolute precondition for incurring liability. Accordingly, the Member States may incur liability for breach of their EU obligations without having to annul the wrongful act, and may be obliged to compensate the injured parties even if the act is not directly effective, but it conferred rights on the party.[132] The right of primary remedies, i.e. right to ask for the revision of a wrongful act, does not constitute a precondition for the secondary legal remedy, i.e. the right to make compensation for a wrongful conduct.[133] However, in terms of compensation in the course of the WTO relationships, the injured parties could hardly prove that the EU institutions, when taking decisions for non-complying with the DSB rulings, *manifestly* and *gravely* disregarded their discretion; this being a necessary criterion for establishing a sufficiently serious breach.[134] Similarly, it would be difficult to construe the WTO Agreement, or the DSU, as able to confer rights or benefits to the applicants, considering that they are typically inter-state instruments.[135]

In light of the above, it has been suggested that if the ECJ finds in the negotiation system of the DSB the argument for the necessity of preserving the political scope for maneuver for the benefit of the Union's general interest, then it would be also justifiable to compensate for the impaired benefits of the individuals.[136] This is precisely because the general interest is being made better off from this strategy of the Union, while the interests of economic operators are not considered from the decision-making bodies. This suggests for an inclusive approach of legal

[130]Thies (2013), p. 73.

[131]Joined Cases C-120/06 and C-121/06 *FIAMM and Fedon v Council and Commission*, [2008] ECR I-6513, para. 184 (emphasis added).

[132]Of particular relevance in this aspect is the ECJ jurisprudence on the liability as developed in the Case C-224/01 *Gerhard Köbler v Republik Österreich*, [2003] ECR I-10239 and Joined Cases C-6/90 and C-9/90 *Francovich et al. v Italy*, [1991] ECR I-5357.

[133]Thies (2013), p. 77.

[134]Thies (2013), pp. 124–125, 179.

[135]Thies (2013), pp. 179–180.

[136]Thies (2013), p. 75.

interpretation that is open to complex economic, social, and political arguments. Following a pluralist approach, the normative arguments are considered cumulatively with other arguments, such as the economics of the allocation of costs between victims of retaliation, the exposure of the Union budget toward compensation claims, the costs and benefits of a wide political room for manoeuver, the observation of the principle of good governance and institutional accountability, etc.

The argument of the ECJ for allocating the incurred damages with the economic operators as part of the normal economic risk of the market cannot be sustained in the context of the principles of free market economy where the world prices, being driven down from the competition, make it very easy for the enterprises to exit the market. Furthermore, the retaliatory system, which allows the countermeasures to cross from one industry to another, makes it impossible for the operators to predict the directions of countermeasures in due time.[137] The countervailing system could be misused by trading partners in order to drive their EU competitors out of the market. Such economic arguments should be part of the analysis of the decision-making processes, when determining the configuration of the Union participation in the DSP.

The system of countermeasures aims to make a prudent public authority, which is found in breach of its WTO obligations, to comply with the DSB ruling within a reasonable period of time (the grace period). The burden on the Union to compensate the injuries of the industry, more than a limitation on the Union's political bargain, could be seen as a constraining instrument for compliance. Indeed, more than a negative pressure to the detriment of the bargaining power, the duty of compensation would constitute for the Union a guarantee for an informed use of discretionary powers. This would improve good governance.[138] In addition, this enhances the democratic legitimacy of the decision-making processes, and brings the issues of a general interest out of the influence of lobbies, by increasing in this way transparency.[139] The prospect of victim compensation may stimulate an internal debate on the management of resources.

As to the management of the burden of compensation, the normative model could provide significant predictions in terms of the parties that have to share the costs. Accordingly, the Union should be regarded fully responsible for claims of compensation raised in the context of the ordinary format of representation. In the other configurations, the burden could be allocated to the default entity that is primarily responsible for the wrongful measure. Hence, although the Union may be designated as a representative of the Member States, the latter are responsible for redressing the injuries suffered from individuals for their wrongful measures.

---

[137]Thies (2013), p. 74.

[138]Joined Cases C-120/06 and C-121/06 *FIAMM and Fedon v Council and Commission*, [2008] ECR I-6513, Opinion of the AG Poiares Maduro, para. 59.

[139]Thies (2013), pp. 194–195.

The compensation may potentially be regulated either on an *ad hoc* or general (permanent) manner by means of legislative acts of the Union, which target those situations that may become subject to compensation as a result of disproportionate and intolerable measures of the Union affecting individual rights of economic operators incurring damages.[140] In this way, the collateral damages of the Union participation in the DSP may be mitigated to the greatest reasonable extent, without hindering the scope for maneuver necessary for the political bodies in the negotiation of compliance with the DSB rulings and recommendations. A successful claim of compensation would offset the unbearable loss incurred from individuals, without requiring the Union to comply with the DSB rulings and recommendations that gave rise to cross-retaliatory measures.[141] In this way, in case that the general interest of the Union would necessitate the continuation of exceptional measures, such as the non-compliance with DSB rulings and recommendations, the Union would have to compensate for the burden imposed on a number of individuals. This thesis could be construed either as a corollary of the principle of equal treatment, or as a corollary of the fundamental right to property, which requires the compensation of individuals for their special sacrifice that they have to bear for lawful conduct that causes damages close to expropriation.[142]

The Union participation in the DSP interferes with the fundamental rights of the individuals protected by the EU legal order. The conduct of the Union and Member States in terms of the WTO membership should not be construed to escape the judicial review, as a guarantee for the predictions of the rule of law and standards of protection of fundamental rights pursuant to the EU general principles.[143] The reparation of damages incurred from individuals as a result of the conduct of the Union in the course of the DSP could be further addressed in light of the fundamental rights and the general principles of the Union law, such as the right to property, the principle to pursue an economic activity, the principle of legitimate expectations, and the right to non-discrimination.[144] These principles, which derive from the rule of law,[145] target primarily individuals, and as such, could be suitable for the construction of their legal protection in terms of compensation. However, considering that the political bargaining power of the Union in the course of the DSP is regarded from the ECJ as pursuing a general interest of the Union, the individuals may be required to sacrifice their interests to this end.[146] Therefore, the prospect of sustaining the claims of compensation for unlawful and lawful acts of

---

[140] Tancredi (2012), p. 267.

[141] Thies (2013), p. 155.

[142] Thies (2013), pp. 157–158.

[143] See also Thies (2013), p. 187.

[144] Thies (2013), pp. 126–127.

[145] Tridimas (2006), p. 4.

[146] Joined Cases C-120/06 and C-121/06 *FIAMM and Fedon v Council and Commission*, [2008] ECR I-6513, para. 183.

the Union is possible only from a theoretical perspective.[147] This theoretical possibility is argued by giving due account to the jurisprudence, which has recognized the normative relevance of the general principles, without however providing for compensation on those grounds.

## VI. Concluding Remarks: The Normative Model in Light of the Principle of Transparency

With respect to the issue of responsibility, the Union participation in the DSP for matters related with the non-conferred competences remains the main challenge of the WTO membership of the Union and its Member States. The responsibility assumed from the Union in the course of the DSP for wrongful acts attributed to a Member State constitutes the central fallacy of the joint responsibility regime. This challenge will not cease to exist even with a more advanced federalization of the Union polity, as long as it is inherent in the very idea of the vertical distribution of powers. Nor would any declaration of powers or any withdrawal of the Member States from the WTO fully resolve the consequences of this participation in the DSP. The challenge does not result from any misconstruction of the WTO Agreement as a mixed agreement *per se*. Rather, this challenge is rooted in the constitutional nature of the Union polity, as well as in the misalignment of the general rules of international responsibility with the Union's responsibility from the WTO membership. In light of these observations, this Chapter patterned a normative model for the Union participation in the DSP, with a view of addressing at best the fallacies of the joint responsibility regime.

The normative model addresses the problems of mixity by establishing a normative framework that regulates the participation of the Union in the DSP as well as the procedural aspect of the representation. This model is conceived as a mediating strategy that balances the contradicting claims by accommodating them through political-decisional processes within the Union. These processes are based on the normative premises of the international law of responsibility, the law of the WTO, and most importantly, the constitutional principles of the EU legal order. The model is conceived in compatibility with the current practice, and revives the current attempts for the formalization of the Union participation in the DSP, such as the draft Code of Conduct, the Regulation (EU) 2015/476 (*re anti-dumping/subsidies*) and the Regulation (EU) 2014/912 (*re financial responsibility in investor-to-state disputes*). These premises support the general idea of proceduralization of the DSP relationships.

The elaboration of the normative model does not differentiate between the function of a prior (formalized) model and a flexible one. However, from the above analysis it could be inferred that the flexible model ensures a better

[147] See also Thies (2013), pp. 147, 149.

adaptability to the dynamic changes in the internal structure of powers, as well as in the external geo-political interests. Accordingly, once the possible configurations are provided in a general framework, the decision-making body, namely the Council, or the Article 207 Committee, decides by taking account of the relevant criteria of subsidiarity and proportionality, in order to take the most optimal decision on whether to centralize the representation at the Union level, or better leave it with the Member States.

The most important part of the patterning of the Union participation in the DSP consists in the decision of the Union legislator to establish a general regulation with this respect. More than a political process, this decision should be preceded from a critical and comprehensive analysis of all the premises related with the participation of the Union in the DSP. This decision is not about formalizing an unwritten practice, or deciding whether the Union or the Member States would be better off if they acted collectively or individually. Certainly, these aspects are instrumental for the decision. However, this decision is about the principles and values that the Union has to defend in its external action in the course of the participation in the DSP. This decision, more than filling the lacunae in the infrastructure of the Union polity, is about the establishment of a credible process that ensures the protection of interests, meets the normative expectations of participants, and addresses their cognitive expectations with equality. More than creating rules for the sake of legal certainty, this decision is about limiting the extreme pursuit of particular formulations of justice. Only in this way, the individual interests are balanced against the utilitarian collective actions, and the legal certainty goals.[148] Hence, the normative model of participation would serve as an adequate framework for reconciling the conflicting interests of the Union and its Member States, and would preclude the fallacies of the joint responsibility regime.

The principle of transparency permeates the normative model of participation in the DSP in two main dimensions. The scope of this principle concerns particularly the principles of legal certainty, legitimate expectations, due process of law, as well as the principles of political processes, such as the principles of conferral, subsidiarity, and proportionality. As to the external dimension, transparency implies the communication of the model of participation to the trading partners, by means of a decision in the context of the WTO Ministerial Conference.[149] This element plays the same function of a declaration of powers in mixed agreements, in that it ensures the third states to be aware of the division of powers in the polity, and to develop their expectations pursuant to the procedures prescribed from the model.

The principle of transparency serves to the principle of legal certainty, inasmuch as it guarantees the trading partners that their interests shall not be hindered as a result of the complicated and confusing structure of powers in the Union polity. Indeed, the safeguard of the interests of the third parties in the internal processes

[148] See further in general, Dowrick (1983), p. 230. Referring also to Wolf and Radbruch (1963) and Radbruch and Lask (1950).

[149] Antoniadis (2004), p. 339.

constitutes an international obligation that is primarily inherent in the nature of the WTO Agreement. This obligation aims to ascertain the trading partners that their interests should not be hindered as a result of the joint membership of the Union and its Member States. Additionally, this obligation is rooted in international law, as an obligation of the Union and its Member States not to use their internal rules of organization as instruments for justifying their failure to perform treaty obligations (Articles 27 VCLT and 27 VCLTSIO).[150] Hence, the management of responsibility in the Union should take into account the interests of third parties, and should not hinder their expectations.[151]

In the context of internal relations, the principle of transparency may exert a greater normative application. The formalization of the participation of the EU in the DSP based on formal proceedings allows the participants to get informed about the content and the implications of this participation. As a result, the normative model would enhance the transparency and the legitimacy by organizing the political-decisional processes in relation with the participation in the DSP on firmed foundations, and make them subject to judicial review from the ECJ.[152] From the procedural point of view, the involvement of the disputed measures in the agenda of decision-making organs in the Union requires the attention of all the participants, and as such, becomes subject to their approval. This art of transparency is far more advanced than the current practice of the abstract participation of the Commission in the DSP. Considering that the object of these proceedings is the analysis of the national measures that are claimed as WTO inconsistent, the Member States may assess in due time the implications of potential countermeasures for their trade interests. Similarly, the European industries and other lobbies may get involved more easily in the proceedings, so that they can express their interests on the matter and offer their expertise.

In this way, the element of transparency serves to a due process of law, which allows the trade interests of the Member States to become subject to administrative proceedings at their inception phase, and, as such, potentially subject to legality review in the ECJ. The current practice of the Union participation in the DSP does not reveal this function of the principle of transparency, and in view of this, the normative model appears advantageous. Furthermore, the transparency of the proceedings serves to the observance of the principles of political processes. Accordingly, a political-decisional process at the Union level on the EU participation in the DSP regarding the defense of a national measure should be able to better observe the principles of conferral, subsidiarity and proportionality. Member States have more chances to observe their residual powers in the context of these proceedings, and the ECJ remains a significant guarantee for ensuring that a DSP is not turned into an instrument for creeping their residual powers.

[150]See in particular on the legal certainty Heliskoski (2001), pp. 121–155.

[151]Heliskoski (2001), pp. 157–158.

[152]Heliskoski (2001), p. 248.

# References


Antoniadis, Antonis. 2004. The Participation of the European Community in the World Trade Organization: An External Look at European Union Constitution-Building. In *European Union Law for the Twenty-First Century: Rethinking the New Legal Order*. Vol. 1: Constitutional and Public Law: External Relations, ed. Takis Tridimas and Paolisa Nebbia, 321–344. Oxford: Hart.

Bogdandy, Armin von. 2005. Legal Effects of World Trade Organization Decision Within European Union Law: A Contribution to the Theory of the Legal Acts of Damages Under Article 288(2) EC. *Journal of World Trade* 39: 45.

Bourgeois, Jacques H.J. 1995. The Uruguay Round Results from a European Lawyers' Perspective: An Introduction. In *The Uruguay Round Results: A European Lawyers' Perspective*, ed. Jacques H.J. Bourgeois, Frédérique Berrod, and Eric Gippini Fournier. Bruges conferences, vol. 8. Brussels: European Interuniversity Press.

Brownlie, Ian. 1998. *Principles of Public International Law*. 5th ed. Oxford, New York: Clarendon Press; Oxford University Press.

Commission of the European Communities. 1996. General Report on the Activities of the European Union 1995: European Commission.

Crawford, James. 2008. *Brownlie's Principles of Public International Law*. 8th ed. Oxford: Oxford University Press.

Crawford, James, and Jeremy Watkins. 2010. International Responsibility. In *The Philosophy of International Law*, ed. Samantha Besson and John Tasioulas, 283–298. Oxford, New York: Oxford University Press.

Cremona, Marise. 2001. A Policy of Bits and Pieces – The Common Commercial Policy After Nice. *Cambridge Yearbook of European Legal Studies* 4: 61.

Dashwood, Alan. 2011. *Wyatt and Dashwood's European Union Law*. 6th ed. Oxford, Portland, OR: Hart.

Dominicé, Christian. 2010. Attribution of Conduct to Multiple States and the Implication of a State in the Act of Another State. In *The Law of International Responsibility*, ed. James Crawford, Alain Pellet, Simon Olleson, and Kate Parlett, 281–289. Oxford, New York: Oxford University Press.

Dougan, Michael. 2007. When Worlds Collide! Competing Visions of the Relationship Between Direct Effect and Supremacy. *Common Market Law Review* 44 (4): 931–963.

Dowrick, F.E. 1983. A Model of the European Communities' Legal System. *Yearbook of European Law* 3 (1): 169–237. doi:10.1093/yel/3.1.169.

Dupuy, Pierre-Marie. 1989. The International Law of States Responsibility: Revolution or Evolution. *Michigan Journal of International Law* 11: 105.

———. 2010. Relations Between the International Law and Responsibility in Municipal Law. In *The Law of International Responsibility*, ed. James Crawford, Alain Pellet, Simon Olleson, and Kate Parlett. Oxford, New York: Oxford University Press.

Eagleton, Clyde. 1928. *The Responsibility of States in International Law*. New York: New York University Press.

Eeckhout, Piet. 2011. *EU External Relations Law*. 2nd ed. Oxford EU law library. Oxford, New York: Oxford University Press.

Frid, Rachel. 1995. *The Relations Between the EC and International Organizations. Legal Theory and Practice*. The Hague: Kluwer Law International.

Gamper, Anna. 2010. On Loyalty and the (Federal) Constitution. *Vienna Online Journal on International Constitutional Law* 4: 157.

Graig, Paul. 2012. Competence and Member State Autonomy: Causality, Consequence and Legitimacy. In *The European Court of Justice and the Autonomy of the Member States*, ed. Hans-W Micklitz and Bruno de Witte. Cambridge, Antwerp, Portland: Intersentia.

Heliskoski, Joni. 1996. The 'Duty of Cooperation' Between the European Community and its Member States Within the World Trade Organization. *Finnish Yearbook of International Law* 7: 59.

———. 2001. *Mixed Agreements as a Technique for Organizing the International Relations of the European Community and its Member States*. The Hague, New York: Kluwer Law International.

Hilf, Meinhard. 1995. The ECJ's Opinion 1/94 on the WTO: - No Surprise, but Wise?. *European Journal of International Law* 6 (1): 245–259. doi:10.1093/ejil/6.1.245.

Hirsch, Moshe. 1995. *The Responsibility of International Organizations Toward Third Parties. Some Basic Principles*. Dordrecht, Boston: Martinus Nijhoff.

Hyett, Stephen. 2000. The Duty of Cooperation: A Flexible Concept. In *The General Law of E.C. External Relations*, ed. Alan Dashwood and Christophe Hillion, 248–253. London: Sweet & Maxwell.

Koutrakos, Panos. 2006. *EU International Relations Law*. Modern studies in European law, vol. 9. Oxford, Portland, OR: Hart.

Kuijper, Pieter. 2010. International Responsibility for EU Mixed Agreements. In *Mixed Agreements Revisited: The EU and its Member States in the World*, ed. Christophe Hillion and Panos Koutrakos, 208–227. Modern studies in European law, vol. 21. Oxford [England], Portland, OR: Hart.

Kuijper, Pieter-Jan. 1995. The New WTO Dispute Settlement System: The Impact on the Community. In *The Uruguay Round Results: A European Lawyers' Perspective*, ed. Jacques H.J. Bourgeois, Frédérique Berrod, and Eric Gippini Fournier, 87–114. Bruges conferences, vol. 8. Brussels: European Interuniversity Press.

MacLeod, I., I.D. Hendry, and Stephen Hyett. 1996. *The External Relations of the European Communities. A Manual of Law and Practice*. Oxford, New York: Clarendon Press; Oxford University Press.

Neframi, Eleftheria. 2012. Mixed Agreements as a Source of European Union Law. In *International Law as Law of the European Union*, ed. Enzo Cannizzaro, Paolo Palchetti, and Ramses A. Wessel, 325–349. Studies in EU external relations, vol. 5. Boston: Martinus Nijhoff.

Orakhelashvili, Alexander. 2010. Division of Reparation Between Responsible Entities. In *The Law of International Responsibility*, ed. James Crawford, Alain Pellet, Simon Olleson, and Kate Parlett, 647–665. Oxford, New York: Oxford University Press.

Pellet, Alain. 2010. The Definition of Responsibility in International Law. In *The Law of International Responsibility*, ed. James Crawford, Alain Pellet, Simon Olleson, and Kate Parlett, 3–16. Oxford, New York: Oxford University Press.

Quigley, John. 1987. Complicity in International Law: A New Direction in the Law of State Responsibility. *British Yearbook of International Law* 57 (1): 77–131. doi:10.1093/bybil/57.1.77.

Radbruch, Gustav, and Emil Lask. 1950. *The Legal Philosophies of Lask, Radbruch, and Dabin*. Cambridge: Harvard University Press.

Schermers, Henry G. 1983. International Organizations as Members of Other International Organizations. In *Völkerrecht als Rechtsordnung, Internationale Gerichtsbarkeit, Menschenrechte: Festschrift für Hermann Mosler*, ed. Hermann Mosler and Rudolf Bernhardt, 823–838. Beiträge zum ausländischen öffentlichen Recht und Völkerrecht, vol. 81. Berlin, New York: Springer.

Tancredi, Antonello. 2012. On the Absence of Direct Effect of the WTO Dispute Settlement Body's Decisions in the EU Legal Order. In *International Law as Law of the European Union*, ed. Enzo Cannizzaro, Paolo Palchetti, and Ramses A. Wessel, 249–268. Studies in EU external relations, vol. 5. Boston: Martinus Nijhoff.

Thies, Anne. 2013. *International Trade Disputes and EU Liability*. Cambridge studies in European law and policy. New York: Cambridge University Press.

Timmermans, Christiaan. 2000. Organising Joint Participation of E.C. and Member States. In *The General Law of E.C. External Relations*, ed. Alan Dashwood and Christophe Hillion, 239–247. London: Sweet & Maxwell.

———. 2010. Opening Remarks – Evolution of Mixity Since the Leiden 1982 Conference. In *Mixed Agreements Revisited: The EU and its Member States in the World*, ed. Christophe Hillion and Panos Koutrakos, 1–8. Modern studies in European law, vol. 21. Oxford [England], Portland, OR: Hart.

Tridimas, Takis. 2006. *The General Principles of EC Law*. 2nd ed. Oxford: Oxord University Press.

Wolf, Erik, and Gustav Radbruch. 1963. *Rechtsphilosophie*. Stuttgart: Koehler.

# Chapter 6
# Summary and Conclusions

This work aimed to elaborate on the international responsibility of the European Union and its Member States arising from their joint membership in the WTO Agreement, and focused on the Union participation in the DSP for matters of non-conferred competences. The WTO membership is characterized of legal uncertainty, particularly resulting from the atypical political and constitutional nature of the Union polity, which creates confusion in terms of the representation in the DSP. Indeed, the lack of a competence clause or a declaration of powers linked to the conclusion of the WTO Agreement makes the EU and its Member States jointly responsible. This joint responsibility regime oversimplifies the structural problems in the Union polity in terms of the distribution of powers. This regime proves fallacious with respect to the devolution of responsibility resulting from the Union participation in the DSP for matters falling within the non-conferred areas of powers, or for measures for which the distribution of powers is unclear. The Union may be deemed jointly responsible for wrongful measures that are instituted from the Member States in the exercise of residual powers. The fallacy consists of the fact that the Union, by virtue of the principle of attributed powers, may not be able to oblige the concerned Member States to comply with the DSB rulings or recommendations and as a result, may become subject to cross-retaliatory measures, which are subsequently devolved to other Member States.

From a theoretical perspective, these concerns were analyzed in light of the problem of fragmentation of international law, by posing the issues of the fallacies in each of the involved legal orders. The responsibility for violation of the WTO Agreement is excluded, yet not isolated, from the majority of the *legi generali*, inasmuch as this Agreement regulates exclusively the issues of compliance with the WTO disciplines. In addition, the EU legal order has its own rules of compliance with international agreements, which are mandatory for the Union institutions and its Member States. The joint participation of the EU and its Member States in the WTO Agreement, which results from the vertical distribution of competences, interferes with the issues of compliance and responsibility in the context of WTO

 
P. Ruka, *The International Legal Responsibility of the European Union in the Context of the World Trade Organization in Areas of Non-Conferred Competences*,
DOI 10.1007/978-3-319-57177-5_6

membership. On the other side, this membership may affect the internal relations in the EU legal order, and may cause constitutional tensions in the federal dimension of the polity. In view of these concerns, in order to substantiate this theoretical discourse into a practical pursuit for a solution for precluding the fallacies of the joint responsibility regime, this work raised two main questions. Initially, by analyzing these fallacies according to *legi generali*, the law of the mixed agreements, and the EU legal order, it highlighted the relevant premises and conditions for the participation of the Union polity in the DSP. These premises, in turn, were employed for the construction of an adequate normative model that regulates the participation and representation of the Union in the DSP, and gives predictions for the management of the issues of responsibility of the Union for matters of blurred or non-conferred competences.

In order to develop a model that explains adequately the nature of the conflict, this work was built on a real case where different facets of the fallacious model of joint responsibility could be observed. A critical assessment of the facts of *EC – Asbestos* revealed the deficiencies of the passive legitimation of the Union in the DSP. In this case, the EU took the defense of a national measure, which, in light of the principle of intertemporal law, was not enacted in the context of EU legislation, but was instituted within the realm of the residual powers of France. Accordingly, the assumption of responsibility of France for the prohibition of import of asbestos from the Commission could not be justified on the basis of the normative framework of the WTO membership. Furthermore, the DSP was indifferent on the *ratione personae* of the Commission in these proceedings. Obviously, this issue would not be relevant in case that the participation of the Union in the DSP would be regulated, or from the constitutional nature of the Union's powers, it could be clearly drawn a causal link between the disputed measure and the attributes of the Union in the area. Rather, the blurred distribution of powers was defined as an argument for the joint participation of the Union and its Member States in the DSP. Absent a legal justification, this participation could be regarded as a pragmatic conduct of the Union, which is deemed unable to produce legitimate consequences for the part of the residual competences of the Member States.

The joint participation in the DSP is determined from the joint responsibility regime, which is the result of the WTO Agreement designated as a mixed agreement without a declaration of powers. The joint responsibility regime has a systemic character, which is determined from the constitutional nature of the WTO Agreement (as a mixed agreement) and the EU legal order. The vertical distribution of powers, characterized of dynamic changes in the scheme of competences, remains a decisive element for the joint responsibility model. The "combination of parallelism, preemption, and material expansion of powers"[1] constitutes the main reason for the formal-substantive gap of the WTO membership of the Union and its Member States. Allegedly, even the designation of the common commercial policy to include the areas of GATS and TRIPS within its exclusive nature, did not

[1]Weiler (1999), p. 175.

resolve this gap, inasmuch as the conferred powers of the Union could be inextricably linked with the residual powers of the Member States. Hence, the Union may be virtually competent for areas falling within the common commercial policy in the external dimension, but internally, the actual power could remain with the Member States.

The review of the *EC – Asbestos* case revealed the insufficiency of the rules of attribution to ensure the attribution of conduct to the wrongdoer, considering that the apportioning of obligations of the Union from the Member States was impossible in the conditions of blurred delimitation of powers. Accordingly, the attribution of responsibilities pursuant to this scheme would remain hostage of the complex distribution of powers in the Union polity. For this reason, the attribution of responsibility in the course of the DSP is attributed to the Union *ex relatione*, hence by virtue of the joint membership of the EU and its Member States in the WTO Agreement, and not by virtue of the rules of attribution. In view of these concerns, the *EC – Asbestos* revealed the necessity to construe a model for the participation and representation of the Union polity in the DSP, which takes into account the ownership of powers and the attribution of responsibility not on a solidarity basis, but rather on the authorship of the wrongful conduct.

As a matter of fact, *EC – Asbestos* was not a hard case. Having been concluded in favor of the French measure, this case did not evidence the constitutional tension between the claims of authority of the Union and its Member States. However, from a theoretical perspective, this case could serve as a relevant scenario for assessing the proposition of the normative model in practical terms. Building on the premises of *EC – Asbestos*, the normative model addressed the deficiencies of the Union participation in the DSP. The model put together the normative premises offered from the international law of responsibility, the law of the mixed agreements, and particularly the WTO law. Additionally, a constitutional framework of selected principles of the EU legal order was adopted as an instrument for criticizing the state of the law and practice of the joint responsibility regime. This consists of three categories of principles flowing from the rule of law, which concern the unity of the EU legal order, the political organization, and the political processes in the polity. It served also for substantiating the normative model of the Union participation in the DSP as an aggregate of processes and principles that determine the conditions for managing the fallacies of the joint responsibility regime. The normative model represents therefore a synthesis of premises from different legal orders, which are construed according to a pluralist approach. The model makes use of the EU legal order, which is conceived as a platform for accommodating tensions of claims from various legal orders in a pluralist manner. This platform solves the conflicts by prioritizing interests based on normative propositions, principles, and values. As such, this model sheds light into new perspectives on the legal scholarship, which cultivate the analysis beyond the traditional lines that pursue the solution of problems within isolated areas of law. In this way, the prospect and the acceptance of the model are more certain, and as such, could provide an adequate level of normativity and legitimacy.

The normative model itself is the result of the constitutionalization processes in the Union polity, and relies on the ability of the Union to adapt to various challenges of fragmentation. It establishes internal political-decisional processes that ensure the justification of answerability of the Commission in the DSP. In this way, the procedural position of the Union in the DSP for matters of non-conferred competences, as well as for matters where the ownership of powers is unclear, is capable to produce legitimate consequences in terms of the allocation of responsibility for the wrongful measures of the Member States. The political-decisional processes in the Union are able to integrate the constitutional principles of the polity, in order to ensure that the interests of all participants are observed. The cumulative deference to others' interests is particularly preferred in an international legal order, where the increasing fragmentation makes the dominance of collective interests jeopardize the individual interests of participants.

As to the choice of the legal form, the normative model can be enacted as a regulation of the Union institutions. The effort of identifying an adequate competence in this regard, inherits the same concerns that permeate the fallacious model of the joint responsibility regime. In order for the normative model to be able to tackle the issue of legitimacy in the course of the Union participation in the DSP for matters falling within the residual powers of Member States, the normative model should be able to deconstruct the thesis of false mixity inherent in the Union membership in the WTO, and terminate the state of dependency of the Union participation and representation in the DSP from the discretionary conduct of Member States, as a factor for increased uncertainty. After considering different alternatives, it was concluded that the virtual nature of the common commercial policy, designated as an exclusive competence of the Union, could compromise the pleading for legal certainty. Rather, it could prove more plausible to propose the adoption of a regulation dealing with the normative model pursuant to Article 352 TFEU. The flexibility clause could be regarded more appropriate in filling the lacunae of the Treaties in the operational domain of the normative model. Although this method could be loaded with procedural hurdles, such as the pursuance of prior approval from the Member States' legislators, it still proves more realistic than the amendment of the Treaties with the relevant instruments empowering the institutions for adopting the normative framework, which needs a particular constitutional momentum.

The main finding of the normative model is to engage the Union and the concerned Member States in internal processes for the formulation of a common position on the DSP, which determine the general guidelines of the representation therein. The common position is underlined by the idea of the unity of representation. This is further maintained in the mandate of representation in the DSP from the Union and/or the concerned Member State. If the parties succeed to formulate a common position, they should be able to construe the format of participation and representation in the DSP, which consists in the designation of the Commission as a solely or jointly participant and representative in the DSP. In addition to the *ordinary* representation, where the Commission alone represents the entire polity (mainly for conferred powers), the model provides for two variations of the *alternated* representation, where the roles of the principal and subsidiary representatives may be alternated between the Union and the concerned Member State. This format concerns disputes falling within the areas of non-conferred powers, or blurred areas of powers. It can produce various configurations that switch the default scheme to an alternated one. Depending on the situation, the default configuration is determined from the ownership of competences (for which the *alternated (competence)* model applies), or from the authorship of the wrongful conduct (which triggers the *alternated (authorship)* format). The alternated format represents the choice of the decision-making body for ensuring an adequate representation in the DSP for the entire polity.

These configurations are relevant also for ensuring the compliance of the Union polity with the DSB rulings or recommendations, as well as for allocating and enforcing the burden of responsibility (mainly the cessation of wrongful act). The prospect of the model in terms of the victims' compensation does not differ much from the current practice. However, with this respect, it can be maintained that the model is more likely to preclude the cross-retaliatory measures. Furthermore, the model could provide a more inclusive approach of interpretation for the judicial-normative processes, which takes into account, in addition to the normative arguments, also arguments of a cognitive nature, such as the economics of retaliation, etc.

The political-decisional processes proposed in the model are capable of accommodating conflicting interests of the participants, given that the model is largely based on the constitutional principles of the Union polity as a *pactum fidelis*. Accordingly, the main decisions in relation with the participation and representation of the polity in the DSP are taken from the Member States and the Union in deference to their reciprocal interests. This precludes the disavowal of interests of the individual states to the benefit of the collective action, which would lead to the unilateral harmonization of residual powers. Instead, the normative model predicts that the decision-making body, either the Council, or the Article 207 Committee, may take the decision to centralize the representation in the Union level only to the extent that the entire polity would become better off. The optimal level of decision-making takes account of the analogy with the principles of subsidiarity and proportionality, which allow an adequate decision-making process. The Member States have their duty of care in terms of precluding excessive levels of responsibility from the joint membership regime.

In order to ensure efficient decision-making in the course of the political-decisional processes, the model proposes the default procedure of consensus for taking decisions. In case that this would fail, the qualified majority voting follows. In the presence of a blocking minority, the failure to take decisions could lead to the parallel representation of the Union and the Member States. This would hinder the effectiveness and unity of the EU legal order. Therefore, in order to prevent this fallacy of the joint responsibility regime, the normative model ensures the obligation of the parties to cooperate. The normative model provides for conciliation committees for resolving the impasses in decision-making, and the duty of loyalty can manifest its normative power therein. However, in case that such conciliation fails, the judicial-normative processes remain a guarantee for the effectiveness of the model. The structural value of the normative model consists in establishing processes that could trigger judicial review proceedings in a timely manner. Hence, the Union and the Member States may end up before the ECJ for resolving their claims in due time, without jeopardizing the unity of representation in the DSP.

The model could choose between the *formalized* or *flexible* approaches of approval of the formats of participation and representation. The former would require a high level of predictability, and would turn the model into a guide for the DSP. The latter represents a more advantageous approach, in that it allows for the adaptability to the new challenges brought from the dynamic nature of Union powers. For both these approaches, it is important that the participation of the Union and the concerned Member State in the DSP does not result in a fallacious attribution of joint responsibility. The proceduralization of the participation in the DSP should make use of the advantages of the collective action, without hindering the residual powers of the Member States. In this way, the nature of powers in the Union polity is precluded from leading to sterile debates that shade off the power of the Union to observe the common interests, which would ensure that the Member States derive all the benefits from the Union as a unified actor in international trade.[2]

As to its practicability, it can be suggested that the model, as a theoretical paradigm, should be able to preclude the fallacies of the joint responsibility regime by construing adequate configurations of participation in the DSP, and by promising for timely management of the consequences of responsibility. The premises of *EC – Asbestos* could evidence this. By definition, the sole participation of the Union in the DSP of the *EC – Asbestos* would have designated the Union responsible for the French measure, in case that it would have been found in violation of WTO law. This would have been a case for vicarious liability of the Union, inasmuch as no principal-agent relationship was established beforehand. Hence, the responsibility of France would be shifted to the Union. This remains however a theoretical possibility, given that France would be considered jointly responsible for triggering the WTO responsibility of the Union. The normative model would have precluded this situation. Accordingly, although the proceedings were instituted against the Union alone, the decision-making body, by taking account of the ownership of powers criterion, would come to the conclusion that the disputed measure falls in the domain of residual powers of France. Hence, the default configuration would be to consider France as the principal representative, and the Union as the subsidiary one. The same conclusion would result even if construing the default configuration pursuant to the authorship criterion. Very likely, the decision-making body would alternate these positions, and would designate the Commission as a principal representative, whereas France would be mandatorily a jointly participant with subsidiary status, or a principal co-representative.

[2]See also Timmermans (2000), p. 247.

In case that the DSB would require the withdrawal of the French Decree, the Union would engage its internal political-decisional processes for transposing the obligation to France, which, pursuant to the default configuration, remains the competent authority to act. This is due to the fact that the normative model does not alter the nature of powers, but provides for temporary configurations (altered ones) for the representation in the DSP. In case that France would refuse to comply, the Union might engage the judicial-normative processes for obliging France to comply with the WTO obligations of the Union, pursuant to Article 216(2) TFEU. The right of recourse of the Union toward France would make possible the reallocation of obligations to France, which should be obliged by virtue of its joint responsibility and the relevant propositions of the normative model, to discharge its formal obligations against Canada. France would be obliged to take appropriate measures for compliance, as a positive and a negative duty of loyalty. The compliance with an act of the Union transposing its virtual obligation into a real obligation for France is construed as an obligation for the latter to ensure the effectiveness of the EU norm. Hence, it can be maintained that the normative model is capable to preclude the fallacies of the joint responsibility regime.

The normative model addresses the structural deficiencies created from the distribution of powers in relation with the DSP participation, by constitutionalizing the political-decisional processes at the Union level. These processes ensure the accommodation of contradicting claims of authority by producing decisions that are the aggregate of interests of all parties considered in a cumulative way. This is a prime expression of the principle of constitutional tolerance, which permeates the infrastructure of the EU legal order. Obviously, the principle of loyalty plays a crucial role in the conduct of these processes and in the implementation of their outcomes. Notwithstanding the doubts relating to its normative value, the principle of loyalty remains the flagship of the constitutional framework regulating the normative model. With its predictions on the voluntary obedience toward the Union's claim of authority, and the cumulative consideration of interests of other participants, the principle of loyalty, as an evidence of the *pactum fidelis* in the Union, substantiates the normative model with effective instruments, which are crucial for the political-decisional processes. With its predictions on the positive and negative obligations, and the self-restricting conduct of participants in deference to others' interests, the principle of loyalty could generate plausible solutions to open questions. As such, it could ensure a sound management of the consequences of the Union participation in the DSP for matters of non-conferred powers, by preserving the ownership of residual powers of the Member States. Although not justiciable in the course of judicial-normative processes, the principle of loyalty offers a firm support for the implementation of the normative model.

This book aimed to argue that the joint responsibility as it stands today is fallacious, in that it circumvents the rules of attribution. Arguably, this could be considered a defective regime of responsibility, which weakens the normative value of international law, inasmuch as it circumvents the deterrent effects of the international law of responsibility. Based on these considerations, the normative model enhances the premises for enforcing the responsibility of the wrongdoer in the

Union polity. It provides the necessary normative framework that allows the Commission to initiate infringement proceedings against the wrongdoer, in order to ensure the compliance with the DSB rulings and recommendations. This legitimates the Commission to act also in areas of non-conferred powers without changing the structure of powers. In this way, by enhancing, from a normative perspective, the guarantees that the international obligations will be observed, the normative model serves to the principles of *bona fide* and *pacta sunt servanda*, which at the same time are prerogatives for respecting the claims of sovereignty of all participants. Hence, the normative model, by formalizing the mediating strategy for all the participants in the polity, ensures the balance between the conflicting collective and individual interests, which are considered in a cumulative manner, and creates the necessary normative framework for enforcing the regime of international responsibility. In this way, the model of participation of the Union and its Member States in the DSP is construed in the spirit of the legal maxim *ubi responsibilitas, ubi ius*, inasmuch as it enhances the regime of responsibility as a premise for justice and unity in the Union polity.

## References

Timmermans, Christiaan. 2000. Organising Joint Participation of E.C. and Member States. In *The General Law of E.C. External Relations*, ed. Alan Dashwood and Christophe Hillion, 239–247. London: Sweet & Maxwell.

Weiler, Joseph H.H. 1999. *The Constitution of Europe: "Do the New Clothes Have an Emperor?" and Other Essays on European Integration*. Cambridge: Cambridge University Press.

# Bibliography

Accetto, Matej, and Stefan Zleptnig. 2005. The Principle of Effectiveness: Rethinking its Role in Community Law. *European Public Law* 11 (3): 375–403.

Amtenbrink, Fabian. 2012. The European Court of Justice's Approach to Primacy and European Constitutionalism – Preserving the European Constitutional Order? In *The European Court of Justice and the Autonomy of the Member States*, ed. Hans-W Micklitz and Bruno de Witte. Cambridge, Antwerp, Portland: Intersentia.

Antoniadis, Antonis. 2004. The Participation of the European Community in the World Trade Organization: An External Look at European Union Constitution-Building. In *European Union Law for the Twenty-First Century: Rethinking the New Legal Order. Vol. 1: Constitutional and Public Law: External Relations*, ed. Takis Tridimas and Paolisa Nebbia, 321–344. Oxford: Hart.

Anzilotti, Dionisio. 1906. La Responsabilité Internationale des Etats à Raison des Dommages Soufferts par des Étrangers. *RGDIP* 10: 5–29.

———. 1999. *Cours de Droit International*. Les introuvables. Paris: LGDJ; Université Panthéon-Assas.

Arnull, Anthony, and Derrick Wyatt. 2006. *Wyatt and Dashwood's European Union Law*. 5th ed. London: Sweet & Maxwell.

Barbier, Sandrine. 2010. Assurances and Guarantees of Non-Repetition. In *The Law of International Responsibility*, ed. James Crawford, Alain Pellet, Simon Olleson, and Kate Parlett, 552–561. Oxford, New York: Oxford University Press.

Bariffi, Francisco J. 2012. Scilingo Case. In *The Max Planck Encyclopedia of Public International Law*, ed. Rüdiger Wolfrum, VII. New York, NY: Oxford University Press.

Barker, John. 2010. The Different Forms of Reparation: Compensation. In *The Law of International Responsibility*, ed. James Crawford, Alain Pellet, Simon Olleson, and Kate Parlett, 599–611. Oxford, New York: Oxford University Press.

Barnet, Hilaire. 2006. *Constitutional & Administrative Law*. UK, US, Canada: Routledge-Cavendish.

Bauböck, Rainer. 2002. Political Community beyond the Sovereign State, Supranational Nationalism and Transnational Minorities. In *Conceiving Cosmopolitanism: Theory, Context and Practice*, ed. Steven Vertovec and Robin Cohen. New York: Oxford University Press.

Bogdandy, Armin von. 2005. Legal Effects of World Trade Organization Decision within European Union Law: A Contribution to the Theory of the Legal Acts of Damages Under Article 288(2) EC. *Journal of World Trade* 39: 45.



P. Ruka, *The International Legal Responsibility of the European Union in the Context of the World Trade Organization in Areas of Non-Conferred Competences*, DOI 10.1007/978-3-319-57177-5

———. 2010. Founding Principles. In *Principles of European Constitutional Law*, ed. Armin von Bogdandy and Jürgen Bast, 2nd ed., 11–54. Oxford, Portland, OR; München, Germany: Hart; CH Beck.

Bogdandy, Armin von, and Jürgen Bast. 2010. The Federal Order of Competences. In *Principles of European Constitutional Law*, ed. Armin von Bogdandy and Jürgen Bast, 2nd ed., 275–307. Oxford, Portland, OR; München, Germany: Hart; CH Beck.

Bogdandy, Armin von, and Michael Ioannidis. 2014. Systemic Deficiency in the Rule of Law. What It Is, What Has Been Done, What Could Be Done. *Common Market Law Review* 51: 1–38.

Bourgeois, Jacques H.J. 1995. The Uruguay Round Results from a European Lawyers' Perspective: An Introduction. In *The Uruguay Round Results: A European Lawyers' Perspective*, ed. Jacques H.J. Bourgeois, Frédérique Berrod and Eric Gippini Fournier. Bruges conferences, vol. 8. Brussels: European Interuniversity Press.

———. 1997. Mixed Agreements: A New Aproach? In *La Communauté Européenne et les Accords Mixtes: Quelles Perspectives?*, ed. Jacques H.J. Bourgeois, Jean-Louis Dewost and Marie-Ange Gaiffe, 83–91. Conférences de Bruges, vol. 11. Bruxelles: Presses interuniversitaires européennes.

Bourgeois, Jacques H.J., and Orla Lynskey. 2008. The Extent to which the EC Legislature Takes Account of WTO Obligations: Jousting Lessons from European Parliament. In *Law and Practice of EU External Relations: Salient Features of a Changing Landscape*, ed. Alan Dashwood and Marc Maresceau, 202–223. Cambridge: Cambridge University Press.

Boyle, Alan. 2010. Liability for Injurious Consequences of Act not Prohibited by International Law. In *The Law of International Responsibility*, ed. James Crawford, Alain Pellet, Simon Olleson, and Kate Parlett, 95–104. Oxford, New York: Oxford University Press.

Brownlie, Ian. 1998. Principles of Public International Law, 5th edn. Oxford; New York: Clarendon Press; Oxford University Press.

Burton, William C. 1998. *Burton's Legal Thesaurus*. 3rd ed. New York: Macmillan Library Reference.

Chalmers, Damian, G.T. Davies, and Giorgio Monti. 2010. *European Union Law. Cases and Materials*. 2nd ed. Cambridge: Cambridge University Press.

Commission of the European Communities. 1996. General Report on the Activities of the European Union 1995: European Commission.

Condorelli, Luigi, and Claus Kress. 2010. The Rule of Attribution: General Considerations. In *The Law of International Responsibility*, ed. James Crawford, Alain Pellet, Simon Olleson, and Kate Parlett, 221–236. Oxford, New York: Oxford University Press.

Corten, Olivier. 2010. The Obligation of Cessation. In *The Law of International Responsibility*, ed. James Crawford, Alain Pellet, Simon Olleson, and Kate Parlett, 545–549. Oxford, New York: Oxford University Press.

Crawford, James. 1999. Second Report on State Responsiblity. DOCUMENT A/CN.4/498 and Add.1-4, date 17 March, 1 and 30 April, 19 July 1999.

———. 2008. *Brownlie's Principles of Public International Law*. 8th ed. Oxford: Oxford University Press.

———. 2010. The System of International Responsibility. In *The Law of International Responsibility*, ed. James Crawford, Alain Pellet, Simon Olleson, and Kate Parlett, 17–25. Oxford, New York: Oxford University Press.

Crawford, James, and Jeremy Watkins. 2010. International Responsibility. In *The Philosophy of International Law*, ed. Samantha Besson and John Tasioulas, 283–298. Oxford, New York: Oxford University Press.

Cremona, Marise. 1982. The Doctrine of Exclusivity and the Position of Mixed Agreements in the External Relations of the European Community. *Oxford Journal of Legal Studies* 2: 393–428.

———. 2001. A Policy of Bits and Pieces – The Common Commercial Policy after Nice. *Cambridge Yearbook of European Legal Studies* 4: 61.

———. 2008a. Defending the Community Interest: the Duties of Cooperation and Compliance. In *EU Foreign Relations Law: Constitutional Fundamentals*, ed. Marise Cremona and Bruno de Witte. Oxford, Portland, OR: Hart.

———. 2008b. Defining Competence in EU External Relations: Lessons from the Treaty Reform Process. In *Law and Practice of EU External Relations: Salient Features of a Changing Landscape*, ed. Alan Dashwood and Marc Maresceau, 34–69. Cambridge: Cambridge University Press.

———. 2012. Member States Agreements as Union Law. In *International Law as Law of the European Union*, ed. Enzo Cannizzaro, Paolo Palchetti and Ramses A. Wessel, 288–324. Studies in EU external relations, vol. 5. Boston: Martinus Nijhoff.

Dani, Marco. 2010. Remedying European Legal Pluralism: The FIAMM and Fedon Litigation and the Judicial Protection of International Trade Bystanders. *European Journal of International Law* 21 (2): 303–340. doi:10.1093/ejil/chq026.

Dashwood, Alan. 1997. Why Continue to Have Mixed Agreements at All? In *La Communauté Européenne et les Accords Mixtes: Quelles Perspectives?*, ed. Jacques H.J. Bourgeois, Jean-Louis Dewost and Marie-Ange Gaiffe, 93–98. Conférences de Bruges, vol. 11. Bruxelles: Presses interuniversitaires européennes.

———. 2011. *Wyatt and Dashwood's European Union Law*. 6th ed. Oxford, Portland, OR: Hart.

Dicey, Albert Venn. 1885. *Lectures Introductory to the Study of the Law of the Constitution*. London: Macmillan.

Dickson, Julie, and John Gardner. 2001. *Evaluation and Legal Theory. Legal Theory Today*. Hart: The Hague.

Dolmans, Maurits J.F.M. 1985. *Problems of Mixed Agreements. Division of Powers Within the EEC and the Rights of Third States*. Asser Instituut: The Hague.

Dominicé, Christian. 2010. Attribution of Conduct to Multiple States and the Implication of a State in the Act of Another State. In *The Law of International Responsibility*, ed. James Crawford, Alain Pellet, Simon Olleson, and Kate Parlett, 281–289. Oxford, New York: Oxford University Press.

Dougan, Michael. 2007. When Worlds Collide! Competing Visions of the Relationship Between Direct Effect and Supremacy. *Common Market Law Review* 44 (4): 931–963.

Dowrick, F.E. 1983. A Model of the European Communities' Legal System. *Yearbook of European Law* 3 (1): 169–237. doi:10.1093/yel/3.1.169.

Dupuy, Pierre-Marie. 1989. The International Law of States Responsibility: Revolution or Evolution. *Michigan Journal of International Law* 11: 105.

———. 1999. Reviewing the Difficulties of Codification: on Ago's Classification of Obligations of Means and Obligations of Result in Relation to State Responsibility. *European Journal of International Law* 10 (2): 371–385. doi:10.1093/ejil/10.2.371.

———. 2010. Relations Between the International Law and Responsibility in Municipal Law. In *The Law of International Responsibility*, ed. James Crawford, Alain Pellet, Simon Olleson and Kate Parlett. Oxford, New York: Oxford University Press.

Eagleton, Clyde. 1928. *The Responsibility of States in International Law*. New York: New York University Press.

Edward, David A.O., and Robert C. Lane. 2012. *Edward and Lane on European Union Law*. Cheltenham: Edward Elgar.

Eeckhout, Piet. 1997. The Domestic Legal Status of the WTO Agreement: Interconnecting Legal Systems. *Common Market Law Review* 34: 11.

———. 2006. The EU and its Member States in the WTO – Issues of Responsibility. In *Regional Trade Agreements and the WTO Legal System*, ed. Lorand Bartels and Federico Ortino, 449–464. International economic law series. Oxford: Oxford University Press.

———. 2011. *EU External Relations Law*, 2nd ed. Oxford EU law library. Oxford, New York: Oxford University Press.

Ehlermann, C.-D. 1983. Mixed Agreements: A List of Problems. In *Mixed Agreements*, ed. David O'Keeffe and Henry G. Schermers, 3–21. Deventer, Boston: Kluwer Law and Taxation Publishers.

Frid, Rachel. 1995. *The Relations Between the EC and International Organizations. Legal Theory and Practice*. The Hague: Kluwer Law International.

Gamper, Anna. 2010. On Loyalty and the (Federal) Constitution. *Vienna Online Journal on International Constitutional Law* 4: 157.

Garner, Bryan A., and Henry Campbell Black. 1999. *Black's Law Dictionary*. 7th ed. St. Paul, Minn: West Group.

———. 2010. *Black's Law Dictionary*. 9th ed. St. Paul, MN: West.

Geiger, Rudolf, Daniel-Erasmus Khan, and Markus Kotzur. 2015. *European Union Treaties. Treaty on European Union, Treaty on the Functioning of the European Union*. München, Oxford: Beck; Hart.

Gomula, Joanna. 2010. Responsibility and the World Trade Organization. In *The Law of International Responsibility*, ed. James Crawford, Alain Pellet, Simon Olleson, and Kate Parlett, 791–801. Oxford, New York: Oxford University Press.

Graig, Paul. 2012. Competence and Member State Autonomy: Causality, Consequence and Legitimacy. In *The European Court of Justice and the Autonomy of the Member States*, ed. Hans-W Micklitz and Bruno de Witte. Cambridge, Antwerp, Portland: Intersentia.

Graig, Paul, and Gráinne de Búrca. 2011. *EU Law. Text, Cases, and Materials*. 5th ed. Oxford: Oxford University Press.

Gray, Christine D. 2010. The Different Forms of Reparation: Restitution. In *The Law of International Responsibility*, ed. James Crawford, Alain Pellet, Simon Olleson, and Kate Parlett, 589–597. Oxford, New York: Oxford University Press.

Grotius, Hugo, Jean Barbeyrac, and Richard Tuck. 2005. *The Rights of War and Peace. Natural Law and Enlightenment Classics*. Indianapolis: Liberty Fund.

Groux, Jean, and Philippe Manin. 1985. *The European Communities in the International Order*. The European perspectives series. Brussels, Washington, D.C: Commission of the European Communities; European Community Information Service [distributor].

Hart, H.L.A. 1968. *Punishment and Responsibility. Essays in the Philosophy of Law*. Oxford: Clarendon Press.

Heliskoski, Joni. 1996. The Duty of Cooperation' Between the European Community and its Member States within the World Trade Organization. *Finnish Yearbook of International Law* 7: 59.

———. 2001. *Mixed Agreements as a Technique for Organizing the International Relations of the European Community and its Member States*. The Hague, New York: Kluwer Law International.

Hilf, Meinhard. 1995. The ECJ's Opinion 1/94 on the WTO: – No Surprise, but Wise? *European Journal of International Law* 6 (1): 245–259. doi:10.1093/ejil/6.1.245.

Hillion, Christophe, and Panos Koutrakos, ed. 2010. *Mixed Agreements Revisited. The EU and its Member States in the World*. Modern studies in European law, vol. 21. Oxford [England], Portland, OR: Hart.

Hirsch, Moshe. 1995. *The Responsibility of International Organizations Toward Third Parties. Some Basic Principles*. Dordrecht, Boston: Martinus Nijhoff.

Horn, Henrik, and Joseph H.H. Weiler. 2003. EC-Asbestos: European Communities – Measures Affecting Asbestos and Asbestos-Containing Products. In *The WTO case law of 2001*, ed. Henrik Horn and Petros C. Mavroidis. American Law Institute reporters' studies. Cambridge, New York: Cambridge University Press.

———. 2004. EC-Asbestos: European Communities – Measures Affecting Asbestos and Asbestos-Containing Products. *World Trade Review* 3 (1): 129–151.

Howse, Robert, and Kalypso Nicolaidis. 2001. Introduction: The Federal Vision, Levels of Governance, and Legitimacy. In *The Federal Vision: Legitimacy and Levels of Governance in the United States and the European Union*, ed. Kalypso Nicolaidis and Robert Howse, 1–27. Oxford [etc.]: University Press.

Hyett, Stephen. 2000. The Duty of Cooperation: A Flexible Concept. In *The General Law of E.C. External Relations*, ed. Alan Dashwood and Christophe Hillion, 248–253. London: Sweet & Maxwell.

Jacobs, Francis G. 2008. Direct Effect and Interpretation of International Agreements in the Recent Case Law of the European Court of Justice. In *Law and Practice of EU External Relations: Salient Features of a Changing Landscape*, ed. Alan Dashwood and Marc Maresceau, 13–33. Cambridge: Cambridge University Press.

Jouannet, Emmanuelle. 1998. *Emer de Vattel et l'émergence doctrinale du droit international classique*. Publication de la Revue générale du droit international public, vol. 50. Paris: Pedone.

Kaczorowska, Alina. 2013. *European Union Law*. Abingdon, Oxon, London: Routledge.

Kapteyn, P.J.G. 1993. De Coraplexe Rechtsorde van het Unieverdrag: Subsidiariteitsbeginsel en Nieuwe Bevoegdheden. In *Europa in de Steigers: van Gemeenschap tot Unie*, ed. K. Hellingman and P. van Dijk, 41–52. Europese monografieën, vol. 40. Deventer: Kluwer.

Kapteyn, P.J.G., A.M. McDonnell, K.J.M. Mortelmans, C.W.A. Timmermans, and L.A. Geelhoed, ed. 2008. *The Law of the European Union and the European Communities. With Reference to Changes to be Made by the Lisbon Treaty*, 4th ed. Alphen Aan Den Rijn, Frederick, MD: Kluwer Law International; Sold and distributed in North, Central and South America by Aspen Pub.

Kelsen, Hans, and Robert W. Tucker. 1966. *Principles of International Law*. 2nd ed. New York: Holt Rinehart and Winston, Inc..

Kerbrat, Yann. 2010. Interaction Between the Forms of Reparation. In *The Law of International Responsibility*, ed. James Crawford, Alain Pellet, Simon Olleson, and Kate Parlett, 573–587. Oxford, New York: Oxford University Press.

Klein, Pierre. 2010. The Attribution of Acts to International Organizations. In *The Law of International Responsibility*, ed. James Crawford, Alain Pellet, Simon Olleson, and Kate Parlett, 297–315. Oxford, New York: Oxford University Press.

Kolb, Robert. 2000. *La Bonne Foi en Droit International Public. Contribution à l'Étude des Principes Généraux de Droit*, 1st ed. Publications de l'Institut universitaire de hautes études internationales, Genève. Paris: Presses universitaires de France.

Koskenniemi, Martti. 2010. Doctrines of State Responsibility. In *The Law of International Responsibility*, ed. James Crawford, Alain Pellet, Simon Olleson, and Kate Parlett, 45–51. Oxford, New York: Oxford University Press.

Kotzur, Markus. 2012. Good Faith (Bona Fide). In *The Max Planck Encyclopedia of Public International Law*, ed. Rüdiger Wolfrum, VII. New York, NY: Oxford University Press.

Koutrakos, Panos. 2006. *EU International Relations Law*. Modern studies in European law, vol. 9. Oxford, Portland, OR: Hart.

Kuijper, Pieter. 1995a. The Conclusion and Implementation of the Uruguay Round Results by the European Community. *EJIL* 6: 222–244.

Kuijper, Pieter Jan. 2010. International Responsibility for EU Mixed Agreements. In *Mixed Agreements Revisited: The EU and its Member States in the World*, ed. Christophe Hillion and Panos Koutrakos, 208–227. Modern studies in European law, vol. 21. Oxford [England], Portland, OR: Hart.

Kuijper, Pieter Jan, and Marco Bronckers. 2005. WTO Law in the European Court of Justice. *Common Market Law Review* 42: 1313–1355.

Kuijper, Pieter-Jan. 1995b. The New WTO Dispute Settlement System: The Impact on the Community. In *The Uruguay Round Results: A European Lawyers' Perspective*, ed. Jacques H.J. Bourgeois, Frédérique Berrod and Eric Gippini Fournier, 87–114. Bruges conferences, vol. 8. Brussels: European Interuniversity Press.

Latty, Franck. 2010. Actions and Omissions. In *The Law of International Responsibility*, ed. James Crawford, Alain Pellet, Simon Olleson, and Kate Parlett, 355–363. Oxford, New York: Oxford University Press.

Lauwaars, R.H. 2008. Institutional Structure. In *The Law of the European Union and the European Communities: With Reference to Changes to be Made by the Lisbon Treaty*, ed. P.J.G. Kapteyn, A.M. McDonnell, K.J.M. Mortelmans, C.W.A. Timmermans and L.A. Geelhoed, 4th ed., 175–272. Alphen Aan Den Rijn, Frederick, MD: Kluwer Law International; Sold and distributed in North, Central and South America by Aspen Pub.

Leiter, Brian. 2011. The Demarcation Problem in Jurisprudence: A New Case for Scepticism. *Oxford Journal of Legal Studies* 31 (4): 663–677.

Lovin, Robin W. 2007. Religion and Political Pluralism. *Mississippi College Law Review* 27: 97.

Luhmann, Niklas. 1981. *Ausdifferenzierung des Rechts. Beiträge zur Rechtssoziologie und Rechtstheorie*. 1st ed. Suhrkamp: Frankfurt am Main.

MacLeod, I., I.D. Hendry, and Stephen Hyett. 1996. *The External Relations of the European Communities. A Manual of Law and Practice*. Oxford; New York: Clarendon Press; Oxford University Press.

Maduro, Miguel Poiares. 2009. Courts and Pluralism: Essay on a Theory of Judicial Adjudication in the Context of Legal and Constitutional Pluralism. In Ruling the World?: Constitutionalism, International Law, and Global Governance, ed. Jeffrey L. Dunoff, 365–379. Cambridge [u.a.]: Cambridge University Press.

Martin, E.A. 2002. *A Dictionary of Law*, 5th ed. Oxford [England], New York: Oxford University Press.

Montgomery, John Warwick. 2002. Subsidiarity as a Jurisprudential and Canonical Theory. *Law & Justice The Christian Law Review* 148: 46.

Mortelmans, Kamiel. 1998. The Principle of Loyalty to the Community (Article 5 EC) and the Obligations of the Community Institutions. *Maastricht Journal of European and Comparative Law* 5: 67.

Neframi, Eleftheria. 2002. International Responsibility of the European Community and of the Member States under Mixed Agreements. In *The European Union as an Actor in International Relations*, ed. Enzo Cannizzaro, 193–205. The Hague, New York: Kluwer Law International.

———. 2010. The Duty of Loyalty: Rethinking its Scope Through Its Application in the Field of EU External Relations. *Common Market Law Review* 47 (2): 323–359.

———. 2012. Mixed Agreements as a Source of European Union Law. In *International Law as Law of the European Union*, ed. Enzo Cannizzaro, Paolo Palchetti and Ramses A. Wessel, 325–349. Studies in EU external relations, vol. 5. Boston: Martinus Nijhoff.

Noyes, John E., and Brian D. Smith. 1988. State Responsibility and the Principle of Joint and Several Liability. *Yale Journal of International Law* 13: 225.

O'Connell, D.P. 1963. State Succession and the Effect Upon Treaties of Entry Into a Composite Relationship. *British Year Book of International Law* 39: 54.

Orakhelashvili, Alexander. 2010. Division of Reparation Between Responsible Entities. In *The Law of International Responsibility*, ed. James Crawford, Alain Pellet, Simon Olleson, and Kate Parlett, 647–665. Oxford, New York: Oxford University Press.

Pellet, Alain. 2010. The Definition of Responsibility in International Law. In *The Law of International Responsibility*, ed. James Crawford, Alain Pellet, Simon Olleson, and Kate Parlett, 3–16. Oxford, New York: Oxford University Press.

Pescatore, Pierre. 1979. External Relations in the Case-Law of the Court of Justice of the European Communities. *Common Market Law Review* 16: 615.

Peters, Anne. 2006. The Constitutionalisation of the European Union — Without the Constitutional Treaty. In *The Making of a European Constitution: Dynamics and Limits of the Convention Experience*, ed. Sonja Puntscher Riekmann and Wolfgang Wessels, 1st ed., 35–67. Wiesbaden: VS Verlag für Sozialwissenschaften.

Petersmann, Ernst-Ulrich. 1986. The EEC as a GATT Member – Legal Conflicts Between GATT Law and European Community Law. In *The European Community and GATT*, ed. Meinhard

Hilf, Francis Geoffrey Jacobs and Ernst-Ulrich Petersmann, 23–72. Studies in transnational economic law, vol. 4. Deventer, The Netherlands, Boston: Kluwer.
Quigley, John. 1987. Complicity in International Law: A New Direction in the Law of State Responsibility. *British Yearbook of International Law* 57 (1): 77–131. doi:10.1093/bybil/57.1.77.
Radbruch, Gustav, and Emil Lask. 1950. *The Legal Philosophies of Lask, Radbruch, and Dabin*. Cambridge: Harvard University Press.
Rau, Markus. 2003. Subsidiarity and Judicial Review in German Federalism: The Decision of the Federal Constitutional Court in the Geriatric Nursing Act Case. *German Law Journal* 04 (03): 223–236.
Rossi, Lucia Serena. 2012. Does the Lisbon Treaty Provide a Clearer Separation of Competences Between EU and Member States? In *EU Law After Lisbon*, ed. Andrea Biondi, Piet Eeckhout and Stefanie Ripley, 85–106. Oxford [England], New York: Oxford University Press.
Sack, Jörn. 1995. The European Community's Membership of International Organizations. *Common Market Law Review* 32 (5): 1227–1256.
Salles, Luiz Eduardo. 2014. *Forum Shopping in International Adjudication: The Role of Preliminary Objections*. Cambridge: Cambridge University Press.
Schermers, Henry G. 1983. International Organizations as Members of Other International Organizations. In *Völkerrecht als Rechtsordnung, Internationale Gerichtsbarkeit, Menschenrechte: Festschrift für Hermann Mosler*, ed. Hermann Mosler and Rudolf Bernhardt, 823–838. Beiträge zum ausländischen öffentlichen Recht und Völkerrecht, vol. 81. Berlin, New York: Springer.
———. 1989. The Suit for Damages as a Means of Pressure on the Member States of the European Community. In *Staat und Völkerrechtsordnung: Festschrift für Karl Doehring*, ed. Karl Doehring, Kay Hailbronner, Georg Ress and Torsten Stein, 883–888. Beiträge zum ausländischen öffentlichen Recht und Völkerrecht, vol. 98. Berlin, New York: Springer-Verlag.
Schermers, Henry G., and Niels Blokker. 2003. *International Institutional Law. Unity Within Diversity*. 4th ed. Boston: Martinus Nijhoff.
Schmidt, Vivien A. 2013. Democracy and Legitimacy in the European Union Revisited: Input, Output and 'Throughput'. *Political Studies* 61 (1): 2–22. doi:10.1111/j.1467-9248.2012.00962.x.
Schütze, Robert. 2012. *European Constitutional Law*. Cambridge, UK, New York: Cambridge University Press.
Simma, Bruno, and Dirk Pulkowski. 2010. *Leges Speciales* and Self-Contained Regimes. In *The Law of International Responsibility*, ed. James Crawford, Alain Pellet, Simon Olleson, and Kate Parlett, 139–163. Oxford, New York: Oxford University Press.
Simmonds, Kenneth R. 1989. The European Economic Community and the New Law of the Sea. In *Recueil des cours: Collected Courses of the Hague Academy of International Law*, vol. VI, 9–166. Collection, Tome 218. Dordrecht: Martinus Nijhoff.
Stern, Brigitte. 2010a. The Elements of an Internationally Wrongful Act. In *The Law of International Responsibility*, ed. James Crawford, Alain Pellet, Simon Olleson, and Kate Parlett, 193–220. Oxford, New York: Oxford University Press.
———. 2010b. The Obligation to Make Reparation. In *The Law of International Responsibility*, ed. James Crawford, Alain Pellet, Simon Olleson, and Kate Parlett, 563–571. Oxford, New York: Oxford University Press.
Stoll, Peter-Tobias. 2012. World Trade Organization (WTO). In *The Max Planck Encyclopedia of Public International Law*, ed. Rüdiger Wolfrum, VII. New York, NY: Oxford University Press.
Tancredi, Antonello. 2012. On the Absence of Direct Effect of the WTO Dispute Settlement Body's Decisions in the EU Legal Order. In *International Law as Law of the European Union*, ed. Enzo Cannizzaro, Paolo Palchetti and Ramses A. Wessel, 249–268. Studies in EU external relations, vol. 5. Boston: Martinus Nijhoff.
Tavernier, Paul. 2010. Relevance of Intertemporal Law. In *The Law of International Responsibility*, ed. James Crawford, Alain Pellet, Simon Olleson, and Kate Parlett, 397–403. Oxford, New York: Oxford University Press.

Thies, Anne. 2006. Cases T-69/00, *FIAMM and FIAMM Technologies*, T-151/00, *Le Laboratoire du Bain*, T-301/00, *Fremaux*, T-320/00, *CD Cartondruck*, AG, T-383/00, *Beamglow Ltd* and T-135/01 *Giorgio Fedon &(and) Figli S.p.A., Fedon S.r.l. and Fedon America USA Inc.*, Judgments of 14 December 2005, Grand Chamber of the Court of First Insurance. *Common Market Law Review* 43 (2): 1145–1168.

———. 2013. *International Trade Disputes and EU Liability*, Cambridge studies in European law and policy. New York: Cambridge University Press.

Thouvenin, Jean-Marc. 2010. Responsibility in the Context of the European Legal Order. In *The Law of International Responsibility*, ed. James Crawford, Alain Pellet, Simon Olleson and Kate Parlett, 861–875. Oxford, New York: Oxford University Press.

Thym, Daniel. 2010. Foreign Affairs. In *Principles of European Constitutional Law*, ed. Armin von Bogdandy and Jürgen Bast, 2nd ed., 309–343. Oxford, Portland, OR; München, Germany: Hart; CH Beck.

Timmermans, C.W.A. 1981. Division of External Powers between Community and Member States in the Field of Harmonization of National Law. A Case Study. In *Division of Powers Between the European Communities and their Member States in the Field of External Relations: Colloquium, 30 and 31 May 1980, Amsterdam*, 15–28. Deventer, Netherlands: Kluwer.

———. 2008a. General Aspects of the European Union and the European Communities. In *The Law of the European Union and the European Communities: With Reference to Changes to be Made by the Lisbon Treaty*, ed. P.J.G. Kapteyn, A.M. McDonnell, K.J.M. Mortelmans, C.W.A. Timmermans and L.A. Geelhoed, 4th ed. Alphen Aan Den Rijn, Frederick, MD: Kluwer Law International; Sold and distributed in North, Central and South America by Aspen Pub.

———. 2008b. The Basic Principles. In *The Law of the European Union and the European Communities: With Reference to Changes to be Made by the Lisbon Treaty*, ed. P.J.G. Kapteyn, A.M. McDonnell, K.J.M. Mortelmans, C.W.A. Timmermans and L.A. Geelhoed, 4th ed., 115–174. Alphen Aan Den Rijn, Frederick, MD: Kluwer Law International; Sold and distributed in North, Central and South America by Aspen Pub.

Timmermans, Christiaan. 2000. Organising Joint Participation of E.C. and Member States. In *The General Law of E.C. External Relations*, ed. Alan Dashwood and Christophe Hillion, 239–247. London: Sweet & Maxwell.

———. 2010. Opening Remarks – Evolution of Mixity since the Leiden 1982 Conference. In *Mixed Agreements Revisited: The EU and its Member States in the World*, ed. Christophe Hillion and Panos Koutrakos, 1–8. Modern studies in European law, vol. 21. Oxford [England], Portland, OR: Hart.

Tinbergen, Jan 1959. The Theory of the Optimum Regime. In *Selected Papers*, ed. L.H. Klaassen [and others], etc. [With a Portrait and a Bibliography.], 264–304. Amsterdam: North-Holland.

———. 1964. *International Economic Integration*, 2nd ed. Amsterdam [u.a.]: Elsevier.

Tinbergen, Jan, Antony J. Dolman, and Jan van Ettinger. 1976. *Reshaping the International Order. A Report to the Club of Rome*. 1st ed. New York: Dutton.

Tomuschat, Christian. 1983. Liability for Mixed Agreements. In *Mixed Agreements*, ed. David O'Keeffe and Henry G. Schermers, 125–132. Deventer, Boston: Kluwer Law and Taxation Publishers.

———. 2002. The International Responsibility of the European Union. In *The European Union as an Actor in International Relations*, ed. Enzo Cannizzaro, 177–191. The Hague, New York: Kluwer Law International.

Tridimas, Takis. 2006. *The General Principles of EC Law*. 2nd ed. Oxford: Oxord University Press.

Uerpmann-Wittzack, Robert. 2010. The Constitutional Role of International Law. In *Principles of European Constitutional Law*, ed. Armin von Bogdandy and Jürgen Bast, 2nd ed., 131–167. Oxford, Portland, OR, München, Germany: Hart; CH Beck.

Verhoeven, Joe. 2010. The Law of Responsibility and the Law of Treaties. In *The Law of International Responsibility*, ed. James Crawford, Alain Pellet, Simon Olleson, and Kate Parlett, 103–113. Oxford, New York: Oxford University Press.

Villalpando, S.M. 2002. Attribution of Conduct to the State: How the Rules of State Responsibility May Be Applied Within the WTO Dispute Settlement System. *Journal of International Economic Law* 5 (2): 393–420. doi:10.1093/jiel/5.2.393.

Weiler, Joseph H.H. 1981. The Community System: the Dual Character of Supranationalism. *Yearbook of European Law* 1 (1): 267–306. doi:10.1093/yel/1.1.267.

———. 1999. *The Constitution of Europe: "Do the New Clothes Have an Emperor?" and Other Essays on European Integration*. Cambridge: Cambridge University Press.

———. 2001. Federalism Without Constitutionalism: Europe's *Sonderweg*. In *The Federal Vision: Legitimacy and Levels of Governance in the United States and the European Union*, ed. Kalypso Nicolaidis and Robert Howse, 54–70. Oxford [etc.]: University Press.

———. 2002. A Constitution for Europe? Some Hard Choices. *JCMS: Journal of Common Market Studies* 40 (4): 563–580. doi:10.1111/1468-5965.00388.

———. 2003. In Defence of the Status Quo: Europe's Constitutional *Sonderweg*. In *European Constitutionalism Beyond the State*, ed. Joseph Weiler and Marlene Wind, 7–23. Cambridge, UK: Cambridge University Press.

Wessel, Ramses A. 2014. Can the EU replace its member states in international affairs? An international law perspective. In *The European union in the world: Essays in honour of Marc Maresceau*, ed. Inge Govaere, Erwan Lannon, Peter van Elsuwege, Stanislas Adam, and Marc Maresceau, 129–147. Leiden, Boston: Martinus Nijhoff.

———. 2008. The EU as a Party to International Agreements: Shared Competences, Mixed Responsibilities. In *Law and Practice of EU External Relations: Salient Features of a Changing Landscape*, ed. Alan Dashwood and Marc Maresceau, 152–187. Cambridge: Cambridge University Press.

Witte, Bruno de, Grainne de Burca, and J.H.H. Weiler. 2011. The European Union as an International Legal Experiment. In *The Worlds of European Constitutionalism*, ed. Grainne de Burca and J.H.H. Weiler, 19–56. Cambridge: Cambridge University Press.

Wolf, Erik, and Gustav Radbruch. 1963. *Rechtsphilosophie*. Stuttgart: Koehler.

The manufacturer's authorised representative in the EU is Springer
Nature Customer Service Centre GmbH, Europaplatz 3, 69115 Heidelberg,
Germany. If you have any concerns regarding our products, please
contact ProductSafety@springernature.com

Printed and bound by CPI Group (UK) Ltd, Croydon, CR0 4YY
30/09/2026
02225649-0019